100 YEARS

SIMON & SCHUSTER

ALSO BY CRAIG WHITLOCK

The Afghanistan Papers: A Secret History of the War

FAT LEONARD

How One Man Bribed, Bilked,
and Seduced the U.S. Navy

CRAIG WHITLOCK

Simon & Schuster
NEW YORK   LONDON   TORONTO
SYDNEY   NEW DELHI

100 YEARS
SIMON & SCHUSTER

1230 Avenue of the Americas
New York, NY 10020

Copyright © 2024 by Craig Whitlock

All rights reserved, including the right to reproduce this book or
portions thereof in any form whatsoever. For information, address
Simon & Schuster Subsidiary Rights Department,
1230 Avenue of the Americas, New York, NY 10020.

First Simon & Schuster hardcover edition May 2024

SIMON & SCHUSTER and colophon are registered trademarks
of Simon & Schuster LLC

Simon & Schuster: Celebrating 100 Years of Publishing in 2024

For information about special discounts for bulk purchases,
please contact Simon & Schuster Special Sales at 1-866-506-1949
or business@simonandschuster.com.

The Simon & Schuster Speakers Bureau can bring authors to your
live event. For more information or to book an event, contact
the Simon & Schuster Speakers Bureau at 1-866-248-3049
or visit our website at www.simonspeakers.com.

Interior design by Paul Dippolito

Manufactured in the United States of America

1 3 5 7 9 10 8 6 4 2

Library of Congress Cataloging-in-Publication Data has been applied for.

ISBN 978-1-9821-3163-0
ISBN 978-1-9821-3165-4 (ebook)

For my parents,
Robert and Marion Whitlock,
with love and gratitude

Contents

It is by no means enough that an officer of the Navy should be a capable mariner. He must be that, of course, but also a great deal more. He should be as well a gentleman of liberal education, refined manners, punctilious courtesy, and the nicest sense of personal honor.

> —*"Qualifications of a Naval Officer," compiled by*
> *Augustus C. Buell from letters written by John Paul Jones*

Midshipmen are persons of integrity. They stand for that which is right. They tell the truth and ensure that the truth is known. They do not lie.... They do not cheat.... They do not steal.

> —*From the Naval Academy Honor Concept*

Chain of Command

Commissioned U.S. Navy officers on active duty, 2023

Promotion for the lowest ranks is swift and nearly automatic. Competition becomes progressively tougher after that. Only a handful make it to admiral.

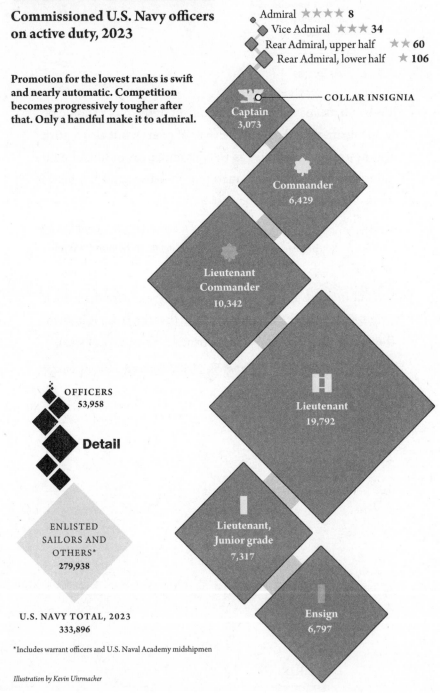

Admiral ★★★★ 8
Vice Admiral ★★★ 34
Rear Admiral, upper half ★★ 60
Rear Admiral, lower half ★ 106

COLLAR INSIGNIA

Captain
3,073

Commander
6,429

Lieutenant Commander
10,342

Lieutenant
19,792

OFFICERS
53,958

Detail

ENLISTED SAILORS AND OTHERS*
279,938

Lieutenant, Junior grade
7,317

Ensign
6,797

U.S. NAVY TOTAL, 2023
333,896

*Includes warrant officers and U.S. Naval Academy midshipmen

Illustration by Kevin Uhrmacher

Ships of the Seventh Fleet

The U.S. Seventh Fleet has about sixty ships and submarines deployed in the Western Pacific and Indian Ocean. Here are examples of three classes of ships that Leonard Francis's company serviced in ports in Asia.

USS MUSTIN DDG 89   Arleigh Burke-class destroyer

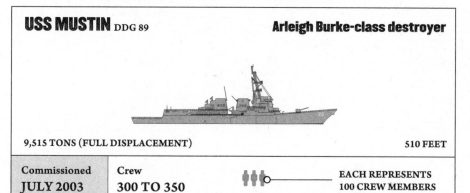

9,515 TONS (FULL DISPLACEMENT)   510 FEET

| Commissioned | Crew | | EACH REPRESENTS |
| JULY 2003 | 300 TO 350 | | 100 CREW MEMBERS |

USS BLUE RIDGE LCC 19   Seventh Fleet flagship

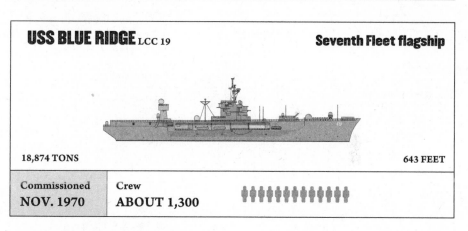

18,874 TONS   643 FEET

| Commissioned | Crew |
| NOV. 1970 | ABOUT 1,300 |

USS RONALD REAGAN CVN 76   Nimitz-class aircraft carrier

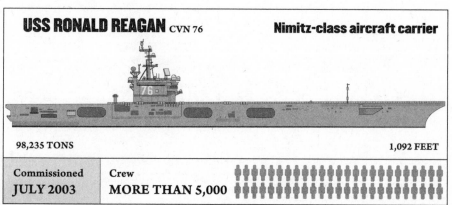

98,235 TONS   1,092 FEET

| Commissioned | Crew |
| JULY 2003 | MORE THAN 5,000 |

Illustration by Kevin Uhrmacher

Prologue

September 2022

It shouldn't have been so easy for a morbidly obese, fifty-seven-year-old felon with two bad knees and kidney cancer to escape federal detention and flee the country. But early Sunday on Labor Day weekend, while nobody was paying attention, Leonard Glenn Francis seized his chance. Having bought off his lone security guard, he cut off the GPS tracking device strapped around his ankle, waddled outside, and climbed into an Uber. About twenty minutes later, he arrived at the Mexican border crossing near Tijuana. By the time the U.S. Marshals Service and the San Diego police realized he was missing, he was on his way to Cuba.

The fugitive wanted posters that appeared a few days later described Francis as an Asian man with black hair and brown eyes, standing well over six feet tall. But his most distinguishing features were his weight—350 pounds—and his nickname, "Fat Leonard."

His crimes: bribing scores of military officers, bilking millions of dollars from defense contracts, and paralyzing the U.S. Navy in one of the worst public corruption scandals in American history.

Federal authorities had gone to extreme lengths to lock Francis up, luring him to California from his base in Southeast Asia in a sting involving dozens of law enforcement agents. After his arrest, however, Francis gradually lulled the Justice Department, a federal judge, and other gullible U.S. officials into lowering their guard. People in the

Navy had always belittled him as Fat Leonard because he was grossly overweight and wheezed as he walked. But his size masked his cunning intellect and disarming persona. He could literally charm the pants off an admiral.

His farcical escape belied the irony that the Navy had long depended on Francis for its own security and sustenance. He owned Glenn Defense Marine Asia, a Singapore-based company that held more than $200 million in defense contracts to resupply U.S. warships and submarines at almost every port in the Western Pacific. In naval jargon, he was a husbanding contractor: a maritime fixer who provided harbor protection, tugs, barges, cranes, food, fresh water, sewage collection, and anything else a nuclear-powered aircraft carrier might need.

For twenty-five years, Francis and Glenn Defense played a critical role supporting the Navy's Seventh Fleet, which ruled the Western Pacific and most of the Indian Ocean with about sixty ships and submarines, two hundred aircraft, and forty thousand sailors and Marines. The Navy's biggest forward-deployed fleet, it guaranteed freedom of navigation through the world's busiest shipping lanes and served as the United States' front line of defense against threats from China, Russia, and North Korea.

In partnering with the Seventh Fleet, Francis perfected a simple but successful business model: He showered Navy officials with gifts and temptations so they would look the other way while Glenn Defense defrauded the federal government. During port visits, the company reaped millions of dollars in illicit profits by overcharging the Navy for virtually everything its ships and crews consumed.

Navy officers knew Francis was cheating Uncle Sam but became mesmerized by his opulent lifestyle and wanted a taste for themselves. When their ships arrived in port, they usually found him smiling on the pier in his Rolls-Royce or armored stretch Hummer, waiting to show them a good time. He treated admirals and ship captains to champagne-drenched feasts at the finest restaurants in Hong Kong,

Jakarta, Singapore, Tokyo, and other cities, dropping $30,000 or more on a single meal.

His most effective bribes were his legendary sex parties. He assembled an armada of prostitutes to entertain Navy officers in Pacific ports from Vladivostok to Sydney, flaunting his VIP status at sex clubs and karaoke bars in Bangkok, Bali, Phuket, and Kuala Lumpur.

Francis's talents as a world-class con artist made him a formidable spy. Had he worked for a foreign power, he would have ranked among the most successful practitioners of espionage in modern history. He recruited a network of moles inside the Navy by targeting officers with personal insecurities, strained marriages, drinking problems, or other vices and vulnerabilities. "Every sailor has a weakness somewhere," he boasted.

Once he reeled them in with sex, booze, cash, and free travel, he expected favors in return. Deferentially addressing him as "Boss," his Navy quislings fed him dirt on his enemies and rigged multimillion-dollar husbanding contracts to his benefit.

Francis's moles included ten Navy officers who betrayed their country by leaking him classified material, a breathtaking security breach that made a mockery of the Navy's counterintelligence defenses. For seven years, his moles fed him military secrets about U.S. ship and submarine movements in the Pacific, highly sensitive information that he exploited for profit.

His informants also helped him run circles around the watchdog agencies that were supposed to protect the Navy from fraudsters and thieves. He neutered the Naval Criminal Investigative Service (NCIS), the Navy's television-famous law enforcement arm, by befriending agents and bribing one of the service's rising stars to leak him investigators' case files. He thwarted twenty-seven criminal investigations of his company before he was finally caught.

James Maus, a Navy officer who served thirty years in uniform and became Francis's nemesis, said the uneducated Malaysian—Francis was a high school dropout—was smarter than anyone he ever met.

"The Soviets couldn't have penetrated us better than Leonard Francis," Maus said. "He's got people skills that are off the scale. He can hook you so fast that you don't see it coming." Maus added: "At one time he had infiltrated the entire leadership line. The KGB could not have done what he did."

Francis's arrest triggered panic in the corridors of the Pentagon. Many of the Navy's senior leaders feared their friendships with him would be exposed. More than ninety admirals came under investigation for interacting with Francis or accepting his lavish dinners and gifts. Among them were the chief of naval intelligence, the commander of all U.S. military forces in the Pacific, the superintendent of the Naval Academy, and two admirals who had served as the chief of naval operations—the highest-ranking job in the service.

All told, nearly one thousand people were swept up in the investigation, including 685 U.S. servicemembers.

The Navy had long led the public to believe it was immune to such rot. In recruiting ads, the sea service cast itself as "A Global Force for Good" and trumpeted its "core values"—*Honor, Courage, Commitment.* Opinion surveys showed that Americans admired and trusted the military more than any institution. With their unblemished, dress-white uniforms, Navy officers carried a reputation for rectitude and the highest standards of character. Most admirals graduated from the venerable Naval Academy in Annapolis, Maryland, where midshipmen commit themselves to a lifetime of honesty and integrity.

While the majority of the 340,000 active-duty personnel in the Navy adhered to those values and served their country with dignity, Francis recognized that for a surprising number, particularly senior leaders, the honorable facade was a sham. The dirty secret was that the Navy tolerated—and promoted—toxic leaders, sexual harassers, flagrant adulterers, and serial liars. For Francis, those people made easy marks.

He exploited an unofficial Navy tradition that abided and even encouraged personal misbehavior as long as it happened far from home.

The Navy had a history of letting sailors go wild during port visits after months at sea, especially in Asia. During the Cold War, a massive, legalized sex industry thrived at Subic Bay in the Philippines, home to the Navy's largest overseas base until the early 1990s. Ports in Singapore, Malaysia, Thailand, Australia, and South Korea also provided U.S. sailors with endless opportunities for mischief. While senior officers were expected to set a sober example and stay away from brothels, Francis discovered that many would succumb to temptations if he provided them in a discreet, upscale setting.

Francis also exploited a culture of entitlement that infected parts of the U.S. military during the wars in Iraq and Afghanistan. Accustomed to civilians placing them on a pedestal in gratitude for their service, some Navy officers felt they were owed something extra. If a wealthy, patriotic businessman like Francis wanted to show his appreciation by buying them a bottle of Dom Pérignon or paying for a five-star hotel suite, what was the problem?

But the biggest factor enabling the Navy's corruption was the dereliction of admirals who tolerated the graft and misconduct instead of treating it as an insidious threat. The gusher of gifts, perks, and extravagant parties was an open secret within the Seventh Fleet and at the Pentagon, even among commanding officers who kept their distance from Francis. Yet no one in a position of leadership had the courage to intervene or admit the Navy had a problem. Instead, the admirals abdicated their responsibility to protect the integrity of the institution and stymied the few who tried to stand up for what was right.

As an investigative reporter, I spent a decade digging into the Fat Leonard scandal. I wrote my first article about the case for *The Washington Post* in October 2013, soon after Francis's arrest in San Diego. Over the next five years, I wrote more than fifty news articles about the criminal investigation, many on the *Post*'s front page. The more I reported, however, the more I realized the story was much bigger and more damning for the Navy than federal authorities were letting on. Fresh leads kept multiplying. I could barely keep track of all the crazy stories I heard about Francis's exploits and the unbecoming conduct of Navy officers who pocketed his bribes.

The most important questions seemed obvious but proved difficult to answer. How could an obese Malaysian high school dropout seduce the leadership of the most powerful navy in the world? How had he gotten away with massive fraud for twenty years? Why had Navy leaders allowed such unlawful and disgraceful behavior to fester? I became convinced that the only way to get to the bottom of the story was to report and write a book.

Navy officials had zero interest in shedding light on the matter and disclosed almost nothing without a fight. Using the Freedom of Information Act (FOIA), I filed dozens of public records requests and a federal lawsuit to pry loose documents, but the Navy slow-rolled my queries for years. Ultimately, it released more than three thousand pages of court-martial proceedings, contracting records, and disciplinary letters, but with most of the names and incriminating details blacked out. Eventually, the Navy grew tired of my questions and informed me in writing that it would no longer respond to my FOIA requests or release any new information.

I kept digging elsewhere and conducted more than 150 interviews. I mined federal and state courthouses, collecting more than thirty thousand pages of transcripts, exhibits, affidavits, warrants, and charging documents. I also obtained court and police records from Malaysia, Singapore, the Philippines, and Australia.

Finally, trusted sources gave me an enormous and invaluable trove of information: federal agents' case files for the Glenn Defense investigation. Comprising several terabytes of data, the confidential case files contain notes of interviews with several hundred people and transcripts of interrogations of dozens of criminal suspects. Critically, the case files included investigators' notes from more than three hundred hours of debriefings with Francis after his arrest. The cache also held millions of emails, text messages, photographs, hotel receipts, travel records, and dinner menus recovered from Francis's electronic devices and his company's computer server.

Combined with my other reporting, this mother lode of primary-source material helped me gain a full understanding of the scandal and write a narrative exposé of how Francis infiltrated the Navy. The consequences, and the Navy's determination to bury its mistakes instead of learning from them, will haunt the service for years.

At a time when the public has become understandably skeptical of anonymous sources in the news media, it is important to emphasize that this book is based on official evidence and documents—most of which the Navy and Justice Department tried to keep secret—as well as on-the-record interviews. None of the dialogue is reimagined. Everything in quotation marks is exactly as people said it, based on contemporaneous audio recordings, notes, emails, and text messages. The source material and attributions are detailed in the Endnotes.

The story of Fat Leonard and the U.S. Navy may be mind-boggling, but every word is based on the facts.

Part One

1986–2005

Chapter One

A Good Whipping

April 1986

GEORGE TOWN, MALAYSIA

The Malaysian police assumed, with good reason, that Leonard Francis would spend much of his life behind bars. The evidence against the twenty-one-year-old hustler was undisputed. They had searched his house and found two unlicensed .38-caliber Smith & Wesson revolvers, fourteen rounds of ammunition, and a bulletproof vest stashed in his bedroom. Under Malaysia's gun-control laws—among the toughest in the world—he faced mandatory prison time. In some cases, those convicted of firearms possession could be sentenced to death.

Detectives had nabbed Francis after receiving a tip that he was involved in the armed robbery of a moneylender. Though this was his first arrest, he was well known to the police. He stood out on the docks in George Town, where his family owned a security company that supplied watchmen to the shipping lines moving cargo through the nearby Strait of Malacca. Flashy and flamboyant, he wore oversized cowboy belt buckles, rode loud motorcycles, and frequented red-light districts near the harbor. Compared with other Malaysians, he looked like a giant: heavyset and six-foot-three-inches tall, with muttonchop sideburns and a bushy crown of jet-black hair.

Francis surrendered without incident when a police inspector found him on the street. He knew right away what the detective wanted. He had gotten mixed up with a loan shark and a crew of gangsters who enlisted him to drive the getaway car during a robbery. Unwisely, he had agreed to hide the loot and the guns in his bedroom. Now someone had ratted him out. "Dumb me," he recalled years later. "Young dumb-dumb."

His case made headlines in George Town, the biggest city on Penang, a steamy island of about 600,000 people off the western coast of the Malay Peninsula. Newspapers dubbed him "the burly businessman" and noted he came from a well-off family. Francis's parents hired three prominent criminal defense attorneys to represent him, but given the clear evidence of his guilt, there was only so much they could do. After seventy-four days in jail, he took his lawyers' advice and pleaded guilty to illegal possession of the guns and ammunition.

The plea deal spared him from the death penalty. But he still faced up to twenty-one years in prison and a whipping—a bloody lashing on the buttocks with a heavy rattan cane.

For the sentencing, Francis's lawyers pinned their hopes on winning mercy from the judge, Madam Ho Mooi Ching, the president of the Sessions Court in George Town. Portraying their client as a hapless fall guy, they admitted he had fallen in with some "undesirable characters" but blamed the gangsters for coercing him to hide the guns from the robbery.

Francis's mother, Felicia, also tried to deflect guilt from her son. In tearful testimony, she told the judge the whole mess was partly her fault because she had separated from her philandering husband but left Leonard behind. She explained that when Leonard was a teenager she'd allowed him to live with his father, hoping that it would discourage her estranged spouse from having affairs. But she said the arrangement only exposed Leonard to more immoral behavior.

A psychiatrist from Penang General Hospital emphasized other extenuating circumstances. The doctor, who had been hired by Francis's parents, recommended to the court that Francis receive "prolonged" psychotherapy, not prison time, for undisclosed mental health issues.

The doctor also urged the judge to spare the defendant a caning because he was overweight and suffered from a blood disorder.

Improbably, the bid for sympathy worked. Though the law called for mandatory prison time, the judge let Francis go free, sentencing him to probation, a fine—and no whipping. "I am giving him another chance," she said, citing his young age, his admission of guilt, and the fact that he and his family had already suffered "public humiliation."

The lenient sentence infuriated the police. Before Francis could walk out of the courthouse, they rearrested him and charged him with three fresh counts of robbery based on other crimes he and the gangsters were suspected of committing.

He was released on bond while his case bounced around the courts for the next three years. In 1989, an appellate court overruled Madam Ho, finding that her decision not to impose a prison sentence "cannot be justified either in law or on principle."

Again, however, Francis got off easy. The appellate court ordered him to serve eighteen months and receive a "whipping with six strokes," a relatively mild punishment for a gun crime in Malaysia. After spending about a year behind bars, he was released early for good behavior.

Even the whipping went better than expected. By coincidence, the Penang prison flogger attended the same church as the Francis family. He landed three blows with the rattan cane. But during the other three swings he somehow missed the prisoner's posterior. Luckily for Francis, the whiffs counted anyway. Malaysian law did not mandate a do-over.

Through it all, Francis learned an important life lesson: With a little luck and the right connections, you could pretty much get away with anything.

Leonard Glenn Francis was born in George Town in October 1964, seven years after the Federation of Malaya achieved independence from Britain. Two centuries earlier, the British East India Company had established a trading outpost on Penang—the island derives its name from a native word for the betel nut—to export rubber and tin from plantations and mines on the Malay Peninsula. The monsoon-swept island attracted waves of immigrants and became home to a mélange of ethnicities: Malays, Chinese, and Indians, with European expatriates mixed in.

Francis's roots extended in all directions. His paternal grandfather was a Scot who arrived in Malaya in the 1930s and managed a rubber plantation in the state of Perak. The Scotsman married a woman of Indian descent and fathered two sons and a daughter. When the Japanese invaded in 1941, he fled to Britain and left his wife and children behind.

After World War II, Francis's father, Michael, joined the British Army while it was embroiled in a long fight with a communist-led insurgency in Malaya. In the early 1960s, he deployed to the British colony of Singapore, where he served as a military policeman rounding up drunken soldiers. There he fell in love with a teenage girl named Felicia Wisidagama, the daughter of a well-to-do Singapore family that traced its ancestry to Portuguese explorers and Tamil merchants from Ceylon, or present-day Sri Lanka.

The couple married and built a life on what appeared to be a solid foundation. Felicia's father owned a firm that provided supplies and stevedores to cargo ships in Singapore. The company had a branch in Penang, about 370 miles away at the other end of the Strait of Malacca. Michael Francis seemed a natural choice to take over that part of the family business, so he and Felicia moved to George Town and raised a family: a girl and two boys. Leonard was the middle child and the eldest son.

Five degrees north of the equator, George Town was a seafaring city known for its colonial shophouse architecture and eclectic street food. Though Malaysia was predominantly Muslim, the Francises were Roman Catholic, and Leonard's parents baptized him in the church. The family attended the majestic Cathedral of the Assumption, the oldest church in Penang. As a youngster, Leonard enrolled at St. Christopher School, a private academy that catered to the children of wealthy rubber planters.

Life in the household soon deteriorated. Michael Francis, a dour man, cheated on his wife and beat her and the children. In the early 1970s, Felicia moved out with Leonard and his siblings and returned to Singapore. "She was traumatized by my father," Leonard recalled. "My father was very violent."

In Singapore, then a city-state of 2.2 million people, Leonard attended private schools while living with his mother, siblings, grandparents, and cousins. By age thirteen he was already six feet tall and joined a team playing American-style football. By his account, he soaked up American culture but was "always messing around" and not interested in school.

Michael Francis remained in Penang to run his branch of the family business. He continued chasing women and the split with his wife widened. Around 1979, Felicia moved from Singapore to England. This time, she took her daughter, Anna, and her youngest son, Andre. But, in a decision that she'd regret, she allowed Leonard to go back to Penang to live with his adulterous father.

Leonard developed a love-hate relationship with his father, who was preoccupied with girlfriends and rarely at home. But Leonard saw both his parents as selfish. "My dad had his own thing. My mom had her own thing. So, everybody went their own way and just kind of left me in limbo," he recalled. "I kind of found my own way on the streets. That's why I became so street smart. I'm a survivor."

As a teenager, Leonard often rode away on his bike and disappeared for long stretches. "My parents thought I was a pretty difficult child to manage," he admitted. In an effort to teach him discipline, Leonard's separated parents agreed to send him to the Uplands School, an international boarding school in Penang that had recently begun accepting day students. Many, like Leonard, came from mixed-race or multiethnic families. They wore school uniforms adapted to the local culture and climate: batik-print shirts and dark green pants, but no coats or ties.

As a ninth-grader, Leonard became chummy with two younger American-Malaysian boys, Jeff and Charles O'Neal. The O'Neals looked up to Leonard. He was popular and spent more time than most boys his age primping in front of a mirror in the school bathrooms. "He had a lot of personality," Jeff O'Neal recalled. "He was a natural-born leader."

It didn't take long for Leonard to get into trouble. One weekend, he and a handful of boarding students at Uplands ventured off campus to party. The school principal found out. He suspended the boarders for violating curfew but expelled fifteen-year-old Leonard because he had illegally driven the group in his father's car. (The minimum driving age in Malaysia was seventeen.)

The episode marked the end of Leonard's formal education. Instead of enrolling at another school, he went to work full-time for his father at the family firm, Glenn Security Services. Though he was young, his imposing size made him a good fit for a company that guarded ships.

By all accounts, Leonard worked hard. He spent countless hours on Swettenham Pier, the shipping terminal on the northeast tip of Penang, where he helped provide security for renowned cruise ships such as the *Pearl of Scandinavia*, the *Princess Mahsuri*, and the *Queen Elizabeth 2*. But it was the cargo shipping lines, with their worldly captains and intrepid lifestyles, that fascinated him the most. He dreamed of becoming a Malaysian version of Aristotle Onassis, the playboy Greek shipping tycoon who won the heart of the widowed American first lady, Jacqueline Kennedy.

Leonard's father lacked his son's work ethic. "He was too busy womanizing to care about making more money," Leonard recalled. And in contrast with his gregarious son, Michael Francis had a grumpy demeanor. Leonard's friends called the old man "Gaddafi" behind his back because he reminded them of the grim-faced Libyan dictator.

Nonetheless, under Michael Francis's leadership, Glenn Security Services built solid relationships with several shipping lines. Business was steady, if modest. But as Leonard learned on the job, he saw myriad other opportunities to make money. Merchant vessels needed water taxis to ferry their crews from ships at anchor, or barges and stevedores to transfer their cargo.

Michael Francis had no interest in expanding, but he didn't object when his son pushed to branch out on his own. Leonard drew up the paperwork to start a new company, Glenn Marine Enterprise, of which he was the sole proprietor. He worked out of his dad's office and borrowed his secretary, but he cut his own deals to sell victuals and cigarettes to cargo ships arriving from Europe, South America, and other far-flung places.

By his late teens, Leonard had already become known for his outsized personality and play-hard mentality. Deepening his fixation with American culture, he loved to dress up like Elvis and listen to Fleetwood Mac. He couldn't watch enough of *The Godfather*, the epic film about an Italian American family of mobsters. He liked shiny things and bought a Kawasaki KZ1300 motorcycle. With a top speed of around 140 mph, the superbike was not only fast but weighed seven hundred pounds: sturdy enough to carry someone of Leonard's stature.

"He had a taste for going big," said Jeff O'Neal, who remained close with Leonard after he was expelled. And he was a charmer. Most respectable families would probably keep their distance from a motorcycle-riding delinquent, but according to O'Neal, Leonard "connected with people really well. It didn't matter who it was. My dad was critical of my friends, but he liked Leonard."

A night owl, Leonard partied in red-light districts near the waterfront, where he hung out with crewmembers from cargo vessels who regaled him with tales of their international adventures.

Penang's nightlife also taught him beneficial lessons about mixing business with pleasure. When he was twenty, he purchased a dive bar in George Town and renamed it Tropicana, in homage to a famous nightclub of the same name in Singapore. Ship captains, after weeks at sea, gladly accepted his offers to get drunk and meet women, especially when he covered their bar bill or invited them to take a girl upstairs for a massage. To his delight, he discovered they would happily do him all sorts of favors in return.

Chapter Two

The Striver

May 1992

PENANG, MALAYSIA

The USS *Acadia* moored on the northeastern tip of Penang at Swettenham Pier with 1,300 sailors. Waiting eagerly was Leonard Francis, who wanted to dazzle his new American clients. In the two years since his release from prison, the twenty-seven-year-old Malaysian had revived his fledgling company, Glenn Marine Enterprise, and expanded its customer base. Besides merchant mariners passing through the Strait of Malacca, he had won a few small contracts from the U.S. Navy to resupply its ships with food, water, and other goods during their sporadic visits to Penang. If he could establish an enduring relationship with the Americans, Glenn Marine's future would be bright.

Francis placed a premium on personal service and ensured that *Acadia* officers had a memorable time during their four-day port call. He invited Commander Harry Guess, the head of the ship's supply department, and three female officers on his staff to a lobster dinner at Eden Seafood Village, a landmark Penang restaurant.*

---

* Military personnel are identified throughout this book by the rank they held at the time of the events described.

Francis cut a vivid figure that evening, wearing sandals, a blue-and-yellow tropical print shirt, and a golden crucifix that dangled from a chain around his neck. While a band blasted tunes and waiters delivered platters of food, he plied his guests with drinks and cigars, and snapped photos of everyone having a grand time. To con them into thinking he was an American at heart—he certainly spoke like one, with no discernible accent—he told made-up stories about his college days at the University of North Carolina at Chapel Hill, a school he'd never attended.

The forty-one-year-old Guess had never been taken to dinner by a husbanding contractor before. As the officer who signed the *Acadia*'s supply invoices, he knew he wasn't supposed to accept freebies from someone who did business with the U.S. government, but the fun-loving Malaysian host insisted on paying. Afterward, Francis took the three female officers out for more drinks and karaoke at the Fun Pub at the Golden Sands Hotel and again covered the bill.

As Francis had intended, his hospitality left an indelible impression on the sailors far from home.

"Dear Leonard: This has been the best liberty port of the deployment, and that is only due to you!" Lieutenant Ruth Christopherson, an assistant supply officer, cooed in a handwritten thank-you note after the *Acadia* left Penang. "You are a wonderful person and a great friend. Thanks so much for everything. With Love, Ruth."*

It was the start of a long and intimate relationship between Francis and the Navy. Over the next two decades, hundreds more officers—men and women alike—would become smitten.

The *Acadia*'s successful visit paid off for Francis right away. Later that month, a U.S. Marine Corps F/A-18 Hornet fighter jet crashed in a

---

* Another young *Acadia* officer who partied with Francis during the port visit, Michelle Coyne Skubic, became a three-star admiral twenty-seven years later—the first female supply officer selected for that rank.

jungle on the east coast of Malaysia during a training mission. The pilot ejected safely, but his copilot was killed, and the Americans had trouble accessing the wreckage. Glenn Marine won another contract to help recover the aircraft.

The firm's budding reputation for reliability emerged at the perfect time. The early 1990s marked a generational realignment of American military power in Asia. Since the end of World War II, the Navy's operations in the Western Pacific had revolved around its huge base in the Philippines at Subic Bay. Covering 262 square miles—about four times as much territory as the District of Columbia—the base teemed with American and Filipino personnel, over 26,000 in total. Subic Bay enabled the Navy to maintain a formidable presence from the South China Sea to the Indian Ocean without its ships needing to travel thousands of miles to bases in Hawaii or California for supplies and repairs.

After failed negotiations to extend the U.S. lease on Subic Bay, however, the Philippines notified the United States in December 1991 that it would have to vacate the premises. The Navy relocated part of its fleet to Japan and began hunting for new places in Southeast Asia to use as rest stops.

The Navy had long-standing arrangements to make port calls in Thailand and Hong Kong, a British colony until 1997. Malaysia, Singapore, and Indonesia were willing, to varying degrees, to host American ships for brief visits. But the Navy also needed husbanding contractors in those countries to service its ships while in port.

Glenn Marine was one of the few Malaysian providers that had experience with foreign navies. Even before Francis absorbed his caning, he had eyed military contracts as a potential stream of revenue. In the mid-1980s, he opened a storefront office near a new Malaysian navy base in Lumut—halfway between Penang and Kuala Lumpur—hoping to win spillover business from visiting warships. Back then, the Glenn Marine office was so small that it shared a squat toilet with other shop tenants. But the location gave Francis a physical presence in a military town, and he won his first defense contract: a minor deal to sell food and water to the *Ali Haider,* a Bangladesh Navy frigate making a pit stop in Lumut.

More opportunities followed. Francis rented a refrigerated shipping container, stuffed it with provisions, and loaded it onto a fishing trawler to resupply navy ships from Malaysia, Britain, Singapore, and Australia when they conducted exercises in the South China Sea. He faced scant competition in what was then a niche market.

"It all just kind of fell in my lap because nobody offered the services," Francis recalled. "Nobody wanted to do it. I did."

To dispel concerns about his youth and inexperience, he advertised that Glenn Marine had been in business since 1946, implying it was the same firm his grandfather had started in Singapore after World War II. To add further seasoning to Glenn Marine's reputation, he sometimes led people to believe his father was the owner.

By the early 1990s, Francis had grown from a burly businessman into a corpulent one, weighing well over three hundred pounds. But his flabby physique didn't diminish his appetite for flirting and carrying on with women. After his stint in prison, he met and married Deanna Gonzales, a lounge singer from Manila. Their first child, Leonardo, was born in 1992. A second son, Marco, arrived two years later.

As a husband, Francis was unfaithful from the start, just like his father. After he expanded his business operations across the Strait of Malacca to Indonesia, he had an affair with a twenty-one-year-old woman named Rose who helped manage Glenn Marine's branch office on the resort island of Bali. "I kind of got a liking to her and hooked up with her," he recalled. "She was a smart girl."

Francis targeted Bali figuring the Navy would find its bars and beaches irresistible for shore leave. Because the island's facilities were inadequate for hosting warships, he partnered with local businessmen to build a jetty and a pier. The Navy took notice and started sending ships Francis's way, though it wasn't all smooth sailing at first. During a 1995 visit to Bali by the USS *O'Brien*, Francis almost drowned when he lost his footing in the surf while attempting to help sailors disembark from Glenn Marine's water taxis.

Commander Tracy Brown, the supply officer for the USS *Blue Ridge*, the Seventh Fleet flagship, met Francis in 1995 when he traveled with an advance team to Port Klang, Malaysia—near the capital, Kuala Lumpur—to prepare for a port call. Francis picked up the officer at his hotel in a beat-up Mercedes with broken seats that looked as if they had been squashed on purpose so Leonard could fit in the car.

The Glenn Marine owner nonetheless impressed Brown as "a bend-over backwards type guy." In fact, many Navy officers admired Francis for his work habits, even as they mocked his physical appearance behind his back. Some called him "Fat Bastard"—a reference to the vulgar, sumo-wrestler-sized character in the *Austin Powers* movies. But as his profile rose, "Fat Leonard" became his dominant nickname in the fleet.

Commander Brown, for his part, disapproved of other sailors making fun of Francis. He considered it disrespectful given how helpful Francis had been to the *Blue Ridge* crew. The Seventh Fleet commander, Vice Admiral Robert Natter, agreed. "Mr. Francis's untiring devotion to United States Navy ship visits is sincerely appreciated," he wrote in a 1997 thank-you letter after the *Blue Ridge* passed through Port Klang and Bali.

Whatever they thought of Francis, one thing many people in the Navy didn't seem to mind was his habit of padding the bills. In Bali, Glenn Marine charged the U.S. government high prices to collect sewage from warships and then illegally dumped the wastewater to save money. As an inducement to look the other way while he cheated, Francis took Navy personnel to Bali's tiki bars, karaoke joints, and massage parlors. Other times, his enticements were more flagrant. He bragged that he once handed a $20,000 bribe to a supply officer who walked away with the cash hidden under his hat.

As the Navy generated additional business for Glenn Marine, Francis saw the potential to lift his company to new heights and did everything he could to cultivate relationships with the Americans. Above all, he targeted young officers with bright career prospects and loose morals.

In 1997, the USS *Boxer*, an amphibious assault ship, made a port call to Bali. By then, Francis's weight had ballooned to over four hundred pounds, so big that the crew helped him board the vessel by hoisting him up to the deck as if he were a piece of heavy equipment. "He was huger than huge then. He was enormous," recalled Robert Gilbeau, who was a lieutenant commander at the time and the *Boxer*'s assistant supply officer.

In a perverse way, Francis's heft enhanced his personal magnetism. Gilbeau, a Naval Academy graduate who would become an admiral, found he couldn't look away.

One night, Gilbeau left the *Boxer* to meet Francis at a bar in Bali to pay some supply bills. He spotted the contractor relaxing in a lounge chair, surrounded by pillows and a harem of attractive women.

"Oh, sit, sit—spend some time!" Francis beckoned.

Gilbeau couldn't resist. The two men began a friendship that would endure for sixteen years and bring unprecedented disgrace to the Navy.

Living alongside one of the most congested shipping lanes in the world, Malaysians saw just about everything pass by their shores: cargo vessels, oil tankers, cruise ships, fish factories, passenger ferries, tugboats, even pirate skiffs. In 1997, about three hundred ships a day transited the Strait of Malacca, the maritime highway connecting the Indian Ocean to the South China Sea. But Malaysians had never beheld anything like the colossal, flat-topped warship flying the American flag as it navigated a narrow channel to reach the northern wharves of Port Klang in late April.

The USS *Independence*, a steel-gray Forrestal-class aircraft carrier, stretched 1,070 feet from bow to stern, about as long as the height of the Eiffel Tower. A floating military base operated by five thousand sailors, the *Independence* could launch up to seventy-five aircraft: Tomcat and Hornet fighter jets; Viking and Hawkeye surveillance planes; Prowler electronic jammers; and Seahawk helicopters. Built in the 1950s, the conventionally powered carrier boasted a top speed of more than thirty knots, or about thirty-five miles per hour. The draft of its hull extended thirty-seven feet below the waterline, so deep that only a handful of harbors in Southeast Asia could swallow it.

The *Independence's* four-day visit was the first by an aircraft carrier to Malaysia, and it created a popular sensation in Port Klang. The U.S. Navy expected a small crowd when it agreed to host an open house aboard the ship. Instead, about 100,000 people showed up, jamming roads leading to the harbor. Malaysians of all ages took the day off to see and touch the symbol of American military might, including ninety-four awestruck kindergarteners who toured a hangar deck and received their own briefing.

Amid the din on the pier, Francis shouted orders from a makeshift command center. Sitting underneath a tent canopy to block the tropical sun, he wore loose-fitting clothes and dripped with sweat as he surveyed the crowds. It was the first time the Navy had entrusted Glenn Marine with a contract for servicing a ship this big and he was feeling the pressure.

Commander Jim Maus, the *Independence's* supply officer, wasn't sure whether the young Malaysian was up to the job. From the ship, Maus watched as Francis parked himself in an enormous chair under his tent. It "was almost comical how big it was," Maus recalled. "He looked like Jabba the Hutt sitting out there." A lanky officer from Northern California, Maus had served two decades in the Navy and dealt with all sorts of husbanding contractors. But he soon discovered Francis was one of a kind.

As the supply officer, Maus led the biggest department on the ship, with a $100 million annual budget. More than 550 officers and enlisted sailors reported to him. He was responsible for meeting the carrier's massive logistical requirements: stores of food and fresh water, hardware inventories, plus replacement parts for the ship's mechanical systems and warplanes. He had no say into which husbanding companies the Navy hired, but he was the one who dealt with the contractors in person. He was also responsible for paying the ship's expenses while in port, which could run more than $100,000 a day. If anything went awry—if the garbage barge didn't show up, if the gangways didn't fit—Maus caught flak.

Francis had impressed Maus—at first. Four months earlier, the Glenn Marine owner had traveled 3,300 miles from Malaysia to the U.S. Navy base in Yokosuka, Japan, the home port for the *Independence* and the rest of the Seventh Fleet. Without an appointment, he boarded the ship and asked to see Maus so he could introduce himself. The supply officer was floored. No husbanding contractor had ever taken initiative like that before. "The guy was unbelievably charming," Maus said.

On a ship engineered to maximize every square inch of space, Francis literally struggled to fit in. The width of the passageways between the bulkheads narrowed to twenty-six inches in places and the obese Malaysian could barely squeeze through. Still, he didn't shy away. Three months later, he showed up unannounced again—this time while the *Independence* was visiting Perth, on the remote western coast of Australia. Francis said he just wanted to touch base before the ship's next stop in Malaysia, 2,600 miles away. "I was thinking, 'Wow, this guy is really prepared for us,'" Maus said. "He didn't mess around."

Once the aircraft carrier reached Port Klang, however, Francis and his staff labored to prove themselves. Glenn Marine delivered pallets of stale bread and bungled the job of providing ground transportation for the crew. Because Port Klang was an industrial zone, Maus had requested a fleet of buses so sailors could spend their shore leave in Kuala Lumpur, an hour's ride away. Instead, Francis arranged for the sailors to travel by rail on a little-used spur line. The train was infested with rats and cockroaches and moved at a snail's pace, triggering an avalanche of complaints.

On a personal level, Francis further irritated Maus by delivering an unsolicited gift to his office on the ship each morning: a Royal Selangor pewter tankard. (Malaysia is a major producer of tin, the main ingredient in pewter.) The tankards were worth about $100 apiece and federal rules prohibited Navy personnel from accepting contractor gifts worth more than $20. Maus, a stickler for ethics, sent them back.

The worst annoyance came at the end of the visit. The Navy had a hard-and-fast rule that supply officers review and pay contractor invoices before leaving port. But as the *Independence* prepared to get under way, Glenn Marine still hadn't delivered its bills, and Francis was nowhere to be found. "I was just absolutely livid," Maus said. "I said, 'Screw it,' and for the only time in my career, I left port without paying." He left a brusque message for Francis with the Glenn Marine staff: If you want your money, meet us at our next stop in Singapore.

Chastened, Francis arrived in Singapore with $300,000 worth of invoices. Maus didn't dispute the amount but exploded when Francis asked to be paid in cash. For Francis, the request wasn't unusual: Merchant ships often paid him in hard currency, and the *Independence* kept several million dollars in its safe, much of it to pay the crew. But disbursing cash was an accounting nightmare for the Navy. Maus told Francis that he'd write him a check and that he could take it or leave it. Francis accepted, but his actions left some sore feelings. "I was so pissed," Maus said.

While neither recognized the significance of the encounter at the time, Maus and Francis had sized up each other and made important first impressions. In the years ahead, their tumultuous relationship would reverberate through the highest ranks of the Navy as they turned into wary associates, then close allies, and finally obsessive enemies, each threatening to destroy the other.

Chapter Three

Ring of Steel

October 2000

ADEN, YEMEN

The USS *Cole* arrived mid-morning on October 12 in Aden, an ancient Arabian port, and anchored at the mouth of the harbor. The guided-missile destroyer had transited the Suez Canal and the Red Sea and needed to stop for several hours so it could take on 220,000 gallons of fuel before continuing north into the Persian Gulf. As the crew started to eat lunch, a small red-and-white motorboat approached. The two men aboard smiled and waved as they drew close to the hulking warship. Unsuspecting sailors on the *Cole* waved back, thinking the skiff had come to collect trash.

In fact, the two men were suicide bombers recruited by al-Qaeda and the motorboat was packed with explosives. The terrorists detonated their cargo and blew a gaping hole in the side of the *Cole* that almost sank the $1 billion vessel. Seventeen U.S. sailors were killed and forty-two were wounded, making it the deadliest assault on a U.S. Navy vessel in thirteen years. The attack presaged the far bigger one that al-Qaeda would inflict eleven months later with hijacked airliners.

Just as the United States was unprepared for 9/11, the Navy had not foreseen that a common motorboat could torpedo one of its powerful warships. The *Cole* disaster instantly upended the Navy's risk calculations for foreign port calls. Unsure of the extent of the maritime threat posed by al-Qaeda, the Navy curtailed ship visits to Yemen and other Muslim countries and upgraded force protection requirements elsewhere.

The shift imperiled the fortunes of Leonard Francis and Glenn Marine Enterprise. Since 1997, he had established a thriving subsidiary— Glenn Defense Marine Asia—to handle military contracts, most of which came from the U.S. Navy. He had moved his hub of operations from Malaysia to Singapore, where the U.S. military maintained a small but permanent presence. After the *Cole* bombing, however, he realized his profitable partnership with the Americans would evaporate if he could not guarantee their ships were safe in his hands.

Under pressure, Francis devised a solution: a floating barrier that encircled a ship to prevent waterborne intruders from getting too close. The primitive contraption was merely a makeshift fence of heavy barges and pontoons linked by steel cables. But in a deft stroke of marketing, he branded it as the "Ring of Steel."

The Ring of Steel sounded impregnable and looked plausible when he showed it to Navy force protection officers. "It was impressive," said Jim Maus, the supply officer from the USS *Independence*. "No little boat is going through that. Bounce off it, maybe." The Ring of Steel was also portable. Glenn Marine could move the components from harbor to harbor and customize the perimeter to suit any ship.

Shaken by the *Cole* bombing, the Navy grabbed the Ring of Steel as a lifeline. It didn't have better ideas to protect its ships in Southeast Asia. Nor did it trust commercial ports or revenue-starved foreign navies to provide adequate security. The only other option was to park ships at well-guarded U.S. bases in Japan and Hawaii.

With the Ring of Steel, Francis not only saved his company, but found a way to expand it. After the *Cole* attack, Glenn Marine became one of a handful of contractors that could meet the Navy's enhanced force protection requirements. Most competitors in the husbanding industry were mom-and-pop operators who couldn't or wouldn't

invest in their own floating barriers. That meant more business for
Francis.

"The Navy went crazy and paranoid over the *Cole*," recalled Commander David Kapaun, an operations officer based in Singapore at the
time. "Leonard jumped on that like you wouldn't believe."

The Ring of Steel's first major test came in April 2001 when the
USS *Blue Ridge*, the Seventh Fleet flagship, arrived in Malaysia's Port
Klang. According to the ship's official command history, "a group of
Malaysians" tried to attack the *Blue Ridge* in "a small boat loaded with
explosives" but was stopped by Glenn Marine's "floating barrier of
barges." The command history credited Francis by name for helping
to "thwart" the attack and said the suspected "terrorists" were later arrested while robbing a bank "to gain more money for explosives."

Curiously, the foiled terrorist attack and bank robbery didn't make
the news or draw public attention, raising the question of whether
they really happened. It's possible that U.S. and Malaysian authorities
hushed up the incidents, but some Navy officials later came to suspect Francis of exaggerating threats and staging fake plots to justify
demand for the Ring of Steel.

If there was an attempted terrorist strike against the *Blue Ridge*, it
didn't deter about two dozen Navy officers from venturing into Kuala
Lumpur on the final night of the port visit to enjoy a swanky dinner
courtesy of Glenn Marine. Francis hosted the officers in a private
room at one of his favorite restaurants: the Chalet, a "grande dame" of
continental cuisine in the Equatorial Hotel. Customized menu cards
appeared with each place setting:

Duet of Oyster Mornay and Kilpatrick

Cream of Wild Forest Mushroom Soup served in Papa Bread

Fresh Gooseliver Panfried with Grapes and Madeira

Mango Sherbet with Pinot Noir in Ice Igloo

"Homard Thermidor"
The Classical Preparation of US Boston Lobster
In Champagne Cream Sauce and Gratinated

*Sabayon du Chalet**

Crepe Suzette

La "Dolce Vita"

Iced Pralines

Francis spent thousands of dollars on the meal, but the expense was nothing compared with the profits he earned from a port visit. He knew if he wined and dined the Americans, they were unlikely to question his exorbitant fees, including for the Ring of Steel, which cost between $50,000 to $100,000 per day. "Everybody had to use the Ring of Steel," he recalled. "So literally, the military's force protection became the golden goose for me."

For ship captains, no price was too high to protect their crews, not to mention their careers. The Navy held them accountable for everything that happened on their watch, regardless of whether they were personally responsible. If a low-ranking seaman screwed up a task that led to a serious accident, the Navy disciplined the commanding officer on the grounds that he or she had failed to ensure the sailor was properly trained and supervised.

The Navy upheld that unforgiving standard after the attack on the *Cole*. A high-level investigation concluded the *Cole* was "a well-trained, well-led and highly capable ship" and that the skipper, Commander Kirk Lippold, was not at fault. Intelligence reporting had also failed to detect any threats in advance of the visit to Aden. But the Navy nonetheless blocked Lippold from promotion and forced him to

---

* The restaurant's signature dessert, a sugary egg-based concoction whipped by hand and served cold.

retire—Pentagon officials and members of Congress decided someone needed to be held accountable for the disaster.

Many commanding officers thought the Navy and Congress treated Lippold unfairly, but the message resonated: Take every precaution. As a result, few ship captains were willing to risk a port visit without the Ring of Steel, no matter the expense—particularly after 9/11 demonstrated that al-Qaeda's attack on the *Cole* was not an isolated event.

Terrorist threats spread to Southeast Asia. In October 2002, an al-Qaeda affiliate bombed Bali's tourist districts, killing 202 people. Seven Americans died and the U.S. consulate was damaged. The Navy reduced its visits to Indonesia, but demand for the Ring of Steel soared in other ports. Glenn Defense's bottom line soared with it.

The Navy's byzantine accounting policies made it easy for Francis to jack up his prices with minimal resistance. Ship captains had no incentive to scrutinize bills for the Ring of Steel because they did not have to dip into their own budgets to pay for it—force protection expenses were covered by Pacific Fleet headquarters in Hawaii. Captain James Dolan, a logistics officer who was friendly with Francis, said Pacific Fleet officials always approved bills for the Ring of Steel, even if it cost "umpteen gazillion dollars," because they knew if "you had a second *Cole*, that the shit would hit the fan."

More broadly, Francis benefited from the Navy's profligate mindset as the United States boosted military spending during the "War on Terror." Between 2000 and 2008, the Navy's annual budget jumped from $89 billion to $165 billion, an 85 percent increase. With so much money, the Navy faced scant pressure to hold down costs, especially for counterterrorism defenses.

Ironically, many Navy officers doubted the Ring of Steel would work in a real crisis. Some mocked it as the "Ring of Gold" or the "Ring of Death." Captain Al Collins, who led naval exercises in Southeast Asia during the early 2000s, said he was "underwhelmed" by the level of protection. "It was either a bunch of barrels or a bunch of barges mated together," he said. "It's nothing sophisticated or fancy."

Some Navy officers guessed that the Ring of Steel might stop small boats but that watercraft more than thirty feet long could go right over the steel cables. There was also nothing to prevent a diver from swimming underneath and planting a bomb.

For reasons that remain unclear, the Navy never subjected the Ring of Steel to rigorous field testing. Five years after Francis began providing the Ring of Steel, the Navy's contracting office in Singapore hired Wackenhut, a security firm, to analyze force protection measures in Southeast Asia. Wackenhut reported the Ring of Steel had "a robust appearance," but noted that it remained untested and "may give a ship's captain a false sense of security while making only marginal contribution to the overall safety of the ship and crew."

The deputy commander of the Singapore contracting office complained that the Ring of Steel was "ridiculously expensive" and calculated that the Navy could have simply surrounded a ship with a perimeter of patrol boats for the same cost. For several years, the Singapore office tried to persuade the Seventh Fleet and Pacific Fleet staffs to define acceptable standards for the use of the Ring of Steel. But fleet officials didn't want to assume responsibility for force protection decisions, preferring instead to leave ship captains with that burden.

Francis's success with the Ring of Steel was an outgrowth of his strategic decision to base Glenn Defense in Singapore. The fast-growing city-state had swelled to around four million people since Francis lived there as a boy and had given the Americans access to an old British military installation after the closure of Subic Bay. Though the site was far too small to replace Subic, the Navy stationed about two hundred personnel in offices in Singapore to manage regional contracts, logistics, and other matters.

Intensely ambitious, Francis wanted to expand beyond the handful of ports he serviced for the Navy in Southeast Asia. To win more contracts and fatten his profit margins, he needed help navigating the inner workings of the Navy bureaucracy, which spoke in a peculiar dialect colored by acronyms and military jargon. With his corporate headquarters in Singapore, he had more opportunities to recruit tutors to teach him the Navy's lingo and feed him inside information about its business dealings.

Navy officials were prohibited from showing favoritism to contractors or working on their behalf. But Francis had a talent for spotting people who, with a little encouragement, would break the rules. He'd start by offering a modest inducement: a drink, an inexpensive lunch, a cigar. If his target took the bait, he'd ratchet up the value of the gifts.

He set his sights on David Kapaun, a Navy commander at the logistics office in Singapore whom he had met in 1999. Francis struck up a casual acquaintance, often bumping into Kapaun on the waterfront. In 2001, while refining his early designs for the Ring of Steel, Francis invited him to a group dinner at a hotel restaurant. The meal was nothing fancy, but Kapaun accepted and had a good time. Soon, they started meeting one-on-one at Singapore's Amara Hotel.

The Glenn Defense owner privately regarded Kapaun as a "silent, quiet weirdo" but viewed him as an ideal candidate to groom as an informant because he drank heavily and was estranged from his wife. Soon Francis began providing Kapaun with free hotel rooms and what he described as "a whole lot of expensive prostitutes." He learned that Kapaun liked Indonesian women and group sex, so he flew multiple prostitutes in from Jakarta.

After his liaisons, Kapaun sent "status reports" to Francis from an anonymous email account. He rated prostitutes by their looks and eagerness to perform his favorite sex acts. ("Anga and Olive. Most enthusiastic double.") In a half-joking attempt to hide the affairs from his wife, Kapaun prefaced the emails with coded references to secret operations ("Senior executives eyes only . . . Do not disseminate").

In exchange, Kapaun served as an unofficial business consultant for Francis and edited Glenn Defense's official correspondence with the Navy. "[Leonard's] written English was terrible," he recalled. He suggested how Francis could tweak his plans for the Ring of Steel to increase the chances that the Navy would pay for it. He coached Francis on the design by sharing photos and presentations of how the Navy protected its ships in other locales. He leaked confidential information about Glenn Defense's competitors and their pricing structures.

For Francis, the help was invaluable. Between 2001 and 2004, Kapaun became instrumental in the transformation of Glenn Defense from a small company into a leading contractor for the Navy. Francis later estimated that he provided Kapaun with $50,000 worth of prostitutes, meals, hotel rooms, tickets, and other gifts.

Even at the time, Kapaun recognized he had crossed the line into illegal behavior. "I knew the banshees might come to roost for me," he recalled. But he thought the worst that could happen was that the Navy might discipline him or drum him out of the service. It never occurred to him that he might go to prison.

Months after the *Cole* bombing, Francis flew to Tennessee to visit Jeff O'Neal, his boyhood friend from Penang, who had moved to a Nashville suburb. They hadn't seen each other in more than a decade. Jeff was shocked by how large his old pal had become. Leonard admitted to his friend that he now weighed about five hundred pounds.

He was too big to fit in a car, so Jeff picked him up at the airport in his truck. Leonard acknowledged that his eating was out of control. In desperation, he'd asked a doctor to wire his jaw so he could only drink liquids. But after a couple of days he gave up and had the wires removed. Before arriving in Nashville, he had visited a doctor in the Midwest—a specialist in gastric bypass surgery—to inquire about getting his stomach stapled. Leonard thought the operation sounded promising and said he planned to go through with it.

Jeff was pleased to see Leonard but noticed some other changes in his friend. While Leonard had always been a showman, he seemed overly intent on advertising his newfound wealth and status.

When they arrived at the O'Neal home, Leonard sprung a surprise: He was carrying $40,000 in cash. Did Jeff have a gun and a safe he could borrow so he wouldn't get robbed? Uh, no, Jeff replied. There wasn't much crime in the Nashville suburbs. Puzzled, he asked Leonard what he was thinking. Why didn't he just use credit cards? The business tycoon smiled but offered no real explanation.

During the visit, Leonard spent hours on the phone negotiating another lucrative contract with the Navy. He and Jeff also went shopping at souvenir stores in downtown Nashville, where Leonard spent about $1,000 on military paraphernalia and patriotic knickknacks emblazoned with U.S. flags and bald eagles. He wanted to decorate Glenn Defense's offices to show how pro-American he was.

The shopping trip left Leonard exhausted. When they got home, he told Jeff he was accustomed to having servants and, dropping a hint, mentioned that his maid in Singapore would take off his shoes for him. "I was like, 'No,'" Jeff said.

Despite his fatigue, Leonard wanted to take a side trip to Memphis. The lifelong Elvis fanatic had to see Graceland. Jeff couldn't take more time off work, so Leonard rented a car: a stretch limousine with a chauffeur. When the limo arrived, Jeff thought it looked like Leonard was going on a prom date or to a homecoming dance, not a two-hundred-mile ride to Elvis's mansion. Leonard climbed in, clutching his bag with what remained of his $40,000 in cash, giddy as a teenager.

"Off he went," Jeff recalled, "off to Graceland."

Chapter Four

Leonard the Legend

September 2003

SINGAPORE

With his shirt untucked and his stomach hanging out, an inebriated Leonard Francis lay atop a banquet table at one of the most exclusive restaurants in Singapore. A prostitute hand-fed him leftover morsels from the $30,000 feast he was hosting. Around the table, his American guests—about two dozen U.S. Navy and Marine Corps personnel—puffed Cohiba cigars from Cuba and swilled Dom Pérignon while a gaggle of young women massaged their necks. One Navy officer present said the scene resembled a "Roman orgy."

For the five-hour party with his American customers, Francis had rented Jaan, a Michelin-starred restaurant on the seventieth floor of a luxury hotel. Through plate-glass windows, the private dining room boasted spectacular views of the Singapore skyline and, in the distance, the twinkling lights of ships on the South China Sea. But the sights inside the restaurant that evening made an even more indelible impression.

One prostitute flashed her breasts at Rear Admiral Robert Conway Jr., the commanding officer of the USS *Peleliu* expeditionary strike group. Colonel Michael Regner, the normally rigid commander of the strike group's 2,200 Marines, mouthed the words to "Y.M.C.A" while a band played the disco hit. One Navy captain was spotted French-kissing a prostitute. As the spectacle unfolded, a few officers watched slack-jawed, unsure how to respond to their superiors' conduct. The rest had the time of their lives.

The evening had started innocently enough. Before the *Peleliu*, a Tarawa-class amphibious assault ship, arrived in Singapore for a port visit, Francis sent an invitation to Conway, offering to host a dinner for him and officers under his command. Like many admirals, Conway was known as a strict, at-times imperious boss. One staff officer described him as a "self-impressed" blowhard.

Conway showed the invitation to a uniformed Navy lawyer on his staff: a member of the Judge Advocate General's Corps, or JAG. Federal gift rules prohibited personnel from accepting gifts worth more than $20 from a contractor—something Conway had been taught repeatedly during mandatory ethics training—but the JAG officer sensed his boss really wanted to go and was looking for cover. The lawyer, whose career prospects depended on staying in the admiral's good graces, said it was probably fine if the event wasn't too fancy. The legal advice was dubious, but Conway embraced it.

On the night of the dinner, Glenn Defense drivers picked up Conway and the *Peleliu* strike group officers from the pier and chauffeured them to Swissôtel The Stamford, the tallest hotel in Singapore. Francis greeted them as they stepped off the elevator on the seventieth floor and summoned them inside the restaurant for cocktails. Most of the Americans had not met their host before and watched spellbound as he snapped his fingers at the waitstaff, ordering whiskey and other spirits for his guests. They admired the views as the sun dipped over the horizon, then gathered inside a private banquet room for the main event.

As the highest-ranking officer present, Conway received the place of honor at the head of the table, with Francis seated at his right elbow, juggling calls and texts on multiple mobile phones. As the seven-course meal progressed, he told the admiral stories, in graphic detail, about his recent gastric bypass surgery and how it had enabled him to shed about 150 pounds.

Close to midnight, about twenty young women whom officers described as "dressed to the nines" and wearing "hooker shoes" suddenly paraded into the room. "This is your entertainment for the evening!" Francis exclaimed. All eyes pivoted to Conway to gauge his reaction. The admiral seemed to be enjoying himself immensely. One woman broke the ice by sitting in an officer's lap. The guests cheered.

One person at the table looked visibly uncomfortable: Captain Cynthia Thebaud, the commanding officer of the USS *Decatur*, a destroyer in the *Peleliu's* strike group. She bit her tongue but emailed Conway's chief of staff the next day to express her displeasure. She wanted the admiral to know that the party flunked what she called the "*Washington Post* Front Page" test—in other words, they would all look like idiots if a reporter found out a defense contractor had bought them a meal that cost $880 per person and provided prostitutes as entertainment.

Conway dismissively told his staff to pass along the complaint to Glenn Defense, but the admiral didn't apologize or express any regrets about the dinner. Instead, he sent Francis a thank-you letter.

"Please accept my sincere appreciation and deepest gratitude for the exceptional support services you provided," he wrote. "Although our stay was brief, you made our stay a memorable one."

Though most people still called him Fat Leonard behind his back, Francis leveraged his magnificent dinner parties to encourage a different nickname: "Leonard the Legend." The banquets were the foundation of his strategy—honed in the aftermath of his success with the Ring of Steel—to expand his business by currying favor with commanding officers, especially admirals.

Over the years, he had learned that rank and perception meant everything in the military. Admirals in the Navy were like the College of Cardinals in the Roman Catholic Church: Both were exclusive clubs with around two hundred members who wielded near-absolute power. Francis knew whenever people saw him glad-handing an admiral, word would spread through the fleet that he was a VIP with connections at the top. Likewise, when admirals pocketed his perks, other officers assumed it was permissible for them to do the same. Most important, he understood that few would dare challenge his fraudulent business practices if they thought he was cozy with the brass.

Most admirals welcomed Francis's flattery. "Their egos allowed them to feel like they should be treated in a certain way, and he certainly scratched that itch," said Captain Ted Algire, a U.S. defense attaché in Hong Kong. Consequently, the Navy "turned a blind eye to anything this guy was doing."

By 2003, Francis had secured the contract for Navy port visits to Singapore and could barely keep up with all the ships crossing the Pacific en route to the Persian Gulf to help fight the wars in Iraq and Afghanistan.

In September 2003, the same month that he hosted Conway and the *Peleliu*, Francis reserved the Jaan restaurant again to impress another admiral. The USS *Nimitz*, a nuclear-powered aircraft carrier, had stopped in Singapore after completing a mission to the Gulf. Francis wanted to meet the head of the *Nimitz* strike group: Rear Admiral Samuel Locklear III, a tall, silver-haired South Carolinian and Naval Academy graduate, as well as a rising star in the fleet. The wives of many *Nimitz* officers—including Locklear's—had traveled to Singapore to see their spouses for the first time in months. Francis invited them, too.

The *Nimitz* affair was slightly more modest than the *Peleliu* party, but still elaborate. Francis seated himself next to Locklear during the eight-course meal, which included caviar, freshly shucked oysters, three preparations of foie gras, lobster Thermidor, beef tenderloin, and baked Alaska. As he did with Conway, Francis engrossed the admiral with a blow-by-blow account of his stomach-stapling operation.

After clearing the plates, the waitstaff handed out Cohiba cigars. When the gathering ended around 11 p.m., Francis handed floral bouquets to the wives and personalized wooden plaques to the officers. All told, it cost Francis upward of $300 per person.

Francis stayed on his best behavior around the wives. But on another night during the port visit, he enticed his old friend from Bali—Commander Robert Gilbeau, newly promoted and now the head of the Nimitz's supply department—to join him at Brix, a loud nightclub at the Grand Hyatt Hotel. Francis said he paid some prostitutes they met there to spend the night with the forty-two-year-old Gilbeau and another Navy officer.

The Nimitz was scheduled to visit Hong Kong next. But after several days at sea, Gilbeau emailed Francis to say the carrier's plans had unexpectedly changed: The ship would be returning to Singapore. Gilbeau suggested visiting Brix for another evening of fun. "Catch my drift?" he wrote.

Francis understood completely. "The Kahuna above has heard our prayers," he replied. "Will be standin by to Welcome you all back home to Papa Leonard soon." He promised that a female friend from their previous night on the town would be "waiting eagerly."

He hastily arranged another opulent dinner at Jaan—the third in less than a month—for Locklear, Gilbeau, and others from the Nimitz strike group. This time, however, the evening would be just for the guys. The officers' wives had left town.

About twenty-five guests, dressed casually in shirts and slacks, crowded around a single long table topped with floral displays of red roses. Francis spent $35,000 on the feast.

After dessert, things turned rowdy. Francis stood on a chair and sang at the top of his lungs while a conga line of graying, middle-aged Navy men shuffled through the restaurant, hands on another's hips. Locklear, normally dignified and tightly composed, beamed as he loosened up with a glass of cognac.

Then the festivities really took a turn. "The doors opened and Fat

Leonard brought in the girls," recalled Commander David Fravor, a pilot who served on the *Nimitz*. "There were probably about fifteen girls, at least, who barged in."

Francis's hospitality, as intended, left an unforgettable impression on the admiral.

"I just wanted to say thank you for the kind invitation to your dinner party," Locklear wrote to Francis a few days later, gushing about the "wonderful" venue and the "incredible" view. "The food was absolutely magnificent!"

Francis recouped his party expenses, and then some, by overcharging the *Nimitz* for the port visit.

Gilbeau, the carrier's supply officer, had the authority to approve major purchases so Francis asked him to buy $200,000 worth of flat-screen televisions for the ship from Glenn Defense. The carrier had no pressing need to acquire televisions in a foreign country, but Francis said he wanted to mark up the price by 40 to 50 percent. "Help out an old buddy," Francis urged in an email. Gilbeau obliged.

Glenn Defense further overcharged the *Nimitz* by claiming it had pumped 450,000 gallons of wastewater from the ship, more than twice the usual amount for a port visit. Francis said Gilbeau agreed to pay the fraudulent wastewater invoice in exchange for a $40,000 cash bribe and two prostitutes. "He doubled it up just so that he could get a kickback from me and get laid, of course," Francis recalled. (Gilbeau confirmed that he approved the wastewater bill but said he didn't realize that it was inflated. He denied taking the $40,000 in cash. "I never accepted a bribe from Leonard Francis.")

In 2004, Glenn Defense won a new husbanding contract to service Navy ships in Hong Kong. With its glittering skyline, tantalizing food, and English-speaking red-light districts, the former British colony had exerted a gravitational pull on American sailors for generations.

To commemorate his expansion to Hong Kong, Francis organized a holiday party for officers from the USS *Abraham Lincoln*, a nuclear-powered aircraft carrier, and three smaller warships in its strike group: the USS *Benfold*, the USS *Shoup*, and the USS *Shiloh*. The ships anchored near Penny's Bay on Christmas Eve and Francis invited the strike group commander, Rear Admiral Doug Crowder, and his officers to a "Christmas Cheer" celebration on December 26.

A Naval Academy graduate from North Carolina, the fifty-two-year-old Crowder was making his eighth visit to Hong Kong. He had never met Francis but thought his staff might appreciate the holiday party. He asked his JAG officer, Lieutenant Commander Scott Thompson, to review the invitation. It was Thompson's first time dealing with Glenn Defense too, and he knew Navy personnel were not supposed to accept gifts from a defense contractor. He emailed the company to inquire about the event.

Over the years, Francis had become adept at fielding queries from Navy lawyers and circumventing ethics rules. He ordered a Glenn Defense staffer to masquerade as a corporate attorney and respond to Thompson, assuring him that the event would be open to other Americans in Hong Kong, including a broad cross section of people from business and government with a diversity of interests. None of it was true. But the description, not coincidentally, mirrored the language in an obscure section of the U.S. Code of Federal Regulations that permitted government officials to accept invitations to professional conferences and other "widely attended gatherings" for free.

Thompson thought the explanation passed muster, but he double-checked with a senior JAG officer on the Seventh Fleet staff in Japan, asking whether he could take Glenn Defense's assurances at "face value." He was told yes. That was good enough for Thompson. He advised the admiral that it was legally permissible to attend the Christmas Cheer party. "I ran the traps, I thought, pretty thoroughly," he recalled. "I was trying to do the right thing."

Most of the strike group officers were thrilled, but one sensed trouble. Commander David Meyers, the head of the *Abraham Lincoln's* supply department, urged the carrier's commanding officer, Captain Kendall Card, not to attend. He thought it was stupid to accept such a blatant overture from a defense contractor and predicted Francis would use the party as an excuse to gouge the Navy for the port visit.

"I said, 'All his profits are coming from overcharging us for services,'" Meyers recalled. "When they said they were going to go, I'm thinking, 'You're the captain of this ship and you've had more ethical training than me, but this seems like a no-brainer.'"

The brass ignored him. On the evening of December 26, Admiral Crowder, Captain Card, and about sixty Navy officers from the strike group—minus Meyers and his staff from the supply department—arrived at Petrus, a resplendent French restaurant on the fifty-sixth floor of the Shangri-La Hotel overlooking Hong Kong's Victoria Harbour. Waiting to greet them was a troupe of bagpipers and a beaming Francis, dressed in a black suit with wide lapels and a red-and-green Santa Claus tie. He had planned his most extravagant dinner yet.

For cocktails, he'd stocked the open bars with Dom Pérignon and Cristal champagne, rare whiskeys, Armagnac brandy, and thirty-year-old vintages of wine from the Château Lafite Rothschild. A Filipino chorus sang Christmas carols while the waitstaff handed out fistfuls of Cuban cigars.

Despite Glenn Defense's representations that a broad cross section of people would attend, only two guests were unaffiliated with the Navy or Francis's firm: a *South China Morning Post* reporter and a priest who volunteered as a U.S. military chaplain in Hong Kong.

Glenn Defense spent more than $60,000 on the dinner, or roughly $800 per person, forty times the federal $20 gift limit. After cocktails, guests gathered around circular tables and luxuriated in a seven-course meal featuring Francis's favorite surf-and-turf delicacies:

Light Boston lobster jelly with Oscietra caviar
*And cauliflower espuma**

Warm black truffle royale with cepe cappuccino

Duck liver confit raviolis with black truffles

Champagne sherbet with peach foam

Boston lobster Thermidor

Beef fillet served with shallots cooked in red wine,
bone marrow potatoes and grilled duck liver,
Bordelaise sauce

Vanilla strawberry flambing Alaska

One officer called it the "fanciest dinner I'd ever been to." Captain Craig Faller, the skipper of the *Shiloh*, sized up the forty-year-old Francis as "full of himself, pretty large and in charge" but couldn't help being amazed. "I won't sugarcoat it and say, you know, it was just a standard party. It was sort of, wow, very nice event, world-class event," he recalled.

But what really caught everyone's eyes were the amorous young women dressed as elves, roaming the restaurant in red-and-white hats, black boots, and skimpy yuletide skirts. Francis introduced them as his Santa Niñas, or Santa Girls. The elves flirted with the American officers all night, giving them hugs, fetching them drinks, and asking whether they had been naughty or nice.

Commander Donald Hornbeck, the skipper of the USS *Benfold*, couldn't believe it when he arrived. "Is this illegal?" he asked a colleague, who assured him the party was legitimate—or at least that the JAG officer had said so. Hornbeck perked up when a blond Santa Niña snuggled in close and showed him her bare thighs. Fortified by a

---

* A foam or froth that is a hallmark of molecular gastronomy.

few drinks, he donned his Ray-Ban sunglasses and crashed the stage to play drums with the band.

Armed with cameras, the Santa Niñas darted around the restaurant snapping photographs of themselves with dozens of tipsy officers. At that point, Lieutenant Commander Thompson realized he'd made a colossal error in judgment by giving his legal blessing to the dinner. "I definitely felt snookered," he recalled.

Other JAG officers at the party worried that the women and their cameras presented a counterintelligence threat. It would be easy to blackmail Navy officers with photos of their drunken behavior with women who appeared to be prostitutes. Making matters worse: Some of the women spoke with Russian-sounding accents.

The counterintelligence risk would become more acute in the years ahead as several of the partygoers ascended in the ranks. Crowder later pinned on a third star and served as the commander of the Seventh Fleet. Card became a vice admiral and chief of Naval Intelligence. Faller became a four-star admiral and held high-ranking jobs at the Pentagon.

The JAGs had been right to worry: Francis kept digital copies of the Santa Niñas' photographs, adding them to his collection of compromising material on senior officers. He expected the dirt might come in handy someday.

The morning of Francis's Christmas Cheer bash, a historic earthquake measuring 9.1 on the Richter scale struck the Indian Ocean seabed off the west coast of Sumatra, about 1,850 miles southwest of Hong Kong. The quake triggered a tsunami that crashed into coastlines in Indonesia, Malaysia, Thailand, Sri Lanka, and India, killing 220,000 people.

As news of the disaster spread, the *Abraham Lincoln* strike group received orders to depart Hong Kong early to conduct a humanitarian relief mission. The day after the party, while the ships prepared to leave, Francis boarded the aircraft carrier to hand out boxes of cigars as gifts and to present Glenn Defense's bills for the port visit.

Lieutenant Chris Statler, the stock control officer in the *Abraham Lincoln's* supply department, had not attended the party. But he heard stories about the scrumptious food, Dom Pérignon, and prostitutes. When Francis handed him a $600,000 invoice for pumping wastewater from the ship, he was incensed. He knew the aircraft carrier didn't generate that much sewage and suspected Glenn Defense was dumping it in the harbor anyway.

Statler accused Francis of padding the bills to cover the costs of the dinner. Francis didn't deny it but demanded full payment. In the end, Statler had to back down. There was a rush to get under way because of the tsunami, and the bills had to be settled before the ship could depart. "He laughed in my face," Statler recalled. "He knew he was going to get paid."

Francis's strategy of kissing up to the admirals was soon vindicated. Two days later, as the *Abraham Lincoln* rushed toward the Indian Ocean to help quake victims, Rear Admiral Crowder took a moment to compose a letter.

"Dear Leonard," he wrote by hand. "Thanks so much for inviting me and so many of my officers to your wonderful dinner . . . And what an event it was!! Everyone is still talking about it! It was great to get to know you and your other guests. And I know that you easily could see what a great time we all had."

Part Two
2006

Chapter Five

Mr. Make-It-Happen

January 2006

SAN DIEGO, CALIFORNIA

Proud-but-teary family members crowded the dock at the North Island Naval Air Station on a balmy winter day, waving tiny American flags as they bade farewell to the Navy's newest aircraft carrier, the USS *Ronald Reagan*. After eighteen months of tests and drills, the $4.5 billion warship was departing Southern California on its maiden deployment. The Navy had not officially announced the *Reagan*'s destination, but everyone in San Diego knew its five thousand sailors were headed to the Persian Gulf to support the wars in Iraq and Afghanistan. Michael Reagan, the fortieth president's son, was on hand to wish the crew good luck. "Win one for the Gipper!" he told them.

As the *Reagan* approached Singapore, its last port of call before the Gulf, the crew trained for the combat mission ahead. But the strike group commander, Rear Admiral Michael Miller, had additional things on his mind: shopping and fine dining.

A mustachioed, fun-loving redhead from Minot, North Dakota, Miller graduated from the Naval Academy in 1974. ("Undoubtedly Mike will go far," the Academy yearbook predicted, "as far as the next bar.") Trained as an S-3 Viking antisubmarine aircraft pilot—his call sign was "Madman"—he flew combat missions in Libya and commanded an air squadron in the first Persian Gulf war. During the late 1990s, he served as a Seventh Fleet staff officer in Asia, where he had fond memories of time spent with Leonard Francis. Now that he was back in the region, the admiral wanted to reconnect.

"Leonard, Rear Admiral Mike Miller, here, checking in," he emailed as the *Reagan* passed through the Java Sea. "Don't know if you remember me or not. . . . We always called you 'Mr. Make-it-Happen' on the staff, since you consistently seemed to find a path to success."

Miller piled on more compliments and invited Francis for a chat in his stateroom once the ship arrived in Singapore. He had some favors to ask. "I'm wondering if you would have any suggestions for where I might find some nice rattan furniture. I'm looking for a comfortable swivel chair or rocker that I can relax in, but have found them cost prohibitive back in the States." The admiral also wanted a digital camera "at a decent price."

"Looking forward to our visit, and renewing our friendship," he concluded warmly.

Despite Miller's chummy tone, Francis barely remembered him. But as soon as he read the email, he understood the subtext. Leonard the Legend's reputation for largesse had circulated through the admiral's old-boy network, and this one wanted a share of the spoils.

He wrote Miller back to say he was happy to oblige.

"Dear Admiral Miller: What a pleasant surprise it was to hear from you, and it is always a pleasure to renew old acquaintances! I sincerely appreciate your kind words. Of course I remember you." He promised to satisfy the admiral's shopping needs and couldn't resist mentioning that he had slimmed down to a svelte 350 pounds since they last met. "You may have trouble recognizing me as I am not the Red oak I once was!" he bragged. "Although I may be only half the size of my former self, I am still 'Mr. Make-it-Happen.'"

More than other branches of the armed forces, the Navy invested its commanding officers with an unusual degree of independence, a tradition dating to the era of sailing ships, when captains ruled with an iron hand during long voyages. Even in the modern era, the Navy bestowed commanding officers with unfettered authority to ensure successful missions and the well-being of their crews. The downside was that they often became accustomed to royal treatment and few subordinates had the courage to chide them for a swollen ego.

During his thirty-two years in the Navy, Miller had earned a reputation as a leader who cared deeply about his sailors but also savored the trappings of his rank. A JAG officer on his staff described him as someone who "has expensive tastes and likes to buy nice things." Francis, who was used to Navy officers extending their hands for freebies, said Miller was in a category of his own, calling him "very entitled" with "two hands and two legs" out. Francis had already been planning one of his patented dinner parties for officers on the *Reagan*, but after receiving Miller's email he rushed to upgrade his usual package of perks for the visiting admiral.

As part of its contract with the Navy, Glenn Defense was required to provide senior officers with ground transportation during port visits. The contract called only for the basics: an air-conditioned sedan and driver. But Francis ordered his personal chauffeur to escort Miller around Singapore in a "British racing green" Jaguar with a plush leather interior.

On the third day of the *Reagan's* visit, Francis invited Miller to tour Glenn Defense's new glass-walled headquarters on Pandan Road, along the waterfront overlooking the Singapore Strait. He also wanted to show off a decommissioned British warship he had purchased. Formerly known as the RFA *Sir Lancelot*, it was built in the 1960s as a logistics landing ship and served in the 1982 Falklands War.

Francis spent $3 million upgrading the ship and renamed it the *Glenn Braveheart*, an allusion to the Scottish martyr William Wallace and Francis's own Highlander lineage. Over four hundred feet long and capable of carrying three hundred people and two helicopters, the *Braveheart* was by far the most imposing ship in Glenn Defense's growing fleet of barges, tugboats, and supply vessels. But it was of little practical use and served mostly as an outlet for Francis's vanity. He held parties on the ship, used it to transport his Rolls-Royces from port to port, and staffed the crew with elite British-trained soldiers from Nepal known as Gurkhas.

Flanked by a Gurkha honor guard and bagpipers wearing kilts, Francis welcomed Miller aboard the *Braveheart* with full VIP honors and gave him a wooden-and-brass plaque. As they chatted inside Francis's office on the ship, Miller admired a collection of burgundy Chesterfield-style chairs and commented that they would look nice in his stateroom on the *Reagan*. Francis had recently bought the chairs for about $1,700 each but took the hint. When Miller departed, Francis instructed an assistant to polish three of the chairs and deliver them to the *Reagan* for the admiral's personal use.

That night, Francis again rented out the Jaan restaurant, to entertain Miller and about thirty other guests from the *Reagan* and the U.S. embassy in Singapore. The event began with cocktails on the skyscraper's helipad, where bagpipers in kilts played in the drizzle. Despite the clouds, one Navy officer was so taken by the high-altitude views that he swore he could see the curvature of the earth.

Because some Navy spouses were present, Francis exercised restraint and did not bring prostitutes. But he did flaunt his new wife, Teresa, a raven-haired "catwalk model" whom he introduced as "Miss Indonesia." The Americans found her captivating—one officer called her "drop-dead gorgeous"—and marveled at Fat Leonard's improbable ability to attract such a beauty.*

At her husband's direction, Teresa sat next to Miller during the meal and hovered over his right elbow. With smug satisfaction, Francis noticed the admiral gazing at her with a "lusty" look on his face.

---

* Francis divorced his first wife, Deanna, in the 1990s. "Hey, I'm a butterfly and there's so much out there," he explained. "Not that I'm a bad husband. It's just that women can't keep up with me."

Miller admitted he found her attractive. "She was very striking, so you wouldn't forget meeting her," he recalled.

On the helipad, Francis and his guests noshed on hors d'oeuvres and drained twenty-four bottles of Dom Pérignon. Then they retreated indoors to assigned seats where embossed menu cards trumpeted another surf-and-turf feast:

*Amuse-Bouche**

Pan Fried Duck Liver And Terrine Au Naturel
Caramelized Mini Pear, Orange-Pepper Reduction

Perigord Black Truffle Crème
Braised Bobby Veal Shank Pastilla

Intermezzo

John Dory† With Nut Crumble
Risotto And Sevruga Caviar, Garlic-Parsley Butter

Grilled Beef Tenderloin Maine Lobster Thermidor
Mashed Potato And Pilaf Rice, Truffle Jus

Grand Cru Dark Chocolate Mousse
Wild Strawberry Coulis, Walnuts Maple Ice Cream

Coffee or Tea
Mignardises

Between courses, Francis and his Navy friends kept the wine steward scrambling. They ordered thirty-one bottles of Bordeaux and seven bottles of Sauternes. After dessert, they sipped twenty-eight glasses of cognac and smoked thirty-six Cuban cigars. At the

---

* A single, bite-sized appetizer—or "mouth amuser" in French.
† A flat, spiny fish with creamy white flesh, served pan-fried or grilled.

end of the evening, the restaurant handed Francis an itemized bill for $28,375. More than half of it was for the booze.

The indulgences didn't end there. Francis honored Miller by presenting him with an elaborate model of the *Reagan*—at a scale of 350 to 1, it was the size of a coffee table—that he'd custom-ordered from a Florida craftsman for $5,150.

The beneficence touched Miller. "Leonard, my thanks to you and Teresa for one of the best evenings of my life," he wrote the next day in an email. "Your generosity is only exceeded by your genuine concern for each and every one of my Sailors, and I will forever be in your debt for the many courtesies that you have extended them . . . and me."

Nothing made Francis happier than knowing an admiral was in his debt. Inevitably, he knew, a time would come when he'd want to call in a favor.

He was also pleased that he had found a way to dodge U.S. government killjoys who wanted to clamp down on his fun. By the time of the *Reagan*'s visit in 2006, Navy contracting officials in Singapore who oversaw husbanding operations across Asia had received numerous reports about Glenn Defense's profligate parties. Some worried Francis had become an "ethics time bomb" and decided an intervention was necessary, though there was only so much they could do to prevent higher-ranking Navy officers from misbehaving.

After the fabled Christmas Cheer celebration two years earlier, they inserted a clause into Glenn Defense's contracts requiring the company to "refrain from providing gratuities, upgrades, entertainment, food, parties and any other prohibited items" to Navy personnel. Commander David Warunek, the head of the Singapore contracting office, said it was highly unusual for the Navy to try to regulate a company's conduct in that manner but called the Hong Kong soiree the "last straw."

The edict had forced Francis to cancel a few events, including a giant beach party for about a hundred people on Sentosa Island in Singapore. But with the connivance of Navy officers who wanted to let the good times roll, he devised a workaround grounded in the same logic as the Pentagon's "Don't Ask, Don't Tell" policy for gays in the military.

Under the scheme, Francis's guests agreed in advance to reimburse him a token amount for a dinner, usually $50 per person. They knew the real expense would be exponentially higher, but as long as they didn't ask and Francis didn't show them the bill, they could claim they had paid for their meal. For the dinner at Jaan, for instance, several officers from the *Reagan* said they paid Francis between $50 and $70 apiece.

The only one who kept a record was Miller. The day after the party, he wrote a personal check to Francis for $550: fifty bucks for the dinner and $500 for the ship model. He wrote a second check for $1,000 for his new stateroom chairs and a third check for $203 to reimburse Francis for a new digital camera.

The checks covered only a fraction of what the items cost. But Miller also gave Francis something priceless: a written endorsement.

Commanding officers had a tradition of sending congratulatory messages known as Bravo Zulus, a Navy term meaning "well done." Bravo Zulus were basically thank-you notes, intended as a public pat on the back. But Francis treasured the letters as a boost to his business and exploited them in a way that none of his competitors did.

Although Navy rules prohibited contractor endorsements, Francis constantly solicited written praise from commanding officers. He showcased Bravo Zulus in glossy marketing brochures and attached them to his bids for Navy contracts. He coveted messages from admirals because their words carried extra weight. If a junior officer were to file a complaint about Glenn Defense's performance, Francis could easily neutralize it with a Bravo Zulu from an admiral.

Two days after the *Reagan* strike group departed Singapore, Miller signed an over-the-top Bravo Zulu applauding Glenn Defense for performing "like a well-oiled machine" and "delivering extraordinary customer service." It singled out Francis by name, saying his "ability to 'make it happen,' regardless of the size of the challenge, is simply without parallel." To Francis's delight, Miller circulated the message widely, copying it to U.S. Pacific Fleet headquarters at Pearl Harbor, the commander of the Seventh Fleet, and even the contracting office in Singapore that had tried to outlaw Glenn Defense's parties.

A few weeks later, Miller sang the Malaysian businessman's praises again in an email to a fellow admiral passing through Asia. "Should you need anything, trust me, Leonard can make it happen," Miller wrote. "If you haven't met him, be sure to greet he [sic] and his beautiful wife Teresa for me when you pull in. Leonard brings an entirely new definition of 'first class' service to the ship."

The compliments were proof that his investment in Miller was paying off.

The *Reagan* departed Singapore on February 11, 2006, and crossed the Indian Ocean to the Persian Gulf. During three months in the Middle East, the carrier's air wing launched more than 6,100 sorties, most of them combat flights in support of the war in Iraq.

Amid the fighting, some officers daydreamed about their epicurean adventures with Francis and longed for more. "I'm still full from that wonderful spread you put on for us in Singapore," Commander David Pimpo, the *Reagan*'s supply officer, emailed Francis on March 30.

In May, the *Reagan* strike group ended its mission in the Gulf and returned to Southeast Asia. Francis was planning to welcome the *Reagan* with another dinner at its next port of call in Kuala Lumpur. But Miller's chief of staff emailed with discouraging news: Navy spoilsports were asking legalistic questions "that may prevent us from accepting your generous offers."

Undeterred, Francis dusted off an old trick. Under federal ethics regulations, Navy personnel were allowed—and often expected—to attend formal events hosted by foreign governments. He went forward with his plans for a ritzy dinner, but in addition to the Americans, he invited a handful of officers from the Royal Malaysian Navy and designated them the official hosts. The Malaysian Navy was perpetually strapped for cash and couldn't afford fancy business meals, so its officers were happy to wink and nod at the arrangement.

The June 4 steak-and-lobster dinner and cocktail reception took place at the Chalet, Francis's favorite restaurant in Kuala Lumpur. Miller and sixteen officers from the *Reagan* strike group attended, along with Captain Claudia Risner, the U.S. naval attaché to Malaysia. While Francis pretended the Malaysian government was hosting such events, Risner said she always made it "crystal clear" to visiting U.S. Navy officers that Glenn Defense was really footing the bill.

"I remember a couple of [admirals] saying, 'Wow, this is really nice of the Malaysian Navy to host this.' And I said, 'the Malaysian Navy is not hosting this.' I said, 'The husbanding agent you pay is hosting this,'" Risner recalled. Still, she said, nobody seemed bothered. "It's not like they bolted from the room or called the cops or anything."

The cost of the Kuala Lumpur dinner exceeded $1,000 per person. In keeping with their Don't Ask, Don't Tell agreement, Miller wrote a personal check to reimburse Francis for his and his officers' share: $50 a head. "Thanks again for the magnificent support," the admiral added in a handwritten note. He also praised Glenn Defense in another effusive Bravo Zulu message: "Mr. Francis can truly do it all—throughout our deployment no one has come even close to his level of service."

Miller and his staff had to rally quickly to regain their appetites. Seven days after the party in Malaysia, Francis hosted another epic dinner at the *Reagan*'s next port of call in Hong Kong.

Several Navy spouses had flown in to spend time with their husbands during the four-day port visit. Miller again reimbursed Francis for the meal at a rate of $50 per person, even though the total bill came to $23,061, about $769 per guest.

Glenn Defense went the extra mile to make the Hong Kong visit memorable in other ways. The company paid $28,000 for several wives of *Reagan* strike group officers to go on a sightseeing and shopping tour, picking them up from the airport in a caravan of Rolls-Royces. Glenn Defense also reserved luxury hotel suites for some officers and their spouses, covering about half of their lodging expenses.

"The service you provide is head and shoulders above all others," Miller crowed to Francis in yet another Bravo Zulu message.

Francis's business was flourishing, and his entertainment expenses were a pittance compared with the husbanding revenue Glenn Defense was collecting from the Navy. A four-day port visit by an aircraft carrier strike group could generate more than $1 million for the company, plus however much extra Francis could earn from phony bills.

During the *Reagan's* last day in port in Hong Kong, for example, Glenn Defense submitted a fraudulent invoice for removing 1.2 million gallons of sewage from the aircraft carrier, far more than its tanks could hold. Lieutenant David Schaus, a junior officer with the Navy's Ship Support Office in Hong Kong, flagged the charges and determined Glenn Defense had overbilled the carrier by $68,000.

It wasn't the first time that Schaus had caught Glenn Defense cheating. Two years earlier, he had confronted Francis about another impossibly high wastewater bill. "He became furious, accusing me of calling him a liar. And I told him, 'I *am* calling you a liar,'" Schaus recalled. "He said, 'Lieutenants don't tell me what to do. Do you know who I am?' He was being profane and banging on the table."

Schaus lost that argument after Francis complained to his superiors, who told the lieutenant to back off. This time, Schaus escalated matters by reporting the *Reagan's* bogus sewage bill to the Naval Criminal Investigative Service.

An NCIS agent reviewed the invoices and confirmed Schaus's allegations. But the agent inexplicably closed the case and wrote a note saying the findings would be referred to the *Reagan's* commanding officer, Captain Terry Kraft, one of the guests at Francis's $23,000 dinner. Nothing happened after that. (Kraft said he was never informed about the NCIS investigation.)

Schaus was stunned that NCIS would let Glenn Defense slide but relearned a harsh lesson: Francis had powerful friends inside the Navy who would protect him. Glenn Defense "was rotten from the first day I worked with them in 2004, and everyone knew they were rotten," he recalled. "Everyone knew what was going on, and it was just accepted as the way it was. If you tried to rock the boat, you got squashed."

Tellingly, nobody in the *Reagan*'s supply department complained about the overbilling. When the ship returned to Hong Kong nine months later, Commander Pimpo—the senior supply officer—emailed Francis to puff him up and see if he was game for another dinner.

"Leonard, you are already a legend in the RONALD REAGAN STRIKE GROUP. Everybody knows 'Leonard' and appreciates your professionalism and class," he wrote. "You guys are the best we've ever seen . . . by a long shot."

Francis fulfilled their expectations. On March 10, 2007, he hosted Pimpo and seventeen others from the *Reagan* for an eight-course spectacle at Spoon, a restaurant at the InterContinental Hotel run by renowned chef Alain Ducasse.

The Malaysian contractor and his beautiful wife greeted the Americans in a private banquet room with caviar appetizers and crystal goblets of Dom Pérignon. They dined on white-asparagus custard, Maine lobster with coral sauce, black truffles, Angus tenderloin "Rossini" style, and Pont-Neuf potatoes. Each course was paired with a different French wine.

Their bellies full, the *Reagan* officers sipped brandy and blew smoke rings from Cohiba cigars. They also autographed a tasseled copy of the menu in homage to their hosts. "Leonard & Teresa—The only thing more precious than this meal is your friendship! Thank you for all you do! God bless," Pimpo scribbled.

As had become customary, the Navy officers paid $50 per person. Francis happily covered the rest of the $20,962 bill. He was investing in relationships with officers with bright futures. In the years ahead, five of his guests from the Hong Kong dinner would become admirals.

Among them was Captain Michael Gilday, the commodore of a destroyer squadron who later rose through the ranks to become the chief of naval operations, the highest-ranking admiral in the Navy. "Thank you for an amazing night!" Gilday wrote to Francis on the commemorative menu. His attendance would remain a secret for the rest of his military career.

Chapter Six

Naked Bribery

January 2006

SINGAPORE

The tiny Republic of Singapore covers about 275 square miles, less than one-quarter the size of Rhode Island. Yet, in 2006, it ranked as the busiest port in the world, moving nearly 25 million containers of cargo. Though scores of American warships visited each year, the U.S. Navy maintained only a small permanent presence. About 250 uniformed and civilian personnel worked out of a two-story office building on a restricted wharf in Sembawang, a former British military base across the Strait of Johor from the southern tip of Malaysia. Their primary mission was to oversee the Navy's contracting and logistical operations for Southeast Asia.

The senior civilian supervisor at the Naval Regional Contracting Center in Singapore was Paul Simpkins, a fifty-one-year-old South Carolinian who had specialized in the fine print of defense contracts since he was a teenager. He served more than two decades as a uniformed contracting officer in the Air Force and attained the rank of master sergeant before retiring from active duty in 1994. He then filled a variety of civilian contracting jobs for the Marines and Navy before arriving in Singapore in 2005 for a two-year assignment. In his new job, he held the power to award millions of dollars in federal contracts.

The child of a single mother, Simpkins grew up poor in the South. The military provided him with a steady career, if not riches, and opportunities to live all over the world. A slim, fastidious man, he was an introvert who rarely socialized with coworkers or discussed his personal life. Few knew that he had been married five times or that his current wife had cancer and was living in Japan. Even fewer knew he was cheating on her with a Chinese girlfriend who would eventually become spouse number six.

During visits to the contracting center, however, Leonard Francis had gleaned tidbits about Simpkins's tumultuous personal life and sensed an opportunity. Beginning in January 2006, he invited Simpkins to meet sporadically for drinks at a bar in the Amara Hotel, a place where they were unlikely to attract attention. The Amara catered to international travelers, not locals, and was nestled in the central business district, far from the Navy's contracting office in the northern district of Sembawang.

Francis wanted to build a rapport without spooking his target. During their first few meetups, he casually mentioned that he was thinking about expanding Glenn Defense's operations beyond Malaysia, Singapore, Indonesia, and Hong Kong. He admitted he wanted more business from the Navy but was impatient with its sclerotic bidding process and needed to sideline his competitors.

After several conversations, Simpkins cut to the chase: What was in it for him?

Francis was pleased. This was a man he could do business with. Ordinarily, he devoted months or years to grooming Navy contacts, but occasionally he got lucky and found someone who was unabashedly greedy. During a subsequent visit to the hotel bar, Francis said he handed over an envelope containing a stack of $100 bills—$50,000 worth. Simpkins smiled, allegedly taking the bribe and sliding it into his jacket pocket.

The payoff marked the beginning of one of Francis's most corrupt and productive relationships. In multiple payments over ten months—while he was simultaneously wining and dining the brass from the *Reagan*—he bribed Simpkins with an additional $350,000 by wiring the money to a Japanese bank account in the name of his cancer-stricken wife. As an added sweetener, he said, he provided Simpkins with prostitutes on more than ten occasions. In exchange, Simpkins served as Glenn Defense's covert enforcer inside the Navy's contracting office in Singapore and rigged government business in the company's favor.

With Simpkins secretly on his payroll, Francis crushed his rivals in the husbanding industry and extended Glenn Defense's reach throughout Asia. His first task for Simpkins was to crack the lucrative Thai market. The Navy had a long history in Thailand. Sailors loved making port calls at the Andaman Sea resort of Phuket and the beach towns south of Bangkok. Since the Vietnam War, the Navy had given its business in Thailand to a husbanding contractor named Chin Ounsathitporn. Nicknamed Papa Chin by the Americans, he received good marks for his service and had rebuffed Francis's attempts to muscle into his territory.

Simpkins moved swiftly to change all that. One month after he allegedly pocketed his first cash bribe, he recommended that the Navy award its husbanding business in Thailand to Glenn Defense. Soon, Navy higher-ups approved a contract worth $7.1 million. Francis was ebullient. "Yes we have conquered Thailand from Chin after 30 years," he boasted to a Navy officer in an email.

Other Glenn Defense competitors suddenly got slammed, too. A few weeks after winning the Thailand deal, Francis fed Simpkins spurious allegations that an Australian husbanding firm had overcharged the Navy for a port visit in the Maldives, an island nation in the Indian Ocean. The complaint was pure hypocrisy—Glenn Defense regularly did the same thing.

But Simpkins seized on the allegations and recommended that officials in Washington suspend the Australian company. He then leaked a copy of the proposed suspension to Francis as proof of his efforts to kneecap Glenn Defense's rival. "I did the research myself," he gloated in an email decorated with several smiley-face emojis.

Sensing his value, Simpkins demanded more bribes. On May 15, Francis reassured him in an email, "the $$ will flow." Over the next eight days, he made good on his word and wired two payments totaling $200,000 to the bank account registered to Simpkins's wife.

For much of 2006, Francis pushed Simpkins to rig another major husbanding contract, this one for the Philippines. Though the Philippine government had forced the Navy to abandon its base at Subic Bay, the archipelago nation still had a mutual defense treaty with the United States and close historical and cultural ties. During the Cold War, the Navy recruited more than 35,000 Filipinos to serve on its ships and gave them a path to U.S. citizenship. By the 2000s, it was not uncommon for sailors of Filipino descent to make up 15 or 20 percent of a Navy crew.

A company called Global Terminals & Development Inc. had handled Navy port visits in the country for years. But when the Philippines contract came up for renewal, Francis wired another $50,000 bribe to the bank account of Simpkins's wife. Two months later, on Simpkins's recommendation, the Navy awarded the bulk of the Philippines contract to Glenn Defense.

The Philippines and Thailand contracts gave Glenn Defense temporary control of most of Southeast Asia.

Suspicious that Glenn Defense had cheated to win the bidding, Rose Baldeo, Global's founder and chief executive, filed an official protest to try to overturn the contract award. The move infuriated Francis and prompted him to resort to more trickery.

"Now the Bitch Rose is suing," Francis complained to a Navy officer in an email. In addition to his admiral friends, Francis maintained an extensive network of informants at all levels of the Navy's chain of command. He asked his moles to dig up dirt on Baldeo. A former low-ranking staffer at the U.S. embassy in Manila sent him police records showing that Baldeo had been charged multiple times for bouncing checks.

The two-bit cases were later dismissed and hardly compared to Francis's far more serious rap sheet for gun crimes in Malaysia. But he leaked details of Baldeo's charges, along with her mug shots, to Simpkins. "For your info and convict file," he wrote. Francis also asked an intermediary to leak Baldeo's file to NCIS agents in Singapore in hopes that they would open an investigation that would disqualify her from doing business with the U.S. government.

This time the dirt-spreading didn't work. Instead, Glenn Defense began to face its own scrutiny. Simpkins's coworkers in Singapore questioned how Glenn Defense had landed the contracts in Thailand and the Philippines given its lack of experience in those countries and mounting complaints about the firm's prices.

Several of Simpkins's colleagues in the contracting command held him in low regard, viewing him as "standoffish" and incompetent. In truth, Simpkins was deeply experienced in the byzantine world of federal procurement. He proved masterful at blocking or delaying directives—from within and outside his office—that might hurt Glenn Defense.

For instance, Commander David Warunek, the contracting command's executive officer, repeatedly pressed Simpkins in 2005 and 2006 to modify future contracts so the Navy didn't have to pay as much for the Ring of Steel. For reasons nobody could explain, the Navy had failed to negotiate a fixed price for the Ring of Steel since Francis began offering it as a service in 2001, which meant Glenn Defense could charge whatever it wanted. Warunek regarded the Ring of Steel as his "pet peeve" and told Simpkins to include the barrier as a competitively bid item in the Philippines contract. Simpkins ignored him. Warunek was scheduled to retire, so Simpkins simply waited for him to leave and preserved Glenn Defense's cash cow through inaction.

Lieutenant Mike Lang, a supply officer based in Singapore, also considered the Ring of Steel a rip-off. In late 2006, he recommended against awarding an extension of the Thailand contract to Glenn

Defense, writing that it would be better "to draw competition from other contractors and drive prices down." Simpkins overruled him and gave the extension to Glenn Defense anyway.

Lang thought it strange that the Navy kept giving Francis more business with little regard for the swelling cost. He also found it suspicious that Simpkins took Glenn Defense's side whenever Navy officials challenged the company's invoices. He filed a complaint with the Naval Supply Systems Command inspector general, asking for an investigation.

"I was just getting sick of the Navy getting bilked for millions of dollars," Lang recalled. "I just said that there's some smelly fish over here and you ought to take a look at it." The inspector general's office took perfunctory steps to open a case, "but that was it. I never heard about anything being done about it."

As part of a bureaucratic reshuffling, the Navy downgraded the status of the contracting command in Singapore in 2006 and had it report instead to a higher headquarters in Japan, the Fleet Industrial Supply Center. The move diminished Simpkins's authority on paper, but with his superiors 3,300 miles away, he gained more leeway to perform illicit favors for Francis.

In June 2006, officials with the Navy's Ship Support Office in Hong Kong tangled with Glenn Defense again over its billing of the USS *Decatur*, a guided-missile destroyer. Once more, Simpkins interceded to squash their efforts. "Do not request any invoices from the ship," he emailed a contracting official in Hong Kong. "Do not violate this instruction." The official, who reported to Simpkins, had to give up the inquiry. As a reward, Francis gave Simpkins business-class, round-trip plane tickets from Singapore to Bangkok. (According to Francis, Simpkins liked to take "dirty weekend" trips to Bangkok, a city with a thriving sex tourism industry.)

Soon thereafter, Simpkins intervened to protect Glenn Defense's longtime scam of overcharging ships for sewage disposal. David

Schaus, the lieutenant in the Ship Support Office who had feuded
with Francis over the *Reagan's* wastewater bill, devised a simple solution to prevent him from cheating again. He proposed installing inexpensive flow meters on ships to measure how much waste was being
pumped, instead of taking Glenn Defense's word for it.

Francis was irate. His company profited enormously from the sewage business. In an email to Simpkins, he attacked Schaus as a "prick"
and demanded that his mole do something.

Again, Simpkins acted decisively. He ordered the Hong Kong office to stop using the flow meters, decreeing that the devices violated
the terms of Glenn Defense's contract. He copied his order to Francis,
who was thrilled.

"Meters solved ha ha," the Glenn Defense boss laughed in an email
to three subordinates.

Schaus couldn't believe it. Every time he tried to blow the whistle
on Francis, Navy higher-ups "made my life hell," he recalled. The following year, he resigned his military commission in frustration. "What
else could I have done to expose this racket?" he asked.

Simpkins left Singapore in June 2007 to take a federal contracting
job in Washington at the Justice Department.* While Simpkins had
boosted Glenn Defense's fortunes, Francis regarded him as a replace-
able asset. He had already recruited other moles in the Navy's contracting office in Singapore to fill the void.

Most uniformed personnel rotated through Singapore every two
or three years. But the Navy contracting command also employed a
cohort of Singaporean civilians as a permanent bureaucracy. From

---

* In later years, Simpkins sought to return to Singapore to work for Glenn Defense. But Francis refused to hire him, reasoning that he could not trust Simpkins
as an employee, knowing he was susceptible to bribes.

years of experience, they understood how inside information could be exploited for corrupt purposes. Francis and his staffers at Glenn Defense cultivated three women who served as husbanding contract specialists, mid-level workers who reviewed invoices and processed payments. The most valuable was Sharon Kaur, who had known Francis since the early 1990s.

Because of their long relationship, Francis trusted Kaur more than Simpkins, her supervisor. After earning a promotion in 2005, Kaur began leaking Glenn Defense a deluge of confidential information: internal emails, competitors' pricing quotes, advance knowledge of questions prepared by contract review boards, anything that might give Francis an edge. Kaur and the other moles in the Sembawang office also kept Francis apprised in real time of the comings-and-goings of their bosses.

With Francis's guidance, Kaur surreptitiously photocopied stacks of Navy records or scanned them onto compact discs. None of the documents was classified but they gave Glenn Defense a competitive advantage and helped the company win contract after contract. Francis estimated that he sent his chauffeur to retrieve material from Kaur's apartment and other rendezvous sites more than one hundred times.

Glenn Defense compensated Kaur handsomely for her spying. Starting in 2006, the company paid for her to take luxury vacations in Bali, Dubai, and Jakarta. Francis said that while Kaur's "body was with the Navy," her "heart, soul and mind" were devoted to him.

But Kaur was a skilled manipulator herself, and she exploited Francis's vanity by telling him how brilliant he was. When they emailed or spoke in person, she addressed him as "Darling." Behind his back, she called him "Mottu," or "Fatty" in Punjabi.

At Christmastime, Francis gave Kaur what he called an end-of-year cash "bonus." In 2008, a holiday gift basket was delivered to her apartment with champagne, chocolates, and cookies. Hidden underneath was a red packet containing 50,000 Singapore dollars.* Another time, Francis alleged, he met Kaur in a parking lot near the Singapore Botanic Gardens and slipped her 50,000 Singapore dollars while they sat in his Range Rover.

On a third occasion, he alleged, he gave Kaur an even larger bonus: 150,000 Singapore dollars. To avoid detection, they arranged to meet at a Toys "R" Us store in Singapore, where he said he discreetly placed a cash-stuffed envelope in her shopping cart as they passed in an aisle.

Kaur's managers, oblivious that she was on the take from Francis, gave her high job performance ratings year after year. They twice honored her with the Singapore office's "On-the-Spot" Award for uncovering a total of $77,000 in excessive charges by husbanding contractors. Not coincidentally, both companies were rivals of Glenn Defense.

"Ms. Kaur's superb performance in aggressively tracking down these overcharges, returning the money to the ships, and sending a clear signal to our [husbanding] contractors that they cannot get away with overcharging the US government is worthy of recognition," read the citation on one award.

For that, the Navy gave her a $250 bonus.

---

* The equivalent of $34,000 USD at the time.

Chapter Seven

Seducing the Seventh Fleet

February 2006

HONG KONG

With the Navy's contracting office in Singapore falling under his control, Leonard Francis shifted his sights to a more daunting target: the USS *Blue Ridge*. Commissioned in 1970 and named after a range in the Appalachian Mountains, the aging vessel was only half as long as an aircraft carrier and bore little firepower. But it was packed with advanced communications gear and served as the command flagship for the Seventh Fleet, overseeing all U.S. maritime operations in Asia. From its headquarters on the *Blue Ridge*, the Seventh Fleet's staff of two hundred directed about sixty other Navy warships and submarines operating in an ocean expanse covering 48 million square miles, about one-quarter of the surface of the earth.

Francis had sought for years to recruit informants on the *Blue Ridge* because the Seventh Fleet staff had final say over the Navy's port visit schedules, logistics, and military exercises in the Western Pacific. But he had found it difficult to sustain relationships. Most officers served two-year tours of duty before moving on. Another hurdle was that the *Blue Ridge* spent half the year docked at the U.S. Navy base in Yokosuka, Japan, visiting Singapore and Malaysia only once or twice annually— limiting Francis's opportunities to cozy up to its officers. Now that Glenn Defense had won husbanding contracts in additional countries, however, he was becoming more familiar to the *Blue Ridge* crew.

The commanding officer of the Seventh Fleet was a three-star admiral who spent most of his time away from the ship crisscrossing Asia to meet foreign military counterparts. In the admiral's absence, the chief of staff—a captain—ran the fleet's day-to-day operations and wielded outsized clout for an officer of his rank. Francis had long dreamed of getting his hooks into whoever held the job.

When Captain Timothy Giardina served as the Seventh Fleet chief of staff between 2003 and 2005, he found it impossible to avoid Francis when the *Blue Ridge* visited ports serviced by Glenn Defense. At each stop, the ship hosted "Big Top" receptions on its main deck for foreign dignitaries and VIPs, invitation-only events featuring the Seventh Fleet band and generous servings of roast beef, California wine, and military pomp. As the husbanding contractor, Francis always finagled his way onto the guest list so he could glad-hand senior officers.

His methods were unsubtle. During one Big Top reception, Giardina complimented Francis on his handmade suit and admired his "blowtorch of a cigar lighter." The next morning, as the *Blue Ridge* prepared to leave port, Francis arrived on the pier to deliver some unsolicited gifts for the chief of staff: a $700 cigar lighter like the one he had showed off the night before; two pewter platters worth about $500 apiece; a pack of twenty-five Cuban Cohiba cigars; and a business card for his tailor.

Giardina declined the presents but said Francis constantly dangled temptations. "Leonard would throw prostitutes at me trying to influence. I mean it really had that kind of feel everywhere we went," he recalled. "You just had to stay away from it."

Francis fared better with Giardina's successor: Captain David Newland, a forty-nine-year-old Californian and UCLA graduate who arrived on the *Blue Ridge* as the new chief of staff in 2005. Married with two sons, Newland had a sterling reputation. One officer who served with him in Japan described him as "ramrod straight," with "impeccable character and integrity." Another called him a "total pro" and unfailingly calm under pressure.

After a quarter-century of climbing the Navy's ladder, however,

Newland recognized that the Seventh Fleet chief of staff job was going to be the apex of his career. Fewer than one in twenty captains won promotion to admiral, and Newland sensed he was unlikely to make the cut. He set aside his ambitions and resolved to milk the benefits of his powerful Seventh Fleet assignment for as long as it lasted.

Newland had an affinity for fine cigars and expensive wine, which made him a sitting duck for Francis. They met during a change-of-command ceremony aboard the *Blue Ridge*, and when Francis offered to host a dinner during an upcoming port visit, Newland enthusiastically agreed. "I knew I wasn't going to be an admiral and I decided to take advantage of Leonard's hospitality," he recalled.

His first taste of Francis's largesse came in February 2006, when the *Blue Ridge* arrived in Hong Kong as part of its annual "Spring Swing" deployment to visit major cities in Asia.

Francis's calendar was exceptionally busy that month. He had just thrown a huge bash on February 9 to welcome the USS *Ronald Reagan* carrier strike group to Singapore and was bribing Paul Simpkins to rig the Navy's husbanding contract in Thailand. But when Francis learned that Newland's wife and the spouses of several other Seventh Fleet staff officers were flying to Hong Kong to meet their husbands for Valentine's Day weekend, he saw an opportunity. He rushed to the city and invited the couples to a "Valentine's Cheer" dinner they would not soon forget.

Francis tried to keep the banquet a secret from the Navy's Ship Support Office in Hong Kong, which had clashed with Glenn Defense over its billing practices since it won the husbanding contract there two years earlier. Because of the feud, Francis developed what one Seventh Fleet officer called "a tremendous level of hatred" for the Hong Kong unit and bad-mouthed its staffers to his allies among the Navy brass.

Despite his discretion about the party, rumors spread that he was planning another of his notorious blowouts for a select group of Seventh Fleet staff officers. One day before the *Blue Ridge*'s arrival, Captain George Foster, the U.S. defense attaché in Hong Kong, urged Commander Steve Barney, the Seventh Fleet's senior JAG officer, to be vigilant. "Mr. Francis has been known to host extremely elaborate and expensive affairs, way over what any reasonable person would consider the fraud/abuse threshold," Foster emailed. "I don't know what he has planned for your folks tomorrow, but it's something to be cautious about."

Barney, who also served as the Seventh Fleet's ethics adviser, then wrote his own email to officers on the ship, warning them to be wary of Glenn Defense. He emphasized that it was illegal to accept anything of value—meals, hotel rooms, taxi rides, souvenirs—worth more than $20 from a federal contractor.

Unaware that Newland was the inspiration for the dinner, Barney sought him out in person and asked him to reinforce the message that Fat Leonard's parties were taboo. Newland assured Barney that he'd take care of it.

Newland did take care of it, but not in the manner the JAG officer presumed. Instead, Newland told a trusted underling to forward Barney's ethics email to Francis—to let him know that his Seventh Fleet guests were still coming to the dinner but to keep it hush-hush.

The "Valentine's Cheer" celebration unfolded the next night in a balloon-decorated banquet room at Petrus, the Michelin-starred restaurant on the top floor of the Shangri-La Hotel. About twenty people attended, including a half-dozen Navy spouses who received floral bouquets and fancy chocolates from Glenn Defense.

The avant-garde menu showcased elements of molecular gastronomy, including champagne espuma and coral powder made from dehydrated lobster roe. The Americans and their genial host also ate Oscietra caviar, gobbled slices of bread topped with foie gras and Wagyu beef, and savored Périgord black truffle, a rare French fungus that is to be served within three days of harvesting. A different wine accompanied each of the eight courses.

"It was one of the most extravagant things I've ever seen," recalled Lieutenant Commander Edmond Aruffo, an officer on the *Blue Ridge*. "I didn't know people lived like that."

Francis spent $20,435 on the meal, or roughly $1,000 a head. To forestall any ethics inquiries, the Navy officers coughed up $50 each so they could claim they had paid their way.

The Hong Kong Ship Support Office learned about the dinner a few days later and sent a complaint up the chain of command to the Navy's regional contracting office in Singapore, accusing Glenn Defense of violating the no-party clause in its contract.

Fortunately for Francis, the complaint landed on the desk of Paul Simpkins, whom he had tempted one month earlier with $50,000 in cash at the Amara Hotel. Simpkins alerted Francis to the Ship Support Office's allegations and suggested he provide a plausible-sounding explanation. "We are getting too many complaints about the event," he emailed. "Need your side of it."

In a formal written response, Francis lied and insisted Glenn Defense had nothing to do with the party. While he admitted that he was present, he claimed a Hong Kong travel agency, Richmond Travel, had independently arranged the banquet for the Seventh Fleet officers and charged them $50 apiece. He assured the Singapore contracting command that everything was on the up-and-up. "Please let me know if you require further clarifications," he concluded.

In reality, Richmond Travel was a front Francis had created for the purpose of issuing bogus expense reports for Navy officers who attended his dinners and stayed at luxury hotels on his dime. But the ploy worked. The contracting command let the matter drop.

The Valentine's dinner thrilled Newland and bonded him with Francis. The Malaysian businessman soon was allowed to wander the *Blue Ridge* without an escort. He began depositing large duty-free shopping bags filled with alcohol and other gifts, including briefcase-sized humidors of Cuban cigars, in Newland's stateroom. "He was in my cabin in every port, just about," Newland recalled.

After Hong Kong, the *Blue Ridge* headed south to Malaysia for a four-day visit to Port Klang. The Royal Malaysian Navy invited senior officers from the Seventh Fleet staff, including Newland and his boss, Vice Admiral Jonathan Greenert, to an official dinner. In fact, Francis secretly paid for the event and swanned around the restaurant mingling with the brass. Afterward, several junior U.S. Navy officers piled into his Hummer and rode to a karaoke bar where they partied with prostitutes.

In return for the hospitality, some officers from the flagship performed special favors for Glenn Defense. Before leaving Malaysia, the crew of the *Blue Ridge* requested a refueling even though the vessel still had plenty of gas. Because the fuel was ordered at the last minute, Glenn Defense billed the ship $1 million—about four times what it would have cost under normal circumstances or if the *Blue Ridge* had refueled at sea with a Navy oiler.

As the *Blue Ridge* departed Port Klang, Francis emailed Newland with another request: He wanted a Bravo Zulu letter, signed by Admiral Greenert, praising Glenn Defense for its performance. Francis explained that it would "assist with blowing away" criticism from his enemies in the Hong Kong Ship Support Office.

It was a bold ask. Greenert conducted himself by the book. He didn't socialize with Francis unless he bumped into him at official events, and he had instructed his aides to refuse gifts from Glenn Defense and other defense contractors. But Greenert rarely stayed on the *Blue Ridge* for more than a few days at a time because his duties required him to fly frequently around Asia. He entrusted his chief of staff to oversee the fleet's day-to-day business, including paperwork that needed his signature.*

In the admiral's absence, Newland didn't hesitate to please his generous new friend. "Can do easy!" he emailed. Within days, Francis received a letter signed by Greenert, lauding Glenn Defense for its

---

* Greenert said his encounters with Francis were straightforward and business-like, and that he had no idea the defense contractor was treating his subordinates on the Seventh Fleet staff to lavish meals and other gifts. "I'm extremely disappointed that this happened," he said in an interview with the author.

"superb services" and "exceptional" reputation. For good measure, the Seventh Fleet staff transmitted a copy of the Bravo Zulu message to the rest of the fleet, including the Ship Support Office in Hong Kong.

Francis loved the testimonial. "Have framed it up next to Teresa's photo, am comparing if it's better looking than my wife, ha ha," he gloated in an email. He sent a copy of the letter to the Navy's contracting command in Singapore to add to Glenn Defense's performance file. When bidding for Navy contracts, not much topped a letter of appreciation from a three-star admiral.

According to Francis, he and Newland reached an understanding: A select group of Seventh Fleet officers would receive a stream of "six-star perks" if they let Glenn Defense charge the Navy "six-star prices" for port services. As part of the bargain, the officers agreed to intervene on Glenn Defense's behalf in billing and contracting disputes with the Navy. (Newland denied doing anything unlawful to benefit Glenn Defense, with the exception of leaking biographical information about another Navy captain whom Francis was trying to recruit as a mole.)

Both sides valued the compact. Navy officers earned a decent salary but were hardly wealthy. A captain such as Newland with more than two decades of service collected about $100,000 in basic pay in 2006, plus extra allowances for housing and dependents, free health care, and pension credits. For officers willing to violate their constitutional oath, Fat Leonard's gifts were an added fringe benefit.

The *Blue Ridge's* next stop on the Spring Swing was Singapore, where Francis had prepared another royal welcome for Newland, his deputy chiefs of staff, other officers, and their wives. He invited them to a feast at Jaan, the skyscraper restaurant.

By then, the balance of power in the relationship had started to shift. Francis continued to spare no expense for his parties, but he became more demanding of favors in return. Meanwhile, his moles on the Seventh Fleet staff grew increasingly subservient. To kick off the evening at Jaan, eight of the Navy guests—the same number that would greet an admiral aboard a ship—stood at attention in their business suits while Francis strode onto the helipad along a red carpet.

As the sun dipped toward the horizon and a breeze kicked up, the celebrants sipped cocktails and Dom Pérignon champagne. As a lover of exquisite bubbly, Newland felt like he had ascended to heaven. When Francis produced additional bottles of Cristal, Newland made a show of dumping his glass of Dom Pérignon over the edge of the seventy-three-story building. Then he smiled and waited for a server to pour him a fresh goblet of Cristal.

Inside the restaurant an illuminated ice sculpture of an American eagle shimmered on a table and a three-piece band provided entertainment. This time, Francis sat at the head of the table with Newland at his right. They and nineteen other guests dove into an eight-course smorgasbord featuring goose livers, duck legs, ox tails, and three different preparations of baby lamb.

Toward the end of the evening, servers wheeled around a cart loaded with cigars and cognac, including Hennessy Private Reserve ($600 a bottle) and Hennessy Paradis Rare ($2,000 a bottle). Francis estimated he spent between $20,000 and $30,000 on the event.

While they drank and smoked, the Navy officers laughed about their insolent disregard for the ethics warning the JAG officer had given them a few weeks earlier. They took their cues from Newland. They knew the chief of staff's blessing of the dinner meant no one would dare to blow the whistle on their escapades. Even the Seventh Fleet chaplain—a Catholic priest—joined in the fun, draping his arm around Newland and mugging for the camera with a thick cigar in his mouth.

But occasionally Francis had to remind people who was really in charge. When the merrymaking began that night, he noticed with displeasure that one person on the invitation list was a no-show: Captain Jesus Cantu, the Seventh Fleet's assistant chief of staff for logistics. Cantu, a Stanford University graduate, oversaw the fleet's supply officers, and Francis wanted to pull him into his orbit. He pressed Newland to find the AWOL guest.

Cantu had been uncomfortable with the idea of dining with Francis, and decided to spend the evening in downtown Singapore instead. Newland reached him on his cell phone and barked that his presence was required. The logistics officer, in blue jeans, protested that he wasn't suitably dressed.

But Newland didn't want to hear excuses. "He said, 'J.C., the champagne is flowing. You need to get your ass down here,'" Cantu recalled.

Cantu scrambled to find a tailor who could measure him for a shirt and a pair of trousers. Within forty-five minutes, he was on his way to the restaurant wearing new duds. He arrived while the champagne was still being poured.

"My initial thought was, 'This is the height of decadence,'" he said. "'I should not be here. We should not be here. This is wrong.' And yet I stayed." He was struck by how Newland acted toward Francis. "Newland deferred to him. He treated him as an equal, if not someone higher."

Newland was hooked. For the remainder of his two-year tour on the *Blue Ridge*, the powerful chief of staff reveled in his relationship with Francis, who granted him the privilege of selecting the menu and wine pairings whenever he threw a dinner party.

"I'm trying to get on Leonard's good side there so I'll get another bottle of wine," he admitted years later. "I was certainly looking for the next dinner and a nice hotel room."

Chapter Eight

Grand Ambitions

April 2006

LAEM CHABANG, THAILAND

A slight breeze stirred the humid, eighty-five-degree air as tugboats gingerly guided the USS *Abraham Lincoln* through Laem Chabang's deep-water harbor toward the pier. It was the first time a large-deck U.S. warship had attempted to dock at a Thai port instead of anchoring offshore. About sixty miles southeast of Bangkok, Laem Chabang was the country's busiest seaport and one of the few in Asia that could accommodate an aircraft carrier.

The concrete pier at Laem Chabang extended for a quarter-mile, long enough to berth the *Abraham Lincoln* with a few yards to spare. The water depth was sufficient to swallow the ship's forty-one-foot draft. But the *Abe* carried two nuclear reactors and enough ordnance to destroy a large city, so the tugboat pilots had no margin for error.

To everyone's relief the ship moored smoothly and safely. For the next four days, as five thousand visiting American sailors explored Thailand's beaches and bars, they enjoyed the convenience of walking off the ship instead of having to endure ferry rides to the pier. Nobody was more pleased with the outcome than Leonard Francis, who'd risked his shirt to make it happen.

It had been several weeks since Francis won the Navy husbanding contract for Thailand by underbidding his rival, Papa Chin. Glenn Defense had no experience in Thailand. Francis thought he could quickly launch operations, but the company had been able to muster only a few support vessels in Laem Chabang. If the *Abraham Lincoln* and the three other ships in its strike group had anchored offshore, Glenn Defense would have been forced to pay top dollar to hire Thai subcontractors to transport the sailors in water taxis. Francis feared he'd lose a ton of money.

The Navy had a thicket of safety standards for nuclear-powered aircraft carriers. Because no carrier had moored pierside at a Thai port before, the *Abraham Lincoln* needed a nuclear-safety waiver from Navy officials in Washington—a requirement that ordinarily would take months to fulfill. Francis had only a few weeks. He frantically reached out to Navy officers whom he had lavished with favors to ask for help.

Among them was Captain David Newland, the champagne connoisseur and Seventh Fleet chief of staff. The lobbying paid off. Ten days before the *Abraham Lincoln* was scheduled to arrive in Thailand, Newland informed Francis that all four ships in the carrier strike group had received clearance to dock pierside. "Just got official word, everybody is approved into Laem Chabang," Newland emailed. "Congrats."

The four-day port visit in April 2006 went off without a hitch. The U.S. ambassador to Thailand wrote a glowing thank-you note to Francis: "I understand that your own extra efforts and new initiatives were instrumental in making this port visit possible." Again, Francis had gambled and won. Glenn Defense earned $1.9 million in revenue from the Laem Chabang port call, including a $500,000 security charge for the Ring of Steel.

Its corrupt business tactics notwithstanding, Glenn Defense generally received positive reviews for the quality and reliability of its service. Even Francis's critics inside the Navy acknowledged that his company had better equipment than most of its competitors and accommodated the Navy's ever-changing needs.

Francis knew that dependability mattered more to ship captains than price and that the Navy would allow him to "make a killing" if he enabled it to accomplish its missions. "No one cared about costs," he said.

Since his days as a teenage entrepreneur, Francis had loved to take risks. Now the Malaysian high school dropout had demonstrated that he could push the most powerful navy in the world to move a nuclear-powered aircraft carrier at his whim. His ambitions escalated as he sought to fulfill his dream—becoming the Aristotle Onassis of the ship-husbanding industry. He drafted plans to win Navy contracts in the rest of Asia and dreamed of expanding into the Middle East.

If he was going to become as rich and famous as a Greek shipping tycoon, he decided he needed to present himself accordingly. The entrance to the new Glenn Defense corporate headquarters on Pandan Road in Singapore featured a wavy, five-story facade of blue steel and glass. The circular top floor—Francis's office suite—resembled the captain's bridge on an aircraft carrier with its panoramic views.

The headquarters showcased Francis's "Wall of Fame," a montage of photographs depicting him with dozens of admirals and other VIPs. The wall sent an unsubtle message: Francis had unmatched connections and power. One visiting Navy commander said the Wall of Fame left him with the impression that Francis had close ties to every four-star admiral for "at least the last thirty years."

As his wealth compounded, Francis wore custom-tailored suits, whitened his teeth, and partied in chic nightclubs with packs of gorgeous women. He rolled around the city like a billionaire. His fleet of vehicles included two Bentleys, two Lamborghinis, two Rolls-Royces, several Mercedes-Benzes, a Range Rover, and his racing-green Jaguar. He imported black Hummers from the United States, including a ten-wheeled stretch model with armor-plated doors, a wet bar, and room for fifteen passengers.

During the early 2000s, Francis lived on Singapore's Cluny Road, a millionaire's row near the Botanic Gardens. But he grew bored and decided the address wasn't glitzy enough. He kept the house for his mother, but he moved several blocks away to an ultra-posh, two-story mansion on Nassim Road that had served as the Royal Embassy of Saudi Arabia.

The mansion was one of the most expensive single-family homes in Singapore. At Christmastime, Francis spent a small fortune to illuminate the property with a grandiose holiday light show. A crew of six workers draped the buildings and palm trees with a shimmering galaxy of blue, yellow, purple, red, and green lights. They also erected a giant snowman, life-size reindeer, a forty-foot-tall artificial Christmas tree, and an amusement-park-sized choo-choo train that chugged along a set of tracks.

The spectacle attracted lines of gawkers and loads of publicity, exactly what Francis craved. "You can't put a value on happiness," he told *The Straits Times*, a Singapore newspaper that covered his light show almost every year. "Christmas is a time of peace and joy, so I wanted to share that spirit."

Glenn Defense had come a long way from the days when Francis ran it from a bare-bones office in Malaysia and had to share a squat toilet. By 2006, the company had expanded into an international conglomerate, with subsidiaries in eleven countries.

Despite the size of his empire, Francis remained a paranoid micromanager. He operated on a strict need-to-know basis, signed all company checks himself, and kept profit-and-loss statements a closely guarded secret. He installed security cameras inside his Singapore headquarters that enabled him to spy on his staff, whom he insisted address him as "Boss." He demanded that employees work at least six days a week and respond to his calls and texts round-the-clock. He carried as many as fifteen cell phones—with different country codes so he could always make and receive local calls—in a handbag that his American friends mocked as a "man purse." Preferring vampire hours, the Boss usually arrived at the office late in the day and stayed until 3 a.m.

Though Glenn Defense was now a multinational company, Francis continued to run it like a family business. His core group of staffers included Andre Francis, his younger brother; Alex Wisidagama, a first cousin on his mother's side; and Neil Peterson, the son of a Malaysian admiral who had worked for Leonard since he was seventeen.

Andre had worked for Leonard the longest but the siblings frequently clashed. Andre felt bullied and claimed that Leonard once punched him in the face after an argument. Leonard also didn't hesitate to put Andre in his place verbally, reminding him: "I am the general and you are the soldier."

Fifteen months after the *Abraham Lincoln* moored pierside in Thailand, however, Leonard and Andre worked to engineer another historic port visit.

The White House was trying to seal a nuclear cooperation agreement with India. At the behest of the Pentagon, the Pacific Fleet ordered the USS *Nimitz* to sail to India as soon as possible and become the first nuclear-powered ship to visit the country. But there was a serious obstacle: The Navy didn't have a husbanding contractor in India capable of hosting an aircraft carrier. Navy officials asked whether Francis could handle the port call on short notice. Rising to the challenge, Leonard agreed—even though he had no husbanding assets in India. Two weeks before the *Nimitz* was scheduled to arrive, he instructed Andre and a flotilla of Glenn Defense barges and support vessels to sail from Singapore to Chennai, a port on India's southeastern coast, 1,800 miles away.

The voyage almost ended in disaster. It was monsoon season, and an Indian Ocean cyclone battered the convoy of ships. Some crewmembers clamored to turn back, but the Glenn Defense fleet sailed on.

The Glenn Defense vessels arrived in Chennai a week later, only to run into more trouble. One of the company's trash barges rammed into the *Nimitz*, denting the hull. And a water taxi carrying U.S. sailors had an accident in rough seas. Nobody was hurt, but the water taxi sank after it reached the pier.

Despite the mishaps, U.S. officials were grateful that Glenn Defense had stepped into the breach. They understood that no other husbanding company could muster enough equipment and transport it thousands of miles to a foreign port at the last minute. "Please accept my sincere appreciation and gratitude for your professionalism," Rear Admiral John Terry Blake, the commanding officer of the *Nimitz* strike group, wrote in a Bravo Zulu letter to Francis. "Despite challenging weather conditions, your team provided the utmost in logistics support and security."

Glenn Defense received a hefty reward for going the extra mile. Because the firm did not have a pre-existing contract with the Navy in India, Francis could charge whatever he wanted. He billed the Navy $4.5 million, the most he ever had for a port visit. Francis was unapologetic. The Navy had asked him to help in a pinch and he delivered. "They couldn't find anybody else to compete with me," he said. "They know there's nobody else."

He gave his brother a $10,000 bonus but kept most of the profits for himself. "Leonard loved doing the difficult ports and making that happen," Andre recalled. "He loved getting the glory."

He also gave something back to senior officers on the USS *Nimitz*. After Chennai, the aircraft carrier visited Hong Kong and Singapore, where Glenn Defense subsidized hotel rooms for more than a dozen officers. In Singapore, Francis treated Rear Admiral Blake and sixteen other guests to a sublime dinner at the Jaan restaurant that cost about $1,000 per person.

As Glenn Defense expanded into new countries, Francis hired several former high-ranking Asian military officers as part-time advisers to take advantage of their clout and connections.

Among them were Mohammed Anwar, a retired Malaysian four-star admiral and former chief of the country's defense forces; Mung-korn Tienchai, a retired Thai admiral and former chief judge of the Thai military; Mateo Mayuga, a retired vice admiral and chief of the Philippine Navy; and Stanny Fofied, a retired Indonesian vice admiral. The all-star roster of retired brass had close ties to the political and military elite in their countries. Just as important, they were familiar faces to U.S. Navy leaders.

With Anwar's guidance, Francis signed a $55 million deal to buy the Port Klang Cruise Center: a trophy property near the Strait of Malacca with one hundred acres of waterfront real estate, a five-story passenger terminal, and a pier the length of a football field. Under its previous owner, the Port Klang Cruise Center served as the gateway to Malaysia for the world's biggest passenger cruise lines, including Cunard, Princess, and Royal Caribbean.

Francis had plans to lure a different kind of giant ship: aircraft carriers. When Glenn Defense handled a carrier port visit, it often grossed over $1 million in revenue—a phenomenal sum for a few days' work. But the number of carriers visiting Malaysia had dried up during the 2000s. The Navy disliked docking at Port Klang's congested container ports, where its ships jostled for space with cargo ships.

By purchasing the Port Klang Cruise Center, Francis could offer the Navy a private pier on a quiet and safe stretch of the harbor. To accommodate carriers, he doubled the length of the pier and dredged the channel. His investment paid off. Twenty-nine warships, including five carriers, visited Port Klang over the next three years.

Francis referred to Port Klang as one of his "Pearl Ports," or a cash cow. Because he owned the cruise center, it was easy for him to jack up prices. Phuket and Laem Chabang in Thailand were also Pearl Ports because laissez-faire authorities in those cities let Francis operate his business as he pleased. In contrast, Navy ship visits to Singapore were far less profitable for Glenn Defense. The base was owned by the government of Singapore, which provided security and other services to the Americans. In addition, Singapore's strict anticorruption laws crimped Francis's ability to bribe and cheat.

Under terms of its contracts with the Navy, Glenn Defense could charge only fixed prices for most husbanding services. But there was a giant loophole. If a ship requested something else—a bigger tugboat, a slightly longer gangway, the Ring of Steel—that didn't meet the exact definition of a fixed-price item, Glenn Defense could charge what it wanted. As a result, Francis pushed ship captains and supply officers to order slightly modified services that were not spelled out in the contract. Those who were friendly with Francis would oblige, knowing they could count on an elaborate dinner, a free hotel suite, or other gifts in return.

If a ship refused to deviate from contract specifications, Francis would use strong-arm tactics to send a message. In his Pearl Ports, he acted like a mafia *capo* running a protection racket, telling Navy officers it would be a shame if something bad happened to their nice, shiny warship because they failed to request extra services.

During one port visit to Phuket, he recommended that the USS *Pinckney* order bigger fenders to keep barges from banging into the guided-missile destroyer. In emails to officers on the ship, he cautioned that the standard fenders, as called for in the Navy's contracts, provided only "limited protection" and that Glenn Defense "cannot be held liable" in case of an accident. The *Pinckney* officers declined because they thought the bigger fenders were unnecessary and the price to rent them was $60,000 extra.

Sure enough, just as Francis predicted, a fuel barge slammed into the *Pinckney* and damaged the warship. Though they couldn't prove it, officers suspected Glenn Defense of engineering the mishap. Either way, the message was clear: It was safer to pay off Fat Leonard than be sorry.

Chapter Nine

The Wedding Planner

September 2006

YOKOSUKA, JAPAN

Officially, Lieutenant Commander Edmond Aruffo, a six-foot-five wiseass from South Philadelphia, served as the Seventh Fleet's protocol officer. As a member of the fleet commander's staff, he managed the admiral's social calendar, planned Big Top receptions aboard the USS *Blue Ridge*, and accommodated foreign dignitaries.

Unofficially, he had been performing the same duties for Leonard Francis for the past ten months. The thirty-seven-year-old Aruffo worked countless hours as the social liaison between the maritime tycoon and his Seventh Fleet moles, scheduling Francis's dinner parties, ordering champagne, organizing guest lists, rounding up prostitutes, and ensuring the unauthorized fun and games ran smoothly. He called himself "the wedding planner," and he took pride in his job.

Now that Francis had curried favor with a core group of Seventh Fleet staff officers, he spent much of his time following the *Blue Ridge* around Asia to cement their allegiance. Aruffo functioned as his day-to-day handler, troubleshooter, and communications conduit to Captain David Newland, the Seventh Fleet chief of staff. The junior officer was in awe of Francis and more loyal to him than his superiors in the

Navy. "I wanted to impress him, and I wanted to make him happy," Aruffo recalled.

When Francis visited Japan in September 2006 to attend a Seventh Fleet change-of-command ceremony, Aruffo drew up a five-day travel itinerary fit for a potentate. The document, titled "Leonard Conquers Tokyo," divided Francis's daily schedule into fifteen-minute segments. On September 9, Aruffo and his wife, Yumie, greeted Francis in the arrival hall of Narita International Airport, carried his bags, and escorted him to the Park Hyatt Tokyo. Aruffo then helped Francis unpack, took him to lunch, and presented a curated list of shopping and sightseeing options.

That evening, Aruffo arranged a splendiferous supper for Francis, Newland, and other officers and their spouses. They dined on foie gras and kuruma prawns at the New York Grill on the fifty-second floor of the Park Hyatt. Mindful of Newland's fondness for champagne, Aruffo had asked the restaurant to set aside eight bottles of Cristal. He also ordered floral bouquets for the wives and reserved $600-per-night rooms at the hotel for the American guests. (Francis, who stayed in a more spacious suite, paid for the dinner and hotel bills.)

The main event on Francis's itinerary was the September 12 ceremony at the Navy base in Yokosuka to mark the Seventh Fleet command handover—from Vice Admiral Jonathan Greenert, who was taking a new assignment at the Pentagon, to Vice Admiral Douglas Crowder. The Navy invited hundreds of VIPs, including an array of diplomats and military brass from around Asia.

Francis's inclusion on the guest list had kicked up a fuss among the Seventh Fleet staff. Three Navy officers tried to block his attendance because of his unsavory reputation. But Aruffo and Newland, who controlled the protocol list, intervened to ensure he could attend.

Crowder, the incoming Seventh Fleet commander, had met Francis two years earlier when he was a rear admiral during the unforgettable Christmas Cheer celebration in Hong Kong. Since then, however, he'd developed what he described as an "uneasy feeling" about the contractor. Crowder felt that Francis had tricked him and his crew into attending the Christmas Cheer party by falsely claiming that it would be a "widely attended" gathering with lots of civilian guests. Moreover, Francis had irritated the admiral for months afterward by asking him to sign an "over-the-top" Bravo Zulu letter praising Glenn Defense. "I didn't like the way he kind of hoodwinked us on the party, and I didn't like the way he was badgering me for a letter of endorsement," Crowder recalled.

After the change-of-command ceremony, Crowder and his wife drove to their new quarters, a house on the base reserved for the fleet commander. He glanced into the backyard and spotted a familiar oversized figure standing there with Aruffo. The admiral couldn't believe Francis, a foreigner without a security clearance, was wandering around the property. He angrily summoned Aruffo inside. "What is Fat Leonard doing in my backyard?" he demanded.

Aruffo made things worse with a smart-alecky explanation. The low-ranking protocol officer informed the admiral that his residence was public property and that visitors were permitted inside the first floor. Crowder blew his stack. "You brought Fat Leonard inside of my quarters? Inside of my house where my wife lives and my fifteen-year-old daughter lives and where I have secure communications?" he recalled shouting. He threatened to fire Aruffo on the spot and later ordered Newland to reassign him. "I called the chief of staff and said, 'He's gone. There's no way he's going to represent me.'" (Aruffo acknowledged giving Francis a tour of the house but denied the rest of Crowder's account, calling it "complete and total nonsense.")

But the wedding planner had friends in high places. With Francis's encouragement, Aruffo remained on the *Blue Ridge* and continued to work for Newland as his executive assistant, which insulated the junior officer from the admiral's wrath.

Crowder tried to keep Francis at arm's length during his tenure as the Seventh Fleet commander. But the husbanding contractor was hard to dodge. Thanks to his moles, he gained entry to Big Top receptions and other events, where he waited patiently for a chance to approach Crowder, shake hands, and pose for a cherished photograph with an admiral.

Crowder said there was only so much he could do to limit his exposure. "When he comes through a receiving line in Manila, three people behind the president of the Philippines, what are you going to do? Cause a scene?"

Aruffo grew up poor with three sisters in blue-collar South Philly. His father died when Aruffo was eight years old. His mother, an Italian immigrant who spoke limited English, took a job in a donut shop. During high school, Aruffo worked the late shift in an aluminum-fan factory to put food on the table. At seventeen, he enlisted in the Navy. He thrived in the service, learned to install software, and made the cut for a highly selective program that placed enlisted sailors on a fast track to become officers. He logged several years on assignments in Japan, where he studied the language and married a Japanese woman.

His career took an unexpected turn in 2005 when the skipper of the *Blue Ridge* invited him to a dinner at the Hyatt Hotel in Singapore and introduced him to Francis. Aruffo was spellbound by the self-made Malaysian businessman and his decadent lifestyle. Aruffo had never heard of foie gras, much less lobster Thermidor. But he loved how Francis treated him like a peer and seemed genuinely interested in his personal background: whether he had kids, why he joined the Navy, what he thought of the stock market, whether he had any vices. Francis further won him over by sharing personal intimacies, including the story of his gastric bypass surgery.

At the end of the night, Francis produced his business card and said to reach out anytime. Aruffo, like many other unwitting targets of Francis's recruiting, was smitten. "For some reason, he considered me a friend. I thought I was fortunate for that," Aruffo recalled.

Aruffo was eager to please. Within a few months of their first meeting, he mailed Francis a compact disc with classified details of the *Blue Ridge's* port visit schedules. He also clicked his heels when Francis and Newland asked him in early 2006 to arrange parties for the Seventh Fleet staff. He came to view Francis as a father figure and called him "Uncle Leonard." Francis boosted Aruffo's ego by addressing him as "capo di tutti capi," or "boss of all bosses" in Italian, a slang honorific from mobster movies.

As the pace and intensity of the dinner parties increased, Aruffo jealously guarded his privileged access to the Glenn Defense owner. If Seventh Fleet personnel tried to join the festivities without permission, he'd cut them off. "Don't want anyone [else] with a direct connection, don't need people running their mouths," he emailed Francis after learning that an officer had circumvented him to ask for a free hotel room.

His colleagues on the *Blue Ridge* found his attitude annoying. "Aruffo was a sly guy, cocky, Italian, tall and thought he was God's gift to the world," recalled Lieutenant Commander Todd Malaki, the flagship's supply officer, who likewise accepted bribes from Glenn Defense. Other shipmates described Aruffo as "a little shady," "very flashy," "a glad-hander," "sneaky," "kind of slick," a "used-car salesman," a "wheeler-dealer," "a greasy dude," and a "partying type of officer" who was only "70 to 75 percent reliable."

Francis acknowledged his protégé could be "overbearing" and was "always getting himself into trouble." But he thought Aruffo was "a smart, cunning guy" and appreciated his devotion. He had bigger plans for him.

In February 2007, with Crowder newly in command, the USS *Blue Ridge* kicked off its annual Spring Swing tour of Asian ports. As he had the year before, Commander Steve Barney, the Seventh Fleet's JAG, emailed staff officers—on February 2, Groundhog Day—to implore them to be on their best behavior and stay away from Francis. But this time he was blunter.

"You must exercise extreme caution," he instructed as the *Blue Ridge* arrived in Hong Kong, its first stop. "Remember that there is no 'other side of the world' exception to the gift rules." He reminded them that "public service is a public trust" and that they could go to jail if they accepted a bribe. "Don't risk your career and everything that you have worked for," he concluded. "It's not worth it."

Again, Barney's warning failed to deter. Aruffo dismissed the JAG as a Grinch who was "always complaining about something." He forwarded a copy of the email to Francis as a heads-up.

Leaked copies of the JAG's email also circulated among the Glenn Defense corporate staff in Singapore. Howard Patty Sr., a retired Navy contracting officer Francis had hired as a vice president, advised the Boss to lower his profile and watch out for rats at his parties. "All it would take is some double crosser with a video camera phone showing [you] and 7th flt drinking top shelf liquor," he cautioned.

But Francis had no intention of scaling back. Though he had a scheduling conflict and couldn't meet the *Blue Ridge* in Hong Kong, he instructed Aruffo to organize a memorable gastronomic evening at the Peninsula Hotel for Newland, other key Seventh Fleet officers, and their spouses.

Aruffo wasn't in Hong Kong either—the Navy had sent him to the Philippines on assignment—but he still was responsible for planning the dinner. He emailed Newland to solicit the chief of staff's wine preferences. "Champagne to start. Rather than one type, I'd like to compare. Dom Perignon, Cristal and Bollinger's," Newland replied. He tacked on a list of French Bordeaux and California cabernets he wanted to sample. The meal cost about $850 per person, including alcohol. Glenn Defense, as usual, took care of the tab.

On February 8, the *Blue Ridge* arrived in Manila for its next stop on the Spring Swing. This time, Francis was waiting on the pier in a bouncy mood. The Navy had recently awarded its Philippines husbanding contract to Glenn Defense. To celebrate, he had booked the penthouse suite at the five-star Manila Hotel, which served as the residence for Army General Douglas MacArthur between 1935 and 1941 while the American commander oversaw the creation of the Philippine Army. A fire destroyed much of the hotel during World War II, but the apartment-sized penthouse was restored and stocked with MacArthur memorabilia, including an oil portrait of the general.

Francis invited Newland, Aruffo, Captain Jesus Cantu, and a few other officers to a party in the MacArthur Suite. The suite had two bedrooms, a formal dining room for ten guests, a kitchen, a living room with couches, a wood-paneled study, and a balcony overlooking Manila Bay. Francis thought the stateliness and rich military history would impress his American friends.

The party started slowly, so Francis directed Aruffo to find prostitutes. Sometimes Aruffo found such requests humiliating, but he always carried out Francis's orders as if he were a senior officer. The wedding planner went downstairs to the hotel bar and brought back some women.

According to Francis, things turned "wild and crazy" and "an orgy" ensued. He said some partygoers opened a glass case in General MacArthur's study that contained a replica of his iconic corncob pipe and used it as a sex toy. Francis posed for a photo with the pipe in his mouth, seated at MacArthur's desk in front of the oil painting of the war hero.

The officers didn't have much time to recover from their night in the MacArthur Suite. The *Blue Ridge* was scheduled to make three more port visits that month. One day after departing Manila, the ship anchored in the Philippines' Cebu City. Francis reserved a block of rooms for Seventh Fleet staff officers at the Shangri-La Hotel, including the presidential suite for Newland. During the port visit, Francis said he hosted another party with prostitutes present. Half-jokingly, he began referring to the *Blue Ridge* as "the Love Boat."

On February 16, the scene repeated itself at the *Blue Ridge*'s next stop in the Philippines: General Santos City, a tuna fishing hub. Francis threw a party aboard the *Glenn Braveheart* and took officers out for more karaoke and bar girls. The General Santos City visit was marred by an incident involving Aruffo, who got into a shouting match with Philippine soldiers at a checkpoint. Violence was narrowly averted— the furious soldiers had threatened to shoot the Navy officer—but Aruffo had to be escorted back to the U.S. flagship.

After the *Blue Ridge* left the Philippines, the Seventh Fleet staff's partying eased into a calmer, but still ostentatious, routine. Francis continued to follow the flagship from port to port during the remainder of the Spring Swing to serve as its five-star concierge. He saw each stop as an opportunity to normalize his corruption of the Seventh Fleet staff and to recruit fresh allies.

One officer on his target list was Commander Robert Gonzales, who had recently joined the Seventh Fleet staff after a tour as skipper of the USS *Stethem*. Francis had met Gonzales a few times and identified a vice he thought he might be able to exploit.

"Gonzales is someone I need to build a strong relationship with, and I know he likes fine wine," Francis told Aruffo in an email. He instructed the wedding planner to add Gonzales to the guest list for a dinner he was hosting at the Jaan restaurant in Singapore on February 24.

Gonzales accepted the invitation after Aruffo told him several senior officers and their spouses would be there, and that the meal would only cost $50 per person. But when Gonzales and his wife arrived, he realized the event broke every ethics rule in the book. For starters, everyone was drinking Cristal on the roof of the skyscraper. Then each guest was presented with an appetizer: a smoky glass globe containing liquid nitrogen. When the waitstaff lifted the globes off the plates, white puffs of nitrogen gas wafted into the air, revealing exquisite preparations of foie gras underneath.

While the culinary show was mesmerizing, "It was unbelievably 100 percent obvious that this wasn't right," Gonzales recalled. As he and his wife left the restaurant at the end of the evening, "We're essentially just turning to each other and going, 'What the hell was that? There is no way that's OK.'" Later, he said, he made clear to Aruffo that he didn't want to be invited to any more social events with Francis. Yet he didn't make a stink or report the flagrant violation of Navy regulations. He sensed that it was "business as usual" on the Seventh Fleet staff and better to keep quiet.

Francis made sure the fun didn't end when the *Blue Ridge* completed its Spring Swing and returned home to Japan in March. He had a more important objective in mind. But first he needed to hook the Seventh Fleet officers a little deeper.

He flew to Tokyo to host another spectacular meal on March 24 for Newland, Aruffo, and other officers at the Oak Door steakhouse at the Grand Hyatt Hotel. They supped on old favorites—foie gras, kuruma prawns, and lobster Thermidor—as well as Sendai tenderloin, a top-grade beef from Japan's Miyagi prefecture. They drank Dom Pérignon and Cristal, an assortment of French wines, and three types of cognac, including Rémy Martin Louis XIII, considered by some experts to be the finest in the world.* To pay homage to their benefactor, the officers posed for photographs while wearing custom-ordered Glenn Defense neckties. Cut from blue-and-gold silk, the ties displayed the Glenn family crest between the stripes.

The good times hit a crescendo three months later when the *Blue Ridge* steamed 4,800 miles from Japan to the Southern Hemisphere to visit Sydney.

Glenn Defense did not yet hold the Navy's husbanding contract for Australia, but Francis and his wife, Teresa, flew down from Singapore to meet the ship anyway. The Seventh Fleet officers he had

---

* For dessert, Francis and his American guests were served "Liberte Sauvage," the winning cake of the 10th Coupe du Monde de la Pâtisserie 2007, a biannual global pastry contest. Aruffo proclaimed it "tremendously tasty."

bonded with over the previous eighteen months were scheduled to leave their posts that summer. Newland and Cantu were transferring from the *Blue Ridge* to new assignments. Aruffo was retiring after twenty years in the Navy. Francis wanted to host a farewell meal.

"Well, this looks like the end of the road for a really great crew, sorry to see so many of them go," Aruffo emailed the Boss. "If all goes off well, this may even be the last time you get to see my sparkling ass in a Navy Uniform!"

Francis paid for a group of officers and their wives to stay at the Shangri-La Hotel in Sydney. On June 17, 2007, they gathered for a "Changing of the Guard" dinner at Altitude, the Shangri-La's house restaurant. The five-course menu featured prawns, scallops, beef loin, and foie gras. In Newland's honor, they ordered seven bottles of Cristal, two bottles of Dom Pérignon, and eleven bottles of wine. The chief of staff posed for a photo next to the sommelier holding both brands of champagne.

Francis collected photographs and memorabilia at most of his parties, partly to build camaraderie but also as insurance. The souvenirs were tangible proof that his Navy moles were on the take, and gave him leverage in case they ever dreamed of double-crossing him.

Most of the Seventh Fleet staffers seemed oblivious that they were placing themselves at risk of blackmail. Besides smiling for the camera, they each autographed a copy of the dinner menu as a memento for Francis.

Aruffo gulped. He recognized that the menu could resurface as evidence in a corruption investigation. "I was almost sure that night would be used in a court of law someday," he recalled. He signed the menu anyway because he didn't want to insult Francis or Newland. Yet the Navy officers' acceptance of the $10,000 dinner wasn't the biggest offense committed that evening.

According to Francis, one of the Seventh Fleet staffers, Robert Gorsuch, a forty-year-old chief warrant officer, handed him an envelope at the restaurant. Inside was the payoff he had long been plotting for: two computer disks containing military secrets.

The disks contained classified spreadsheets of the Navy's projected ship movements in Asia for the next eighteen months. Satiated at last, Francis tucked the envelope into his man purse and flew back to Singapore.

He had breached the Seventh Fleet's intelligence firewall. The unauthorized leak of classified information was the key to a scheme to make him even wealthier. It also marked the start of the worst self-inflicted espionage debacle to hit the Navy since the Cold War.

Part Three

2007–2011

Chapter Ten

Leaky Embassies

December 2006

MANILA, THE PHILIPPINES

Six months before he received the disks with classified ship schedules, Leonard Francis flew to Manila to cement another advance. Glenn Defense had just won the Navy husbanding contract for the Philippines, and he wanted to recruit a mole inside the U.S. embassy to support his business interests—no easy task. American embassies in Asia had sophisticated counterintelligence defenses to fend off Chinese, Russian, and North Korean spies.

Francis had a simple plan to penetrate the embassy. He asked an intermediary to help him arrange lunch with Michael Brooks, a Navy captain assigned to the diplomatic outpost as the naval attaché. Francis had not previously met Brooks, who served dual roles as a liaison to the Philippine Navy and as an intelligence collection officer. But Francis had a talent for putting people at ease and conning them into doing what he wanted.

They lunched at the Hyatt Hotel near Manila Bay a week before Christmas. Francis was patient and methodical with his targets, but he felt an instant chemistry with Brooks. By the time he paid the waiter, he had persuaded the Navy officer to work covertly for Glenn Defense. The next day, Brooks emailed Francis a note thanking him for the meal and addressing him as "Boss." He also attached his first leak: proprietary details of past Navy ship visits handled by Glenn Defense's competitors in the Philippines.

Francis relied on a tried-and-true formula to maintain Brooks's loyalty over the next two years. On scores of occasions, he supplied the naval attaché with prostitutes or other gifts. In return, Brooks acted as his spy inside the U.S. embassy, a bayside compound near Manila's Rizal Park, advocating for Glenn Defense with Navy commands, the State Department, and the government of the Philippines.

By bribing a military intelligence officer, Francis had become an acute threat to U.S. national security. Defense attachés hold highly sensitive jobs in the intelligence world, with access to an array of diplomatic, military, and economic secrets. Even if Brooks wanted to stop cooperating, Francis could force him to continue by blackmailing him with evidence of his encounters with prostitutes, an age-old nightmare for intelligence agencies.

One by one, Francis was corrupting the Navy's power centers in Asia. By early 2007, he had infiltrated the Seventh Fleet staff by winning the allegiance of David Newland, Ed Aruffo, and others on the USS *Blue Ridge*. He also had bought off the Navy's contracting command in Singapore and compromised a flotilla of admirals and ship captains. Now he had a naval attaché under his thumb in a strategically vital embassy.

Captain Brooks made himself a sucker of a target for Francis. A helicopter pilot and veteran of the first Persian Gulf war, he had previously served as a naval attaché to Pakistan. When he arrived in Manila in June 2006, he was forty-eight years old. He knew it was reckless for an intelligence officer to go anywhere near a prostitute, but he was approaching the end of his military career and threw caution to the wind. "I lost my moral compass," he later admitted.

Francis said he discovered that Brooks led two separate personal lives: one with his wife and two daughters, and the other spent "whoring." Whenever Francis visited Manila, he provided Brooks with prostitutes and hotel rooms; when the Boss wasn't around, he gave Brooks a cash allowance to spend on sex. On top of that, Francis said he paid running tabs for two prostitutes Brooks slept with on a regular basis.

When he wanted a date with a call girl, Brooks sent Francis coded messages, saying that he was in the mood for "high tea" or "chocolate shakes." According to Francis, Brooks was so hungry for sex that he sometimes asked for tea and shakes several days in a row.

Francis bent over backward to make things convenient, reserving rooms for Brooks at the five-star Shangri-La Hotel in Manila. "It was right across the street from my house," Brooks recalled. "Anytime Leonard came into town, it was girls at the hotel." If the Navy officer was pressed for time, he'd show up for a quickie wearing gym clothes.

While he hid his philandering from his family, Brooks didn't conceal his relationship with Francis and invited the defense contractor over to his house multiple times for dinner. Francis came bearing gifts: fine wine, iPods for the kids, perfume for mom, a Breitling watch for dad. He even chartered a limousine to take one of Brooks's daughters to her high school prom. When the family vacationed in Thailand, Glenn Defense paid for meals and tour guides.

Years later, Brooks confessed he had been a fool. "It was just fucking stupidity," he said. "I hang my head in shame." He said Francis gained his trust by talking about his admiral friends and making the lower-ranking attaché feel just as important. "Did I fall into the trap of Leonard Francis? Yeah," he said. "Leonard had high-level connections. And they were people I never saw, but he would drop names. You know, Admiral This, Admiral That." Brooks knew Francis "ran with . . . the upper crust" and he wanted to be treated the same way.

The investment paid off for Francis at a critical stage. Though the Navy had awarded him its main husbanding contract for the Philippines, his position was tenuous. The contract was good for only one year, and his local rival, Global Terminals & Development Inc., had filed an official protest seeking to overturn the deal. Global had also retained a smaller contract to service U.S. ships visiting Subic Bay, undermining Glenn Defense's hold on the country.

Francis used Brooks to steamroll Global. He slipped Brooks talking points so he could lobby other U.S. officials in favor of Glenn Defense and spread unfounded rumors about Global's safety and performance records. From his embassy post, Brooks leaked internal correspondence to Francis about how U.S. officials were handling the contract dispute. The campaign worked. After several weeks, the federal government dismissed Global's protest.

Brooks was positioned to assist in other ways. As the naval attaché, he was partly responsible for evaluating Glenn Defense's performance in the Philippines. In November 2007, he secretly allowed the company to ghostwrite its own job evaluation. Not surprisingly, the evaluation praised Glenn Defense to the heavens, lauding the firm's "world-class service," "unsurpassed husbanding support," and "exceptional" performance as something "never before experienced in the Philippines."

Separately, Brooks gave his own "strongest recommendation" that the Navy extend Glenn Defense's contract. Francis was elated with the job his mole was doing. "We are looking great!" he emailed his staff. Shortly afterward, the Navy extended Glenn Defense's contract.

In another scheme, Brooks arranged for Glenn Defense's vessels to receive diplomatic immunity. Ordinarily the contractor's ships and barges needed to pass inspection, clear customs, and pay taxes when they crossed international waters to visit Philippine ports. But Brooks declared that the ships were allied with the U.S. Navy and should be treated as sovereign territory. As a result, they bypassed inspection and Glenn Defense did not have to provide crew lists or inventories to Philippine authorities.

Francis said it was "unheard of" for a contractor to be granted unfettered access to foreign waters and given the same legal status as the U.S. Navy. With the diplomatic clearance, he said, he could have smuggled in "nukes" or drugs. "I'm not even a U.S. citizen and I had diplomatic immunity!" he recalled.

Overall, Francis credited Brooks with giving a huge boost to Glenn Defense's revenue. The number of U.S. ship visits to the Philippines roughly doubled during Brooks's two-year tenure as naval attaché. The company's diplomatic immunity expired after Brooks departed Manila in July 2008. But by then, Glenn Defense had firmly established itself as the dominant U.S. Navy contractor in the Philippines. It would not relinquish its grip willingly.

From a young age, Francis understood the importance of schmoozing military attachés. In his early twenties, he became a familiar face at foreign embassies in Kuala Lumpur, trying to drum up husbanding business from the Australians, British, French, and Americans. Over time, he built a network of contacts at U.S. embassies throughout Southeast Asia.

Many U.S. embassy officials in Asia knew Francis was dodgy but couldn't resist fraternizing with him. Military attachés viewed him as an enticing source of information because he loved to gossip and had local contacts the Americans were dying to meet.

Captain Clayton Grindle, who served as the U.S. naval attaché to Malaysia from 2008 to 2011, and later as defense attaché in Hong Kong, called Francis a "slippery character" and a "master manipulator" and said, "I tried like hell to not get wrapped up with Leonard." Nonetheless, they built a rapport and often met for dinner or coffee.

Grindle said he tried to milk Leonard for information about the Chinese and Malaysian governments. He also asked Francis to broker meetings with Mohammed Anwar, the retired Malaysian military chief who'd joined Glenn Defense. Francis obliged. He knew he could use the meetings as bargaining chips to demand favors in return.

Though he had no formal training, Francis possessed all the traits of a skillful spy. "Leonard Francis would have made a wonderful intelligence officer," Grindle said. "He tries to feel you out, he tries to understand your weaknesses, he looks for that stuff. And he starts with vices. The first thing he does with somebody, 'Do you have vices?'"

In Indonesia, Francis tried that exact approach with A. W. Moss, a military intelligence officer assigned to the U.S. embassy in Jakarta. Moss said he tried to avoid Francis at first "because I knew Leonard was slimy," but relented and met him for dinner.

"He puts his arm around my shoulder and he goes, 'A.W., tell me, what are your vices?'" Moss recalled. "Direct approach, right? I've been in this business for many years, okay? I know where this is going." Sure enough, Francis asked Moss to join him for a nightcap at Jakarta's Alexis Hotel, a magnet for high-class prostitutes.

Moss declined the offer but continued to meet Francis for meals, drinks, and cigars. Part of his job was to gather intelligence from corrupt local officials and other dubious characters. But he acknowledged that Francis fell into a special high-risk category and that he should have kept his distance.

"Just meeting with this guy was a stupid thing," Moss said. "I didn't have to meet the guy, and I did because I was curious."

Another embassy official who hobnobbed with Francis was Captain Adrian Jansen, who served as the U.S. naval attaché in Indonesia and later as the defense attaché to China. A brilliant officer by most accounts, Jansen held two master's degrees and spoke five languages, including Bahasa Indonesian and Mandarin. Jansen thought Francis was a "scumbag" and, like others, rebuffed his invitations to dinner at first. But, like others, he eventually succumbed. He said he wanted to build a relationship with another bigwig on Glenn Defense's payroll: Stanny Fofied, a retired admiral from the Indonesian Navy.

Francis was keenly aware of what Jansen wanted. He and Fofied invited the American naval officer to join them for four boozy meals in Bali and Jakarta. The first cost $737 per person, the second $1,055, the third $1,147, and the fourth—a lunch—$180. Francis paid for everything, including the bill for Jansen's wife, who came along for three of the meals. Like a good spy, he snapped photographs and kept the receipts, which gave him leverage over Jansen if he needed it.

Though Jansen didn't give Francis anything improper in return, the photographs and receipts would surface years later when he became an admiral, threatening his military career.

"Did Leonard play me? Yeah, he played me. He played me real good," Jansen recalled. "I played the fool on that one, because he had a lot of dirt on me. . . . Obviously, in hindsight you can look at it and think how stupid, but it was too late. . . . I had no clue."

Chapter Eleven

Dirty Secrets

October 2007

YOKOSUKA, JAPAN

Leonard Francis was hungry for more American military secrets. Most spies hide in the shadows; Francis took the opposite approach. At 10 a.m. October 24, a sunny Wednesday, he rolled up to the main gate of Yokosuka Naval Base in a chauffeur-driven BMW.

Yokosuka ranked as the Navy's largest overseas installation, with 24,500 servicemembers and civilians occupying a 579-acre peninsula at the mouth of Tokyo Bay. Patiently waiting at the gate was Robert Gorsuch, the chief warrant officer on the Seventh Fleet staff who four months earlier had allegedly given Francis classified ship schedules during the Changing of the Guard dinner party in Australia.

Gorsuch had worn his Navy uniform for twenty-two years. Throughout his career, the military had entrusted him with sensitive assignments: working at the White House and for the secretary of defense, plus serving in support of the wars in Kosovo and Afghanistan. But Gorsuch had lapped up Francis's dinner-party largesse and, like other minions on the Seventh Fleet staff, now obediently called him "Boss." At the gate, he escorted Francis past the security checkpoint to the pier where the USS *Blue Ridge* was moored.

Most of the crew knew Francis by sight, and his presence on the flagship with Gorsuch raised no eyebrows. While making the rounds with Francis under the pretense of official business, Gorsuch handed him an envelope with two computer disks. They contained classified spreadsheets, marked SECRET, with updated ship schedules. Francis tucked the envelope into his bag and returned to the main gate and his waiting BMW. Mission accomplished.

If nothing else, Francis had proved with astonishing ease that a foreigner could stroll into a U.S. military headquarters, grab a bunch of classified material, and leave without triggering alarms. Just as astonishingly, the sailor who leaked the secrets had no qualms about doing so. He casually offered to do it again.

"No worries about helping you out—any time my friend," Gorsuch emailed Francis that evening. "It was my pleasure."

The Navy classified its ship schedules for obvious reasons: to make it harder for hostile forces to track vessels or prepare an attack. Partly out of a need for secrecy and partly because the schedules were always in flux, the Navy would wait to notify husbanding contractors that a ship was coming to port until thirty to sixty days before arrival. Around the same time, the Navy would inform the contractor of a ship's logistical requirements for the port visit: its specific needs for food, water, fuel, sewage disposal, equipment repair, security, and transportation. Contractors had limited time to prepare, but the short notice was part of the cost of doing business with the Navy.

By obtaining classified ship schedules several months in advance, Francis could boost Glenn Defense's bottom line by millions of dollars. The company serviced more than 150 ship visits a year in Asian ports that were hundreds or thousands of miles apart. With prior knowledge of Navy ship movements, the company could save money by pre-positioning its equipment—barges, tugboats, cranes, the Ring of Steel—instead of having to rush from port to port at the last minute.

As a foreigner, Francis didn't possess a U.S. security clearance. It was against federal law for anyone to give him classified material. But he persuaded Gorsuch and other Seventh Fleet staff members to leak him ship schedules anyway, arguing that Glenn Defense could provide better service to the Navy if it had more time to prepare for port visits. Plus, he rationalized, most of the information was classified at a low level—usually CONFIDENTIAL or SECRET, as opposed to TOP SECRET.

By definition, however, the unauthorized disclosure of CONFI-DENTIAL ship schedules could be expected to "damage" national security by increasing vulnerability to hostile forces, according to U.S. classification standards, while leaks of SECRET information could result in "serious damage." Regardless, the leakers knew what they were doing was illegal and tried to cover their tracks.

In summer 2007, Gorsuch hunted for a secure way to communicate privately with Francis from the *Blue Ridge*. The Navy could monitor government email and snoop on private providers, such as Yahoo and AOL, that sailors logged onto from the ship. But Gorsuch discovered the Navy didn't track or block access to a site called Cooltoad. So he created an anonymous email address: lyinginthedark@cooltoad.com.

Francis's desire for ship schedules became an obsession. He pestered Gorsuch with follow-up requests and pressed him to send secrets via Cooltoad so they wouldn't have to meet in person for a handoff. Even with Cooltoad, however, Gorsuch couldn't leak the information as quickly as Francis wanted. Because he often traveled with the Seventh Fleet commanding officer, he spent limited time on the *Blue Ridge*. When he was away from the ship, it was harder to access military servers and copy secrets without leaving electronic fingerprints.

Under pressure from the Boss, Gorsuch transferred his leaking duties to a new mole: Lieutenant Commander Steve Shedd, the Seventh Fleet staff's policy and planning officer for South Asia. A Naval Academy graduate from Long Beach, California, who yearned to command a ship one day, Shedd had been carefully groomed for the illicit assignment.

A few months before his retirement from the Navy, Lieutenant Commander Ed Aruffo—Francis's wedding planner—had asked Shedd whether he'd be interested in attending the fancy dinner in Sydney with the fleet's chief of staff and other captains. Shedd leaped at the chance. Before arriving on the *Blue Ridge*, he had been told his chances of being selected for a command job were "very precarious." To improve his odds, he needed a glowing performance evaluation during his Seventh Fleet tour. As he put it, having an opportunity to "rub elbows" with his superiors in a relaxed setting seemed like a godsend. "I honestly thought I hit the lottery in terms of political networking," he recalled.

At the coat-and-tie dinner, Shedd noticed the other officers kowtowing toward Francis. Afterward, Aruffo explained how the Glenn Defense owner paid for lavish meals and hotel rooms for a select group on the Seventh Fleet staff. Because Aruffo was preparing to leave the Navy, he asked Shedd whether he'd be interested in taking over his role as the wedding planner.

Taken aback by the overt unscrupulousness of the scheme, Shedd felt he was "in deep-crap territory." He had to decide on the spot whether to join. If he said no, the senior officers would almost certainly ostracize him and give him low marks on his performance evaluation.

Though he realized he would be "crossing the bribery line," he said yes. "It only took me a few seconds." He figured everyone would have to honor a code of silence. "We had an understanding of mutually assured destruction," he said. "We would all go down in flames or it would all be protected."

In November 2007, Shedd set up an anonymous email account— usna95@cooltoad.com, a reference to his graduation year from the Naval Academy—and began leaking classified ship schedules to Francis, emailing them eleven times over the course of nine months.

Francis was pleased with his new mole's willingness to leak military secrets on demand. He thought Shedd had the potential to be a long-term asset. Along with the usual bribes—dinners, hotel rooms, prostitutes—he rewarded Shedd with a set of his-and-her Swiss watches worth $25,000. He also treated Shedd, his wife, and their three children to a weeklong vacation at a Malaysian resort, spending $30,000 on airfare, lodging, room service, and spa visits.

The seamlessness with which Shedd had joined the conspiracy represented a breakthrough for Francis: He had found a self-sustaining way to infiltrate the Seventh Fleet staff. Instead of having to start fresh every year or two because of the turnover of personnel, he could push his collaborators to recruit their own replacements.

Francis's own networking investments also paid off. Captain Donald Hornbeck, who recently joined the Seventh Fleet as its deputy chief of staff for operations, had been a Francis pal since he was a commander and they met at the Christmas Cheer celebration in Hong Kong. Francis had hosted an expensive promotion party in Hornbeck's honor at Raffles—the hotel that invented the world-famous Singapore Sling, a fruity gin cocktail—and arranged a culinary internship for Hornbeck's oldest son in Kuala Lumpur. A forty-seven-year-old Texan, Hornbeck was introverted when sober but turned into a wild man under the influence of alcohol. Francis nicknamed him "Bubbles" because he guzzled so much champagne.

On May 1, 2008, the USS *Blue Ridge* arrived in Laem Chabang, Thailand, for a three-day visit. Francis invited Shedd, Hornbeck, and two other Seventh Fleet captains—Bruce Loveless, the fleet's intelligence director; and James Dolan, the logistics chief—to visit him in Bangkok for a night of fun. As the social planner and junior officer, Shedd had to coordinate the trip and coddle his superiors. He arranged for a Glenn Defense driver and passenger van to pick them up in Laem Chabang and secured a cooler of beer, or "roadies," for them to drink during the hour-long drive up the coast to Bangkok.

The officers arrived in the city center, met Francis, and checked in at the Conrad Hotel, where the Boss had prepaid for their rooms. Then they piled into his limo and headed to Pegasus, a members-only sex club where, as Francis described it, "a lot of craziness goes on."

At the club, Francis had reserved a large private room, furnished with five couches arranged in a semicircle. A bartender mixed drinks and the Navy officers toasted their host. A few minutes later, about twenty prostitutes wearing cocktail dresses entered the room and settled on the couches alongside the five male guests. For the next ninety minutes they drank and socialized. "It was festive," Dolan recalled, "a lot of boobs flying." Hornbeck showed his wild side, tearing his clothes off and dancing naked. According to Shedd, the officers took women back to the hotel, thanking Francis on the way out.

Shedd described the scene as "kids in a candy store" and emailed Francis two days later to report the officers "were all smiles on the drive home over their 'one night in Bangkok.'"

But a worry gnawed at Shedd. After their fling at the club, it dawned on him that Francis could blackmail the officers if they refused to carry out his orders. Their overgrown frat-boy behavior had at first seemed harmless, if boneheaded, but now he realized it posed a national security threat, especially for Loveless. As an intelligence officer, the forty-four-year-old Loveless was an obvious target for honey traps: the age-old spy trick of compromising someone with sex. According to Shedd, Loveless's "egregious" conduct of consorting with prostitutes had reached the "holy shit" stage, but the "dumbass" captain failed to see it.

A soft-spoken Naval Academy graduate from Chattanooga, Loveless at first impressed Francis as a poker-faced "spook" with intellect. He guessed that Loveless was destined to become an admiral, assessing him as an "up and comer" and another "good investment." But soon he too became dumbstruck by the officer's stupidity.

A few days after leaving Thailand, the *Blue Ridge* made a port call in Singapore, where Francis spent $20,000 on two dinners, as well as female escorts, for some of his Seventh Fleet moles. According to Francis and other witnesses, Loveless became infatuated with a Mongolian prostitute and tried to impress her by sharing his business card—which identified him as a Navy intelligence officer. The perplexed woman showed the business card to Francis, who became furious at Loveless and lectured him about the need for discretion. When Francis's staffers at Glenn Defense headquarters heard about the episode, they joked about it for months. They thought it was hilarious that the besotted officer was named Loveless.

Francis later said that he had provided Mongolian prostitutes to the Seventh Fleet officers as a "new flavor," adding: "What I gave them was beyond their wildest dreams."

Indeed, before the *Blue Ridge* departed Singapore on May 10, Hornbeck emailed Francis to report that he had also "really enjoyed my new Mongolian friend." Shedd likewise reported that the officers "were all grins this morning" and that "Hornbeck said he couldn't have survived another night in Singapore with you!"

Then, as thanks, Shedd emailed Francis another set of classified ship schedules.

As the *Blue Ridge* continued its tour of Southeast Asian ports that spring, Francis and the Seventh Fleet captains grew more reckless.

On May 12, the flagship pulled into Jakarta, the Indonesian capital, and Francis booked a suite at the Shangri-La Hotel to entertain his friends. Because of security threats, however, the Seventh Fleet commander imposed liberty restrictions on the crew, meaning all personnel had to stay on the ship unless they had official business elsewhere.

Several staff officers resolved to go ashore anyway to party with Francis and "get hookers," according to Shedd. The problem was that Vice Admiral Douglas Crowder, the fleet commander who had grown to disdain Fat Leonard, was scheduled to be at the Shangri-La for an official event. If the admiral spotted them, they would get in deep trouble for disobeying the restricted-liberty order. To minimize the risk, Shedd learned when the admiral was supposed to arrive and depart from the hotel and arranged to use a different entrance.

Shedd said he and three captains arrived undetected at Francis's hotel suite, where the Boss was waiting with several prostitutes. Francis insisted on conducting business first, calling the officers one at a time into the suite's study. While sitting at a desk with his man purse, phones, and files arrayed in front of him, he debriefed each officer for about thirty minutes. "They were going to listen to my agenda before the pants came down," he recalled.

After several hours at the hotel, the officers returned to the ship at twilight with the admiral none the wiser. Two days later, Shedd repaid Francis by emailing him more classified ship schedules.

The partying resumed when the *Blue Ridge* arrived in Manila on May 22. Glenn Defense had won an extension of its Navy husbanding contract for the Philippines and Francis was eager to celebrate again, this time without restraint.

Francis reserved the presidential suite and several other rooms at the five-star Makati Shangri-La Hotel. A butler took food orders and served drinks. For three days straight, about a dozen Navy officers filed in and out of Francis's cavernous suite, socializing with women and draining the hotel's entire supply of Dom Pérignon. Among the guests were Shedd, Dolan, Hornbeck, Loveless, and Captain David Lausman, the *Blue Ridge's* skipper.

The depraved scene shocked even veteran philanderers. "I went by that room and holy—debauchery like nothing you've ever seen before," said Captain Michael Brooks, the naval attaché who liked "high tea" and "chocolate shakes." He said the suite looked like a "disaster," with plates scattered on the floor and inebriated officers smoking cigars, women splayed on their laps.

As the hours and days went by, the scene turned from bad to

worse. According to Hornbeck, Francis got "out of control" drunk and ate a wineglass. It was a bizarre party trick: Francis liked to show he could chew chunks of glass without spitting blood. The grisly sight disturbed Navy officers who hadn't seen it before.

Francis further creeped out his American guests by losing his temper with the women, most of whom were college students or office professionals who did sex work on the side. When one tried to join the Navy officers for breakfast in the suite, Francis humiliated her, yelling: "What's this whore doing here?" According to Shedd, Francis ordered the woman to undress while he berated her. In tears, she obeyed.

Francis erupted at another prostitute that night, throwing her across the room, and threatening to douse her face with acid and toss her out a window. Shedd said he became "tremendously alarmed" and tried to calm Francis but didn't know what had triggered him. He said Francis soon lost it again, threatening to get an Uzi to "shoot these bitches."

Despite the outbursts, none of the Navy officers dared to cross Francis by telling him he was out of line. Instead, they laughed it off and expressed their gratitude to the misogynistic thief who was bribing them to betray their country. "I finally detoxed myself from Manila," Shedd emailed Francis five days later. "It's been a while since I've done 36 hours of straight drinking!!!"

The *Blue Ridge* returned to Japan. In October 2008, as Shedd neared the end of his assignment on the Seventh Fleet staff, Francis flew to Tokyo to throw another party. This time there were no prostitutes because Francis had brought along a new girlfriend. He hosted a dinner and took Shedd, Dolan, Hornbeck, and another officer to karaoke bars in Tokyo's red-light Roppongi district before they headed back to their hotel.

Shedd had turned in for the night when he heard a loud commotion in the hallway. He investigated and said he found a "quite intoxicated" Dolan hammering on the door to the room where Francis and his girlfriend were staying.

"Let me in!" Dolan kept shouting. "I want to fuck! Let me in!"

Shedd didn't know where Francis had gone and rushed to defuse the situation. He said he explained to Dolan that the woman was off-limits and not a prostitute. Then he put his arm around the captain and tried to coax him back to his room.

"Get your fucking hands off me!" Dolan yelled. He shoved Shedd, igniting a scuffle.

Shedd said he grabbed the drunken Dolan in a headlock and marched him down the hall. Dolan went into a tirade. He threatened to court-martial Shedd for assaulting a senior officer.

"Captain, no problem, we'll deal with it in the morning," Shedd replied. "But right now you need to go into your room." He said Dolan eventually calmed down and did as he was told.

Shedd had intervened out of self-interest. He needed to stay on Francis's good side, because he was planning to ask him for a giant favor. Despite all the gifts and bribes he had pocketed, the lieutenant commander was drowning in debt and desperate for a bailout. The next day, in Francis's hotel suite, he explained his plight and presented a spreadsheet that itemized his debts. Then he asked Francis for a $100,000 loan.

Francis didn't say much but looked cross. "I'll think about it," he said.

Shedd could tell he wasn't going to get the money. He realized that Francis saw him as a "washed-up asset," since he was leaving the *Blue Ridge* in a few days to take a new Navy posting in Tennessee.

But Shedd didn't leave entirely empty-handed. He received superlative ratings for his job performance on the Seventh Fleet staff, ranking second out of sixteen lieutenant commanders in his group. Though his written evaluation didn't mention it, his willingness to compromise his morals and his hard work as the wedding planner saved his career. In the years ahead, he would win promotion and fulfill his dream by taking command of a ship: the USS *Milius*, a guided-missile destroyer. He'd owe his prestigious new position to Fat Leonard.

By the time of Shedd's departure from the Seventh Fleet staff, there was no shortage of candidates to replace him as a Glenn Defense mole. With Shedd's help, the Boss recruited three new supplicants to take over the duties for leaking ship schedules: Lieutenant Commander Alexander Gillett, Commander Mario Herrera, and Lieutenant Commander Jose Luis Sanchez. Though all were married, they dubbed themselves "the Wolfpack," a moniker inspired by the hit movie *The Hangover*, about four pals and their wild bachelor's party in Las Vegas.

Gillett was a thirty-one-year-old Royal Australian Navy sailor embedded on the USS *Blue Ridge* as an exchange officer. Shedd had introduced him to Francis at a Hong Kong dinner that Gillett described as "probably the most extravagant, salubrious surrounds I've been in." He addressed Francis as "Big Kahuna," or "BK" for short.

Herrera, a forty-year-old deputy operations officer on the Seventh Fleet staff, grew up in San Antonio. Another Wolfpack member described him as a muleheaded sailor with "crazy-ass bug eyes."

Sanchez, a thirty-five-year-old native of Albuquerque, New Mexico, served as the Seventh Fleet's deputy logistics officer and inherited the wedding planner role from Shedd. Like Francis, he struggled with his weight and he affectionately called the contractor "Lion King," or "LK." A mentor acknowledged that Sanchez looked "a little bit like a stumblebum" and "wasn't the brightest of bulbs." Another Seventh Fleet officer labeled him "just a big mouth, braggart, showoff."

The Wolfpack officers craved Fat Leonard's approval and could be cringingly servile. In November 2008, Gillett emailed Francis from his anonymous account—dingo11@cooltoad.com—to make sure a batch of military secrets he had leaked were up to snuff. "If the information I sent to you last week wasn't what you expected or you had questions please let me know and I will get the answers for you," Gillett wrote. "Please be in touch with your needs."

In fact, the ship schedules were not to Francis's liking. He wanted to change the itinerary for the USS *Boxer* expeditionary strike group and reroute ships to his Pearl Ports. "Lets work a plan and send the [ships] away from Singapore and to Penang or Phuket," he instructed. His wish was granted; after other officers intervened, the *Boxer* added Phuket to its schedule.

Francis rewarded Gillett and other members of the Wolfpack when they visited Hong Kong a few days later. The Boss flew in prostitutes from the Philippines and Indonesia, spending a total of $55,000 on meals, alcohol, and lodging. The group partied in the presidential suite of the Shangri-La Hotel in Kowloon, where Francis mesmerized his newest class of moles by chewing wine goblets and spitting glass shards across the room.

Chapter Twelve

The Nemesis

November 2008

SINGAPORE

The past eleven months had been a nightmare for Jim Maus. At the beginning of 2008, after a three-decade career in the U.S. Navy and retiring as a captain, the former supply officer took what seemed like a terrific gig working for Glenn Defense as a senior executive in Singapore. He earned $25,000 per month, plus a fully furnished apartment and private-school tuition for his son. But after less than a year on the job, his life fell apart. The Great Recession hit. Glenn Defense laid him off. His marriage crumbled.

The strangest part of the whole tribulation had been working for Leonard Francis. Maus had clashed with him when they met in 1997, during the historic visit by the USS *Independence* to Port Klang. But a decade later, Francis sweet-talked him into joining Glenn Defense. Francis hired Maus because he had a strong reputation in the Navy and loads of connections among supply officers. He profiled Maus in corporate brochures and granted him a fancy title: vice president for worldwide operations.

The fifty-four-year-old Maus embraced his new job at first and didn't mind addressing Francis as "Boss" like the rest of the staff. Francis told him to pitch contracting deals to his old Navy shipmates, so he arranged a few business trips to Hong Kong and California. While in Singapore, he enjoyed corporate perks like his membership at the American Club, but he soon ran out of things to do. Francis gave him few assignments, excluded him from his inner circle, and didn't even invite him to any Glenn Defense dinners or parties. Strangest of all, Francis was inscrutable about the company's finances. Maus spent much of his time reading or daydreaming in his spacious office. "I felt I wasn't earning my money," he recalled. "Sometimes I'd just walk around the harbor and look at the ships. It was ridiculous."

Though the company appeared to be swimming in money, there were signs that something was amiss. Maus noticed that another Glenn Defense executive hadn't decorated the walls in his office or put any keepsakes on display. One day, he asked why. His colleague said he kept only one personal possession at work: a coffee mug. Hinting that Glenn Defense was a financial house of cards, the executive explained that he didn't want to leave anything important behind if the company suddenly shut down.

Maus hadn't spoken with Francis in a month when he received his layoff notice out of the blue, on the Saturday after Thanksgiving in 2008. Still, Maus had no hard feelings and was grateful for his $75,000 severance payment. "I fully understood. I wasn't doing much anyway."

Feeling depressed and washed up, Maus caught a break a few months later when a former colleague, Rear Admiral Thomas Traaen, the Pacific Fleet's deputy chief of staff for logistics, threw him a life preserver. Headquartered at Pearl Harbor, the Pacific Fleet oversaw naval operations for half the globe, including the Seventh Fleet and the San Diego–based Third Fleet. The Pacific Fleet's port visit expenses were soaring at a time when the recession was straining the Navy's budget. Though Traaen hadn't seen evidence that Glenn Defense or other husbanding contractors might be involved in criminal activity, he wanted to get the costs under control. He had an open government job for a civilian to analyze husbanding bills. He thought Maus would be perfect for the role: someone with industry experience who could navigate the Navy's hidebound bureaucracy.

Maus accepted and moved to Hawaii. He had been a figurehead when he worked for Glenn Defense and had no insight into the company's daily operations or billing practices. But after a few months he organized a team of junior Navy officers to collect data on the fleet's port visit expenses and the problem soon became obvious: Glenn Defense was gouging the Navy for à la carte services. Ship visits to Francis's Pearl Ports cost double or triple what they did elsewhere.

Much of the blame lay with the Navy. Commanding officers ordered gold-plated services without much thought. Meanwhile, incompetent procurement officials overlooked loopholes in contracts that Glenn Defense exploited. Whenever the Navy protested a bill, Glenn Defense got its lawyers involved and usually won on appeal.

"It was clear Leonard was playing us. You had to be stupid not to know that. I mean, good Lord," Maus recalled. "But he won all the time, so it was like, how do you take it on? Our current process didn't stop him."

Maus recognized it was a waste of time to protest excessive bills after the fact. The only way to hold down costs was to make ships cut back the amount of à la carte services they ordered. But that was a hard task. Ship supply officers weren't contracting experts. They often failed to realize they were requesting something that wasn't a fixed-price item.

For example, Glenn Defense might offer to make a sewage barge available twenty-four hours a day to ensure a ship's holding tanks didn't overflow while in port. The idea sounded good. No Navy officer wanted to risk polluting a foreign harbor. But Glenn Defense would neglect to mention that round-the-clock service wasn't covered by the Navy's standard contract, which meant the company could charge whatever it wanted.

In late 2009, Maus began organizing weekly teleconferences with representatives from an alphabet soup of Navy commands throughout the Pacific. The group analyzed samplings of upcoming port visits and reviewed the logistical services ships were ordering. Each week, Maus focused on a different item—force protection, tugboats, refueling—and looked for strategic ways to save.

One breakthrough came when Maus and his team persuaded Navy commands to install flow meters on all ships, to measure exactly how much water and sewage were being pumped out of their tanks. Navy officials had known for years that Glenn Defense scammed them by overstating how much wastewater it removed during port visits. But Francis and his moles had defeated prior attempts by individual supply officers to use the inexpensive flow meters. This time, with the edicts coming from Pacific Fleet headquarters and other Navy commands, Glenn Defense couldn't do anything about it. The company lost a lucrative source of sham revenue.

While Maus generally had the backing of the Pacific Fleet leadership in his mission to control costs, he had to overcome bureaucratic resistance within the Navy. Some mid-level officials in Singapore and Japan didn't like being confronted by tough questions about soaring costs or the implication they had done a poor job—and a few were secretly on the take from Francis. Maus slowly won most of them over with reassurances that he wasn't trying to make them look bad and that they would share in the credit for saving taxpayer dollars.

Maus knew some people in the Navy would suspect him of having a vendetta against Glenn Defense because he had been laid off. But he insisted that, in many ways, he was a fan of the company. He thought it provided reliable, high-quality service—especially in remote parts of the world where the Navy had little presence.

"There was never an intention to put him out of business," recalled Maus, who said he was unaware of the extent of Glenn Defense's graft or that Francis was bribing Navy officers for classified information. "I was just trying to get a fair price for services. There was nothing personal about it, because I knew how good [Glenn Defense] was, as far as providing services no one else could provide."

Personal or not, Maus's cost-cutting campaign spelled trouble for Glenn Defense and represented the first existential threat to its corrupt business model.

Maus held his weekly teleconferences on secure military communication networks. But that didn't stop Francis from listening in. One of his moles, Jose Sanchez, the deputy logistics officer on the Seventh Fleet staff, was invited to all the meetings and reported everything back to the Boss.

Francis paid close attention to Maus's efforts but wasn't unduly worried. He had walled off his former employee from the company's secrets and figured he would be easy to outsmart. "Maus is stirring shit now that he has moved back across the fence. He will self destruct in due time," he smugly predicted in an email to Sanchez.

To outmaneuver Maus, Francis tried recruiting additional moles who could sidetrack or slow-roll the cost-cutting campaign. He targeted Sanchez's new boss, Captain James Piburn, the Seventh Fleet deputy chief of staff for logistics.

A supply officer who graduated from San Diego State University, Piburn had never met Leonard Francis or worked with Glenn Defense before he reported to the USS *Blue Ridge* in 2009. During Piburn's first week on the job, Sanchez introduced him to Ed Aruffo, the original wedding planner on the Seventh Fleet staff. After retiring from the Navy in 2007, Aruffo had moved to England to attend business school at Cambridge University and work for Barclays Bank. Two years later, Francis recruited him to return to Asia to run Glenn Defense's office in Yokosuka and oversee the company's new husbanding contract with the U.S. Navy in Japan.

Aruffo acted friendly and offered to take Piburn out for a beer at the officers' club in Yokosuka so they could build a rapport. Piburn didn't realize he was being recruited. But he had no interest in getting chummy with a contractor and turned Aruffo down cold.

Aruffo, Sanchez, and Francis were undeterred. As a captain, Piburn was one of the highest-ranking officers to participate in the weekly port visit teleconferences with Pacific Fleet headquarters. Francis wanted to compromise him by digging up dirt.

"Let's study Capt Piburn," Francis emailed Sanchez. "Every sailor has a weakness somewhere?"

"Will pull out the magnifying glass on Piburn and find out," Sanchez promised.

But Piburn proved an elusive target. He was happily married, loved his job, and had no obvious vices. Another Seventh Fleet officer described him as a "Boy Scout." Francis and his moles grew frustrated at their inability to find blackmail material and began mocking Piburn privately as Captain "Pubic Hair."

"In case I haven't said this at least once daily, Piburn is a moron," Aruffo complained in a February 2010 email, four months after he made his first overture to the captain.

"Piburn is a Cancer," Francis agreed.

Piburn eventually caught wind of his status as a reviled figure at Glenn Defense. During a visit to Thailand, the naval attaché at the U.S. embassy in Bangkok informed him that "Leonard hates your guts." Piburn was surprised. "I said, 'I don't know why. I'm not trying to drive him out of business. I'm just trying to make sure he doesn't rape and pillage the American taxpayer.'"

In that sense, Piburn saw eye to eye with Maus, and they became natural allies as the cost-cutting campaign built up steam in 2010 and 2011. Their partnership enraged Francis, partly because it was depriving him of tens of millions of dollars in potential revenue, but also because he felt Maus had gotten one over on him. Francis, ordinarily a master at sizing up people, had underestimated his former employee, and became obsessed with finding a way to take him down.

"This is a personal agenda driven by my Ex staff," he vented to one of his moles in a text message. "I take th[e] hits like a man but back stabbing by Ex staff . . . to get at my Company I will not accept."

• • •

Francis and Maus had more in common than either man would have liked to admit. Both had overcome painful relationships with their fathers and adversity as young adults, relying on grit and hard work to build successful careers.

Maus grew up in Los Altos, California, a small town forty miles south of San Francisco. His father, a country club golf pro, abandoned the family when Jim was ten years old, without paying child support for him or his sister. His mother took a job as a secretary but earned barely enough to pay the bills. Meanwhile, as a mediocre student with short hair and conservative views, Jim didn't fit in with the hippies in Northern California. He had no idea what he wanted to do with his life.

When he turned eighteen in 1971, at the beginning of his senior year in high school, about 190,000 U.S. troops were in Vietnam. The number of conscripts had been waning since the height of the war, but Jim received an unlucky number in the draft lottery. Rather than risk being inducted into the Army or Marine Corps and getting stuck in Southeast Asia, Maus visited a Navy recruiting office and signed up for a reserve officer training program. "Jesus, I'd better do something. If I don't do anything, I'll be a ground-pounder," he recalled thinking.

Maus never intended to make a career in the military, but he found he loved it. His assignment as a young officer to a tight-knit aviation fighter squadron gave him confidence and purpose for the first time.

Vietnam combat veterans in the squadron taught him that "you do whatever it takes to win. You don't lose. Period," he recalled. "As a young ensign, having that imprinted on me was—I never thought that I would lose. I always thought I was the best there was in the Supply Corps. I just did."

Maus carried that attitude for the next thirty years. It drove him at Pacific Fleet headquarters, even though he was now his late fifties and struggled with a bad back. He knew that the cost-savings drive would anger Francis and that the Malaysian would retaliate, but he didn't care. "When it came to taking on Leonard, who had never lost, who used to brag about that, I said, 'Well, shit. Yeah, right, pal. Let me figure this out.'"

Francis hated to lose, too. In February 2011, he decided to go over Maus's head. He flew to Honolulu to meet an old contact, Rear Admiral Timothy Giardina, the deputy commander of the Pacific Fleet. Francis had met him several years earlier when he was a captain, serving as the Seventh Fleet chief of staff. Giardina was one of those officers who knew Francis was trouble but couldn't resist his allure. When he was with the Seventh Fleet, he had tried to fend off Francis's overt gift baiting, yet accepted his invitations to two dinners, including one at the Jaan restaurant in Singapore. Now that Giardina had risen in the ranks, Francis wanted to call in a favor.

They met for a Sunday champagne brunch at the Ala Moana Hotel, a Honolulu landmark. Giardina was on guard because he knew Francis would try to butter him up. "He's got a big-ass shopping bag that looks like Santa Claus . . . to give me gifts and he gives me a big hug. 'Oh, it's been so long, Admiral. Good to see you back in the Pacific,'" Giardina recalled. "I just said, 'Leonard, how many times do you have to try and give me gifts?' and 'Please just send them back.'" He said he insisted on paying his share of the meal.

But the deputy fleet commander listened as Francis moaned about Maus, called him a disgruntled employee and griped that the cost-cutting program was a vendetta against Glenn Defense. He demanded that the Navy open an ethics review of Maus's conduct.

Personally, Giardina had no problems with Maus and thought he was doing a good job for the Pacific Fleet. He agreed with Maus's assessment that while Glenn Defense provided "the best service," it was "charging us through the nose" and the Navy needed to curtail its port visit expenses.

But during the brunch, the admiral left Francis with the impression he was sympathetic to his concerns. He encouraged Francis to file any complaints about Maus with the Pacific Fleet legal staff. "There was clearly bad blood between them," Giardina said. "Maus wanted to cut Leonard's piece of the pie. . . . And there was talk on the staff that he had a personal bone to pick with Leonard."

Francis took Giardina's advice. Three months later, an attorney representing Glenn Defense sent a blistering forty-page complaint to the Pacific Fleet, urging the Navy to relieve Maus of his duties. The letter accused Maus of "retaliatory activities" because Glenn Defense had fired him for "unsatisfactory performance." The complaint further alleged Maus had misused Glenn Defense's "confidential proprietary information and trade secrets," and made "false and disparaging statements" about the firm.

The letter landed on the desk of Edward Hanel Jr., the top civilian lawyer at the Pacific Fleet. He discussed the matter with Giardina. The admiral indicated he was open to giving Glenn Defense what it wanted—Maus's scalp. "His reaction was, 'Well, do we need to suspend Jim at this point?'" Hanel recalled.

It was a pivotal moment. If the Pacific Fleet agreed to suspend or fire Maus, that would probably spell the end of the cost-cutting campaign. Glenn Defense could carry on as usual, overcharging for port visits and defrauding the Navy.

But after conducting a brief review, Hanel told the admiral no. He had gotten to know Maus over the previous two years and had participated in the weekly teleconferences. Maus had always been composed and professional, with an instinct for asking the right questions. Hanel thought he was an asset for the Pacific Fleet: someone with business sense who also understood how the Navy worked.

It helped that Maus had paperwork to disprove Glenn Defense's allegation that he'd left the company under a cloud. He showed Hanel a copy of his layoff notice. Signed by Francis, the letter said the decision to let him go had been "a difficult one to make" and was due solely to "the sudden global economic recession." It thanked Maus for his "contribution and support."

Hanel drafted a tough reply to Glenn Defense's attorney. It denied the request to suspend Maus and chided the firm for providing no hard evidence to back up its accusations. Hanel showed his letter to Giardina, who approved it without further discussion.

Maus had survived. But it wouldn't be the last time Francis would push his admiral friends to get rid of him.

Chapter Thirteen

Mikey

December 2010

SIHANOUKVILLE, CAMBODIA

The USS *Mustin* dropped anchor a few miles offshore in the blue waters of the Gulf of Thailand. The guided-missile destroyer's skipper, Commander Michael Misiewicz, gazed at the Cambodian coastline and tried to contain a lifetime of emotions welling up inside. He wanted to stay composed in front of his crew of three hundred sailors. He was the only reason they were here. The U.S. Navy had arranged the port of call so Misiewicz could visit the country of his birth, a place he had not seen in thirty-seven years.

Back then his name was Vannak Khem, a six-year-old boy trying to survive in an impoverished, war-battered country. His aunt worked as a housekeeper for Maryna Misiewicz, an American servicemember with the Women's Army Corps who worked in the U.S. embassy in the capital, Phnom Penh. Maryna grew fond of the headstrong little kid with the big brown eyes. She took him fishing and fed him popcorn and showed him American movies. Her Army colleagues adored him too and gave him an American nickname: Mikey.

The genocide that would kill an estimated 1.5 million to 3 million Cambodians hadn't yet begun, but Khmer Rouge insurgents were circling Phnom Penh and Vannak's family saw the evil on the horizon.

His aunt and father begged Maryna to adopt the boy and take him to safety in the United States. At first she said no. "I could not imagine taking him from his mother and father," she recalled. But as conditions worsened in Cambodia, she reluctantly agreed and brought him to America in 1973. She raised him as a single mother and gave him her Polish American surname.

Michael Vannak Khem Misiewicz grew up in corn country in northwest Illinois, in the town of Lanark, population 1,500. He was the only nonwhite kid in school but strove to fit in—and succeeded. In the summers, he baled hay and detasseled corn. He attended Trinity Lutheran Church and read voraciously. He wrestled, ran track, played baseball and basketball and was all-conference in football, all the more impressive given that he was as small as a Little Leaguer: only five-foot-four and 150 pounds. He shed the nickname Mikey, preferring Michael or Mike. Classmates at Lanark High School elected him president four years running, and the town voted him king of the annual Fireman's Ball. At age eighteen, he enlisted in the Navy, but the service soon realized he was officer material and sent him to the Naval Academy in Annapolis, the crucible for its leaders.

In the fall of his second year as a midshipman at the academy, Mike received a phone call that upended his life again. A private investigator hired by his birth family had tracked him down and delivered the first news he had heard about his Cambodian relatives in sixteen years. He learned that his mother, two brothers, and a sister had survived the Khmer Rouge's killing fields. They had lived in refugee camps in Southeast Asia before arriving in Texas as church-sponsored immigrants. But his father and two other sisters, along with sixteen other relatives, had died in the genocide.

A family reunion was hastily arranged for Veterans Day weekend. Mike's birth mother, Yen Touch, sobbed for hours when they met. But the joy was laced with intense pain, as Mike, in a state of near-shock, absorbed details about his family's suffering. He thought about dropping out of the Naval Academy to help his family adjust to life in the

United States. But he couldn't bring himself to leave Annapolis. He graduated in 1992, married his high school sweetheart from Illinois, and recommitted himself to a career in uniform, though he remained in close touch with his long-lost relatives.

Now, almost two decades later, as the commanding officer of a Navy destroyer visiting the port of Sihanoukville, Michael Vannak Khem Misiewicz had come full circle. Cambodian relatives he hadn't seen since he was a toddler hopped in a small boat to meet the *Mustin*. Among them was his seventy-two-year-old aunt Sokha, who had helped persuade his American mother to adopt him.

"Chumreap suor, Om," Misiewicz said in Khmer as he hugged her for the first time since he had fled Cambodia. "Greetings, Auntie."

The Navy knew Misiewicz's life story would strike a chord with the public, and it wasn't about to miss the opportunity. A Seventh Fleet public affairs team choreographed the reunion and invited dozens of journalists to witness it. The underlying message: Only in America could a child fleeing genocide grow up to become the commanding officer of a warship, dedicating his life to defending freedom. "Anything is possible," Misiewicz told reporters. "You see that we are a melting pot of people from almost every country in the world."

The Navy brass had big ambitions for Misiewicz beyond the visit to Cambodia. For years, his superiors had given him glowing job evaluations. "PHENOMENAL LEADER," blared one. "KEEP MIKE ON THE FAST TRACK!" read another. Several colleagues predicted it was only a matter of time before he made admiral.

Navy leaders didn't know that Leonard Francis had ambitions for their superstar officer as well. He'd met Misiewicz when the *Mustin* visited Malaysia a year earlier. Always on the lookout for new moles, Francis heard Misiewicz had a bright future in the Navy and poked around his background for vices to exploit. He discovered vulnerabilities underneath the officer's shiny facade: His marriage was a wreck, and he was always short on money.

Misiewicz also struggled with personal insecurities despite his professional success. As an immigrant torn from his birth family, he craved acceptance. No matter how hard he worked or how high he climbed, he felt like he never quite fit in. Seeking to establish a friendship, Francis lent an empathetic ear. He too was the by-product of different cultures and knew what it meant to feel like a perpetual outsider. "He had me convinced he was my true friend," Misiewicz later admitted.

Shortly after the *Mustin's* visit to Cambodia, Misiewicz received new orders: In early 2011, he would report to the Seventh Fleet staff. Francis couldn't believe his good luck when he heard Misiewicz would be working on the USS *Blue Ridge,* and he resolved to take their budding relationship to a higher level. If he could get Misiewicz in his pocket, odds were good the military secrets would keep coming and his Pearl Ports would stay busy.

Francis crafted a recruitment plan. He instructed Ed Aruffo, manager of Glenn Defense's operations in Japan, to buddy up to Misiewicz before he left for his new position aboard the *Blue Ridge.* Aruffo began playing pickup basketball with Misiewicz and taking him out for drinks. He also gave Misiewicz tickets for his family to see the *Lion King* musical in Tokyo.

Misiewicz's wife, Marcy, didn't like her husband's new friend. She thought Aruffo was "a cheesy, smarmy used-car salesman." She had heard rumors about Glenn Defense and warned Mike to steer clear. But their marriage had grown cold, and Mike didn't want to hear it. "I'm sure it just came across as another ping from the nagging wife that pushed him farther away," Marcy said. "It was much like watching a ball of yarn unravel and I was helpless and powerless to do much about it."

In February 2011, Misiewicz joined the Seventh Fleet staff as its deputy operations officer, replacing Commander Daniel Dusek, another mole who had leaked classified ship schedules to Glenn Defense dozens of times in exchange for fancy meals, hotel stays, and prostitutes.

Hoping to bring Misiewicz fully on board, Aruffo flew from Japan

to Manila to meet the *Blue Ridge* and host a traditional "hail and farewell" party for the two officers—hello to Misiewicz and goodbye to
Dusek. Aruffo reserved the MacArthur Suite at the historic Manila
Hotel, the site of a legendary Glenn Defense blowout four years earlier. But he didn't quite have Fat Leonard's knack for organizing debauchery.

The night before the party, Aruffo emailed Francis—who was
traveling and couldn't make it to the Philippines—for advice on finding prostitutes. "Do you have a place/person to use for girl delivery?"
he wrote. "I would like to drop off four or six girls."

Francis rolled his eyes in disbelief. "Girls for delivery you're in
MANILA DUDE they are everywhere," he chided. He supplied the
number for a Manila madam he called his "chief sex officer" and suggested that Aruffo order "a dozen to go."

Aruffo ordered half that number and hosted a dinner on Valentine's Day for several Navy officers, followed by beer and prostitutes
in the MacArthur Suite. Dusek passed out, but Aruffo and Misiewicz
kept partying. They went to a bar that featured a boxing ring where
customers could tussle with scantily clad women. One thing led to
another, and a shirtless Misiewicz—the Navy's new poster child—
ended up flat on his back on the mat while a gaggle of female fighters
downed body shots off his torso. Aruffo snapped a photo and sent it to
Francis, who saved it for his blackmail files.

"Just wanted to say thanks for showing me a great time while in
Manila," Misiewicz emailed Aruffo afterward. "Should have happened
25 years ago! Appreciate everything brother."

Aruffo's recruitment plan seemed to be working. He persuaded
Misiewicz to create an anonymous Gmail account so they could communicate covertly. "I am grooming Mike to be a good mole, he is starting to follow through," Aruffo informed Francis.

Then disaster struck. On March 11, 2011, an epic 9.0 magnitude
earthquake shook the seabed off the coast of Japan. Thirty-foot-high

tsunami waves crashed onto Japan's main island of Honshu, killing more than nineteen thousand people. Three nuclear reactors in Fukushima prefecture melted down and released dangerous levels of radiation.

The *Blue Ridge* had just arrived in Singapore for a port visit, and Francis had lined up prostitutes and hotel rooms for Misiewicz and three other officers. But the ship received orders to head to Japan immediately to oversee a U.S. humanitarian relief mission. For the next several weeks, Misiewicz was swamped with work and had little time for his new friends at Glenn Defense. The demands on the Seventh Fleet staff were "brutal," he recalled. "It was pretty much the hardest job I ever had."

The U.S. military evacuated hundreds of Navy families from Japan, including Misiewicz's wife and kids, because of the radiation. Once the mission ended, however, with his family back in the United States for several months, Misiewicz had more time on his hands.

Francis and Aruffo brainstormed about ways to take advantage. "We gotta get him hooked on something," Francis mused in a May 2011 email. Aruffo suggested that Francis take Misiewicz on a trip to Bangkok, a hub for sex tourism.

A different opportunity presented itself a few weeks later. Misiewicz confided to Francis that he longed to visit Cambodia again. His aunt was sick and needed medicine, but Misiewicz didn't have the money to get there or to help with her treatment.

Francis pounced. He bought Misiewicz plane tickets from Japan to Cambodia and paid for him to stop over in Malaysia so they could hang out for a few days. He reserved a hotel room for Misiewicz in Kuala Lumpur and provided him with several prostitutes of "different flavors." He also gave Misiewicz medicine to take to his ailing aunt and about $1,500 in pocket money.

The Malaysian businessman and the Cambodian American officer made for an odd couple. Francis, loud and gregarious, towered nearly a foot over the introverted Misiewicz and outweighed him by two hundred pounds. But they bonded while partying in Kuala Lumpur and began calling each other "Big Bro" and "Little Bro."

Misiewicz showed his gratitude after he returned to Japan from his jaunts in Cambodia and Malaysia. On the Fourth of July, he emailed Francis and Aruffo a coveted set of ship schedules for the first time. "Take care gents, thank you for the best leave (w/o kids that is) ever!" he wrote.

He was hooked. "We got him!!:)" Aruffo cheered in an email to Francis.

"You bet," Francis replied, signing his email, "the Godfather."

"All hail!!!" Aruffo added.

By leaking national security secrets, Misiewicz was jeopardizing his high-flying career. He almost got caught right away.

The day after he emailed the ship schedules to Francis, an anonymous whistleblower coincidentally contacted the Naval Criminal Investigative Service to report concerns about his behavior. The tipster suspected Misiewicz of committing espionage, reporting that he had recently traveled to Cambodia under furtive circumstances. The implication was that Misiewicz might be committing treason by selling military secrets to his native country.

The whistleblower had it half-right—Misiewicz had indeed leaked sensitive material to a foreigner, but it was to Francis, not someone in the Cambodian government. Still, the tipster correctly flagged Misiewicz as a security threat. The information threatened to unravel Francis's entire criminal racket and his penetration of the Seventh Fleet staff.

Protecting the Navy's secrets is a core component of NCIS's mission. But luckily for Francis, agents in the NCIS field office in Yokosuka, Japan, didn't treat the tip about Misiewicz with urgency. They knew he had visited Cambodia when he commanded the *Mustin* and figured he returned for personal reasons.

They also had little desire to investigate a ballyhooed officer the Navy had showcased as an American success story. "This dude was the golden boy of the Seventh Fleet," said Commander Ron Thornton, another staff officer who partied with Misiewicz and Francis. "He was the golden child—with the admiral, with the chief of staff, with everyone." An NCIS agent performed some perfunctory background checks on Misiewicz and put the case on the back burner.

Unaware that someone had reported him to NCIS, Misiewicz continued to leak classified material to Glenn Defense. But he found he could never quite satisfy his Big Bro. Francis wanted ship schedules on demand, not just when his mole found it convenient. After paying for the plane tickets, the hookers, his aunt's medicine, and other bribes, Francis considered Misiewicz to be on his "payroll" and expected more in return.

"I am disappointed with Mike," Francis groused to Aruffo in an email. "We are not a nonprofit organization," he complained in another note. "He has to deliver port visits, stick his neck out."

"As yet, he hasn't been worth the effort," Aruffo agreed. "We both worked to bring him aboard, took good care of him, but he needs to change his work ethic."

In late August 2011, Misiewicz made amends. He informed Francis that he had successfully lobbied the Seventh Fleet to extend a visit by the USS *John C. Stennis* carrier strike group to Port Klang. The carrier would stay at the Pearl Port for five days, generating $1.3 million in revenue for Glenn Defense.

"See, you ask—I deliver! LoL!" Misiewicz wrote.

Francis couldn't have asked for a better-placed mole. As the Seventh Fleet's deputy director of operations, Misiewicz had easy access to ship schedules and more influence over itineraries than other Glenn Defense informants did. But Francis worried the officer's unstable marriage was distracting him from his leaking duties and pushed him to sort it out. First, Francis offered to pay for a divorce lawyer so Misiewicz could make a clean break. Then he changed his mind and urged

Misiewicz to kiss and make up, buying a Gucci handbag for the commander to give his wife.

The faltering marriage neared collapse when Marcy Misiewicz and the couple's four children returned to Japan from the United States. In September 2011, during an argument at their home in Yokosuka, Mike allegedly became violent and grabbed Marcy, pushing her up the stairs. Marcy reported it to the Seventh Fleet staff, which issued a protective order requiring Mike to stay away from his spouse for several days.

When Aruffo heard about the incident, he became alarmed that the Navy might reassign Misiewicz and deprive Glenn Defense of its well-placed mole. "He has been feuding with his wife, he hit her and left a couple of bruises, she promptly showed them off to a doctor who called police," Aruffo warned Francis in an email.

A couple weeks later an NCIS special agent got around to pursuing the whistleblower's tip about Misiewicz's trip to Cambodia and contacted Marcy for an interview. When the agent, Trevor Moss, asked whether she knew why NCIS wanted to meet with her, she replied that she assumed it was about her quarrels with her husband. Instead, the agent explained it was because NCIS was investigating an espionage complaint against her husband.

The spying allegation stunned Marcy. Crying, she acknowledged the couple's marriage was fraying. She described how Mike had engaged in two affairs and sometimes stayed out drinking until 5 a.m. But she couldn't believe he would sell out his country. She told Special Agent Moss there was nothing mysterious about Mike's visit to Cambodia, though she was upset Mike had not spent the time with her and their kids instead.

But Moss failed to grasp just how turbulent the Misiewiczes' home life had become. Documents suggest he was unaware of the protective order that the Seventh Fleet staff had recently imposed in response to the domestic violence complaint. After the interview, Moss wrote in a report that he "expressed some sympathy" for the Misiewiczes' marital problems and advised Marcy "to contact NCIS if violence, abuse and/ or neglect are introduced into the relationship."

Marcy, worried her spouse might now be in deeper trouble, didn't want to say anything that might incriminate him relating to national security. When the agent asked if she knew whether Mike had any "suspicious foreign contacts," she said no—choosing not to share her concerns about the time he was spending with Francis.

By then, NCIS had uncovered other troubling evidence. Records from Commander Misiewicz's Navy-issued cell phone showed he had called a woman in Malaysia ninety times over a 120-day period.

After speaking with Marcy, the NCIS agent interviewed Mike about the espionage allegations. Misiewicz explained, truthfully, that he had gone to Cambodia to see his sick aunt. When Moss asked him about all the phone calls to the Malaysian woman, however, he lied, claiming she was a "family friend." He denied having affairs or sex with anyone other than Marcy. In fact, the Malaysian woman was his steady girlfriend, and he had seen her—along with Francis—during his stop-over in Malaysia on the way to Cambodia.

Adultery is a crime under military law, but Moss had little interest in pursuing a case that seemed to be about a philandering husband in an unhappy marriage. He accepted the Misiewiczes' statements at face value and closed the espionage investigation six days later, blind to the fact that the officer had been giving classified information to a foreigner for women, cash, and free travel.

"This investigation revealed marital stress (suspicions of adultery, lack of intimacy) vice indications of espionage as the information most likely misconstrued by the anonymous tipster," Moss wrote in his counterintelligence report, which was classified as SECRET. "This investigation is closed."

Misiewicz got unbelievably lucky. He had survived a counterintel-ligence investigation that should have landed him in the brig. Some criminals might have been chastened by such a close call. But rather than change his ways, Misiewicz escalated his reckless behavior.

In October 2011, two weeks after NCIS closed its case, Misiewicz flew to Singapore, where Francis treated him and a former Naval Academy classmate to dinner and supplied them with prostitutes. The next month, Misiewicz and another Seventh Fleet staff officer traveled to Tokyo, where Francis allegedly paid $20,000 for them to dine, party with prostitutes, and stay at the Ritz-Carlton. In December, Francis bought plane tickets for Misiewicz to go on another vacation to Cambodia to see his relatives.

In exchange, Misiewicz became one of the most productive moles Francis ever had, feeding him ever more classified material and advocating for Glenn Defense's Pearl Ports. The corruption would continue unabated until NCIS finally discovered just how dirty the Seventh Fleet's golden boy really was.

Chapter Fourteen

The Special Agent

June 2011

SINGAPORE

Commander Mike Misiewicz wasn't the only person dodging uncomfortable questions from U.S. Navy law enforcement officials. On June 15, 2011, Glenn Defense corporate headquarters received an email from Tony Sanz, an NCIS agent stationed in Singapore, asking for a meeting to discuss "some billing discrepancies" in Thailand.

Sanz had secretly opened a criminal investigation into Glenn Defense after the firm billed the Navy for $110,000 in wharfage and dockage fees accrued during a 2010 joint military exercise with the Royal Thai Navy. The expense was another one of Leonard Francis's scams. The Thai government exempted U.S. Navy ships from paying to dock at its military ports, but Glenn Defense tacked the invented fees onto its husbanding invoices anyway, hoping the Americans wouldn't notice the brazen rip-off.

In fact, Navy contracting officers had noticed and asked NCIS to open a fraud case, a step that jeopardized Glenn Defense's husbanding contract in Thailand—and potentially the rest of its business with the Navy in Asia.

Still, Francis wasn't worried. He was accustomed to running circles around NCIS. He scoffed at Sanz's email and blew off his request for a meeting.

From experience, Francis knew that NCIS didn't take fraud or corruption seriously. The agency had sharply de-emphasized such cases after 9/11, when counterterrorism became its primary mission. Before then, NCIS had 140 special agents around the world assigned full-time to investigating financial crimes. By 2002, there were just eight—and none in Asia.

Francis was untroubled for another reason. Over the years—even as he was ripping off the Navy, bribing its officers, and filching classified information—he had made himself indispensable to NCIS as an intelligence asset. Agents relied on him as an informant because he had a wealth of contacts in Southeast Asian maritime and security circles. He knew NCIS did not want to lose him as a source.

On top of all that, Francis was effectively acting as a double agent. Unbeknownst to NCIS, the consummate con artist had penetrated the agency by cultivating his own mole on the inside: a highly decorated official who was in a position to leak Francis whatever he wanted.

The Naval Criminal Investigative Service had about two thousand personnel stationed around the world, more than half of them civilian special agents with badges and arrest powers. The agency traced its roots to 1882 in the Office of Naval Intelligence, and broadened its mission during the world wars to pursue counterespionage and criminal investigations.

In 1991, the agency bungled the biggest investigation in its history: the Tailhook sexual assault scandal. The case was triggered when a female Navy officer alleged that gangs of drunken male aviators had molested her and other women during a convention in Las Vegas. After investigating for six months, the agency tried to close the case by pinning the blame on a handful of suspects, ignoring evidence that scores of women had been victimized while hundreds of male officers—including nearly three dozen admirals—participated or stood by and did nothing.

Amid public anger over the cover-up, members of Congress ordered the Pentagon to clean house by replacing much of the Navy's leadership, including the admiral who commanded the law enforcement agency. To prevent uniformed brass from interfering with investigations again, the Defense Department restructured it under a civilian boss who reported to the secretary of the Navy, a political appointee.

NCIS maintained a low public profile until 2003 when Hollywood seized it as the inspiration for a new television cop show. Starring Mark Harmon as Special Agent Leroy Jethro Gibbs, *NCIS* became the most watched TV series in America. Navy leaders loved the publicity and the glamorous way the show portrayed its personnel, though the action-packed, cliffhanger scripts lacked any pretense of authenticity.

Leonard Francis had dealt with NCIS agents since the early 1990s. Back then, the agency had only a handful of agents stationed in Singapore. But after the USS *Cole* attack and 9/11, as the Navy upgraded the protection of ships in foreign ports, the number of agents in Singapore rose. In 2005, NCIS expanded its Singapore operations into a full-fledged field office for Southeast Asia, responsible for about two dozen countries and territories.

Because Francis had an intimate knowledge of ports in the region, as well as a shared interest in safeguarding U.S. ships, he became an important contact for NCIS. John Smallman, a special agent based in Singapore from 2002 to 2006, and other NCIS personnel registered Francis as a confidential source—a cooperating witness. Smallman said he often cajoled the Malaysian for intelligence over drinks and cigars because "he just had a ton of information." He viewed the Glenn Defense owner as a cunning opportunist but admired his work ethic and how Francis seemed to know more about the inner workings of the Seventh Fleet than NCIS did.

"Everyone knew Leonard was dirty, but so what—business at ports is dirty, business in Asia is dirty," recalled Smallman, who worked as an FBI agent and a JAG officer before he joined NCIS. "I liked the guy, warts and all." Smallman refused to utter Francis's nickname, even when the contractor wasn't present, because he thought it was disrespectful. "I never busted his balls about being fat. Everybody called him 'Fat Leonard.' But I'll tell you what—it hurt his feelings."

Francis was less sentimental. He played the game, pretending to befriend agents such as Smallman so they would lower their guard. He knew there was nothing inherently special about NCIS personnel that made them immune to temptation.

In 2004, he met Mike Michell, a former New York City cop serving as an NCIS counterintelligence officer on the Seventh Fleet staff. Given the sensitivity of his job, Michell had a special obligation to stay out of trouble. But he couldn't resist Francis's invitations to go clubbing in Hong Kong and other cities.

Francis noticed that Michell liked to "sit and talk" at bars with prostitutes. To encourage the habit, he said he'd give Michell a few hundred dollars in cash when they went out so the NCIS agent could pay a chatty bar girl to spend the night with him. In exchange, Michell became a source for Francis. He blabbed about internal politics on the Seventh Fleet staff and divulged details about planned ship movements, even though other agents said he knew it was a "big no-no" to share ship schedules with contractors.

Michell's vices eventually became too much of a liability. In April 2006, he was relieved of duty from his counterintelligence post after a colleague found him passed-out drunk after curfew while on shore leave, according to his direct supervisor at the time. NCIS reassigned Michell but wouldn't find out for years that he had been a mole for Francis.

It was common knowledge among NCIS special agents that Francis lavished Navy officers with gifts, but they saw unethical behavior as a problem for the uniformed chain of command to deal with. Nor did they care much about his contract disputes with the Navy. "A lot of us were like: 'Yeah, you know, whatever.' People just weren't paying attention to fraud stuff," Smallman recalled.

NCIS field offices in Singapore and Japan frequently received fraud and overbilling complaints about Glenn Defense. Starting in 2006, when the Hong Kong Ship Support Office reported Glenn Defense for faking sewage invoices, NCIS opened twenty-seven criminal investigations into the company. But unmotivated or incompetent agents never dug up enough evidence to bring charges, and each case was closed.

In one such case, in 2007, NCIS received an anonymous letter, accompanied by incriminating paperwork, alleging that Glenn Defense overcharged for port fees, security guards, and other services during a visit by the USNS *Fred W. Stockham* to Subic Bay in the Philippines. But NCIS closed the case after Navy contracting officials in Singapore—some of whom were on the take from Francis—made excuses for Glenn Defense.

Two years later, NCIS opened another investigation after Glenn Defense was caught attempting to bilk the Navy with $740,000 in fake fuel receipts from a fictitious supplier in the Philippines. The company did not contest the allegations and withdrew the bills. But NCIS still allowed Glenn Defense to walk away without penalty, reasoning that because the Navy had not actually paid the bogus invoices yet, "there appears to be no loss to the U.S. Government."

Sometimes NCIS appeared incapable of performing the most rudimentary checks. In 2009, the agency opened a counterintelligence investigation into Glenn Defense after realizing it lacked basic background information about the firm's employees and had no way of knowing whether they posed a security threat to ships or crews. But NCIS soon hit a wall. While the Navy's contracts with Glenn Defense required the firm to conduct background checks on its staff and subcontractors, nowhere was it written that the company had to share the results—or even its employees' names—with the Navy. Instead of finding other avenues to pursue the investigation, NCIS gave up and closed the case.

The lax enforcement encouraged Francis to cheat more. Submitting inflated or invented bills became the rule, not the exception. "I don't think there was an invoice that came out of Glenn Defense that wasn't doctored in some way," Ed Aruffo recalled.

In 2010, however, Glenn Defense's tactics began to catch up with the company. First, Special Agent Sanz opened his investigation into the bogus dockage fees in Thailand. Then NCIS agents based in Japan opened a separate case into allegations that Glenn Defense was receiving kickbacks from subcontractors in that country.

Francis was unfazed at first. But when the cases remained active after several months, he grew more concerned. He had plenty of moles embedded throughout the Navy, but he had lost his best source inside NCIS four years earlier when Michell was reassigned. He needed better intel about law enforcement and decided to try to recruit another special agent.

The most promising candidate was John Beliveau Jr., an NCIS special agent assigned to the counterterrorism squad in Singapore. Beliveau had a reputation for immersing himself in his work, but Francis knew he was a bachelor and had picked up hints that he was vulnerable.

A native of Lewiston, Maine, Beliveau grew up in Pennsylvania and attended Villanova University on a Naval Reserve Officer Training Corps (ROTC) scholarship. He made the dean's list but was plagued by anxieties, including an irrational fear of everyday chemicals such as detergent and bleach. After he graduated and reported for duty in the Navy, he was diagnosed with obsessive-compulsive disorder and discharged from the service. His dreams of a military career dashed, he moved back to Pennsylvania to live with his mother and receive treatment for depression.

He worked as an investigator for the Pennsylvania attorney general's office, but his health problems worsened after he was diagnosed with a cancerous bone tumor in his thigh. Doctors removed part of his pubic bone, compounding his insecurities about sex and women.

In 2002, a colleague urged him to try again for a career in the Navy as a civilian agent with NCIS. The agency hired him, and he seemed to flourish, serving three years in San Diego and three years in Japan as the personal security adviser to the Seventh Fleet commander.

He first saw Leonard Francis in Kuala Lumpur during a 2006 Big Top reception aboard the USS *Blue Ridge*. Francis arrived in a Rolls-Royce, wearing a hand-tailored, dark gray suit with a stiff, raised collar that reminded Beliveau of the James Bond villain Dr. No. Beliveau watched while Francis glad-handed the admiral and a retinue of other senior officers. "He was affable, eccentric, with a jolly laugh," he recalled. "Definitely a smooth operator."

Beliveau moved to Singapore in 2008 to join a NCIS counterterrorism squad as a liaison to Timor-Leste, a small island nation that had won independence from Indonesia a few years earlier. Beliveau impressed his bosses and was named an NCIS Special Agent of the Year in December 2010 for his role in a human-trafficking investigation. But his anxieties and compulsions returned in force after he witnessed a Timor-Leste gang behead a rival with a machete. He later told a psychiatrist that the traumatic episode left him "shocked, numb and scared out of my fucking mind."

To cope, Beliveau drank and sought solace from prostitutes. In Singapore he frequented Brix, a club in the basement of the Hyatt, and Tiananmen KTV, a karaoke lounge. Both places were magnets for prostitutes as well as favorite haunts of Francis, who befriended the NCIS agent. He sensed that Beliveau craved intimacy and companionship. Instead of bribing him the usual way with lobster Thermidor and $1,000 bottles of wine, Francis became his buddy.

"He was a good groomer," Beliveau said. "He would be patient about it, like not pushing too much or too far."

The forty-two-year-old NCIS agent was fit and good-looking. But he was agonizingly shy, particularly around women. When he con-fided to Francis that he'd never had a serious girlfriend, the Malaysian businessman offered to play matchmaker.

In March 2011, Francis arranged for Beliveau to spend a weekend in Bangkok with a woman named Joyce who he said happened to be in the Thai capital on business. He emailed Beliveau a photo of his date, a twenty-eight-year-old Filipina who looked like a fashion model.

"Joyce your kind of babe?" he teased.

"Nice. You bet," Beliveau replied. "Hopefully, I'm her kinda guy, hehe."

In fact, Joyce was a part-time college student from Manila who worked as a prostitute on the side. She'd met Francis a few years ear-lier and he provided lots of business. He paid her about $665 per day, plus expenses, and flew her to Hong Kong, Kuala Lumpur, and other cities to entertain clients, including U.S. Navy officers. She called him "Papi" and knew the shipping industry had made him rich but didn't ask questions beyond that. She agreed when Francis offered to fly her to Thailand to spend a few days with an American friend named John.

With high hopes for romance, Beliveau checked into the Dusit Thani, a five-star Bangkok hotel known for its modernist architecture. Joyce joined him there, and they got acquainted on a dinner cruise along the Chao Phraya River. But Beliveau ruined the mood by drink-ing too much. He got sick, blacked out, and woke up hungover, yet kept bingeing all weekend.

His date was horrified. "Gosh john is unbelievable," Joyce emailed Francis in broken English. "I haven't met a guy drinking as early as 9am and drink the whole day also. Its sound exagarating but its true. And when he is drunk he is crazy." Despite his alcohol-induced meltdown, Beliveau wanted to see Joyce again and asked to visit her in Manila. Joyce was petrified. She emailed Francis and pleaded with him not to make her do it. "Papi honestly I had a hardtime with him," she wrote.

Francis didn't push her. He was fond of Joyce and knew Beliveau was a handful. He would find another way to hook the agent.

When Beliveau returned to Singapore, Francis fixed him up with other prostitutes and continued to nurture their friendship. Over drinks, he listened empathetically while the federal agent moaned about his terrible luck with women and other grievances. "I was kind of like his fake friend," Francis said.

After a few months, Francis carefully vented his own frustrations. He mentioned that other NCIS agents were investigating Glenn Defense's operations in Japan and Thailand. But he insisted he hadn't done anything wrong, claiming he had been unfairly netted in disputes between the Navy and other parties.

Beliveau swallowed the explanations and offered to help. He knew he could get fired, or worse, for interfering with the investigations—a fundamental betrayal of his oath as a federal law enforcement officer. But he rationalized that he was assisting both Glenn Defense and the Navy by trying to resolve the conflict. The depressed and clingy agent had grown accustomed to Francis paying for his prostitutes and bar bills. He wanted to believe the Malaysian businessman's promise that they would be friends for life. "I would be distraught and almost crazed if I thought I would lose this way of living, or him," he recalled.

During the summer of 2011, Beliveau began coaching Francis on how to respond to inquiries from NCIS agents investigating the cases in Thailand and Japan. Then he stepped further over the line by downloading investigators' case files from a shared NCIS database. Sometimes he printed copies and slipped them to Francis when they met for dinner.

The leaked files showed the criminal investigations into the fabricated invoices in Thailand and kickbacks in Japan were gathering momentum and, for the first time, posed a serious threat to Glenn Defense. Beliveau also tipped off Francis when NCIS questioned witnesses or met with federal prosecutors, and he provided insights into the personalities and reputations of his NCIS colleagues. For Francis, the information was invaluable. It gave him a full understanding of what NCIS was up to and enabled him to remain a step ahead of investigators.

While Beliveau had proved his value as a mole, he became progressively high-maintenance and erratic. He bombarded Francis with texts when he was off duty, especially while drinking.

"Im so drunk hehe, but I gou a lot of ideas for u, u got stupid people for u, I got the solution, give me 3 weeks," Beliveau sloppily texted in January 2012.

"Yeah Bro take it easy I appreciate tr Intel but do care abt yr health n condition," Francis responded.

Sometimes it was hard to distinguish the puppet master from the marionette. Beliveau knew the confidential NCIS files gave him tremendous leverage. When he wanted attention, he didn't hesitate to boss Francis around.

One evening in Singapore, he messaged Francis to drop whatever he was doing and meet him at a club. Beliveau wanted to show off a prostitute he had booked for the evening ("She a hotty, what u think," he texted when Francis arrived at their table). He demanded money so he could pay his date, making clear it was the price he was charging for an NCIS file he had brought with him. Francis complied.

In private, Francis disdained Beliveau as "a nut case" with "this really split personality like Jekyll and Hyde." He was unaccustomed to anyone treating him this way, but he tolerated the prima donna behavior. All things considered, it was a small price to pay to protect his empire of fraud and corruption. For now, he remained a step ahead of NCIS. But unlike the other twenty-seven closed cases involving Glenn Defense, the agency's twin investigations in Thailand and Japan would not go away.

Part Four

2011–2012

Chapter Fifteen

Spousal Privileges

August 2011

HONG KONG

Despite his well-deserved reputation for lechery and lewdness, Leonard Francis was a master of seduction when it came to the spouses of senior Navy officers. But his motivations were more tactical than romantic. Winning the hearts and minds of the spouses made it easier to buy off admirals and ship commanders. From experience, he knew some wives could be just as greedy as their husbands.*

With that in mind, Francis set aside a few hours on a Friday afternoon for a shopping trip to Pacific Place, a hotel-and-office complex in Hong Kong filled with luxury-brand boutiques. He was looking for gifts to impress the wives of two senior officers aboard the USS *George Washington*, an aircraft carrier making a four-day port visit. Far from a novice shopper, he had studied the two women closely during previous get-togethers, taking mental notes of their wardrobes and color preferences. He stopped in the Versace store and consulted with the store manager, Pinky, a longtime acquaintance. At her suggestion, he purchased a black handbag with gold-plated lettering. Then he ducked

---

* In 2011, 87 percent of U.S. Navy officers ranked lieutenant commander or higher were men.

into a Gucci store and bought a leather purse with the coveted gold Gucci crest and a quality-control tag attesting to its authenticity.

The next day, he hosted an intimate dinner at Spoon, the renowned French restaurant at the InterContinental Hotel. Officially, the guests of honor were Rear Admiral J. R. Haley, the commanding officer of the USS *George Washington* strike group, and Captain David Lausman, the aircraft carrier's skipper. But Francis's primary targets for the evening were their spouses, Charlene Haley and Carol Lausman, who had flown to Hong Kong to catch up with their husbands for a few days.

To put the women at ease, Francis brought along one of his steady girlfriends, Leticia Murakami Acosta, a Japanese-Brazilian beauty he introduced as his fiancée. (Francis and his second wife, Teresa, had since divorced.) The meal was another majestic spread, featuring delicate hen pheasant with chestnut velouté and white truffles, as well as line-caught sea bass, *forestiére* style. As the satiated guests left, Francis kissed the ladies on their cheeks and handed them a final treat: the Versace bag for Carol and the Gucci purse for Charlene, each wrapped tastefully in a shopping bag marked with the brand's logo.

The women knew they were forbidden from accepting posh freebies from a defense contractor, never mind the dinner, which cost $320 per person—the Navy's $20 gift limit applied to spouses, too. But like their high-ranking husbands, they felt entitled.

Charlene Haley was "overjoyed" with the Gucci purse and wanted to keep it, but a guilty feeling bothered her husband. In December 2011, after consulting with a JAG officer on his staff, Admiral Haley sent Francis a Christmas card along with a personal check for $215. In a handwritten note, he explained that he needed to reimburse Francis for the fair-market value of the gift. At the same time, he admitted he was undervaluing the purse to get around the Navy's "seemingly illogical ethics rules."

"Char + I hope that this card arrives as you and your family are enjoying a fantastic holiday in warm Singapore!" Admiral Haley wrote. "The enclosed money is not your 'Santa's Present'—it is my endeavour to avoid the ethics guys. Char loved the purse you gave her—it is seldom that I can choose a purse that is not 'exchanged' yet you do it on the 1st try!! Anyway . . . she loves it and to keep it I need to 'pay you for it' according to the lawyers. So . . . I went online and found a similar purse for $215 US—not the same and far less than it's worth or that you paid for it, but it satisfies the lawyers."

Unlike Charlene Haley, Carol Lausman frowned at her present. When she unwrapped the $2,500 Versace handbag in her hotel room, she immediately decided to return it—not because she was a purist on ethics, but because one of the gold-plated decorative letters on the purse had cracked. She emailed a Glenn Defense staffer to complain and asked to have the handbag repaired.

Francis fumed when he learned his plan to butter up Carol Lausman had left egg on his face. He ordered another Glenn Defense employee in Hong Kong to rush over to the *George Washington* and retrieve the defective purse from the ship's supply officer before the aircraft carrier could leave port. Then he dispatched yet another staffer to go to the Versace store and demand a replacement handbag from Pinky.

"I am very disappointed that they sold me a damaged product as I have been a regular customer to their store for many years," he vented in an email. Pinky apologized profusely and supplied another purse, which Glenn Defense delivered to Carol Lausman at the Navy base in Japan. This one, she kept.

The saga of the broken purse marked a rare misstep for Francis, but his determination to make amends reflected the importance he placed on keeping Navy spouses happy. In his crafty mind, he saw the grand tastes of some Navy wives as a weakness waiting to be exploited.

Many Navy spouses became fond of Leonard, viewing him with a mix of pity and fascination. Admiral Haley said the wives "tended to keep track of Leonard because he's kind of a unique individual" who displayed a vulnerable side, confiding in the women about his struggles with obesity. "I would say a majority of the wives really—I think they feel sorry for him is what it amounts to." At the same time, they were perplexed by his inexhaustible supply of attractive girlfriends. "He always has these women who, you look at them and say, 'Why are you with this guy?'" Haley added.

Francis's most steadfast supporter among the Navy wives was Carol Lausman. Though she'd turned up her nose at the first Versace handbag, she had known Francis for years and said she considered him almost like family.

Originally from Michigan, Carol was a six-foot-tall college jock whose exploits on the softball and basketball teams at Wayne State University in Detroit earned her a spot in the school's Hall of Fame. She fell in love with another student, David Lausman, a six-foot-six athletic trainer known as "Too Tall." When he joined the Navy as an aviator, they married and she followed him around the world, including to postings in Florida, Maryland, California, South Carolina, Rhode Island, Hawaii, Washington state, and Japan.

She first met Francis around 2006, shortly before her husband took command of the USS *Blue Ridge*. The Lausmans didn't have children and Carol had lots of time to travel. She flew from their home in Japan to ports in Southeast Asia when the *Blue Ridge* pulled in for a visit. Francis said he often invited her to dinners that he hosted for his Seventh Fleet moles—unless he was planning an after-party with prostitutes.

Carol became accustomed to Francis's generosity. The Glenn Defense staff acted as her personal concierge and travel service, picking her up at the airport and making reservations at five-star hotels, according to Francis and Aruffo. She was on a first-name basis with Francis's chauffeur, who knew her favorite shopping haunts.

During one trip to Singapore, Francis assigned a female executive from Glenn Defense headquarters to hang out with Carol for a few days. They played golf at the exclusive Tanah Merah Country Club and toured the botanical gardens. "Loving it here and having a glass of champagne as I type," Carol emailed her husband from the Shangri-La Hotel as she waited for the *Blue Ridge* to arrive.

The next night, Francis hosted an $11,000 dinner for the Lausmans and several other officers. Carol was enjoying herself so much at Francis's expense that she suggested roping him into another meal two days later. "I was thinking we could go out to a nice dinner on Friday and invite Leonard," she emailed her husband. "Of course we would pay . . . yea right, but at least we could try."

Carol introduced Francis to the wives of other senior Navy officers. In 2010, she invited two other spouses, including the wife of an admiral, to a small dinner in Singapore that Francis hosted without their husbands present. Carol told the other women beforehand that it was common—and normal—for Francis to pay for the meal and not to worry about it.

The arrangement sounded good to the other spouses. They let Francis cover the $3,300 bill and kept coming back for more. Over the next three months, Francis took Carol and her two friends out repeatedly, buying them brunch at the Ritz-Carlton in Singapore and an $8,600 dinner at a rooftop restaurant in Bangkok.

The meals enhanced Carol's status with the other wives, and she became fervently loyal to Francis. "Thank you for a wonderful weekend, and especially thank you for all your kindness wherever we go," she wrote in a Christmas card. "Love Always, Dave + Carol XXOO."

Francis estimated that over the six years the Lausmans were stationed in Japan, he spent more than $100,000 on the couple. (The Lausmans disputed the amount as an exaggeration. David Lausman's attorney denied that the officer did anything illegal to benefit Francis and called the defense contractor "completely untrustworthy.")

Francis understood why some Navy wives felt entitled. Life as a military spouse required considerable personal sacrifice, especially for those stationed overseas. Few had the opportunity to pursue their own careers. Every couple of years, they had to pull up stakes to follow their husbands to new postings. When ships deployed for several months at a time, spouses shouldered full responsibility for life on the home front. The Navy demanded a lot. If Francis offered them a fringe benefit, what was the harm?

In exchange, some Navy wives served as recruiters for Francis. In his description, they "spread the gospel" about Glenn Defense and boosted its reputation with Navy officers and their spouses.

In 2007, Francis was struggling to mend his frayed relationship with a hostile Navy captain who headed the contracting command in Yokosuka, Japan. He asked Rose DeGuzman, the spouse of one of his moles on the Seventh Fleet staff, to help him make inroads with the captain's wife. Rose agreed to run a "shaping" operation by telling the wife that Francis was brilliant and brokering an introduction.

Francis chatted up the wife at a change-of-command ceremony. Afterward, Rose reported back that he had "bedazzled" the spouse and that she had swooned in his presence. "It's so cute, but she even told me how she touched your hand and could feel the warmth," she emailed. "I told her besides being the savvy business man you are, that you are such a good family man and husband." But Rose hit a wall with the captain himself, who told her that he couldn't stand Francis and wanted nothing to do with him.

Sometimes Francis played matchmaker. When Commander Hee-dong Choi, the skipper of the USS *Chafee*, mentioned that he was thinking about settling down but could use help wooing his girlfriend, Francis stepped into the breach. He arranged a romantic weekend for the couple in April 2009 while the *Chafee* was in Kota Kinabalu, Malaysia, reserving an executive suite at the five-star Shangri-La Hotel and decorating the room with flowers and a bottle of Dom Pérignon.

The getaway was a smashing success, but Choi needed a little more help persuading his girlfriend, Cassie, a banker with JPMorgan

Chase, to marry him. Francis told the Navy officer to let him take care of everything. He had an inspired idea.

Two months later, during a visit by the *Chafee* to Singapore, he staged an elaborate marriage proposal for Choi on the roof of the seventy-three-story Swissôtel The Stamford. Francis arranged for a three-piece jazz ensemble to serenade the couple on the helipad, where they snuggled on a sofa settee and drank champagne as the sun went down. After a seven-course rooftop dinner, with loose pink and red flower petals strewn on the table, Choi popped the question. He got the answer he wanted and gave all the credit to Francis.

"I never in a million years could have imagined or planned such an awe inspiring event," Choi wrote in a thank-you letter on official Navy stationery. "From the sunset to the moonrise, it was like a fantasy come true. Both Cassie and I cannot thank you enough. You gave us the most memorable night of our lives." He added two sentences that brought a smile to Francis's face: "I am forever in your debt. And if there is anything I can do for you in the future please let me know."

Francis had spent $18,000 on the event, but felt it was worth every cent. Choi was now beholden to him. Over the next four years, amid the bliss of married life, the Navy officer provided him with a stream of inside information about naval exercises, personnel changes, the NCIS investigation, and other sensitive matters.

Chapter Sixteen

Change of Command

September 2011

ANNAPOLIS, MARYLAND

People gawked at the big man in the blue pinstriped suit and gold silk tie as he sauntered into the U.S. Naval Academy's Alumni Hall. Leonard Francis drew attention in any crowd, but his presence on this overcast morning, among the one thousand VIPs gathered for a high-powered military change-of-command ceremony, turned more heads than usual. He flashed mischievous smiles and shook hands with admiral after admiral in the audience. He was among friends.

It took hubris for a serial fraudster under criminal investigation by NCIS to visit the Navy's inner sanctum and mingle with its highest-ranking leaders. The Naval Academy, on the Chesapeake Bay, had served as the hallowed training ground for the sea service's officers since 1845. Above all, the school emphasized absolute devotion to virtue and honesty. The Naval Academy Honor Concept prohibited midshipmen from lying, cheating, or stealing, under any circumstances. Anyone caught committing a violation, no matter how minor, risked expulsion. Graduates were expected to uphold the lofty standards for their entire careers.

Outwardly, the Navy brass assembled at Alumni Hall looked like models of rectitude in their immaculate summer dress uniforms, sporting virginal-white jackets and trousers. But Francis knew that the officers' commitment to ethical purity was overblown and that their honor code had an unspoken and self-defeating corollary: Snitching was considered a cardinal sin. Francis had learned that even the most upstanding officers would not dare to out their crooked shipmates for taking his gifts and bribes. Their silence and tolerance perpetuated the culture of corruption that had infected the Navy.

The ceremony in Annapolis marked a changing of the guard for the chief of naval operations, or CNO, the top job in the Navy and "one of the most revered and fabled titles" in the U.S. military, as one speaker described it. Twenty-nine admirals had filled the role since World War I, including legends such as Fleet Admiral Chester Nimitz, the hero of the Pacific theater during World War II, and Admiral Arleigh Burke, the father of the modern Navy.

Francis had known the outgoing and incoming CNOs—Admiral Gary Roughead and Admiral Jonathan Greenert—for years and wanted to flaunt his familiarity with both men. When he received an invitation to the leadership conclave, he jumped at the chance. He cleared his schedule for the long trip from Singapore to Annapolis, twelve time zones away.

With NCIS bearing down on his company, Francis moved to protect his flanks. First, he wanted to make a public demonstration of his proximity to power that would force federal investigators to reconsider whether he was a target worth pursuing. Second, he wanted to reinforce his friendships with admirals in case he needed them to intervene on his behalf.

In remarks during the ceremony, Greenert forecast dark times ahead for the Navy. "I see the storm warnings out there, and I see the clouds forming. Folks, we are in for some heavy weather." He was referring to anticipated cuts to the Navy's budget, but the metaphor also applied to the threat personified by the large Malaysian guest in the audience. In the years ahead, Hurricane Leonard would wreak far more havoc on the Navy than constrained budgets.

Many officers lauded Greenert—a member of the Naval Academy's

Class of 1975—as an honorable leader and a respected boss. He had
maintained a professional relationship with Francis during his two
years in command of the Seventh Fleet without falling into the Glenn
Defense gift trap. But the admiral had nonetheless failed to prevent
Francis from infiltrating his staff during a period when the debauchery and corruption in the fleet had spiraled out of control.

Though Greenert said he was personally unaware of the graft,
Navy tradition holds that commanding officers are responsible for
upholding standards and must be held accountable for everything on
their watch—and that ignorance is no excuse.*

The retiring CNO, Admiral Roughead, was culpable in the same
manner. He had extended the invitation to Francis to join the ceremony in Annapolis, placing the Glenn Defense owner on his "Personal
A-list" of guests. Francis had attended a previous change-of-command
ceremony for Roughead, in Hawaii in 2007, when he was the commander of the Pacific Fleet. Over the years, Francis had found him re-
ceptive to flattery. Now that Roughead was retiring from active duty,
the Glenn Defense owner had designs to bring the admiral deeper
into his fold.

Roughead graduated from the Naval Academy in 1973. Thirty-
eight years later, he had returned to his alma mater to retire as a four-
star admiral with all the pomp and circumstance the service could
muster. During the ceremony, Navy Secretary Ray Mabus—the service's top civilian—praised Roughead's "genius" and his "steadfastness
in holding naval leaders to exceptionally high standards of conduct."

The comments were an allusion to an embarrassing issue that
had bedeviled the Navy during the latter half of Roughead's four-year

* Greenert said he was unaware of any "rumor or innuendo" about Francis's illicit conduct with Navy officers during his time as the Seventh Fleet commander,
or later, as he climbed the ranks to become CNO. In an email to the author, he
said that "there was more that, collectively, could have been done to preclude this
from going on so long."

tenure as CNO. Since the beginning of 2010, the service had fired twenty-nine commanding officers for poor performance, a near-record number. About half were relieved of command for personal misconduct such as sexual harassment, adultery, or drunkenness.

In public statements and media interviews leading up to his retirement, Roughead said the terminations showed that the Navy had no tolerance for misconduct by senior officers and that it would never bend its expectations of integrity. In one of his final acts as CNO, he issued a stern reminder to all prospective commanding officers in the fleet. "It is your responsibility to meet the highest standards of personal and professional conduct at all times," he wrote. He emphasized that federal law required them to "guard against and suppress all dissolute and immoral practices" and that Navy regulations dating to the Revolutionary War mandated that they provide a "good example of honor and virtue."

Amazingly, however, none of the sacked commanding officers had gotten in trouble for misbehaving with Francis. It was as if Navy leaders were contorting themselves to overlook his penetration of the fleet. For example, among the brass who lost their jobs was Captain Donald Hornbeck, a longtime Francis crony. The Navy fired Hornbeck in May 2011 after a jilted lover reported he had been carrying on two extramarital affairs. Yet Navy officials who investigated him missed the evidence of his corrupt friendship with Francis, including his participation in Glenn Defense sex parties.

From his seat in the Alumni Hall audience, Francis understood the talk about virtue was a lot of hot air. At a reception after the ceremony, he posed for photos with Roughead and Greenert, and chatted up a half-dozen other admirals whom he had lavished with meals and gifts over the years.

Nobody shied away. To the contrary, Francis received red-carpet treatment. The Naval Academy superintendent happened to be his old friend Mike Miller, the former commanding officer of the USS *Ronald Reagan* carrier strike group. Miller, who had since been promoted to vice admiral, took time from his busy schedule to give Francis a personal tour of Buchanan House—the superintendent's on-campus residence—and arranged for him to visit the marbled crypt of John Paul Jones, the Revolutionary War hero, under the Naval Academy chapel.

Francis left Annapolis feeling enraptured and reinvigorated. "The ceremony was a near-religious experience—I was personally moved to witness an event so symbolic and so critical to the Navy's continuum of leadership," he emailed Rear Admiral J. R. Haley, another commanding officer he was chummy with. "It was truly a remarkable day, and provided a great opportunity to catch up with so many friends."

Francis treasured invitations to change-of-command ceremonies. They afforded him a prime opportunity to flatter admirals in person. More importantly, his presence reminded everyone else in the Navy of his VIP status.

Navy protocol officers controlled admission to the exclusive events, with invitations reserved for high-ranking military leaders, politicians, counterparts from foreign navies, and family members of those being honored. Yet Francis was a master at wheedling his way onto the guest lists.

Two weeks prior to the gathering in Annapolis, on September 7, Francis had gained entry to another ceremony aboard the USS *Blue Ridge* in Yokosuka, Japan, where Vice Admiral Scott Van Buskirk handed command of the Seventh Fleet to Vice Admiral Scott Swift.

For weeks beforehand, Francis's anticipated presence had triggered concern among the Seventh Fleet's senior staff. Captain Jim Piburn, a leader of the cost-cutting campaign targeting Glenn Defense, and a Seventh Fleet JAG officer met with Van Buskirk and strongly advised the outgoing fleet commander to declare Francis persona non grata for the event.

The admiral, who had known Francis for years and had written multiple Bravo Zulu letters praising Glenn Defense, seemed to get the

message. He nodded and thanked the officers for bringing the matter
to his attention. Piburn assumed it was settled. On the day of the ceremony, he was shocked to see Francis glad-handing his way across the
deck of the *Blue Ridge*.

"I look over and there's Leonard, and my hair stands up on the
back of my neck," Piburn recalled. Furious, he tracked down a junior
aide on Van Buskirk's staff and demanded, "What the hell is Leonard
doing here?" The aide confessed that the admiral had ignored Piburn's
warning and invited Francis anyway.

"I was so pissed because we'd done everything possible to ensure
that Leonard did not show up," Piburn said. Yet part of him wasn't surprised. He respected Francis as a formidable rival, recognizing his unmatched skills at manipulating the Navy's power structure. "We never
made the mistake of thinking that we were smarter than Leonard. All
we could do was the best we could do, and if we turned out to have
lost, we'd go, 'Damn it,' and then move on."

The intensifying NCIS investigations did nothing to curtail Francis's
presence at Navy change-of-command ceremonies. If anything, his
legal troubles made him more determined to show his flag.

In January 2012, four months after the ceremony in Annapolis,
staffers from the Pacific Fleet and their family members gathered at
the command boathouse in Pearl Harbor, Hawaii, to celebrate the
forthcoming retirement of Admiral Patrick Walsh, the fleet's leader.
The change-of-command ceremony was scheduled for the next day.
Instead of a big social gathering, Walsh and his successor had decided
to hold "a very intimate, small party," according to Ed Hanel, the Pacific Fleet's top civilian lawyer.

Hanel was pleased to have merited an invitation. He relaxed and
sipped a drink while a group of schoolgirls performed a hula, then
he turned his head "and about two feet behind me, lo and behold, is
Leonard Francis."

"I must admit, I kind of swore to myself, 'What are *you* doing here for crying out loud?'" Hanel recalled. He and other Pacific Fleet staffers had been working long hours to prevent Glenn Defense from gouging the Navy, yet here was Francis ingratiating himself with the fleet's leadership.

The next day, a bigger crowd gathered at an open-air pavilion overlooking Pearl Harbor for the change-of-command ceremony. Hanel snagged a seat in the rear next to Jim Maus. Their eyes widened as they watched Francis make his way to the front to take a reserved VIP seat in the second row. "We kind of looked at each other and laughed," Hanel said.

After the ceremony, Francis posed for photographs with Admiral Walsh and the incoming commander, Admiral Cecil Haney. Both admirals later insisted they had no idea how Francis was able to gain admission.

Haney said he had never met Francis before. Walsh acknowledged he had met Francis previously—the admiral had attended two official dinners with him in Malaysia—but didn't know who had invited him to his retirement. "Leonard Francis had a way of showing up at all kinds of ceremonies," Walsh said.

In this case, however, Francis's technique was straightforward. One month before the change of command, he had sent a polite email to Walsh's chief of staff, asking for an invitation to the "prestigious event" and saying he "would be honored" if he could attend.

The chief of staff, Captain Bill Kearns, told Francis not to worry. He was already on the list. "Admiral Walsh looks forward to seeing you," he replied.

Six weeks after the Pacific Fleet event, Francis returned to Hawaii to pay homage to yet another pair of four-star admirals he considered old friends. In a ceremony at Camp H.M. Smith, Admiral Samuel Locklear, the former commanding officer of the USS *Nimitz* strike group, succeeded Admiral Robert Willard as the head of the Pacific Command, the joint headquarters for all military forces in the region.

Afterward, Francis stayed in Hawaii for a few days to enjoy the island paradise and conduct a little business. He hosted a dinner for several Navy officers and their wives at Nobu, a branch of the famous Japanese fusion restaurant chain, on Waikiki Beach. The party of ten savored plates of toro sashimi, salmon, lobster, and Japanese beef, along with four bottles of Cristal. Francis covered the $8,100 bill.

It was the last time Francis enjoyed a visit to the United States for a change-of-command ceremony. The next invitation to land in his inbox would trigger his downfall.

Chapter Seventeen

The Ghostwriter

March 2012

The job interview took place over lunch at the Halekulani Hotel on the oceanfront in Waikiki, about a thirty-minute drive from the U.S. Navy base at Pearl Harbor. The candidate was Captain Jeffrey Breslau, the chief of public affairs for the Pacific Fleet. An expert in global crisis communications, Breslau had shaped the Navy's talking points in the aftermath of the 2011 tsunami in Japan and the death of North Korean dictator Kim Jong-il. More importantly, he knew how to communicate with three- and four-star admirals. After years of working for fleet commanders, he understood how to plant ideas in their heads.

The interviewer, Leonard Francis, was impressed by the Navy captain. He wanted to hire someone who could help with public relations and reputation management, but he also envisioned Breslau as an admiral whisperer who could help him influence the brass. The Pacific Fleet cost-cutting campaign run by Jim Maus was crimping Glenn Defense's bottom line and reinforcing perceptions that Francis was a shady businessman. Breslau had smart suggestions about how he could punch back and get his message out more effectively. Francis offered to hire the captain on the spot with a big raise from his Navy salary.

Breslau had been planning to stay in the Navy for a few more years.

But he was tempted by the money and floated an alternative arrangement. Would Francis be willing to employ him to moonlight as a part-time consultant? The hitch was they'd have to keep their deal quiet. It would be a conflict of interest for Breslau, and he would be in legal peril if anyone found out.

The proposal intrigued Francis. For two decades, he had seeded informants throughout the Navy. But this would be his first paid helper on the Pacific Fleet staff. Headquartered at Pearl Harbor, the Pacific Fleet oversaw the Seventh Fleet and the San Diego–based Third Fleet, which was responsible for protecting the seas between Hawaii and the West Coast. Having the Pacific Fleet's top flack under his thumb would extend his clout and give him an added layer of protection against Maus and the NCIS investigations that were still threatening his company.

After their lunch, Francis and Breslau hatched a plan. The Navy captain agreed to serve as a shadow spinmeister and image consultant. They would communicate discreetly via Skype, personal email, and phone calls. Francis would pay Breslau by depositing funds into a bank account for an anonymous-sounding company: JJHS International, Inc. Breslau wouldn't touch the cash until he retired from the Navy. His security clearance was coming up for renewal and counter-intelligence officials would ask whether he had ever taken money from a foreigner. This way, technically, he could say no. "I just said I'll not take any money," Breslau recalled, acknowledging that he "wrongly rationalized" that the arrangement was legal.

The Idaho Falls native was risking his stellar reputation and career by working clandestinely for Fat Leonard. The son of a Navy veteran, Breslau had earned respect in the military as a savvy strategic communicator. The Navy employed more than two thousand public affairs officers, and he was one of the best. While some colleagues on the Pacific Fleet staff viewed him as "a smooth operator" with a "huge ego," they admitted he was personable and highly competent. Breslau's bosses drenched him with praise in his performance evaluations, lauding him as "exceptionally talented," "exceedingly qualified," an "unflappable leader," and a "superstar" who deserved to pin on an admiral's star someday.

But the allure of extra cash proved irresistible to Breslau. The forty-six-year-old officer had remarried after a divorce and now had a three-year-old son and an infant daughter to support. Plus, he was close pals with Heedong Choi, the officer who wowed his girlfriend with the $18,000 marriage proposal on a helipad in Singapore. Choi, who had since been promoted to captain, couldn't stop talking about his rich Malaysian friend and encouraged Breslau to work for him.

Breslau dove in. Three weeks after their lunch in Honolulu, he presented Francis with an "action plan." They would build support for Glenn Defense by leveraging "key influencers," a reference to admirals with whom Francis was already cozy.

He also shored up one of the Boss's greatest weaknesses by agreeing to draft his business correspondence with the Navy. While Francis was a charmer in person, the high school dropout was a terrible writer. Breslau was fluent in the Navy's lingo and became Francis's dedicated ghostwriter, crafting messages in a style and tone designed to put admirals at ease.

Francis felt like he had struck gold. He loved Breslau's "good solid ideas" and his Miss Manners–like advice on navigating military protocol. "I like your ghost writing it truly helps me," he wrote in a text message.

"Glad to help," Breslau replied.

Meanwhile, a chronic headache for Francis had turned into a migraine, and he enlisted his spin doctor's expertise to find a cure. His nemesis, Maus, kept ratcheting up the Pacific Fleet's oversight of husbanding expenses by limiting Glenn Defense's ability to gouge the Navy for à la carte services. Maus estimated the effort was saving the Navy about $25 million a year and depriving Francis of a huge source of profits.

But the pain Maus was inflicting on Glenn Defense went beyond financial losses. He had reported the company to NCIS after his Pacific Fleet team discovered in early 2012 that the firm had been submitting phony subcontractor invoices for port visits in Thailand. Ship supply officers had paid the bills—which were written in Thai—even though they couldn't read them. Maus asked another Navy officer's Thai-speaking girlfriend to translate the documents into English, and she exposed them as fake surcharges for nonexistent services.

Unaware that NCIS was already investigating Glenn Defense for suspected fraud in Thailand, Maus and Ed Hanel, the top Pacific Fleet lawyer, showed the fabricated bills to NCIS's Pearl Harbor Office. The Pearl Harbor Office remained tight-lipped about the existing case, for reasons of confidentiality, but passed along the fresh evidence of wrongdoing to colleagues in Asia, adding fuel to the investigation.

Francis soon found out from his moles that Maus had reported him to NCIS. Livid, he asked Breslau to help devise a "whisper" campaign to undermine his former employee. Under the plan, Francis would arrange one-on-one meetings with several admirals under a variety of pretenses. Then, he would bring up Maus, portraying him—falsely—as a resentful former Glenn Defense executive who had gotten canned for poor performance. The objective was to discredit Maus's cost-savings campaign with the Pacific Fleet as a vendetta and get him fired. "It was almost always tied to Maus," Breslau recalled.

It was also the height of disloyalty: Breslau was backstabbing a fellow senior official on the Pacific Fleet staff who was trying to prevent Glenn Defense from bilking U.S. taxpayers. But Breslau expressed no qualms about betraying his shipmate. He was more concerned about staying in the shadows while he helped Francis with his dirty work.

"Important not to compromise me even to your closest Navy brothers," he cautioned Francis in an email one month after they started collaborating.

"Rest assured your identity is protected," Francis promised.

• • •

The ghostwriter's next major assignment was to set up a dinner date between Francis and Admiral Gary Roughead, the recently retired chief of naval operations.

Seven months had passed since Francis flew halfway around the world to Annapolis to attend Roughead's change-of-command ceremony. Since then, the sixty-year-old admiral had moved to Palo Alto, California, to become a distinguished military fellow at the Hoover Institution at Stanford University. The Silicon Valley sinecure was fitting for Roughead, an elder statesman of the military establishment who admitted in an email to Francis that he wanted "the freedom, to put it bluntly, to make some money" by consulting and sitting on corporate boards.

Though he was no longer on active duty, Roughead retained sway at the Pentagon and within the admirals' old-boy network. Francis wanted a personal audience to bolster their friendship and spread rumors about Jim Maus. He sent Roughead a series of fawning emails that Breslau had drafted, asking for the admiral's "informal guidance regarding a couple of issues of concern." Roughead took the bait and accepted Francis's invitation to dinner on May 1 at Quattro, a restaurant at the Four Seasons Hotel in Palo Alto.

In preparation, Breslau spent several days refining a six-page, three-thousand-word set of talking points to guide Francis through every step of the evening. After an "initial warm greeting" and chitchat about their families, he instructed Francis to start a conversation about geopolitical tensions in the South China Sea, followed by a reminder of Glenn Defense's history as a reliable partner to the Navy.

After that, he advised Francis to change the subject to Maus by confiding that his "unethical" former employee was trying to "vilify" and "blackball" Glenn Defense. He told Francis to argue that Maus's campaign, which had led the Navy to cut back on its usage of the Ring of Steel, was jeopardizing sailors' lives—a ridiculous assertion.

Breslau suggested that instead of pressing Roughead to take concrete action, Francis should ask for his counsel, with the hope that he would later take the initiative to whisper in other admirals' ears. "The goal is to get Roughead to offer solutions without making him feel as though you are pressuring him to make phone calls or trying to personally influence the contracting process," Breslau wrote in his talking-points memo.

Besides bad-mouthing Maus, Francis wanted to gauge Roughead's willingness to work directly for Glenn Defense as a consultant or lobbyist. Francis had grand plans to expand his husbanding business in the United States and South America. Hiring the retired chief of naval operations would be a coup—and might deter Maus and NCIS from stirring trouble. "That's exactly what he was trying to do, is obviously use senior officers for protection," Breslau recalled. He discouraged Francis from making any job offers to the admiral over dinner, however, pointing out that federal law prohibited Roughead from lobbying the Navy for at least one year after his retirement.

Francis offered to pick up Roughead at his Palo Alto home at 5:30 p.m., a tactic designed to give them more time together. To his delight, Roughead accepted, and Francis's driver chauffeured them to the Four Seasons in a Cadillac Escalade. During the meal, Francis mostly stuck to his prescribed talking points, but he couldn't resist bringing up Glenn Defense's expansion plans and suggesting that Roughead would make a great business partner.

Roughead was noncommittal, but he politely listened to the complaints about Maus and left the door open to seeing Francis again soon.

"Thank you for your visit and for an absolutely enjoyable dinner last night," he emailed the next day. "I really enjoyed our wide ranging conversation—we must do it more often. . . . Warm regards, Gary."

• • •

Francis hustled back to Asia for the next stage of his whisper campaign against Maus. Thanks to Breslau's ghostwriting magic, he had enticed two admirals and a captain into having dinner on May 16 in Japan.

Breslau had drafted an email to Rear Admiral J. R. Haley, the commanding officer of the USS *George Washington* carrier strike group, to see whether he and his Gucci-purse-loving wife, Charlene, might "care to share a meal" and "catch up"—it had been a while since their last swanky dinner in Hong Kong. Haley responded by inviting Francis to dinner at the U.S. Navy base in Yokosuka, along with Rear Admiral Dan Cloyd, the commander of Navy forces in Japan, and their spouses. Also attending would be Captain David "Too Tall" Lausman and his wife, Carol.

The invitation sent Francis over the moon. To be the guest of honor at a brass-packed dinner on the largest U.S. Navy base in Asia would send another unmistakable message to the fleet that he was tight with people at the top.

From his home in Hawaii, Breslau went into overdrive, writing and revising a six-page set of talking points and coaching Francis on how to maximize the opportunity. He told Francis to bring his girlfriend, Leticia Murakami Acosta, as his date. "She can help distract the other spouses and give you a better opportunity to talk with your friends about what you need to discuss," Breslau said. "Plus, she can also carry the flowers. You only have two hands."

The invitation called for casual attire, but the evening was organized with military precision. An admiral's aide greeted Leonard and Leticia at the front gate of the base at 6:15 p.m. and escorted them to Haley's official quarters, a modern two-story home on Halsey Road.

The guests came bearing gifts for the hosts: Leticia with floral bouquets and Leonard with two heavy bags, one for the Haleys and one for the Cloyds. Each bag contained a $120 bottle of Miss Dior

Eau de Parfum; a $395 bottle of Domaine Leflaive Bienvenues-Bâtard-Montrachet (1996); and a $275 bottle of Château Haut-Brion, Cru Classés de Graves (1994). Francis quickly stashed the gifts in the kitchen so the hosts wouldn't notice them until after the party was over. He didn't want to risk the possibility that they insist he take them back.*

After cocktails at the Haleys', the group walked next door to the Cloyds' residence for dinner. While Leticia distracted the wives, Francis buttonholed the admirals and delivered his talking points, focusing on Maus. He accused his former employee of "unethical practices" and holding a personal grudge. If the Navy didn't do something about Maus, he implied, he might be forced to take legal action.

Once he was done carping about Maus, Francis resumed his sunny demeanor and spent the rest of the evening charming his hosts. The next day, Breslau drafted a flowery thank-you note for Francis to send to the Haleys. "The food was fantastic, the conversation was enjoyable as always, and the entire evening is definitely one to remember," he wrote. "Your friendship means a great deal to me."

The whisper campaign was swiftly gaining momentum. A few days later, Francis flew to Thailand to corner Vice Admiral Scott Swift, the new Seventh Fleet commander, during a reception aboard the USS *Blue Ridge*. Breslau drafted a meticulous plan of action, urging Francis to focus on strengthening his rapport with the three-star commander. Afterward, Francis reported that his twenty-minute chat with Swift went "extremely well" and gloated that the admiral's wife "kissed my cheeks."

The next month, Breslau prepared an "Executive Brief" for another round of admiral encounters in Tokyo. Again, he told Francis

---

* Based on ethics advice from his JAG officer, Cloyd's staff later shipped his gift bag back to Glenn Defense. Haley turned over his bottles of wine to the USS *George Washington* after a different JAG officer ruled the alcohol was a "perishable" item and didn't need to be returned. Haley's wife kept the perfume.

to nurture his relationships with the senior officers instead of just launching broadsides against his antagonist. "Dance around the Maus issue but tread very lightly," he wrote. "Don't want to come across as too obvious."

Though Francis could be mercurial, he generally followed Breslau's scripts and praised the public affairs officer as a "brilliant strategist" and an "awesome mentor and advisor." He grew confident that the admiral-whispering tactics would pay off. "We have made new inroads and will work in the shadows with retired [admirals] to shut Maus up," he emailed a Glenn Defense subordinate. "It's not easy but we have a strategy now."

As insurance, Breslau and Francis devised a ruse to file a dubious complaint against Maus with the Pacific Fleet inspector general. They hoped it would trigger a misconduct investigation and get him suspended, if not fired. Breslau put Francis in touch with Mark Zaid, a Washington power lawyer who represented government whistleblowers, for advice.

Francis was hopeful the idea would work. He thought Zaid was a "pit bull" and couldn't wait to unleash him on his archenemy. "I will finish Maus off this time," he vowed in a text to one of his moles.*

Before he could strike, however, Francis was outflanked.

In July 2012, Cecil Haney, the four-star admiral in charge of the Pacific Fleet, transmitted a stern message warning the 150,000 sailors and civilians under his command to think twice before taking any perks from husbanding contractors. The two-page instruction reminded commanding officers that they were "expected to maintain the highest ethical standards for themselves and their crews" and that henceforth all personnel would have to file a report with JAG officers anytime

---

* Francis later backed off the idea and no complaint was filed.

they accepted a gift, dinner, or favor from a husbanding contractor, no matter the value.

The message did not mention Francis by name, but it was aimed squarely at him. In the past, officers didn't have to report Francis's exorbitant meals or freebies as long as they maintained the fiction that the gifts were worth less than $20. Now they would be required to tell the JAGs and provide documentation.

Francis was enraged. While the new mandate wouldn't stop him from bribing people or holding parties in secret, it would make it harder to entertain and recruit. He complained that the message would render Glenn Defense radioactive and "spook" people from being seen with him.

He sensed who was responsible. "Maus is behind this and . . . it is part of his campaign to try and isolate me," he vented in an email to two moles on the Seventh Fleet staff. He accused Maus of having "a massive bias agenda."

In fact, Maus *was* behind it. Along with others, he had been pushing the Pacific Fleet to tighten its ethics standards for two and a half years, arguing that the Navy had to stop Francis from wining and dining officers if it wanted to prevent Glenn Defense from overcharging for port services. But the timing of the message from the fleet commander was coincidental. Maus had no idea that Francis and Breslau had been trying to kneecap him by whispering to the admirals and plotting to get him fired.

Francis sought guidance from Breslau. His ghostwriter preached patience, reminding him that his moles were still leaking him real-time updates about Maus's cost-cutting campaign and doing their best to thwart it from within.

"I know you are familiar with the principles of Judo—using an opponent's momentum against him," Breslau wrote in an email. "You know nearly every move Maus has and is making and he does not know this. To use an American football term, you have his playbook. . . . This is a marathon and not a sprint; don't allow emotion to drive your decisions."

For Francis, containing his emotions was easier said than done. But he treasured Breslau's advice. He wired a total of $65,000 to the officer's bank account as compensation for his treachery.

Chapter Eighteen

Spy vs. Spy

August 2012

YOKOSUKA, JAPAN

Marcy Misiewicz, the long-suffering partner of Commander Mike Misiewicz, the golden boy on the Seventh Fleet staff, finally sealed the fate of their fragile marriage in August 2012 by reporting his illegal conduct to his chain of command and the NCIS office in Yokosuka. Marcy had been genuinely shocked a year earlier when an NCIS agent had investigated the espionage allegations against her husband. She and Mike were estranged at the time, but she'd instinctively defended him and didn't mention her suspicions about his carousing with Fat Leonard and Ed Aruffo. Since then, however, she had become fed up with his lying and cheating, which worsened as his corrupt friendship with Francis intensified.

The final straw came in July when Commander Misiewicz took their three eldest children—ages thirteen, ten, and seven—on a vacation to Cambodia while Marcy stayed in Japan with their two-year-old. Mike told his wife they were going to see his birth family in Cambodia, which was partly true. But when the children returned home two weeks later, they couldn't stop talking about their unexpected side adventures in Singapore and Malaysia with their dad's buddy, Mr. Francis, and another special friend—a woman.

Marcy fumed. She had devoted herself to Mike since high school in rural Illinois and had forsaken a career to raise their family and follow him to Japan. Snitching was taboo in a military culture that venerated loyalty. But Mike had treated their twenty-year marriage with open contempt. If that weren't enough, now he was exposing her children to Francis and his immoral lifestyle.

"He was my husband. I loved him. We had a life together. But I had known forever that something was off," Marcy recalled. "I was concerned about who he was involved with, and what was going on. I was piecing stuff together."

She shared her suspicions with a senior officer on the Seventh Fleet staff, who referred her to NCIS. On August 14, 2012, Marcy took her teenage son, Merrick, to the NCIS office on the Navy base in Yokosuka. At her urging, he repeated the story about his vacation to NCIS Special Agent Erika Mariner. Merrick recounted how his siblings and their father stopped in Singapore on the way to Cambodia and spent three days at the Shangri-La Rasa Sentosa, a beachfront hotel. While there, they went to a fancy restaurant with the amiable Mr. Francis, whom Merrick sardonically described as "a big guy. He doesn't miss too many meals."

Merrick said his father had warned him: "Don't be bragging that you ate dinner with Mr. Francis." The boy added, perceptively, "I think it's because the Navy does business with [him]." Moreover, Merrick said it wasn't the first time Mr. Francis had treated him and his siblings to an expensive night out. For Father's Day, the Glenn Defense owner had taken them and their dad to Nobu in Tokyo for sushi.

After visiting Singapore and Cambodia, the Misiewicz children and their dad stopped in Malaysia. Merrick told the NCIS agent that they spent a few days in Kuala Lumpur with "Miss Hani," another friend of their father's, who showed them the Petronas Towers—the tallest twin skyscrapers in the world—an amusement park, and other sights. Merrick's ten-year-old sister, Macy, confirmed the details in a separate interview with NCIS. Their mother suspected Miss Hani and

Mike had been carrying on a long-distance affair. She provided NCIS with bank records, credit card statements, and other documents as evidence.*

Marcy thought she was reporting her husband to NCIS for infidelity and accepting gifts from a defense contractor. But Mariner, the special agent, stunned her by saying Mike was caught up in something bigger. Mariner revealed that NCIS had been investigating Francis since 2010 on suspicion of defrauding the Navy of millions of dollars. Now it appeared he had compromised—and perhaps controlled— her husband, an influential Navy officer on the Seventh Fleet staff. Marcy's bank and credit card records would help investigators establish that Francis was not just overcharging the Navy for port services but bribing key personnel.

For NCIS, Marcy's unexpected cooperation was the second major break in a rapidly intensifying investigation. After failing for a decade to make anything stick against Francis, NCIS agents had recently turned the tables by recruiting their own moles inside Glenn Defense: Two low-level female staffers in the company's Bangkok office were helping NCIS as informants.

In June 2012, one informant had agreed to wear a wire to record conversations with Yin Settaphakorn, Glenn Defense's country manager for Thailand, home to a fast-growing division of Francis's husbanding empire. NCIS agents hoped they could dupe Yin, a loyal Francis lieutenant, into incriminating herself and the Boss on tape.

Francis had hired Yin when she was twenty-six years old after Glenn Defense won its first U.S. Navy contract for Thailand. He was impressed by the Bangkok native's skill set. Like him, she was Catholic and spoke fluent English. She had lived in Mississippi as a high school student and knew how to deal with Americans. Plus, she was

---

* Investigators determined years later that Francis had underwritten the family vacation, buying plane tickets for Misiewicz and his kids, giving the Navy officer cash and encouraging his relationship with Miss Hani.

single, which meant Francis could expect her to work around the clock.

Yin became one of the few women Francis trusted. She adopted his management style, acting as an unforgiving taskmaster toward Glenn Defense underlings but as a deferential charmer with Navy personnel. At Francis's direction, she doled out free hotel suites, beach vacations, spa treatments, shopping excursions, and other perks to select Navy officers when they visited Thailand. During a port call by the USS *Ronald Reagan* to Phuket in 2009, she presented the skipper with a six-imperial-liter bottle of Château Mouton Cadet wine, valued at $3,000. In 2010, she welcomed officers from the USS *George Washington* carrier strike group to Pattaya with a swank, $20,000 dinner at the Dusit Thani Hotel.

Tony Sanz, the NCIS special agent leading the Thailand investigation, suspected Yin and Francis of recouping the gift expenses by ripping off the Navy during port visits. But the overbilling was more pervasive than he knew. In October 2011, for example, Glenn Defense billed the Navy $2.8 million for fuel and other services during a visit by the USS *Mustin* to Laem Chabang. More than half the amount was fraudulent, based on fake invoices from fictitious subcontractors.

Sanz coaxed one of his informants into wearing a recording device during a lunch with Yin in Bangkok. The informant tried to bait Yin into admitting that Glenn Defense was falsifying invoices, by implying that a former coworker had taken a stash of documents from the office and was threatening to report the company for fraud.

Unaware she was being taped, Yin fumed that the coworker was "evil," "a psycho," and "a fool" and complained, "She's going to cause problems for everybody . . . . I don't understand why she is doing it. Why does she hate us so much?" But she stopped just short of confessing to a crime.

Even so, NCIS agents were thrilled with their progress. The informant had performed well and was willing to try again. For the first time in three years, they thought they were playing offense instead of defense with their investigations.

They were wrong.

On August 17, three days after Marcy and Merrick Misiewicz met with NCIS in Japan, Special Agent John Beliveau Jr.—Francis's hard-drinking mole inside the law enforcement agency—logged into an internal NCIS case management network and searched for investigative reports filed from Asia containing the word "Glenn."

Beliveau had moved from Singapore to Quantico, Virginia, the site of NCIS headquarters, four months earlier to take a new assignment as a supervisory special agent in charge of local investigations. But he still secretly worked for Francis, who was elated that his mole had risen so high in the agency.

NCIS's counterintelligence defenses should have flagged Beliveau as a risk. He drank too much and was depressed and burdened by debt. The service knew about his money troubles, because it was garnishing his wages, but his 2010 Special Agent of the Year award neutralized any doubts about his reliability. As a result, nobody noticed that Beliveau was checking K-NET, the case management network, every few weeks for updates on the Glenn Defense investigations and leaking reports to Francis, often dozens at a time.

When Beliveau read the notes about Yin and the two NCIS informants in Bangkok, he realized Francis was in serious trouble. He ducked out of the office and contacted the Boss.

"I have 30 reports for u, not good, ur girl in Thailand fd up and got caught on tape," he texted.

"No way!" Francis replied. He asked for details but didn't take the threat seriously at first, trying to laugh it off.

"OK ur in denial," Beliveau texted. "I warned you about this, ill send, u read"

Wary of leaving electronic tracks, Beliveau used a burner cell phone to text Francis and chat with him on Skype. He also had taught Francis a simple but effective technique for sharing sensitive files. He set up two anonymous email accounts—bugsdaffy100@gmail.com and samcoyote500@gmail.com—for them to use jointly. Instead of transmitting the NCIS reports over the internet, however, he saved them as draft emails. Then Francis logged into the accounts using shared passwords and copied the reports from the draft folder. Nobody had to hit "send."

Along with updates about the Thailand investigation, Beliveau included the NCIS report detailing the interviews with Commander Misiewicz's family. Francis flipped when he read the confidential reports and warned Misiewicz that his wife had "fucked things up" by ratting them out. Yet he still hoped things would blow over.

Beliveau was less optimistic. He didn't know Misiewicz personally or the extent of his relationship with Francis. But the veteran federal agent recognized that if Misiewicz was a suspect, NCIS would search his military communication records and obtain a search warrant for his personal email and phone accounts.

The long-distance relationship between Francis and Beliveau ran hot and cold. Beliveau asked Francis to pay for his vacations and gifts for a prostitute he saw irregularly in Manila, but he mostly craved attention and approval. He showed great initiative as a mole, volunteering advice on how to respond to every twist in the NCIS investigations. Yet he could be demanding or even threatening if he felt neglected, especially when he binge-drank.

"You give whores more money than me ☺. Don't get too busy that you forget your friends," he emailed Francis shortly after moving to Quantico. "I can be your best friend or worst enemy. . . . I am not an amateur [but] I feel you are treating me that way."

Beliveau's dark moods drove Francis up the wall, but he didn't want to lose his asset. "You are a sore Bitch and I have not forgotten you Bro ☺" Francis responded. "how do I send you a gift?"

Beliveau was a priceless source, but Francis had moles embedded elsewhere to apprise him of what NCIS was doing.

For years, Francis had been bribing Jose Sanchez, the deputy logistics officer on the Seventh Fleet staff, with prostitutes in exchange for classified ship schedules. As Sanchez earned a promotion to commander and took on new assignments for the Navy, he briefed Francis on the stalled NCIS investigation into Glenn Defense's kickbacks in Japan and Jim Maus's cost-cutting campaign with the Pacific Fleet.

In May 2012, Sanchez became the second-ranking officer at the Navy's Fleet Logistics Center in Yokosuka, which made him even more valuable. A pudgy-faced New Mexican, he idolized Francis and hungered for approval just as much as Beliveau. "Hey boss, how are things?" he emailed Francis before starting his new job. "Just wanted to check in to see how things are going and if I can be of any assistance."

Sanchez tipped off Francis to fresh complaints that U.S. consular officials in Japan had received about Glenn Defense. More importantly, he alerted Francis to yet another set of fraud allegations involving the company that the Yokosuka logistics office wanted to refer to NCIS. The warnings helped Francis defuse both threats before they could metastasize into full-fledged investigations.

Meanwhile, other criminal cases kept popping up. In late 2012, NCIS opened a joint investigation with South Korean authorities amid suspicions that Glenn Defense had illegally dumped wastewater after a port visit by the USS *George Washington*. But again, a loyal Francis mole ran interference.

Captain Heedong Choi, the Korean American officer who let Francis pay for his fairy-tale marriage proposal on the helipad in Singapore, offered to contact a South Korean admiral and make the dumping investigation go away. "I just wanted to make sure you are protected," Choi reassured Francis in an email. "Many times success breeds enemies. I'm always here for you, just let me know how I can help."

Francis's skill at dodging threats left him feeling cocky. He ignored Beliveau's warning to distance himself from Mike Misiewicz. He said he partied with the officer during a USS *Blue Ridge* port visit to Busan, South Korea, splurging for prostitutes, Korean barbecue, and soju. Two weeks later, he met Misiewicz again in Singapore at the Tiananmen KTV karaoke club, paying for Japanese food and more prostitutes.

Misiewicz was hooked on the sex and unrestrained nightlife, which blinded him to his growing vulnerability with NCIS. "Mike wanted to go out and meet girls wherever he went and it didn't matter what was going on, whether he had work to do or not," Ed Aruffo recalled. "He said, 'Hey, let's go to a club. Let's go to a bar.' His expectation was that . . . Leonard had these big credit cards and he could go out and do that sort of thing."

Misiewicz had reason to believe he was untouchable. When Francis tipped him off to his wife's disloyalty, he told his Big Bro not to worry. He had learned the Navy was planning to award him the Legion of Merit, a decoration for exceptionally meritorious conduct. The award was usually reserved for higher-ranking officers, but the Navy wanted to recognize Misiewicz for his performance after the earthquake and tsunami in Japan.

When Marcy heard about the award, in November 2012, she felt sick. After reporting Mike to NCIS, she had packed up her belongings in Japan and moved back to Illinois with their four kids, cooperating all the while with investigators.

Now she worried the real reason the Navy had honored her bribe-taking husband was to inoculate him from legal trouble. Mike reinforced her fear in December when he visited Illinois to see the children. She said he was livid and accused her of "trying to bite the hand that feeds you." She assumed someone in the Navy had tipped him off about her conversations with NCIS. Feeling burned, she abruptly stopped talking to investigators.

When word got back to Francis that a critical witness had gotten cold feet, he felt even more invincible.

Chapter Nineteen

The Birthday Ball

October 2012

SINGAPORE

The stench of entitlement from the U.S. Navy officer corps permeated the Shangri-La Hotel's grand ballroom in the heart of Singapore.
About six hundred guests downed flutes of champagne and devoured
canapés at a resort built to pamper heads of state and international
VIPs. On the dimly lit parquet floor, Navy officers glowed in their
dress-white dinner jackets and gold cummerbunds, outshining the
diplomats, business executives, and other civilians wearing standard-
issue black ties and evening gowns.

For Americans based in Southeast Asia, it was the social event
of the year: the United States Navy Ball, held in honor of the 237th
birthday of the two-vessel navy founded by the Continental Congress
in 1775. Supporters of the Navy hosted balls around the world annually to commemorate the occasion. But the 2012 celebration in Singapore stood out for its splendor and shady accounting. To stage the
event, organizers raised between $100,000 and $125,000, much of it
thinly disguised kickbacks from defense contractors.

Most Navy officers present had heard rumors that the platinum
sponsor of their birthday ball—Glenn Defense—was under criminal
investigation by NCIS. But few worried that their embrace of the firm

might taint them. The master of ceremonies sang Leonard Francis's praises from the stage while banners on the walls touted Glenn Defense as a stalwart friend of the Navy.

Glenn Defense had contributed more than any defense contractor to underwrite the event, purchasing $16,000 worth of tickets, supplying free transportation to the hotel, and loaning six museum-sized models of U.S. warships for guests to gawk at. Glenn Defense had also donated $5,000 for the after-party and a rich assortment of door prizes, including several Apple computers, $5,000 worth of Harley-Davidson gear, and the coup de grâce: a $30,000 pair of his-and-hers gold Rolex watches.

The birthday ball was a turnabout from Francis's typical bribery schemes. Usually, he was the one pursuing the officers, beckoning them to attend his posh dinners during port visits. But for the Navy Ball, the people in uniform were the aggressors—and they weren't shy with their demands.

Glenn Defense had sponsored the ball in Singapore, off and on, for more than a decade. Two years earlier, the firm offered free vacations to Phuket, Bali, and Penang as door prizes. But the ball organizers turned up their noses and pressed instead for pricier trips to faraway destinations. "Are locations such as Australia, New Zealand, Beijing, Seoul, Egypt, Paris, Rome, Tahiti, or Rio de Janeiro off the possibility list?" a Navy officer on the planning committee asked in an email. Unwilling to go that far, Glenn Defense countered with a $5,000 holiday to the Maldives, a $3,000 trip to Phuket, and four cruise tickets to Port Klang.

Shaking down defense contractors to pay for parties and prizes was patently unscrupulous. To senior Navy leaders, however, the annual birthday ball in Singapore was not just a luxury—it was a priority. They craved the perks and attention, and invited the Singapore military's top brass, foreign diplomats, and business titans to celebrate with them. "The Navy wanted bigger and brighter to impress all the guests," said the chief planner of the 2012 ball, Commander Troy

Amundson, who later went to prison for taking bribes. "The leadership had no problem with this. I was doing exactly what I was supposed to do, and they were happy about it."

After a decade of U.S. wars and surging defense budgets, an expectation of special treatment had taken root in the Navy. Many officers felt they were owed something extra for enduring long deployments at sea and missions to support the fighting in Iraq and Afghanistan. The American people fed such attitudes by placing uniformed personnel on a pedestal, thanking them for their service with discounts and freebies. The further one got from Washington, the easier it became to stretch the norms of acceptable conduct. In Asia, Navy officers pocketed favors they knew would be taboo at home.

The scene at the 2012 birthday ball in Singapore shocked and nauseated some of the guests. John Durkin, an American business executive in Asia who had served in the Navy as a supply officer during the 1980s, attended with his wife on a whim. Almost a quarter-century had lapsed since he'd had anything to do with the Navy, and he was taken aback by how standards had changed. "I was expecting a boring Navy birthday event and what I got was the Predators' Ball," he recalled.

Durkin was particularly appalled by the smiling presence of Admiral Samuel Locklear, the head of the U.S. Pacific Command and an old acquaintance of Francis's. Locklear had traveled all the way from his headquarters in Hawaii to give the ball's keynote speech and lauded the Glenn Defense owner in his remarks.

Durkin couldn't believe the admiral tolerated the giveaway of the Rolex watches and other door prizes. "There's a four-star admiral in charge of the entire theater of operations, one of the most senior officers in the whole U.S. military, sitting there and not doing anything. That's basically giving everyone a green light for graft." Disgusted, Durkin and his wife left early. He thought about reporting the event to the FBI or the Navy's inspector general but figured nothing would come of it.

The evening also troubled someone sitting with Locklear at the head table: David Adelman, the U.S. ambassador to Singapore. A bespectacled attorney and former Georgia state senator, Adelman had been appointed to his post two years earlier by President Barack Obama.

Since arriving in Singapore, the forty-eight-year-old Adelman had developed mixed opinions about Navy officers. He admired the Navy for the fundamental role it played in ensuring free trade and security in Southeast Asia, a focus of the Obama administration's foreign policy. At their core, U.S. relations with Singapore hinged on strong maritime and defense partnerships.

But the ball reinforced Adelman's suspicion that many Navy officers in Singapore had fallen in love with privilege, living in upscale housing and driving luxury cars. Given that the U.S. government was grappling with budget cutbacks and embassy staffers had gone without raises, it seemed in poor taste to throw a party that cost more than $100,000. "It was important to display some modesty," he said. "The whole night felt over the top."

Like the Durkins, Adelman and his wife left early because the ball made them uncomfortable. Before that night, he had been unfamiliar with Glenn Defense and its owner.

A year later, in one of his last official acts as ambassador, he would approve a secret operation to bring Leonard Francis to justice.

The birthday ball was a racket in more ways than one. To circumvent federal regulations that barred government employees from accepting gifts worth more than a token amount, the annual gala was officially hosted by the Singapore chapter of the Navy League of the United States, a nonprofit group of Navy alumni and supporters.

In reality, active-duty Navy personnel did almost all the planning and fundraising. Technically, they were supposed to volunteer their time, but most worked on the ball committee as part of their military duties. The lead organizers were judged on the ball's success in their official fitness reports, or performance evaluations.

The way the event was structured almost certainly violated federal ethics rules—not that anyone bothered to enforce them. Financial controls were nonexistent, making the ball ripe for graft. The price of ball tickets depended on whom you asked. Many senior officers got them for free. Envelopes of cash from ticket sales were left lying around Navy office cubicles. After the 2012 gala, some officers reported as much as $30,000 in revenue had gone unaccounted for.

Navy personnel hit up American companies and defense contractors in Singapore to subsidize the birthday ball. Most donated modest sums compared with Glenn Defense, which occupied a category of its own.

Francis knew his ability to make or break the party gave him leverage, and he didn't hesitate to squeeze. Though he had sponsored the Singapore event since the early 2000s, he "gave the Navy Ball the middle finger" one year and refused to participate because Glenn Defense was mired in "a pissing contest" with the Navy over a contract, according to a Navy official.

In other years he strung along anxious ball organizers for months before rescuing them with a plump donation at the last minute, a tactic he used to get his hooks into Amundson, the 2012 ball chairman.

Amundson was what Francis called a "turncoat"—a sailor who disdained Glenn Defense at first but changed his mind once he got a taste of the benefits. A tall Minnesotan, Amundson joined the Navy as a flight officer and flew combat missions in Iraq. The forty-five-year-old had been posted in Singapore since 2008 to coordinate military exercises and earned high praise for his work, including the Legion of Merit.

He traveled frequently in Southeast Asia as part of his duties but refused Glenn Defense's husbanding services and ignored invitations to Francis's parties. But like many other officers, he eventually caved in. In the summer of 2012, his boss in Singapore ordered him to take charge of the upcoming birthday ball, a chore that he detested. Amundson was nearing the end of his military career and thought the ball planning was beneath him. His marriage had also hit the skids, and he'd become moody and bitter.

"In my mind, I was done, done with the Navy, just waiting for retirement," Amundson recalled.

Francis recognized a patsy when he saw one. While making plans for the banquet, he invited Amundson and six other Navy officers for a night out at the Tiananmen KTV karaoke bar. His sources had told him that Amundson had a thing for Asian women of different ethnicities, so he hired several Vietnamese and Mongolian prostitutes. Amundson was delighted. He became an ardent mole for Glenn Defense, leaking proprietary information about military exercises.

Francis exploited his sponsorship of the 2012 ball to the fullest. He knew gossip had spread about the NCIS investigations and wanted to reassure all the guests that Glenn Defense had friends in high places. He was thrilled when Locklear gave him a shoutout in his keynote address and even happier when the admiral and his wife sidled up to him on the dance floor in full view of the crowd.

He also used the evening to target another officer: Commander Jerry King, a supply officer who ran the Navy's Fleet Logistics Center in Singapore.

A graduate of Texas A&M with two decades of Navy experience, King had arrived in Singapore a year earlier and antagonized Glenn Defense by challenging invoices and questioning contracts. Francis bad-mouthed him to others as "a cock" and wanted to neutralize him as a threat.

At first, Francis tried to intimidate the Navy officer by placing him under obvious surveillance. King noticed that people carrying cameras often followed him around Singapore, especially when he had meetings away from the base with other defense contractors. On one occasion a short, middle-aged Chinese woman with a giant telephoto lens tracked King for an entire evening at the Boat Quay, a popular nightlife district, while he was having dinner with two Navy officials. The incident rattled King, and he assumed Francis was behind it.

Other Navy officials he worked with in Singapore had also reported being under surveillance, including one who received an anonymous text message warning that her life was in danger.

King had remained a thorn in Glenn Defense's side, however, so at the birthday ball Francis shifted tactics to see whether he could compromise him.

The high point of the annual event was the "Lucky Draw" to award the dazzling array of door prizes. This year, all eyes were on the pair of gold Rolex watches—the most ostentatious items ever given away. The winner was supposed to be chosen at random from a bowl filled with duplicate ticket stubs for all active-duty military personnel who were present.

The several hundred guests didn't know that Francis had rigged the raffle by arranging for the ticket to be drawn beforehand in secret. His handpicked winner: Commander Jerry King.

A few minutes before the Lucky Draw was officially set to unfold on stage, Amundson, the ball committee chairman, whispered to King that he had already won. King was shocked—and sensed a trap. Given his direct role in the Navy's business dealings with Glenn Defense, he knew people would assume the Rolexes were a quid pro quo. At minimum, he'd be reassigned, or maybe end up in jail.

In a panic, King told Amundson there was no way he could accept and to hurry up and draw another ticket. Moments later, the $30,000 watch set was awarded to an exuberant enlisted sailor, clueless that he was really the runner-up.

But the attempted bribe frazzled King's nerves. He had been hiding his own secret. For months, he had been meeting confidentially with an NCIS agent and helping with the investigation into Glenn Defense's billing scams in Thailand. He wondered whether Francis had sniffed him out and worried the defense contractor would try to silence him one way or another.

Chapter Twenty

Loose Lips Sink Ships

November 2012

TOKYO, JAPAN

Commander Mike Misiewicz walked into the Ritz-Carlton Hotel in midtown Tokyo around nine o'clock on a Thursday night, carrying a thick brown envelope stuffed with forty pages of military secrets. He was allegedly accompanied by his boss, Captain David Haas, the director of operations on the Seventh Fleet staff and a longtime Glenn Defense ally. They were looking forward to an evening of business and pleasure after spending a long hour in Tokyo's notorious traffic, chauffeured by a driver Leonard Francis had dispatched to pick them up from the U.S. Navy base in Yokosuka.

Francis greeted his friends in the hotel lobby and escorted them to his suite on the fifty-third floor of the Midtown Tower, the second-tallest in the city. As usual, the Boss took care of business first. He accepted the envelope from Misiewicz and sat alone at a U-shaped desk, studying the classified documents one by one while the Navy officers relaxed on a pair of tan sofas in an adjoining living room. The papers were stamped SECRET and listed the Navy's projected port visits in Asia for the next fourteen months—the kind of intelligence that Francis cherished.

But the documents also included material Francis hadn't seen before: highly sensitive details of the Navy's ballistic missile defense operations in the Pacific. Unlike ship schedules, which the Navy declassified a few weeks before a port visit, the missile defense information was an enduring secret. In the wrong hands, it could present a grave threat to the safety and operations of U.S. and allied forces.

After Francis finished examining his latest trove of classified information, he joined the Navy officers in the living room. He had depended on Misiewicz more than any other mole for leaked ship schedules over the past eighteen months. But the officer was preparing to leave the Seventh Fleet for a new assignment in Colorado. Francis wanted advice on whom he could recruit as a replacement. Misiewicz and Haas suggested a few candidates who might be willing to cross the line and secretly work for Glenn Defense.

With their business out of the way, Francis tucked the documents into his man purse and escorted the Seventh Fleet officers to Seventh Heaven, a strip joint in Tokyo's Roppongi district that catered to foreigners. By the time the sun came up, the Boss had blown nearly $7,000 on food and entertainment. The bleary-eyed officers caught a ride from Francis's driver back to the Navy base in Yokosuka.

While the tryst in Tokyo fit a years-long pattern of criminal behavior by Seventh Fleet officers, the episode stood out for its sheer recklessness. Francis and his moles knew NCIS was closing in, yet they continued to shamelessly break the law.

Six days earlier, John Beliveau Jr. had tipped Francis off to a new threat. NCIS had recruited another confidential informant—this one in Japan—who had worn a wire and recorded Francis during a meeting with a Navy logistics official. Meanwhile, NCIS's investigation into Glenn Defense's billing scam in Thailand was building momentum, and the agency had opened fresh investigations into the company's operations in Hong Kong and South Korea. NCIS was turning up the heat, but Francis remained as cocksure as ever, convinced he could outsmart anyone.

Misiewicz and Haas also acted with surprising nonchalance.

It was one thing to cheat on their wives and take bribes from a defense contractor. But for Misiewicz to leak classified information to a foreigner—especially missile defense secrets that China, Russia, or North Korea would pay dearly for—bordered on treason. He was betraying his oath to defend his country and putting shipmates at risk. (Haas acknowledged accepting prostitutes, meals, and hotel rooms from Francis but said he didn't know that Misiewicz was passing classified material to Glenn Defense.)

Since World War II, the Navy had drummed the mantra "Loose lips sink ships" into millions of sailors and the public to reinforce the urgency of safeguarding secrets. Everyone in the Navy understood that mishandling classified information, even inadvertently, could land them behind bars. In 2012, a machinist's mate assigned to the USS *Alexandria*, a nuclear-powered attack submarine, was caught storing unauthorized photos of his workspace on his personal phone. He was sentenced to a year in prison. In the late 1980s, a Marine sergeant received ten months in jail after he accidentally left classified documents in a gym bag while cleaning out his office.

The punishment was far more severe for those who deliberately leaked military secrets to foreigners. In 2009, a federal judge imposed a ten-year prison sentence on an enlisted sailor from the destroyer USS *Benfold* for giving ship schedules to Islamist extremists in Britain.

Even so, the Seventh Fleet moles thought they could get away with their crimes and left plenty of fingerprints. Misiewicz once blundered by cc'ing Francis on an official email to a long string of Navy personnel, including intelligence officials, a misstep that could have drawn attention to their relationship.

"Brother you must have copied me by mistake on your internal emails," Francis chided the officer in a message on a separate channel after discovering the screwup. "I don't think they noticed. Stay calm we are ok."

"Oh crap. I hate the auto feature on outlook," Misiewicz replied.

"Now I am worried, there is some spook kind of guys on this email. I can't believe I did that."

Misiewicz tempted fate in other ways. Most of the time, he used an email account featuring Francis's initials—lgflittlebro@gmail.com—to communicate. He amateurishly copied and pasted ship schedules into the body of emails and sent them unencrypted to leonard.glenn.francis@gmail.com. Other times, at night, he slipped printouts under the door of the Glenn Defense office building next to the U.S. Navy base in Yokosuka.

He knew what he was doing was wrong, but Misiewicz naively trusted Francis, calling him "very pro-U.S. and patriotic" and assuming he would never endanger U.S. national security. Another reason for his insouciance was that he felt protected by his forty-four-year-old boss, Captain Haas, the Seventh Fleet's director of operations.

A fellow Naval Academy graduate, Haas had earned the trust of prominent admirals. As a youth in Colorado, he grew close to a neighbor, retired Admiral Arleigh Burke, a former chief of naval operations and one of the most admired leaders in the Navy's history. (Haas called him "Uncle Arleigh.") As an officer, Haas's mentors included Admiral Robert Willard, the retired head of the U.S. Pacific Command, and Vice Admiral Scott Swift, the Seventh Fleet commander.

According to Francis, he and Haas had been chums for almost a decade. The Glenn Defense owner described Haas—a musclebound fitness freak who competed in triathlons—as "wild" and a "beast" and gloated that they were "in bed" together.

From the start, Francis had pegged Haas as a "bright star" with the potential to help Glenn Defense in the future. Haas became an aide to the vice chief of naval operations at the Pentagon and later the commanding officer of the USS *Thach*, a San Diego–based frigate. Francis nurtured their relationship, treating the married officer to dinners and entertainment when he visited ports in Asia.

The investment paid off when Haas joined the Seventh Fleet staff on the USS *Blue Ridge* in 2011. As head of operations, he played an important role in determining ship schedules. Haas never gave Francis classified information himself, but he used his clout to steer ships to Glenn Defense's Pearl Ports, according to Francis and multiple Navy officers. (Haas and Misiewicz denied that they had the authority to singlehandedly schedule port visits, noting that the fleet commander had to approve such decisions.)

In September 2012, for instance, with Francis pulling the strings, Haas and Misiewicz lobbied to change the itinerary of the aircraft carrier USS *John C. Stennis*, pushing for the ship to visit Kota Kinabalu, Malaysia, with only two weeks' notice. The port had never hosted a carrier, and Glenn Defense was the only company that could provide husbanding services there at the last minute, giving it carte blanche to charge sky-high rates. Navy logistics personnel and other officers pushed back against the schedule change and predicted Glenn Defense would gouge the Navy. But Haas and Misiewicz squashed their protests, with one officer saying he was ordered to "shut the fuck up and do what you're told." Sure enough, Glenn Defense billed the Navy $2.7 million for the four-day port call, about five times what it would have earned for a visit scheduled in advance to other ports in the region.

Afterward, Francis crowed about his triumph over the "pork chops," his derisive term for the Navy logistics personnel who arranged for ships' food and supplies. "We ambushed them ha ha," he wrote in an email to an underling. "I love it when my plan falls in place like a Movie," he added, calling it a Glenn Defense "Box Office Classic."

The pork chops took notice of Haas's and Misiewicz's suspicious behavior. The Seventh Fleet's assistant chief of staff for logistics observed that Haas "consistently, routinely and often" protected Glenn Defense. Commander Jerry King, the supply officer who'd refused the gold Rolex watches at the Navy birthday ball and was secretly helping NCIS, figured Misiewicz was either "completely dirty or living on a different planet."

Yet King and other straight arrows felt powerless and frustrated by senior Navy leaders' unwillingness to crack down. When a JAG officer heard Haas brag about having social plans with Francis during a USS *Blue Ridge* port visit in Australia, the lawyer reported the encounter to NCIS, but nothing seemed to come of it. Critics of Glenn Defense couldn't understand why NCIS appeared to be sitting on its hands. In fact, the investigations were heating up but agents wanted to keep their progress a secret.

Thinking that they were untouchable, Haas and Misiewicz saw little need to restrain themselves. When the *Blue Ridge* was docked at its homeport in Yokosuka, they often traveled to Tokyo to party with Francis, giving his credit cards a workout at the Ritz-Carlton, Nobu, Seventh Heaven, and karaoke clubs in the red-light district. When the *Blue Ridge* was at sea, Francis met them in Singapore, Jakarta, and other cities. All told, over a two-year period, Francis spent $90,000 on prostitutes, meals, hotel rooms, and other favors for Haas and about $95,000 on Misiewicz.

After Misiewicz departed the Seventh Fleet staff in December 2012, Glenn Defense needed only a few weeks to find another mole.

Dan Layug, a petty officer first class assigned to the Navy's Fleet Logistics Center in Japan, was a natural choice. He was already on Francis's payroll as an all-purpose source of inside information. Once a month, he visited the Glenn Defense office in Yokosuka to pick up an envelope with $1,000 in cash. Sometimes Glenn Defense sweetened the pot and gave him free hotel rooms, video game consoles, a digital camera, or other electronics.

In January 2013, Glenn Defense broadened Layug's duties and asked him to leak the Seventh Fleet ship schedules on a regular basis. The twenty-five-year-old sailor embraced the assignment and felt little pressure to cover his tracks. Layug used his badge to access a secure room on the USS *Blue Ridge*, logged onto a classified computer terminal, and printed out the schedules on pink paper from a classified printer. Then he took the documents home.

There, Layug scanned the documents and transmitted them to Glenn Defense, unencrypted, from his personal email account. Other times, he drove to the Glenn Defense office parking lot at night, rolled down the window of his dark sedan, and handed over a stack of pink paper in exchange for his $1,000 monthly allowance. Nobody from the Navy seemed to notice.

By 2013, Francis had become a world-class recruiter of spies. Over a seven-year stretch, he had persuaded ten members of the U.S. Navy to divulge state secrets—a number without parallel in modern history. In addition, he had enticed a dozen other individuals, including John Beliveau Jr., Paul Simpkins, and Commander Troy Amundson, to leak law enforcement files or proprietary Navy information.*

Time and again, Francis penetrated the Navy's counterintelligence defenses with astonishing ease. One particularly shocking example happened in May 2011 when three senior officers from the USS *Carl Vinson* carrier strike group met Francis on the rooftop lounge of the Ritz-Carlton Hotel in Hong Kong. Over cocktails, the officers blabbed about how their crew, several days earlier, had dumped the body of al-Qaeda leader Osama bin Laden into the Indian Ocean— even though the Pentagon had ordered personnel on the carrier to keep quiet about the operation.

But for someone so good at prying loose classified information, Francis could be lax about safeguarding the material.

He left printouts of ship schedules scattered around his office and home in Singapore, along with hard copies of emails from moles. He stuffed thousands of pages of documents into cardboard boxes and stored them in an unguarded warehouse in Malaysia. He found it hard

---

* An eleventh servicemember, Lieutenant Commander Alexander Gillett, the Royal Australian Navy officer assigned to the U.S. Seventh Fleet staff, also leaked classified ship schedules to Francis.

enough to keep track of all his cell phones, laptops, thumb drives, and email accounts, much less remember the passwords. His main concessions to security were to install a secret drawer in his office desk and surveillance cameras to spy on Glenn Defense employees.

Beliveau, who knew firsthand how easy it was for federal agents to monitor electronic communications, hounded Francis to delete old emails and message caches. Francis agreed to use encrypted messaging apps such as Viber, Skype, and WhatsApp more often but rarely erased his digital footprints.

While there is no evidence that Francis sold or bartered U.S. military secrets to foreign intelligence services, they would have found him an easy target. He saved purloined ship and submarine schedules— as well as copious amounts of compromising material about senior U.S. Navy leaders—on Glenn Defense's lightly protected computer servers.

In fact, Francis knew the Chinese government had developed a keen interest in Glenn Defense's operations. The Chinese navy and a shipping company owned by the Chinese government had hired Glenn Defense on a few occasions as a husbanding subcontractor.

Meanwhile, the defense attaché at the Chinese embassy in Singapore had become golfing buddies with Glenn Defense's IT manager, a man of Chinese ethnicity. Had U.S. counterintelligence officials been aware of the relationship, it would have given them night terrors.

Part Five

2013

Chapter Twenty-one

Family Man

January 2013

SINGAPORE

An anguished text lit up Leonard Francis's smartphone late on a Sunday afternoon.

"Leonard, pls don't hide my children to me," the message read in broken English. "am still there mother hope u still remember that. u know that I love them so much."

Five minutes before midnight, another text arrived. "i just wanna see my children."

Francis ignored the messages and the sender: Morena De Jesus, the unmarried mother of two of his children, five-year-old Leandro and four-year-old Luisa. Francis had absconded with the kids three years earlier after tricking De Jesus, who was from Manila, into leaving the babies with him for a few days. Since then, the children had lived with their father in splendor in his mansion on Nassim Road in Singapore. He refused to let their mother anywhere near them.

Unlike the other women with whom Francis had fathered children, Morena wouldn't give up and took him to court, trying to win custody of Leandro and Luisa. Francis had enough legal problems as it was, with a posse of NCIS agents breathing down his neck and Chinese security officials snooping around his company. But sometimes

those felt like minor annoyances compared with the unending personal dramas that threatened to suffocate him.

His home life resembled a royal circus. He resided in Singapore
with all five of his kids but none of their mothers. Taking a page from
King Henry VIII's book, he treated women as expendable objects
once they stopped bearing him children. After Leandro and Luisa,
his youngest was three-year-old Don Enrique, whom he had likewise sired out of wedlock. Because Francis traveled so often and kept
strange hours, he delegated child-rearing duties to his own mother
and a workforce of nannies, cooks, and drivers. His college-age sons,
Leonardo and Marco, two princes with their own time-consuming
melodramas, also lived at home intermittently.

Francis modeled his sex life after that of an Ottoman sultan, using
his wealth to attract a harem of lovers willing to sleep with an obese
older man. He replaced his two ex-wives with two mistresses who rotated through Singapore for visits. He also paid an assortment of masseuses and prostitutes to tend to his needs in cities across Asia.

On the surface, Francis acted as if he reveled in all the excitement.
"I don't think I could live a boring life," he boasted. "I'm an alpha male,
high-maintenance kind of person, you know? So that's why I can't live
with one woman. One woman couldn't handle me."

In truth, his domestic juggling act had grown more precarious
by the month, and he could barely keep the plates spinning. Moreover, the stress was aggravating his health, a baleful omen for a hard-
drinking, big-bellied forty-eight-year-old man. His bad knees and bad
back were generating plenty of business for his chiropractor. On top of
it all, he needed a root canal.

Anxiety over possibly losing Leandro and Luisa gnawed at him. He
had always bullied his former partners into submission and couldn't
believe Morena was pushing back. He derided her as "just a little bar
girl," who like his other mistresses knew what she was getting into.
"They came to me with their eyes open. They weren't blind. They
all knew I had multiple wives and partners and I was a playboy," he

recalled. "It wasn't like, 'Oh, I'm innocent. I was this Virgin Mary from the convent.'"

Morena had mesmerized him when he first glimpsed her in 2004 at the Amara Hotel in Singapore. She was a twenty-three-year-old beauty with lustrous dark hair and a shy smile, working as a reception-ist as part of a hotel management training program. She came from a poor Catholic family and wasn't looking for a boyfriend. But Francis was undeniably charming, and he disarmed her with an invitation to church. "When I first met him, he is good," Morena recalled. "I think this guy is a good guy."

When her six-month training program ended, she returned home to the Philippines. But Francis continued to woo her. He told her that he was divorced from the mother of his two sons, Leonardo and Marco, which was true. But he neglected to mention that he had since remarried and had an ulterior motive.

Francis wanted more children and had become fed up with his sec-ond wife, Teresa, who had not become pregnant. He decided to try his luck with Morena instead. He sent money, rented her an apartment, and helped care for her extended family in Manila. Shortly after Glenn Defense won its husbanding contract to service U.S. Navy ships in the Philippines, Morena became pregnant. When Leandro was born in September 2007, Francis moved Morena and their baby to a condo-minium. Francis visited sporadically and promised they'd get married but kept putting it off.

In early 2008, Morena shared some welcome news with her jet-setting boyfriend: She was pregnant again. She gave birth to Luisa in October and for a time lived blissfully with her two wavy-haired babies. Shortly after Luisa's first birthday, however, a Glenn Defense staffer shocked Morena by revealing the real reason Francis was reluc-tant to marry: The Boss still had a wife. Not only that, he had another part-time girlfriend in Manila, the mother of little Don Enrique.

The news was too much for Morena. She told Francis she wanted to end their relationship and keep the kids. Francis exploded. He bombarded her with threatening messages, calling her a "bitch prosti-tute" and worse. "You had a good life for five years. Now go back and rot in the provinces with the worms," he texted.

When Morena stood her ground, Francis suppressed his rage and tried to win her back with money, gifts, and beguiling promises of connubial harmony. In December 2009, he induced Morena to bring their children to Singapore for an extended stay.

Morena gullibly believed that Francis wanted her to live in his mansion with the rest of his family. But when she arrived in Singapore, she found he had rented her a small apartment two miles away. He allowed Luisa and Leandro to stay with him but forbade Morena from visiting, claiming his two teenage sons would disapprove.

Five months later, Francis persuaded her to leave the kids with him for a few days so she could return to the Philippines to take care of a passport issue. When Morena arrived in Manila, however, she discov-ered that he had evicted her from the condo. Francis also locked her out of her bank account, canceled her return ticket to Singapore, and blocked her phone calls. He had duped her into abandoning Leandro and Luisa.

In her eyes, Francis had abducted her children, "as simple as like that," she recalled. "He left me with nothing."

Morena may have been naive, but she loved her children fiercely. She scraped together money to file a custody petition with a Manila court. A year later, the court ruled in her favor and ordered Francis to hand over Leandro and Luisa. When Francis failed to comply or to re-veal the children's whereabouts, the judge in Manila issued a warrant.

Francis appealed the custody order and argued it didn't apply to him because he was a Malaysian citizen. But the oustanding warrant meant he faced arrest if he set foot in the Philippines, crimping his ability to manage his business operations there.

Morena continued to press her case in the courts and pricked Francis's cold conscience with a stream of plaintive texts, begging to see her kids.

As a young man in Penang, Malaysia, Leonard Francis built a thriving business selling victuals and cigarettes to cargo ships passing through the Strait of Malacca. But he also relished living on the edge, a trait that got him expelled from school and sentenced to prison.

Francis, right, plays guitar next to a friend in Penang, Malaysia. Growing up, he developed a love for the flashy side of American culture. An Elvis fanatic, he sported bushy sideburns and oversized belt buckles. "He had a taste for going big," recalled Jeff O'Neal, a childhood friend.

Francis charms two officers from the USS *Acadia* whom he took out for dinner and drinks in Penang in 1992. Lieutenant Ruth Christopherson, right, wrote him a mushy thank-you note. "Dear Leonard: This has been the best liberty port of the deployment, and that is only due to you!" At left is Lieutenant Junior Grade Michelle Coyne Skubic, who later rose through the ranks to become a three-star admiral.

Captain Jim Maus first encountered Francis during a historic visit by the USS *Independence* to Port Klang, Malaysia, in 1997. Maus later worked briefly for Glenn Defense before turning into Francis's biggest nemesis.

Rear Admiral Samuel Locklear III, left, pretends to lift Fat Leonard off the floor at a Singapore dinner party in 2003 (Francis is actually standing on a chair). Locklear's antics would come back to haunt him when he was under consideration to become chairman of the Joint Chiefs of Staff.

A natural showman, Francis leads a troupe of bagpipers at a "Christmas Cheer" celebration for officers from the USS *Abraham Lincoln* in Hong Kong in 2004. Francis dazzled his American customers by throwing increasingly ostentatious dinner parties.

Francis, left, spent more than $60,000 on the Christmas Cheer party and hired Santa Niñas—or Santa Girls—to mingle with his guests. "What an event it was!" Rear Admiral Doug Crowder, right, the *Abraham Lincoln* strike group commander, effused in a thank-you note.

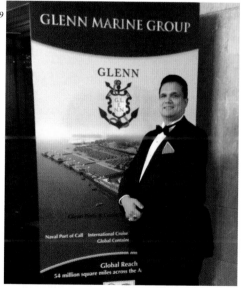

In 2005, Francis moved his corporate headquarters to this glass-walled building in Singapore. His top-floor executive suite resembled the captain's bridge on an aircraft carrier. Employees had to address him as "Boss."

Ever since he was a teenager, Francis dreamed of becoming a maritime tycoon like Aristotle Onassis, the Greek shipping magnate and playboy.

To win more business and sideline his competitors, Francis bribed key officials in the U.S. Navy's contracting command in Singapore, including Paul Simpkins, left.

Sharon Kaur, right, another contracting officer based in Singapore, received a holiday gift basket from Francis that contained champagne, chocolates—and a $34,000 cash bribe. Kaur knew how to exploit Francis's vanity, calling him "Darling" to his face and "Fatty" behind his back.

Francis's favorite place for entertaining was Jaan, a Michelin-starred restaurant in Singapore that customized its menus. Many senior Navy officers saw Francis as a rich fairy godfather who gave them a taste of an unattainable lifestyle.

Francis raises a toast at Jaan in 2006. Captain David Newland, left, the powerful Seventh Fleet chief of staff, let Francis wine and dine him after he was passed over for promotion. "I knew I wasn't going to be an admiral and I decided to take advantage of Leonard's hospitality," he recalled.

Newland, second from right, brandishes a Cuban cigar after dinner. He blew off ethics warnings to stay away from Francis's parties. Lieutenant Commander Ed Aruffo, right, helped arrange the festivities as the "wedding planner." Even the fleet chaplain—Captain William Devine, a Catholic priest, second from left—joined in the fun. At far left is Captain Jonathan Will, another Seventh Fleet staff officer.

Francis gives Rear Admiral Mike Miller a tour of the *Glenn Braveheart*, a decommissioned warship that Francis sometimes used as a party boat, in February 2006. Francis described Miller as "very entitled" with "two hands and two legs" out, expecting perks and gifts.

The USS *Ronald Reagan* prepares to visit Port Klang, Malaysia, in June 2006. Francis referred to Port Klang as one of his "Pearl Ports," because a lack of regulatory oversight enabled him to jack up prices and gouge the Navy.

The USS *Decatur*, a guided-missile destroyer, rests at anchor in Hong Kong harbor in June 2006. The U.S. Navy's Ship Support Office in Hong Kong often accused Glenn Defense of overbilling but was stymied by corrupt Navy contracting officers in Singapore.

A wine steward presents a bottle of bubbly during a 2007 cocktail party on the helipad of a Singapore skyscraper. Francis often indulged Captain David Newland, left, a champagne aficionado, with the world's priciest brands, including Cristal and Dom Pérignon.

Francis socializes with Seventh Fleet officers at a 2009 Big Top reception aboard the USS *Blue Ridge* in Tokyo. Lieutenant Commander Jose Sanchez, right, was one of Francis's most valuable moles. Captain James Dolan, second from right, was a fixture at Glenn Defense parties. At far left is Lieutenant Commander Alan Munoz, another Seventh Fleet staff officer.

Commander Michael Misiewicz hugs his aunt, Samrith Sokha, during an emotional return to his native Cambodia as skipper of the USS *Mustin* in December 2010. Misiewicz escaped the Cambodian genocide as a child when he was adopted by an American servicemember.

Commander Misiewicz lets women drink shots off his bare chest at a Manila bar during an evening of fun paid for by Glenn Defense in March 2011. Francis hooked Misiewicz with prostitutes and other bribes after the officer reported to the Seventh Fleet staff.

Francis's colorful personality and his obesity—his weight fluctuated between three hundred and five hundred pounds—belied a cunning mind that enabled him to infiltrate and compromise the Navy's senior leadership. "The KGB could not have done what he did," Captain Jim Maus said.

Francis hosts a brunch for Navy couples at the Ritz-Carlton Hotel in Singapore in 2010. He wooed officers' wives with gifts so he could get closer to their husbands. Carol Lausman, second from left, considered Francis almost like family. Her spouse, Captain David "Too Tall" Lausman, sits at far left.

24   The USS *Blue Ridge* docks pierside in Jakarta in April 2011. As the Seventh Fleet flagship, it served as the headquarters for all maritime military operations in the Western Pacific and Indian Ocean.

Francis shakes hands with Admiral Gary Roughead, the chief of naval operations, at his change-of-command and retirement ceremony at the U.S. Naval Academy in September 2011. Francis later tried to recruit Roughead to work for him at Glenn Defense.

Francis stands with Admiral Jonathan Greenert, the incoming chief of naval operations, at the Naval Academy in 2011. Francis loved hobnobbing with admirals at change-of-command ceremonies, but his weakness for the VIP events later lured him into a trap.

Commander David Morales poses with Francis at the 2011 Navy birthday ball in Singapore, the service's social event of the year. Officers aggressively lobbied Francis to help finance the annual gala, which could cost more than $100,000.

Admiral Samuel Locklear III, right, the head of U.S. Pacific Command, cuts the cake at the 2012 Navy birthday ball in Singapore with Seaman Joshua Glaser. Locklear gave the keynote address—and a shoutout to Francis, the lead sponsor.

Captain Jeffrey Breslau, left, takes command of a public-affairs detachment at a ceremony in Norfolk, Virginia, in August 2012. While on active duty, Breslau secretly worked as Francis's paid ghostwriter, advising him how to communicate with admirals.

Morena De Jesus, left, and Francis hold their two children, Luisa and Leandro, in Manila. According to De Jesus, Francis later abducted the children and defied a court order awarding her custody.

Francis with Maisa Dourado, one of his two Japanese-Brazilian girlfriends, next to a Rolls-Royce at his mansion in Singapore.

Francis with Leticia Murakami Acosta, his other Japanese-Brazilian girlfriend. "I'm an alpha male," he said. "That's why I can't live with one woman. One woman couldn't handle me."

Commander Steve Shedd speaks aboard the USS *Milius* as he takes command of the destroyer in San Diego in March 2011. Shedd leaked a stream of classified material to Francis and dined with him the night before his arrest.

Captain David Haas, a key mole on the Seventh Fleet staff, enjoys a drink with Francis in June 2013. Francis bragged that he and Haas—a longtime friend— were "in bed" together.

32

33

Vice Admiral Ted "Twig" Branch departs a Navy installation in Virginia in September 2013. The Navy cut off Branch's access to classified material after Francis's arrest but inexplicably allowed him to keep his job as director of naval intelligence for three more years.

Rear Admiral Bruce Loveless also had his security clearance suspended in 2013 after Francis told investigators that the admiral had given his business card—which identified himself as an intelligence officer—to a Mongolian prostitute. Loveless acknowledged socializing with the woman but denied having a sexual relationship with her.

John Beliveau Jr., an NCIS supervisory special agent, arrives with his attorney at the federal courthouse in San Diego in December 2013. Beliveau pleaded guilty to leaking sensitive law-enforcement files to Francis for prostitutes and bribes.

Francis adjusts a cosmetic face mask during one of his "spa days" at the U.S. Attorney's Office in San Diego. Federal officials granted him extraordinary privileges while he was a prisoner after he agreed to provide incriminating evidence against hundreds of Navy officers.

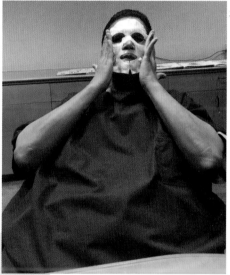

A paralegal dyes Francis's hair while he prepares for a debriefing by federal agents in the U.S. Attorney's Office. In reward for his cooperation, the criminal mastermind was permitted to hire staff who gave him manicures, pedicures, and foot rubs.

Rear Admiral Robert Gilbeau enters the federal courthouse in San Diego in 2016, accompanied by Bella, his fluffy white therapy dog. Gilbeau was treated for a mental breakdown in Afghanistan after Francis's arrest. He became the first active-duty admiral to be convicted of a federal crime.

Federal authorities offered a $40,000 reward for information on Francis's whereabouts after he escaped from home detention in September 2022 and fled the country.

WANTED
By U.S. MARSHALS

Name: FRANCIS,LEONARD GLENN

Sex.. MALE

Race.. WHITE OR WHITE HISPANIC

Height.. 6'02"

Weight.. 350 pounds

Eyes.. Black

Hair.. Black

After sixteen days on the lam, Francis was captured at the international airport in Caracas by Venezuelan authorities acting on an Interpol alert. He remained in Venezuela until December 2023, when he was returned to the United States in a prisoner swap.

"Tell to my children that am always love them. Hugs n kisses for Leandro n Luisa," she wrote in March 2013. "Leonard we are talking about our children here not u n me. . . . u have no rights to hide them u r not God. I just want to see them because they are my children not only yours."

Most of the messages went unanswered, but occasionally one hit a nerve. When Morena informed Francis that she was planning to show up unannounced on his Singapore doorstep for a family visit, he contacted his family-law attorney in a panic.

"Morena claims to be in Spore and wants to see the children! Pls call," he texted.

He regained his composure after a brief legal consultation and dismissed Morena's requests to see the kids. "Don't keep bothering us," he wrote in May 2013. "You are not sincere and play games!"

Despite Morena's wishes and the court order, he would never surrender control of the children.

Francis led a hypocritical personal life. He had an enormous appetite for sin, yet he considered himself a "deep, deep practicing Catholic" because he carried a rosary, attended Mass, hung crucifixes in his home, and donated to the Little Sisters of the Poor. He quoted Psalm 121 in Glenn Defense's corporate brochures and in the signature block of his emails: "The LORD will guard your coming and going, both now and forever."

Nonetheless, he was selective about observing the Ten Commandments and repeatedly shattered one in particular: Thou shalt not commit adultery. He took perverse pride in his philandering but erupted in a fury if he suspected any of his wives or girlfriends of developing a wandering eye.

In his late forties, he formed unconventional "temporary wife" relationships with Leticia Murakami Acosta and another young woman, Maisa Dourado. Both were Brazilian-Japanese and their mixed ethnicity enchanted him. He subsidized their living expenses in Brazil and Japan and flew them to Singapore for alternate visits.

There were downsides to carrying on with two girlfriends. Francis showered them both with jewelry, designer clothes, and electronics but sometimes lost track of which gifts he'd given to whom. Inevitably, the two women learned about each other, which led to jealous recriminations.

The personal distractions caused problems for Francis at work. His Glenn Defense minions resented having to shoulder extra work while he jetted off to Brazil to party with his girlfriends during Carnival. Edmond Aruffo, the retired Navy officer who ran Glenn Defense operations in Japan, griped to a colleague in an email that the Boss had lost focus. "He was just here and spent all his time drinking. I saw him for twenty minutes out of his four days here."

Aruffo had once idolized Francis but grew tired of his act after three years of working for Glenn Defense. He quit in a huff in 2012 and returned to the United States without another job lined up. "Leonard never has clean, cordial breakaways. He did all he could to piss me off before I left," Aruffo complained in a message to a friend.

Discontent at Glenn Defense worsened in 2012 when Francis, claiming the firm was losing money, told his staff he needed to slash payroll. Some workers didn't get paid for two or three months. A few desperadoes pirated fuel from the company to resell on the black market. When Francis found out, he fired the ship captains for negligence, further infuriating his employees.

They became even angrier when Francis continued to squander money on luxuries. During the holidays, he again lit up his mansion with $100,000 worth of Christmas decorations. He also expanded his fleet of limousines, shelling out $500,000 for a new Rolls-Royce Phantom. When one longtime aide suggested that maybe it was time to start driving a Toyota, Francis said the Rolls was critical for maintaining appearances.

"Glad he continues to have fun," Howard Patty Sr., Glenn Defense's vice president for contracts, groused to Aruffo, warning that a "perfect storm is developing over the horizon, and it will be devastating." In an email, he likened the situation to a *Twilight Zone* episode about a guy who finds a lamp with a genie and makes a wish to become a powerful ruler.

"His wish was granted," Patty added, "and he found himself as Adolf Hitler in a Nazi bunker under attack at the end of the war."

Chapter Twenty-two

Baiting a Trap

April 2013

SEAL BEACH, CALIFORNIA

The FedEx package arrived on a Thursday at the NCIS Resident Agency for Los Angeles, an ugly one-story tan building on a small U.S. Navy base in Seal Beach, overlooking Anaheim Bay. The envelope contained a compact disc from Google headquarters in Mountain View, California. A two-page letter explained that the CD was the company's response to a federal search warrant seeking records associated with an anonymous email account, lgflittlebro@gmail.com.

The CD contained an email cache that portended trouble for Commander Mike Misiewicz. He had set up the account sixteen months earlier to transmit classified ship schedules to his Big Bro, Leonard Glenn Francis, and had lazily neglected to delete the files. NCIS already suspected Misiewicz of pocketing bribes from Francis. But the emails showed he also had been leaking military secrets to a foreigner—a far more serious offense—and divulged other damning details of their corrupt relationship.

The emails on the CD represented a breakthrough for NCIS and fundamentally changed its investigations into Glenn Defense. Agents had discovered the lgflittlebro@gmail.com address while combing through Misiewicz's Navy email account and information provided by his wife, Marcy. NCIS had sent the search warrant to Google on March 8, and the company provided the CD four weeks later. Thanks to the emails, NCIS now had hard evidence not just of a billing racket run by Glenn Defense, but of a quid pro quo bribery scheme, in which Francis had provided a Seventh Fleet officer with prostitutes and free travel in exchange for classified information and other favors.

Coincidentally, agents had recently presented preliminary findings from their investigations of Glenn Defense in Thailand and Japan to federal prosecutors with the U.S. Attorney's Office for the Southern District of California. The prosecutors thought those cases looked promising. Though more work needed to be done before the cases could be presented to a grand jury, investigators had progressed enough to start thinking about how they might capture Francis and bring him to justice.

They knew they had to tread lightly. Francis had moles everywhere.

Seven months earlier, Captain Marty Fields had just arrived in Japan to take a new assignment as the commanding officer of the Navy's Fleet Logistics Center in Yokosuka when he received a confidential visit from NCIS. Special Agent Erika Mariner, the investigator who had interviewed Misiewicz's wife and children, wanted to brief him about the criminal cases involving Glenn Defense in Japan. First, though, she made Fields sign a nondisclosure agreement. While NCIS had vetted his background and thought he could be trusted, Mariner warned him that his new deputy in Yokosuka, Commander Jose Sanchez, was suspected of being a Glenn Defense informant.

NCIS needed Fields's permission to secretly access the Yokosuka office's contracting records, hard drives, cell phones, fax machines, and other communications systems on a regular basis. Investigators didn't want to risk tipping off Sanchez or anyone else, so Fields often had to let NCIS technicians into the office at midnight to snoop around and clone his staff's electronic devices.

The secrecy weighed heavily on Fields. He was prohibited from telling his chain of command about the investigations. NCIS also cautioned him to act normally around Sanchez. Meanwhile, Fields caught flak from Pacific Fleet headquarters in Hawaii for not being more supportive of Jim Maus's cost-cutting efforts. Fields wanted to help, but NCIS had ordered him not to change the way his office did business. The agents didn't want Glenn Defense to think anything was amiss. "I'm feeling pressure from everybody," Fields recalled. "I'm getting my ass kicked."

At that point, NCIS had briefed only two Navy officers about its criminal investigations into Glenn Defense: Fields and Commander Jerry King, the officer in Singapore whom Francis had tried to corrupt with the Rolex watches at the Navy birthday ball. By February 2013, however, NCIS agents had decided it was necessary to bring a few more Navy logistics officials into the fold. If Francis were to be arrested, Glenn Defense would almost certainly cease operations within a matter of days, leaving Navy ships high and dry in ports throughout Asia. Investigators told Fields, King, and the other logistics officials to draw up secret plans to replace Glenn Defense with new husbanding contractors at a moment's notice.

NCIS and the logistics team scheduled a strategy session in March to discuss the contingency plans. Because of fears that Francis had bugged Navy offices in Yokosuka and Singapore, however, they met thousands of miles away, at a well-guarded submarine base in Bremerton, Washington.

As agents scurried to gather more evidence against Francis, they confronted another dilemma: Where to arrest him? The United States had extradition treaties with several Asian countries, including Singapore, Malaysia, and Japan. But the legal process moved slowly, and some NCIS officials worried that their extradition request would be denied or that Francis would bribe local authorities to block his transfer. The safest option would be to arrest him in the United States, but agents feared he would be reluctant to visit because he knew Glenn Defense was under investigation.

Fields suggested stringing a trail of bait. First, he would invite Francis to Japan for a friendly chat about improving the Navy's day-to-day relationship with Glenn Defense. Then he would invite Francis to a follow-up meeting with some admirals in the United States that summer. Fields knew the Glenn Defense owner loved to hobnob with the brass at change-of-command ceremonies and figured he would find the temptation irresistible.

The first stage of the plan clicked when Francis accepted Fields's invitation to Japan. By happenstance, the meeting was scheduled for April 11—one week after the Google package arrived at the regional NCIS office in Los Angeles.

The pieces were falling into place. In the days leading up to the meeting, agents rushed to analyze Misiewicz's emails to see what else they could glean from his communications with Francis.

Francis flew to Japan on April 8, three days early. Relaxed and confident, he brought his youngest kids and a nanny so they could visit Tokyo Disneyland while he conducted business. He knew NCIS had him under scrutiny, but he felt safe thanks to his moles.

His most loyal informant was Sanchez, who served as the executive officer—or second-in-command—at the Fleet Logistics Center in Yokosuka. Sanchez eavesdropped on Fields's conversations and texted updates to the Boss about the comings and goings in the office. He had warned Francis that Fields was in contact with NCIS and tipped him off about the secret meeting in Bremerton, though he was unable to learn details about what had been discussed.

Francis had also been pressing John Beliveau Jr., the turncoat NCIS agent, for more updates. On April 9, Beliveau logged into the K-NET case management database from his office in Quantico, Virginia.

He typed in the search term "glenn marine" and downloaded seventy-six reports, saving them on a CD that he took home.

As Beliveau skimmed the reports in his apartment, he noticed that NCIS had a search warrant pending for one of Francis's email accounts, leonard.glenn.francis@gmail.com. Agents hadn't received anything from Google yet, but Beliveau's eyes bugged out. He immediately texted Francis.

"They got a warrant for ur gmail account. I'm worried I might be in there," he wrote. "did u delete all my emails like we talked about?"

Francis reassured him that he had cleaned out the account months earlier. He was more interested in reading what else was in the NCIS reports. He asked Beliveau to copy them to a draft folder in a different account they shared, samcoyote500@gmail.com. Beliveau promised he would that night.

The next day, Francis studied the NCIS reports on his laptop while sitting in his hotel suite near Tokyo Disneyland. He read updates on the investigations of his billing scams in Japan and South Korea. But what seized his attention was the revelation that NCIS had obtained Misiewicz's emails from the lgflittlebro@gmail.com account, as well as two other Gmail addresses that the Navy officer used.

Fuming, Francis contacted Beliveau on Skype to commiserate and assess their exposure.

"My boy Mike Miez just hung himself—dick," he griped.

"Yes he did . . . his own stupid fault . . . they will hammer him," Beliveau replied. "Dumbo didnt delete anything for several years. That guys a piece of work . . . thats why I delete everything."

In a strange way, Beliveau felt invigorated by the bad news. He had no social life in Virginia and spent his free time drinking alone, watching HBO and old episodes of *Star Trek*. He felt gratified that Francis needed him.

Hours later, after Beliveau had fully absorbed the implications, he messaged Francis again on Skype with a more acute assessment. He cautioned that Misiewicz was a liability and would probably be indicted. He predicted NCIS would try to flip Misiewicz into becoming a cooperating witness and urged Francis to protect himself with "Sopranos" tactics—a reference to the fictional New Jersey mafia family—in case Misiewicz tried to secretly record their conversations.

"Don't trust him and never email or text him and never speak on phone with him," Beliveau wrote. "Only in person and with noise and protect yourself against bugs. He is their leverage against you. Unless you have a life or death hold on him or will pay his retirement, you are vulnerable."

Francis took the warnings seriously, but he still thought he could outsmart federal agents. He had eluded NCIS for many years and saw no reason why he couldn't wriggle out of this fix, too. At worst, he figured the Navy might sue Glenn Defense and debar it as a federal contractor. He never dreamed the Americans might try to arrest him.

He was unimpressed by two of the NCIS special agents now leading the investigation: Erika Mariner, the agent in Japan, and Amanda Blair, a Singapore-based agent who specialized in economic crimes. Francis disrespected women in general and doubted these female agents could bring him down. In his online chats with Beliveau, he mocked Mariner as "the Japan bitch" and "the genius agent" because she had been after him for so long and had failed to make anything stick.

While his kids frolicked at Disneyland, Francis went ahead with his appointment at the Navy base in Yokosuka. Captain Fields opened the meeting by emphasizing that the Navy needed to reduce its soaring port visit expenses. But he surprised Francis by saying he wanted to find a "win-win" approach that could generate more business for Glenn Defense. Before parting, Fields asked whether they could continue the dialogue sometime with his bosses at the Navy's global logistics command in San Diego. Unaware that it was a ploy to lure him to the United States, Francis eagerly said yes.

Francis flew back to Singapore and contacted Beliveau on Skype a few days later. He had finally digested the large batch of NCIS reports and was horrified by the summary descriptions of Misiewicz's emails. He told Beliveau he was "embarrassed" he had been loose-lipped in his communications with Misiewicz and couldn't believe the "stupid cock" had failed to safeguard his Gmail account. He knew it would provide NCIS with a pile of fresh leads.

"Yeah, I know . . . emails kill," Beliveau responded. "Your buddy isn't a smooth operator." He advised Francis to adopt a paranoid mind-set. "Just don't do any favors for any Navy fucker until this blows over," he said. "Don't even trust your admiral buddies."

For the umpteenth time, Beliveau reminded Francis to double-check his own Gmail accounts to ensure there was nothing still there—including in the draft folders—that could land them in trouble. "If they find that you sent me [anything], im screwed."

Francis told him they had nothing to worry about.

"I cleaned it out 6 months back," he said.

"Nice," Beliveau replied.

That same day, across the Pacific Ocean, another package arrived at the NCIS regional office in Seal Beach. It contained a letter and CD from Google, this time responding to a search warrant for the email account leonard.glenn.francis@gmail.com.

The CD held a ton of incriminating emails. Francis had tried to delete them but waited too long. NCIS had asked Google to preserve the email account several weeks earlier, so while Francis thought he had erased everything, the company had a backup copy. It was a fateful misstep. If he had acted a few days sooner, he would have been in the clear.

NCIS analysts sifted through the emails and gaped. A cursory review showed that Francis had suspicious relationships with more than thirty Navy officers, including many on the Seventh Fleet staff. Their investigation, which had started as a tedious overbilling inquiry three years earlier, was now a major public corruption case.

The bribery and fraud were only part of it. Francis's emails revealed that other officers besides Misiewicz had been leaking him classified ship schedules, which meant NCIS had a vast counterintelligence problem on its hands. Worse, agents discovered that one of their own—Beliveau—had been tipping off Francis to their every move.

Special Agent Cordell "Trey" DeLaPena III was in Bangkok pursuing leads into Glenn Defense's fraud scheme in Thailand when an NCIS agent rushed up to share the news about Beliveau. The agents recognized that they needed to revisit their entire approach. First, they had to plug the leaks. Second, they had to reframe their assumptions about the case. Was Francis an espionage agent working on behalf of a foreign power? How badly had the Navy been compromised?

"At that point, everything changed," DeLaPena recalled. "We had a significant problem and [we] did not know how far it went."

DeLaPena had joined the NCIS team digging into Glenn Defense eight months earlier. He was on loan from the Defense Criminal Investigative Service (DCIS), a sister law enforcement agency that reported to the Defense Department's inspector general. DCIS kept a low public profile, but its agents specialized in contract fraud, a weakness at NCIS. It also had a West Coast branch in Long Beach, California, that was near the NCIS regional offices for Los Angeles and San Diego.

DeLaPena was only twenty-six years old and looked even younger. An Air Force brat who'd graduated from the University of Virginia with an accounting degree, he had signed on with DCIS after investigating white-collar crimes for the Department of the Interior. The Glenn Defense case was his first DCIS assignment. It would consume him for the next ten years.

As soon as he and other investigators learned that Beliveau had been giving their case reports to Francis, they hurried to contain the damage. DeLaPena had been working with the two confidential informants in Thailand who had recorded conversations with former colleagues at Glenn Defense. Worried that Francis had smoked out the informants' identities via purloined K-NET files and might try to silence them, he raced to arrange a meeting in Bangkok so a federal prosecutor and other agents could interview them in person. The debriefings lasted five days.

Meanwhile, thousands of miles away, Francis's emails triggered a crisis in Washington, D.C.

At Joint Base Anacostia-Bolling, a military installation near the confluence of the Anacostia and Potomac Rivers, activity stirred inside an unmarked, two-story building next to NCIS's Washington Field Office. The building housed a secretive unit with a nondescript name—the Office of Special Projects—that handled national security cases involving counterespionage and counterintelligence. On April 29, it began investigating a former NCIS Special Agent of the Year: John Beliveau Jr.

Agents could tell from Francis's emails that Beliveau had been leaking updates from the Glenn Defense investigations for about a year and that, in return, Francis had paid for Beliveau to go on sex trips to Southeast Asia. They saw no evidence that Beliveau had disclosed classified information. But because Misiewicz had done so, agents had to assume the worst.

Ordinarily, NCIS would have immediately suspended Beliveau's security clearance and his access to law enforcement databases. But investigators knew that if Francis caught the slightest whiff of suspicion around Beliveau, he would make himself scarce. Their plan to arrest him would collapse.

Instead, NCIS leaders decided to allow Beliveau to remain on the job until they could lure Francis to the United States. The gamble was fraught with risk. They could only hope that Beliveau wouldn't give away top secret material or try to flee the country.

"The thing that really kept me awake at night is my agent doing something nefarious and giving information to the bad guy that could possibly compromise the whole shooting match," recalled Mark Ridley, NCIS's acting director at the time. As a preventive measure, Special Projects assigned a clandestine team to place Beliveau under physical surveillance and monitor his electronic communications. In its internal reports, the team referred to Beliveau by a code name: "Blue Wolf."

The fifty-year-old Ridley brooded over whom he could inform at the Pentagon without inadvertently tipping off Francis. For the past two years, he and other NCIS supervisors had briefed Navy Secretary Ray Mabus, a civilian, about their criminal investigations of Glenn Defense. Now he had to tell Mabus that NCIS had a traitor in its ranks. Mabus couldn't believe his ears. "Holy shit. Are you kidding me?" he thought.

Ridley and Mabus had never gotten along. Ridley started his law enforcement career as a jail guard in Nevada before joining NCIS and climbing the management ladder for a quarter-century. Mabus, sixty-four, was a Harvard-educated patrician who had served as governor of Mississippi and U.S. ambassador to Saudi Arabia before he took charge of the Navy. But the two men agreed on one thing: The Navy's uniformed chain of command needed to be kept in the dark about the Glenn Defense mess.

Ridley and Mabus were desperate to avoid a repeat of the devastating Tailhook scandal, in which many Navy leaders tried to cover up their personal involvement. The NCIS director and Navy secretary realized that scores of admirals had deployed to Asia during their careers and that it was likely, if not probable, most had crossed paths with Francis. Any of them could have been compromised or still be tight with the husbanding contractor.

For example, Ridley and Mabus knew that Admiral Jonathan Greenert—the chief of naval operations and the highest-ranking officer in the Navy—was the former commander of the Seventh Fleet. And the head of Greenert's personal security detail on the Seventh Fleet staff? None other than John Beliveau Jr.

Maybe the relationship was a coincidence. Investigators hadn't uncovered any problematic communications between Greenert and Francis. But Ridley was adamant that they could not breathe a word to the chief of naval operations or other admirals who had served in Asia. Mabus concurred.

Chapter Twenty-three

Party On

June 2013

BANGKOK, THAILAND

Wasted and livid, Leonard Francis screamed objections at the unflappable young woman behind the check-in desk of the Conrad Hotel as she politely refused his demands. Yes, she understood that Mr. Francis was a VIP guest who regularly patronized the five-star business hotel, near the U.S. embassy in the Thai capital. But no, she was not permitted to give him card keys so he could escort several prostitutes, whom he had brought back from a members-only sex club, to the restricted floors where his two U.S. Navy friends were staying.

"Yes its 3 am I am drunk and very angry," Francis seethed in a message to his driver. "Really arrogant bitch!" He vowed to take his business to the St. Regis next time. "Go to hell I won't go back ever again."

The indignity in the Conrad's lobby was Francis's latest aggravating setback, and his short temper was erupting with greater force than usual. The warrant for his arrest in the Philippines was still active because he refused to relinquish custody of two of his toddlers. One of his adult sons, Leonardo, had been hospitalized while at college in Massachusetts. Federal agents continued to stalk Glenn Defense on multiple fronts. Now his visit to libertine Bangkok—or "Bang-cock" as he liked to call it—had gone awry.

As usual, Francis had been trying to blend business with pleasure in what he later admitted was a "desperate" bid to recruit new moles. Glenn Defense's entire business plan centered on graft. To stay afloat financially, he needed a constant supply of corrupt Navy officers in key positions. But many of his dwindling gang of loyalists had finished their tours of duty in Asia, and Francis was straining to find replacements. With rumors spreading about the NCIS investigations, Navy officers who once clamored to join his hedonistic parties now treated him like a contagious pathogen.

He had been pestering Captain David Haas, the randy triathlete who served as the Seventh Fleet's head of operations, to anoint someone new on his staff to do Glenn Defense's bidding. But Haas was making only a halfhearted effort, and he was soon due to depart the Seventh Fleet for another assignment. Haas mentioned he would be overnighting in Bangkok during a flight connection. Francis decided to seize the moment and nag him further in person.

Francis thought a brief visit to Thailand would also be a good opportunity to deepen his relationship with Commander David Morales, the Navy's deputy director for contracting operations in Singapore. Dark-eyed and buff with a killer smile, Morales was a married Naval Academy graduate who loved to party. He began his career as a pilot, but now held a boring desk job. He jumped when Francis invited him at the last minute to tag along for a whirlwind, overnight trip to Bangkok, promising to pay for his flight and hotel, and have him back in Singapore the next morning. "He was just fun to hang out with," Morales recalled.

Francis had met Morales two years earlier when the officer was chairman of the 2011 Navy League birthday ball. They became friends and immersed themselves in Singapore's luxury nightlife scene. At Pangaea, a decadent "ultra-lounge" with crocodile-skin sofas, they swilled a $10,000, six-liter bottle of champagne beneath a shower of sparklers. They attended a Gucci fashion show and a Julio Iglesias concert, with front-row seats to both. On another occasion, as a housewarming present, Francis gave Morales four liters of caipirinha—a Brazilian cocktail—and four Spanish suckling pigs worth $450 apiece. "Thanks for oink oinks x 4," the Navy officer texted in gratitude.

Their June 22 trip to Thailand started out smoothly. The pair flew business class on Singapore Airlines, landing in Bangkok at 8 p.m. After a concierge fast-tracked them through immigration and customs, a chauffeur picked them up in a BMW 7 series limousine and escorted them to Pegasus, the ritzy sex club where Francis was a member. The palatial club was bedecked with crystal chandeliers, marble tables, elephant tusks, and stuffed tigers. But the main attraction was the women. Perfumed and pedicured, they wore silky evening gowns and could converse in four languages: Thai, English, Korean, and Japanese.

A mamasan, or madam, welcomed the guests from Singapore to a private VIP suite that Francis had reserved for an additional $4,000. The suite came with its own butler, a DJ, and unlimited food and drink. A parade of girls entered. According to Francis, Morales reacted with "shock and awe" and felt "like a rock star" as they "selected the ones that were suitable for our evening romp." (Morales acknowledged that "working girls" were present but denied selecting any for himself.)

Partway through, Francis slipped out to pick up Captain Haas, who touched down at the airport shortly before midnight. They rejoined Morales at Pegasus and spent a couple of hours drinking, singing karaoke and socializing with women. Afterward, they rode in separate vehicles to the Conrad Hotel. Francis had seven prostitutes in tow, planning to share them with his Navy friends.

Around 3 a.m., Francis arrived at the hotel with the women. He was so inebriated, however, that he fumbled the handoff. He said that after Morales and Haas took the elevator to their rooms, he belatedly discovered he lacked key cards to the officers' floors and couldn't bring them the prostitutes. After making a loud scene in the lobby and drawing the attention of the hotel manager, he was forced to abandon his plans and let the seven women go. (Morales gave a slightly different account, saying there were only four prostitutes, with none intended for him. Haas, in his version, said he was unaware Francis was trying to send women to his room.)

Regardless, Francis appeared to be losing his touch. It was his second botched recruiting mission to Bangkok in a fortnight. Eight days earlier, he had dinner at the Conrad with a female U.S. Navy officer who served as a liaison to the Thai military. Francis tried to charm the officer but again drank too much. He irritated the waitstaff, loudly interrupted other people's meals, and creeped out his target, who said she "just wanted to get out of there."

His quest to embed a new informant on the Seventh Fleet staff also hit a wall, but not for lack of trying. Besides the trip to Bangkok, he chased Haas all over Asia that summer, allegedly plying him with meals, prostitutes, and spa treatments in Singapore, Kuala Lumpur, and Sydney—all while pleading for help finding a reliable mole. Haas tried to broker a succession plan with a couple of candidates. Yet Francis failed to seal the deal and "baptize" any of them, as he put it, into his shrinking network. "Most of the other officers were scared and didn't want to get involved with us," he recalled.

In Washington, NCIS leaders felt their own pangs of anxiety. They'd taken steps to plug the hemorrhaging leak from their K-NET database. Agents ceased filing case updates that might alert John Beliveau Jr., the renegade agent, that his cover had been blown or that they had recovered the emails Francis thought he'd deleted. But they needed to walk a delicate line. Beliveau was smart, and they knew he would interpret a prolonged absence of reporting as a sign that something was amiss. They couldn't hold off much longer.

Agents sensed Francis had become jittery, and some doubted the plan to lure him to San Diego would work. They discussed alternatives, including an outlandish idea to capture him the next time he boarded a U.S. warship in an Asian port. Because Navy vessels were sovereign territory, proponents said they could lock Francis in the brig and float him across the ocean to Hawaii, or strap him into a military aircraft on the flight deck and bring him to the United States that way.

These far-fetched plans were debated at the Pentagon in confidential meetings between Navy Secretary Ray Mabus, NCIS Acting Director Mark Ridley, and Paul Oostburg Sanz, the Navy's general counsel. "We didn't think Singapore would extradite, and so the question we kept batting around was, 'OK, if we can lure him onto a U.S. ship, is that good enough?' I mean, it was for terror suspects coming after 9/11. . . They would kidnap them and put them onto a U.S. vessel," Mabus recalled. While the kidnapping option might have been legal, they decided it was politically impractical. The government of Singapore, a key U.S. defense partner, would no doubt react angrily to an American plot to abduct a prominent business executive living on its territory. Moreover, prosecutors from the U.S. Attorney's Office in San Diego worried they would lose jurisdiction if the Navy transported Francis by ship to Hawaii and handed him over to federal authorities there.

Instead, NCIS leaders settled on another risky approach. They would plant false updates into K-NET saying that the Glenn Defense investigations were shutting down, citing a purported determination by federal prosecutors that the cases were too flimsy to bring charges. If Beliveau believed the bogus reports and passed them to Francis, maybe the Malaysian would let down his guard and visit the United States. While Francis thought he had the upper hand in his tussles with NCIS and had always ducked criminal charges in the past, he would undoubtedly stay away if he sensed he might be arrested.

On July 3, while most federal employees were streaming out of NCIS headquarters in Quantico to get an early start on the four-day holiday weekend, Beliveau logged into K-NET and reviewed sixteen new files. He downloaded seven reports onto his desktop computer and burned them onto a CD to take home.

He read the files at his apartment. It looked like prosecutors were throwing in the towel on the Glenn Defense fraud cases one by one. Hoodwinked, he texted Francis with the good news.

"Fyi Thai case was closed. US Atty declined not enough evidence and no manpower," he wrote. "Korea closed also but Japan case still open."

"Awesome!" Francis replied. He couldn't believe his luck: The reason the American government apparently thought he wasn't worth prosecuting was that he had stolen too little money. "$$ not sexy 😊 ," he added.

That weekend, Beliveau elaborated in a Skype chat. "The Thai case was the best possible case and it was closed," he told Francis. "Japan case was sent for attorney review, my guess it will be declined also. If they didn't take all of them in one bundle, not much luck it will be accepted by [U.S.] attorneys."

Francis thanked Beliveau for his "stellar advice." In an aside, he mentioned that he was thinking about flying to America in several weeks. Maybe they could meet up then.

Contrary to what Francis and Beliveau believed, the Glenn Defense investigations rocketed ahead. NCIS and DCIS analysts combed through Francis's emails and followed trails leading to dozens of Navy personnel. Agents obtained warrants to search the private email accounts of new targets, including Commander Jose Sanchez and Sharon Kaur, the mole who had once met Francis at the Toys "R" Us in Singapore.

The illicit web—and the size of the threat it posed to national security—kept expanding. After obtaining a search warrant for Francis's Facebook account, investigators found messages to Bruce Loveless, the former head of intelligence for the Seventh Fleet who had given his business card to a Mongolian prostitute. Loveless had just been promoted to rear admiral and a senior intelligence post at the

Pentagon. Given his rank and the sensitivity of his job, digging into his relationship with Francis became a priority. Ten other Navy officers surfaced in Francis's Facebook messages. Their names were added to the list of suspects.

Agents still fretted that their false flag operation with the K-NET files might unravel so they doubled down on the deception. On July 16, NCIS Special Agent Amanda Blair traveled to Phuket to meet another agent who had been kept out of the loop and two former Glenn Defense employees who had been cooperating with the investigation. Blair repeated the lie that the cases had stalled because of prosecutorial disinterest, hoping the misinformation would filter back to Francis and reinforce his belief that he was off the hook. Meanwhile, NCIS agents obtained search warrants for Beliveau's personal AT&T cell phone and three private email accounts he had with Google, Microsoft, and Yahoo.

Like Francis, Beliveau was losing his edge, despite the fake good news he'd discovered snooping through K-NET. Plagued by loneliness, he descended further into a fog of depression and drink. The onetime Special Agent of the Year had soured on NCIS and complained about the "amateurs" and "ignorant unintelligent fucks" he worked with. He blew smoke at Francis by saying he was thinking about leaving his post at Quantico for a job in the private sector or an assignment in Afghanistan. Desperate to keep his prize mole in place at NCIS headquarters, Francis counseled patience and reminded him, "Cocks everywhere u go."

But Beliveau had no other friends and grew needier and more resentful.

"As I see it I saved your business at a great risk to my career and liberty," he texted Francis in late July. "You have no idea what I have to dodge to get what you want."

Francis usually tried to humor his mole, but this time he snapped. "Stop being dramatic nd chill," he retorted.

Francis's mood brightened when he received an invitation to the change-of-command ceremony in mid-September for the Navy's global logistics command in San Diego. Navy officials wanted him to arrive a couple days early so he could meet two admirals and give a presentation on the money-saving ideas he had discussed in April with the logistics officers in Yokosuka.

It was the final piece of bait, and Francis swallowed it.

Thinking he was free of his unpleasant legal troubles, Francis merrily planned to do other things during his visit to sunny Southern California. He scheduled a consultation with a plastic surgeon in Irvine. He contacted his former protégé Edmond Aruffo, the ex–Seventh Fleet wedding planner who was now living in San Diego, and asked him to arrange a dinner party while he was in town. "Work n play!" Francis instructed. "TOP SHELF strip clubs."

By early September, Francis felt loose and carefree. He bragged to Aruffo on the phone that he had been working out with a fitness instructor and wanted advice on where to shop in Beverly Hills for "high-end" XXL body-building gear, steroids, and "fat burner" supplements.

Skeptical that Francis had really committed to an exercise program, Aruffo told him that getting "ripped quick doesn't work" and warned him away from steroids. "That will screw up your liver. And you'll grow a third nipple on your back, weird shit," he lectured.

Francis laughed. He said he hoped the steroids would help him grow "a dick extension" instead.

While Francis was making wisecracks, U.S. authorities were signing paperwork to put him behind bars.

During the first week of September, an NCIS agent walked into the U.S. embassy in Singapore for a one-on-one briefing with Ambassador David Adelman. Speaking in strict confidence, the agent explained how NCIS and DCIS, with the Department of Justice, had been investigating Francis for years. They intended to arrest him in California in a few days but needed Adelman's approval because they were tricking a permanent resident of Singapore into leaving the country. Adelman thought the fraud case against Francis sounded "airtight" and signed a form authorizing the sting. But he felt sick when the agent told him that numerous U.S. Navy officials were also suspected of corruption. "It was heartbreaking," he recalled.

On September 12, James McWhirter, a DCIS special agent based in Long Beach, California, signed a twenty-one-page affidavit and submitted it under seal to a magistrate judge in San Diego, seeking an arrest warrant for Francis on a charge of conspiracy to commit bribery. The judge approved the request along with identical warrants for the arrests of Beliveau and Commander Mike Misiewicz, who was working in Colorado with the U.S. Northern Command. The three targets were clueless. Beliveau had checked K-NET three days earlier and thought the investigations still looked dead in the water.

On Friday the 13th, in Singapore, Francis hosted a celebratory dinner with Commander Morales, Captain Jesus Cantu, and another Navy officer in a private room at Tatsuya, a posh Japanese restaurant in the Goodwood Hotel. Afterward, the Boss, Morales and Cantu went to the Brix nightclub and the Tiananmen KTV karaoke bar.

Francis had twisted Morales's arm for ship schedules prior to the dinner, but the officer tried to set boundaries. "Unclassified good but can't do the classified," he wrote in a text. "Don't want to be exiled to Russia for the rest of my life." Francis half-jokingly replied that if Morales was exiled to Venezuela, with its beaches and pretty girls, "I will join you."

On Saturday, the Boss slept in late at his mansion on Nassim Road and made final revisions to his PowerPoint presentation for the Navy brass in San Diego.

The following day, September 15, Francis packed and put on a comfortable tracksuit for the long transpacific flight. Running late as usual because of a barrage of business calls and family demands, he arrived at the Singapore Airlines first-class counter a few minutes before departure. Fortunately, the check-in staff had a golf cart waiting to rush him to the aircraft.

He boarded, eased into his oversized seat, and relaxed as the plane took off for California.

Chapter Twenty-four

Busted

September 2013

SAN DIEGO, CALIFORNIA

A plainclothes surveillance team of fourteen federal agents—nine from DCIS and five from NCIS—staked out the foreign-arrivals terminal at Los Angeles International Airport, blending into the harried masses of travelers on a hot Sunday afternoon. Around 2:30 p.m., an agent spotted Leonard Francis in his rumpled tracksuit trudging alongside Alex Wisidagama, his forty-year-old cousin who had joined him on the flight from Singapore. A thirteen-year Glenn Defense veteran, Wisidagama held the lofty title of general manager for global government contracts. But sometimes he functioned as a glorified servant, carrying the Boss's luggage and tending to his personal needs.

From a distance, agents observed Francis and his cousin flash their red passports at the immigration counter, pass through customs, and climb into a black Cadillac Escalade outside the terminal. The agents followed the SUV for 125 miles as it sped south on Interstate 5 to the Marriott Marquis hotel on West Harbor Drive in downtown San Diego. They arrived at 5:10 p.m.

The surveillance team formed the vanguard of an extraordinary force. More than one hundred law enforcement officers had been assembled to seize Francis, shut down his company, and round up his key moles in one fell swoop. Over the next two days, agents received orders to make arrests, interrogate suspects, and execute search warrants in seven states—California, Colorado, Florida, Hawaii, Illinois, Nebraska, and Virginia—and the District of Columbia. They also fanned out worldwide to conduct interviews and searches in Singapore, Japan, the Philippines, Indonesia, South Korea, Thailand, Hong Kong, and Australia. The meticulously scheduled operation unfolded in seven time zones. Neither DCIS nor NCIS had attempted anything on this scale before.

Secrecy was so tight that many agents and foreign law enforcement partners were not told the names of the targets or the nature of the investigation until a few hours beforehand. Authorities did not want to tip off the suspects, especially Francis, and give them a chance to flee or destroy evidence. Once the arrests began, investigators would have to lock down their targets quickly and seize their phones to prevent them from warning others with a last-second call or text.

James McWhirter, the DCIS special agent who had sworn out the arrest warrant for Francis, knew from experience that much could go wrong. The forty-seven-year-old was the antithesis of the Hollywood caricature of a hotshot federal agent: short and puffy-eyed, with thinning brown hair that he defiantly gelled into a spiky pompadour. He had spent his law enforcement career toiling in unglamorous parts of the federal bureaucracy: four years with DCIS, ten with the U.S. Army Criminal Investigation Division, nine with the Defense Contract Audit Agency, two with the U.S. Postal Service. Fat Leonard was literally and figuratively the biggest crook he had ever chased.

The agents could have grabbed Francis as soon as he stepped off the plane in Los Angeles, but McWhirter and federal prosecutors wanted him to attend his meeting the next day with the Navy logistics officials in San Diego. If he let down his guard, they hoped, maybe he would incriminate himself during his presentation or lead them to moles they hadn't discovered yet.

The surveillance team watched as Francis and Wisidagama checked into their rooms on the twenty-first floor of the blue-glass Marriott, overlooking San Diego Bay. At 8:20 p.m., the targets left the hotel and walked south several blocks to the Gaslamp Quarter, a nightlife district where Francis had asked Ed Aruffo to make a reservation at Nobu, his favorite Japanese chain restaurant. Joining them for dinner were two Glenn Defense employees—contract guru Howard Patty Sr. and Rivers Cleveland, a retired Navy officer and U.S.-based adviser—who had flown in to help with the presentation the next day. Also present was Steve Shedd, the former Seventh Fleet officer and leaker of classified ship schedules, who had ascended the ranks to become commanding officer of the USS *Milius*, a San Diego–based destroyer.

For the next three and a half hours, the group gossiped and gorged on rare Wagyu beef, Tasmanian trout, bluefin tuna sashimi with jalapeño, lobster smeared with wasabi pepper, and other delicacies. For dessert, one person—no prizes for guessing who—still had room for a slice of tiramisu. At 11:45 p.m., Francis pulled out his Visa to pay the $2,694 bill, plus a $553 tip. It would be his last tasty supper for a long time.

Agents followed in the dark while Francis and his cousin toddled back to the Marriott on foot. Satisfied that the targets were calling it a night, they terminated the surveillance at half past midnight.

Francis slept in the next morning, Monday, September 16, and refilled his belly with a late breakfast at the hotel. He rehearsed his presentation in a business suite attached to his bedroom. At 1 p.m., he met Wisidagama, Patty, and Cleveland in the lobby. A red GMC Denali picked them up at the valet stand and drove them a quarter mile northwest to the Navy Broadway Complex, a twelve-acre collection of aging office buildings and warehouses on the waterfront.

The Glenn Defense executives entered Building 1, a seven-story structure that dated to the early 1920s and served as the headquarters of the Naval Supply Systems Command-Global Logistics

Support. They were escorted to a conference room on the top floor and welcomed by Captain Marty Fields, who had invited Francis to the meeting and flown in from Yokosuka, and Captain Bert Heck, the command's lead contract executive.

Heck was oblivious to the sting operation and also had no idea that federal agents had installed a spy camera and microphone in his conference room. Investigators had briefed his boss, Rear Admiral Jonathan Yuen, Fields, and two other participants in the meeting but swore them to secrecy. They were instructed to act normal and told that Francis would probably be apprehended later that day.

Francis put on a bravura performance. At the start, he played the China card, reminding his American hosts that another superpower was flexing its muscles in Asia. He mentioned that Glenn Defense had worked a few times as subcontractors for the Chinese government but pledged that his company would stick with the U.S. Navy "for as long as I am able." During the PowerPoint presentation—titled "Partnering to Save Costs"—his team shamelessly claimed that Glenn Defense could generate $100 million in savings for American taxpayers if the Navy extended the company's husbanding contracts.

"Our mission at Glenn Marine, of course, is to provide the best value solutions to our customers," Patty said. "We really mean that."

The two-hour meeting ended pleasantly at 3:45 p.m. Francis and his entourage rode back to the Marriott and gathered in his suite to discuss how things went.

A few minutes later, McWhirter and a colleague, NCIS Special Agent Shannon Rachal, knocked on the door. "Hi, is Mr. Francis here?" McWhirter asked. Francis waved from his chair and summoned them inside.

McWhirter identified himself as a DCIS agent. Instead of whipping out handcuffs, however, he asked whether they could speak in private. He had some questions about the meeting Francis just had with the Navy's logistics team, hinting that one of the participants was suspected of accepting bribes from a Glenn Defense competitor.

"The real issue, uh, how do I put this—we've got an issue of people taking money and so on," McWhirter said. "And it's real sensitive. Have you heard of that before?"

It was another ruse. McWhirter was wearing a wire and wanted to see whether he could record Francis lying to a federal agent.

Francis sized up McWhirter and thought he could outfox him. A lawyer would have advised Francis to remain silent, but he decided to make a show of cooperating. He signaled for Cleveland, Patty, and Wisidagama to leave the room and said he'd meet up with them later.

Sounding earnest, Francis told the agents he didn't have any personal knowledge about Navy officers taking bribes but could envision his competitors trying something shady. He also pointed the finger at Jim Maus, implying that his antagonist and former employee was corrupt. He encouraged McWhirter to dig in those directions. "You are on something hot, to be honest with you."

"You think so?" McWhirter said hesitantly, playing dumb. To test Francis's reaction, he tossed out the names of a few other Navy people and suggested they might be dirty. Then, after dancing around the heart of the matter, he innocuously asked Francis whether he was friends with any admirals or had ever given them gifts.

"We don't do things like that," Francis said. "I mean the most we would have done in the past was having a drink, eat, you know, but it's in a group, not one on one. It was sociable." He couldn't resist taking another shot at Maus and the Pacific Fleet's ethics directive that had clamped down on his hospitality. "Now, you can't do anything," he complained.

McWhirter asked Francis what he meant. Was he still buying dinners or paying for gifts?

Oh no, Francis said, catching himself. "There's nothing. Nothing, nothing, nothing."

"Nothing?" McWhirter asked.

"Nothing," Francis repeated. "It's been years and years and years."

McWhirter nodded. He apologized in advance for the next

question. "Okay. Okay. Ummm. I have to get this on the record," he said. "Have, at any time, you ever given a bribe?"

"No," Francis lied.

The agent moved on. Like a smooth-talking boa constrictor, he was slowly, methodically, squeezing his prey.

"Okay, I want to put this delicately. And I need you to be really honest with me," he said. "There have been some allegations regarding..."

Francis knew what was coming and interrupted him. "Yeah, I know. I heard about all that," he said, mentioning the investigation looking at Glenn Defense's operations in Thailand. "These rumors go around everywhere."

McWhirter pressed gently, bringing up allegations that Glenn Defense had falsified invoices for Thai port visits. Francis deflected, blaming the Thai navy and his own "disgruntled employees" for any problems. "Our books are open. You can check them," he promised.

The agent nodded some more as he took notes. He acted like it was a formality. "Have you ever directed somebody to create false invoices personally?" he asked.

Francis lied again. "No, personally, no. I don't practice that. I mean, I know the rules of the game."

After ninety minutes of questioning, McWhirter started to bring the interview to a close. He turned to his partner. "Anything else we should ask, Shannon? I mean, help me out on this. I think I have asked everything I can think of." She shook her head no.

Francis grinned and said he'd be happy to answer follow-up questions by email. "I'm here to cooperate and work with you guys and help you all out." But the loquacious Francis couldn't quite bring himself to shut up. Looking for sympathy, he prattled on about tough economic times and how he'd had to downsize his company's workforce from 1,200 to 500, even though Glenn Defense still handled hundreds of Navy port visits a year.

McWhirter let him keep talking. After several minutes, he tried to wrap up the interview again with a final question: So just to be absolutely clear, he asked, Francis had never bribed anyone, or provided any gifts, or authorized any false billing, or made up any bogus invoices himself?

"No, no, no, no," Francis said, lying four more times.

McWhirter thanked him and asked for a business card. Francis apologized that he didn't have any with him. He laughed and assured the agents he was an honest businessman.

"I'm out of Singapore," he said. "The squeakiest and cleanest country."

He shook hands with the agents and bade goodbye. "Nice meeting you."

"Pleasure meeting you too, Mr. Francis," McWhirter said.

The agents turned and exited the room, which was the signal for a team of armed agents waiting nearby to make their move. They burst into the suite.

"Hands up! I said hands up!" one agent commanded. "Show me your hands up!"

"On the ground, on the ground!" another yelled as they pinned Francis, pulled his arms behind his back, and handcuffed him.

McWhirter marked the time: 6:12 p.m. Fat Leonard was down. But the dominoes were only beginning to fall.

As soon as Francis was apprehended, evidence technicians swarmed through his adjoining hotel room suites to seize and catalog everything that didn't belong to the Marriott.

The most critical items were Francis's electronic devices: two iPhones, a Nokia cell phone, a BlackBerry Torch, an iPad, and a Fujitsu Lifebook laptop. Analysts later determined that together they contained more than a million text messages, emails, photographs, and documents dating to 2005.

Technicians found Francis's man purse containing three wallets with four credit cards, $10,570 cash in U.S. currency, and a plastic bag with money from Singapore and Brunei. Another $1,045 in cash lay in a desk drawer. They also bagged up three unopened boxes of Cuban Cohiba cigars, two Ulysse Nardin luxury watches, and a third Swiss watch from Chopard.

Another team of agents took Wisidagama into custody on a material witness warrant. He was not being charged with a crime—yet—but the warrant meant he could be detained to prevent him from fleeing the country or contacting other suspects while the investigation proceeded.

Rivers Cleveland, the U.S.-based adviser for Glenn Defense, was staying in a room three levels up on the twenty-fourth floor. DCIS Special Agent Michelle Hendricks and NCIS Special Agent James Curry—who were also recording with a wire—cornered the shell-shocked retired Navy captain, told him Francis had been arrested, and asked whether he would talk voluntarily.

"Sure," Cleveland replied. "I mean, I have no idea what's going on, so yeah."

Under questioning, Cleveland told the agents he met Francis in 2003 when he was the U.S. defense attaché in Singapore. Francis hired him in 2006 to oversee a new Glenn Defense subsidiary in the United States, but the business never really got off the ground and had no other employees. Cleveland minimized his involvement, saying he received only a $1,500 monthly retainer and rarely met with Francis in person.

The agents looked skeptical. They told him Francis had been arrested on suspicion of bribery and fraud. More arrests were likely. Now was his chance to come clean. "This is opportunity time," Curry said.

Cleveland denied knowing anything about Glenn Defense defrauding the Navy, though he admitted Francis had bought him dinners when he was the defense attaché. "He liked to party pretty hard," he said. He agreed to cooperate and permitted the agents to take his iPhone and laptop.

The last person interrogated at the Marriott was Howard Patty Sr., the retired Navy officer Francis had hired in 2006 as a Glenn Defense vice president. Yet another team of investigators—NCIS Special Agent Denise Harding and DCIS Special Agent Walter Brown—told the fifty-seven-year-old Patty up front they weren't going to arrest him. But they asked whether he would be willing to talk.

"Well, yeah," Patty replied. "I'm just curious as to, you know, what the situation is."

Patty knew far more than Cleveland about Glenn Defense's business practices. He had worked for the company fulltime for seven years, first in Singapore and then remotely from Texas. But he remained cool under pressure and volunteered precious little information. Unlike Francis, he kept his answers short, saying "I'm not aware" or "I don't recall" dozens of times.

Partway through the interview, McWhirter joined the inquisition to play the role of bad cop. He grilled Patty about Glenn Defense's "fictitious" invoices in Thailand and accused him of lying. He warned that investigators could prove Glenn Defense had defrauded the Navy of $10 million over an eight-month period in Thailand alone.

"I am basically telling you the truth on what's happening. I'm not blowing any smoke up your ass," McWhirter growled. "You can go that dishonest route, but it's only going to get you in more trouble."

Patty parried each thrust. "I don't do the invoices," he said calmly. "I don't know anything about fictitious things."

McWhirter pushed harder. "If I hooked you up to a lie detector test, you'd come back with the same answer?"

"I would," Patty said.

After three hours, the agents gave up. Patty signed a form giving investigators permission to take the aging Nokia cell phone that Glenn Defense had given him, but he refused to hand over his laptop or his personal BlackBerry.

By then, agents in other states and countries had rolled into action. Singaporean authorities raided Francis's mansion and the Glenn

Defense corporate offices on Pandan Road, confiscating desktop computers, laptops, boxes of business records, cell phones, and thumb drives.

Francis's family knew he was in California and had no idea what to do in his absence. "Hey dad, we had a situation at the house today," his son Leonardo, texted. "Should I be worried?"

He never received a reply.

Chapter Twenty-five

Shock Waves

September 2013

WASHINGTON, D.C.

John Beliveau Jr. rose early on Monday, September 16, and pulled on a blue polo shirt with the NCIS logo sewn on the chest. He had a long commute ahead of him. Instead of his usual quick dash to the NCIS building at Quantico, he needed to head north on Interstate 95 through Northern Virginia's miserable rush-hour traffic to Joint Base Anacostia-Bolling in Washington. He had scheduled a session at the firearms range to requalify as a federal law enforcement officer on his Sig Sauer P229 pistol.

He could tell something had gone horribly wrong when he rolled up to the gate and found the base on lockdown. The news on his car radio reported an active shooter at the Washington Navy Yard, a bustling workplace for fourteen thousand people about three miles north. At 8:16 a.m., a mentally disturbed government contractor had walked out of a fourth-floor bathroom in a building housing the Naval Sea Systems Command and randomly opened fire with a sawed-off Remington 870 shotgun. For more than an hour, the gunman strode through cubicles, hallways, and stairwells, killing twelve people before he died in a shootout with police. The pandemonium paralyzed Washington for hours.

Beliveau talked his way past the closed gates at Anacostia-Bolling by showing his NCIS credentials. He bypassed the firearms range and drove to the block on Mitscher Road that housed NCIS's Washington Field Office. The entire office was abuzz. A makeshift command center had been set up to organize the response to the Navy Yard massacre.

Jawad Mashny, the field office's assistant special agent in charge, looked up when he spotted Beliveau and said, "I'm glad you're here." Mashny, a former Marine gunnery sergeant, looked anxious and asked whether they could speak in his office. He closed the door and said a counterintelligence case needed immediate attention. He couldn't share details yet but asked Beliveau to join him for a classified briefing at the National Security Agency headquarters at Fort Meade, Maryland, about thirty miles away. Beliveau thought the timing was odd given the bedlam at the Navy Yard, but he assumed the matter was important because it involved the super-secret NSA.

Mashny said that he would drive but that they couldn't bring their weapons to Fort Meade for security reasons. He opened a cipher-lock safe behind his desk to store their sidearms. Beliveau thought this was odd too, but he had never visited the NSA and figured it was normal procedure for the spooks. On the way to the parking lot, Mashny said he needed to stop briefly at the nearby NCIS Office of Special Projects. After they entered the unmarked building, he told Beliveau to wait in the squad area so he could speak alone to a supervisor.

In fact, Mashny had deftly maneuvered Beliveau into a trap.

For the past four months, a team from the Office of Special Projects had kept the former NCIS Special Agent of the Year under tight surveillance. The original plan was to arrest him at Quantico later that day while Leonard Francis was meeting with Navy officials in San Diego. But agents had to improvise when they learned Beliveau was coming to Anacostia-Bolling for his firearms test. Then they had to adjust on the fly again when the base went into lockdown because of the Navy Yard shooting. Luckily, Mashny had intercepted Beliveau and disarmed him.

Beliveau looked around the squad room and recognized a couple of faces: Dave Brown, a supervisory special agent with whom he had served in Yokosuka, and Eric Maddox, a special agent whom he sometimes bumped into at Quantico. Brown said hello and suggested they go into a vacant office to chat. He introduced Beliveau to another visitor, Eleanor Gailey, a special agent from DCIS.

The amiable mood changed as soon as they sat down. The Special Projects agents wanted to talk about Leonard Francis. They opened a folder and showed Beliveau printouts of emails they had obtained from the Google search warrants. "You know, Leonard is not your friend," Brown said with a patronizing tone.

"Am I under investigation?" Beliveau asked. "If I'm being investigated, then I want a lawyer."

That ended the conversation. Gailey stood up, told Beliveau he was under arrest, and read him his Miranda rights. On cue, two other agents entered the room, handcuffed him, and removed the NCIS badge from his belt.

They ordered Beliveau to strip off his NCIS polo shirt and replace it with a plain khaki one. They didn't want it to be obvious when they transported him to the federal lockup that they had a dirty agent in the ranks.

That afternoon, Commander Mike Misiewicz, carrying only a backpack, walked into the Colorado Springs airport terminal to board a flight to Tennessee for a meeting at a Navy command near Memphis. The former Seventh Fleet golden boy had been stationed in the Rocky Mountains for almost a year as a staff officer with the U.S. Northern Command. But life was nowhere near as fun as it had been aboard the USS *Blue Ridge*, a.k.a. "the Love Boat."

He'd rented a tiny bedroom in a group house on Mosquito Pass Drive because he was almost broke from his divorce. The workweek had just started, and he was already exhausted from travel. He'd spent the weekend trying to mend his tattered relationship with his four kids, getting home at 2 a.m. after the fourteen-hour drive from northwestern Illinois.

His Monday turned from bad to worse when a team of law enforcement officers arrested him at the airport and took him to nearby Peterson Air Force Base. He didn't take them seriously at first. He waived his Miranda rights and agreed to talk to two federal agents without a lawyer present, saying he was "curious" to hear what this was all about.

One of the agents was Erika Mariner, who, unbeknownst to Misiewicz, had been investigating him nonstop for twenty-five months, ever since his estranged wife had reported his suspicious contacts with Francis to the NCIS office in Yokosuka.

Mariner introduced herself and asked whether Misiewicz wanted a snack.

"I'm good," he replied. "It depends on how long this takes."

The interview began at 3:30 p.m. Colorado time—while Francis was still presenting his PowerPoint slides in San Diego—and lasted two and a half hours. Mariner started gently, asking Misiewicz about his children and simple questions about his Seventh Fleet assignment. He claimed the tour was "brutal" on both his marriage and his health.

Asked whether he had met anyone from Glenn Defense, Misiewicz said he was friends with Edmond Aruffo, but he neglected to mention their hijinks with prostitutes and other misdeeds. After some prodding, he acknowledged crossing paths with Francis. "I mean, I know Leonard. Everybody knows Leonard," he said, praising him as "a pretty shrewd businessman."

The interrogators squeezed a little harder. They told Misiewicz his name had come up as part of a "very big" investigation into Glenn Defense and informed him—prematurely—that Francis had been arrested.

"Oh, wow," Misiewicz said, genuinely surprised. But he insisted that his relationship with Francis was "professional" and that he had never accepted gifts or done anything unethical.

After some more jousting, the agents bore down. Mariner told Misiewicz he had a special obligation to tell the truth, reminding him that the Navy had glorified him when he returned to Cambodia three years earlier at the helm of a U.S. warship.

"You were welcomed there with a fricking king's reception, I mean, that must have felt amazing, and knowing you have those roots and you overcame so much and you became an American. You're a hero," she said. "When people think of the military and heroes and people thank you for your service, that's what they're thinking of."

She said investigators knew that he had pocketed gifts from Glenn Defense. She would give him one more chance to come clean.

"Did you ever ask them for anything, any items of value, no matter what it is? It could be a new Porsche, a thousand dollars, fancy dinner?"

"No," Misiewicz lied.

"Nothing?" Mariner pressed. "Nothing you can think of?"

"No," he repeated. "No."

Thinking he was calling the agents' bluff, Misiewicz made the fatal mistake of demanding proof of their allegations. Mariner obliged by quoting from his emails with Francis, reciting in excruciating detail how he had leaked military secrets in exchange for prostitutes and paid vacations.

"You were a little lap dog," she spat. "You're a commander . . . right now in the world's most powerful navy and you're referring to Leonard Francis as 'Big Bro.' I mean, is that honorable?"

"You got wrapped up in the world that they had and you wanted to be a part of it, you liked being surrounded by that. You liked the hoochie mamas that he had around him all the time," she added. "That was enticing to you, and like Pavlov's dog, [Francis] knew what was going to make you salivate and they knew how to hit that button. They're like, 'Hey, we know the Blue Ridge is traveling over here, let's get some girls over there for Mike and the boys. Hey, let's set them up in this hotel. Hey, let's go out drinking and partying.'"

The Legion of Merit recipient stayed quiet. But the NCIS agent pressed on, mentioning three of Misiewicz's girlfriends by name and sarcastically asking whether he was still dating them. Finally, she zeroed in on one thing he still cared about: his kids.

"Today is already a bad day for the Navy. Let's not make it worse, okay?" Mariner said. "When you are looking back on this moment and Merrick [and] Maddox, needing that figure in their life, you know, is Dad the kind of guy that we want to look up to, that we want to emulate? Is he the guy that lied and ran from things or is he the guy that stood up and admitted, 'Shit, you know what? You're right. I was wrong. I messed up. How do I fix this?'"

After two hours of questioning, Misiewicz wore down. He grudgingly confessed, admitting his relationship with Francis was improper, that he accepted gifts and free airfare, that he gave classified information to a foreigner, that he knew it was all wrong.

Yet part of him remained in denial. He defended Francis as a devoted friend of the Navy who was unfairly saddled with a seedy reputation. "His company delivers, and I've seen that," Misiewicz said. "I trusted Ed and Leonard that it was again to benefit us and benefit them."

By the time the agents stopped the voice recorder at 6 p.m., there was still no indication the Cambodian American hero fully understood that Francis was a con man who had groomed and exploited him because he was a sucker for girls, booze, and free travel.

After nightfall, 1,500 miles away in Tampa, Florida, a large team of federal agents swarmed the Camden Preserve apartments. A manager had given them the passcode to the gate. They climbed the exterior stairway to the third floor of a stucco building and banged hard on the door to Unit #605.

The local time was 8:50 p.m.: about an hour after Misiewicz's interrogation ended in Colorado and twenty-two minutes before Francis would be tackled to the ground in his San Diego hotel suite.

Commander Jose Luis Sanchez answered the knock. He had just finished gulping down takeout from Steak 'n Shake, anticipating a quiet evening alone. One agent waved a warrant to search the premises. Two others ordered him to step outside.

After completing his unofficial tour of duty as Francis's chief eavesdropper at the Fleet Logistics Center in Yokosuka, Sanchez had spent the past three months working at U.S. Central Command headquarters in Tampa.

Now forty years old, the beady-eyed officer was losing his hair, gaining weight, and—like Misiewicz—taking a beating from a divorce that had left him marooned in a sparsely furnished one-bedroom walkup. But he was smarter than he looked. Before the agents could ask a question or get him to incriminate himself, he said, "I want to talk to an attorney."

Sanchez stood in the third-floor breezeway while the agents from DCIS and NCIS picked through his flat. He knew Francis was in San Diego for a big meeting. The Boss had texted him earlier to say his visit was going well.

Unlike the others, Sanchez was not under arrest. The warrant authorized the agents only to search his apartment and seize certain items. For some reason, his two cell phones were not on the list. He had left them inside, and now the Samsung was ringing almost nonstop. One number, listed as "Baby," kept calling from Japan. Another was from New York. A third was Sanchez's estranged wife, Priscilla, who lived three and a half hours away in Jacksonville. Agents were banging on her door too, with a subpoena for the couple's bank records.

The agents searched for two hours. Once they left, Sanchez rushed inside and picked up a phone to warn Francis on Viber, an encrypted app.

"Emergency, apartment raided by 15 federal agents tonight . . . had me on the ground with guns pointed at me," he tapped with his thumbs. "Working with my lawyer Mo . . . Confiscated computer and other papers . . . shud I throw away this phone . . . some reason this was not taken."

It was too late. He never heard from Francis again.

As Sanchez answered his door in Tampa, a fourth team of federal agents arrived at a far nicer home in Hawaii on Ford Island, a Navy-owned spit of land in the middle of Pearl Harbor. The two-story residence on Catalina Drive stood close to the shoreline in a neighborhood that offered some of the most picturesque military housing in the world, with the Battleship Missouri Memorial and other World War II landmarks within walking distance.

Carol Lausman, the tanned wife of Captain David "Too Tall" Lausman, had spent the day playing golf. She welcomed the agents into their home and told them not to worry about taking off their shoes.

"Dave!" she called to her husband. "It's NCIS!"

The fifty-nine-year-old captain had just retired from the military on September 1 after completing a final assignment with a task force in Hawaii. But the couple were in no rush to leave Ford Island, and the Navy was allowing them to stay a few extra months.

The visitors got right down to business. NCIS Special Agent Patricia "Jo" Dempski maneuvered Captain Lausman into one room to speak with him alone while the other agents diverted his spouse into the kitchen.

Wearing thick glasses and short black hair, Dempski was at least a foot shorter than Too Tall. She told him up front she was investigating fraud allegations involving Glenn Defense. Would he answer questions voluntarily?

"Sure," Lausman shrugged.

For the first hour, he talked down to her, giving long-winded answers to queries about his service in the Seventh Fleet as commanding officer of the USS *Blue Ridge* and the USS *George Washington*. He recalled his first encounter with Leonard Francis, at the 2004 Christmas Cheer party in Hong Kong. "He's as tall as I am and probably another 150 pounds heavier," Lausman said. "You can't miss him."

Things went downhill from there. Lausman fibbed incorrigibly, saying he never let Francis buy him dinner or pay for hotel rooms at the Shangri-La. "I've gone through all the ethics trainings," he assured Dempski.

Like Misiewicz, he defended Francis as a man of virtue. He described once becoming furious with a female admiral who complained that Francis was a thief. "What the hell you saying, lady?" Lausman recalled thinking. "To besmirch somebody behind their back, calling them, 'that Fat Leonard, what a frickin' thief,' that was the quote she used! I mean, why make fun of his body weight?"

Dempski let him drone on. After a while, she interrupted: Had he heard anything about Francis providing prostitutes?

"I have not, I have not seen any, I have not heard of any pro—the prostitute thing I've never heard about before," he stammered. "You know, and—and the prostitute thing or the—the escort ladies, I guess is the better term, I have not—I have never even seen that whatsoever."

In the kitchen, Carol Lausman spun her own web. Yes, she acknowledged to the other agents, Leonard was a friend, but he was a family man, not a partier. No, neither she nor Dave ever let Leonard treat them for dinner. They knew the rules. No, she couldn't recall accepting gifts from Glenn Defense.

One agent asked whether Francis had given her a black purse—a reference to the $2,500 Versace handbag she received in Hong Kong. Upon reflection, Carol said she did recall a purse, but she dismissed it as a cheap little thing that she gave away, probably to Goodwill.

After two and a half awkward hours, the agents left when Captain Lausman declined to let them search the property.

Late that night, sometime between 10 p.m. and midnight, Lausman rummaged through a closet and pulled out two pieces of computer hardware: a two-inch-long USB thumb drive and a notebook-sized, 200-gigabyte external hard drive that was labeled with a bright red sticker:

This medium is classified
SECRET
U.S. Government Property

Against regulations, Lausman had taken the classified drives home from the USS *George Washington*. Among other things, they contained communications about ship movements and tons of his emails.

Suddenly worried that his secrets might fall into the wrong hands, he placed the devices on a flat surface and pulverized them with a hammer.

Chapter Twenty-six

Panic Attacks

September 2013

NORFOLK, VIRGINIA

The strike force of federal agents knew its next window of opportunity would be brief. Luckily, they had managed to apprehend Leonard Francis, his cousin Alex Wisidagama, Commander Mike Misiewicz, and the NCIS double-crosser John Beliveau Jr. without incident.* But the prisoners had to go before a federal magistrate the next day, a Tuesday, September 17. At that point, the arrests would become a matter of public record, and the U.S. Attorney's Office in San Diego was planning to issue a press release. So investigators rushed to ambush other suspects while they still had the element of surprise.

When Captain Jeff Breslau parked his Kia Sorrento at Norfolk Naval Station around eight o'clock Tuesday morning, the forty-seven-year-old officer found two agents from NCIS and DCIS waiting for him outside his building. At first, he didn't think it was unusual. Norfolk was the largest navy base in the world, home to seventy-five warships and 77,000 servicemembers. All sorts of people crossed his path each day. But when the agents told him to cancel his appointments so

---

* Commander Jose Sanchez and Captain David "Too Tall" Lausman remained free but would be charged later.

they could question him about Glenn Defense, a wave of nausea and fear engulfed him.

Breslau had served the past year in Norfolk as the commanding officer of a joint public affairs unit. But investigators knew from their trove of emails that he had been moonlighting as a ghostwriter for Glenn Defense, and that he'd even supplied talking points for Francis's presentation in San Diego the day before. The agents asked Breslau why he hadn't disclosed his outside employment to the Navy and why he was helping Francis.

In a panic, Breslau made several far-fetched claims to dodge culpability. He said he wasn't really working for Francis, just providing "advice." He insisted he wasn't personally "taking any money," though he later admitted Francis had paid $65,000 to a start-up Breslau co-owned.

He also portrayed himself as Francis's better angel. "I told him that he's got to be honest," Breslau recounted. "I've told him things like he's got to stop buying gifts for admirals and captains."

The investigators nodded. Each had a Sony digital voice memory stick in his pocket that was surreptitiously recording the interview. If Breslau wanted to hang himself with his answers, that was fine by them. His statements would be admissible in court.

Petrified of appearing uncooperative, Breslau blabbed for more than two hours. He finally shut up when the agents asked to search his home computers. "Now you guys are scaring me a lot," he said, declining to give his consent.

The agents left, saying they'd be in touch. Breslau raced to find an attorney. He feared, correctly, that it was just a matter of time until his life and career came crashing down.

Eleven hundred miles away at Offutt Air Force Base, near Omaha, Nebraska, two agents from NCIS and DCIS waited outside the home of the next target: Rear Admiral J. R. Haley, director of global operations at U.S. Strategic Command, the military headquarters in charge of nuclear weapons.

The agents had come for the fifty-five-year-old Haley earlier but found only his wife at home. By the time he returned, his spouse had already informed him of the reason for the visit: The agents wanted to know about gifts Francis had given them when the admiral was based in Japan as commanding officer of the USS *George Washington* carrier strike group.

A fast-talking Texan, Haley was congenial at first, offering the federal lawmen sodas and beers. But when the agents read him his rights and said he was suspected of possible criminal violations involving Glenn Defense, he exploded. Two-star admirals weren't accustomed to being accused of criminal behavior.

"If Leonard's guilty, you need to get all his money back and hammer him till the cows come home. But if you're gonna charge me with something and treat me as a suspect, I'm not interested in discussing it," he snapped. "I'm not interested in getting caught up in some entrapment thing. I've watched that happen before."

The agents, who were covertly recording the conversation, said it was up to him. The interview was voluntary. They prepared to leave, but Haley told them to hold on and said he had nothing to hide. "I guess the bottom line is I want to help you."

Haley acknowledged that Francis was "a friend" and that Glenn Defense had booked hotel rooms for him and his wife at the Shangri-La, but he said he didn't realize the company had subsidized their lodging expenses. He admitted that Francis had bought them dinners and given his wife Dior perfume and a Gucci purse that "made her very, very happy." He said that he repaid Francis in kind by hosting him for dinner at his official quarters in Japan and that he'd tried to reimburse Francis for the purse with a personal check for $215 that went uncashed.

When the agents asked whether he had heard about Francis

providing prostitutes to Navy officers, Haley sounded shocked. He swore he never would have tolerated such a thing.

"You gotta be shittin' me," he said. "I'd have been on that like white on rice. . . . If you told me he's involved in fraud I'd be like, well, 'OK, let's call a cop car.' If you told me he was offering an escort service I'm gonna go high and right because that's the stuff that shows up on the front page of the *Navy Times*."*

By the end of the two-hour interview, Haley was back to his affable self, joshing with the agents and assuring them his dealings with Francis were aboveboard. As they stood up to leave, he laughed and said, "This is not going to show up on NCIS TV or whatever?"

The agents chuckled. "It's very possible," one said.

In a belated attempt to make things right, Charlene Haley surrendered the Gucci purse and what was left of the Dior perfume to investigators. NCIS tagged both items as evidence and shipped the purse to Gucci America, Inc., which determined it was genuine and appraised its value between $1,200 and $1,400.

That evening in San Diego, agents sought to track down Edmond Aruffo and Steve Shedd, the two officers who had served as Francis's wedding planners on the Seventh Fleet staff years before. The surveillance team had observed them dining with Francis at Nobu two nights earlier, and analysts had been poring over their email traffic. The emerging evidence indicated they had played pivotal roles in the bribery scheme.

Agents wanted to corner Aruffo and Shedd at their residences because that was often the best place to persuade suspects to confess. For obvious reasons, people typically don't want their bosses or colleagues to see them talking to federal investigators at the office. The agents just hoped the wedding planners would return home before they heard about Francis's arrest.

---

* "High and right" is military slang for losing one's temper.

Shedd lived with his wife, Lauren, and their four children in Coronado, an idyllic resort town across the bay from downtown San Diego. Flanked by two palm trees, their home had a three-car garage and was a short walk from the beach. Two of the Shedd kids were racing around on kick scooters when NCIS Special Agent James Curry and DCIS Special Agent Michelle Hendricks rolled up an hour before sunset.

They were greeted amicably by Lauren Shedd, who said her husband was on his way back from work. She welcomed them inside while she rounded up her "rugrats" for a bath. At the time, Steve Shedd was the skipper of the USS *Milius*. It wasn't unusual for NCIS to pay him a visit if a sailor under his command got into trouble. Lauren saw no reason for concern.

When Shedd arrived, he ushered the agents to the patio and asked how he could help.

"So, who are we investigating?" he said, unaware that the agents were secretly recording him.

"Well, this is the tough part," Curry replied. "We are actually here to talk to you."

When the agent informed Shedd he was a suspect in a fraud investigation involving Glenn Defense, the officer was gripped by "total shock" and "absolute panic," as he later described it. He knew he had betrayed his country when he first leaked classified ship schedules to Francis, but he never dreamed he would get caught—there were too many senior officers involved in the bribery ring.

Curry asked how well he knew Francis and whether he had done anything—legal or illegal—to benefit Glenn Defense. Desperate and with no inkling of how much his interrogators knew, Shedd lied and then lied some more.

"I would like to just state—and I will say this officially and under oath—that I accepted no money or gifts at all," he declared.

In fact, he had accepted $105,000 worth of bribes from Francis over the years and had barely finished digesting their $3,100 meal from Nobu. But the destroyer captain had no intention of taking responsibility. "It's 100 percent true. I'm not sure what other evidence you have or whatnot, but I'll just leave it at that."

As soon as the words left his mouth, however, Curry showed him a printout of a damning email indicating, in detail, that Francis had paid $30,000 for the Shedd family to take a weeklong vacation in Singapore and Malaysia five years earlier.

Shedd read the email and knew he had screwed himself. "Yeah, I'm not going to comment now," he said.

"Oh, that's all on that one?" Curry replied sarcastically.

After a few more questions, Curry told him that Francis had been arrested.

The news floored Shedd. He gave up and said he wanted a lawyer. "Am I going away in handcuffs tonight?" he asked.

The agents told him no, there was no warrant yet for his arrest. But the extent of his involvement was so obvious that Curry counseled him not to do anything rash.

"I just have to make sure that you are okay mentally right now. I mean I know it's kind of a blow and this is a really tough place to do it, at the house," Curry said.

"I am good," Shedd responded unconvincingly. He knew the handcuffs would come.

The other wedding planner reacted differently.

At 8:05 p.m., two agents rapped on the door of a three-bedroom condominium in Carmel Mountain Ranch, a suburb in northeastern San Diego.

A child answered. "Hello, is your daddy home?" asked DCIS Special Agent James McWhirter.

Ed Aruffo thrust his lanky six-foot-five-inch frame into the doorway and trained a gimlet eye on the agents. He sensed danger.

McWhirter introduced himself and his partner, Shannon Rachal of NCIS, and got right to the point. They were investigating Glenn Defense and wanted to talk to Aruffo about his stint on the Seventh Fleet staff and the three years he spent as Glenn Defense's country manager for Japan. "I'll be straight up with you. Leonard Francis right now is currently in our custody."

Aruffo laughed nervously. Francis hadn't returned his texts or phone calls since they ate at Nobu. Now he knew why.

McWhirter told him this was his opportunity to confess and cut a deal before others pinned the blame on him. "You know Leonard," he said. "He'll sell his kids probably to get out of jail. . . . Leonard is going to be saying, you know, 'Ed did that on his own. He was my rogue employee.'"

Aruffo had a love-hate relationship with Francis but figured the agent was right. He made a snap decision to forgo a lawyer and cooperate. "In no uncertain terms, my highest priority is my children and my wife," he said. "I am willing to help."

He didn't want his wife or their two kids to overhear him confessing, so he drove with the agents to Marie Callender's, a nearby chain restaurant known for its comfort food. They sat in a quiet corner booth and ordered water, iced tea, and Diet Coke.

Aruffo claimed he was terrified of Francis and feared retaliation for "running my mouth." Twice, the Italian American from South Philly referred to Francis as "the Godfather."

McWhirter reminded him that Francis was behind bars. "Even Vito Corleone in the movie, they all go down." The agent had a hard time believing the overweight Malaysian could really inspire such nightmares. He asked Aruffo why he spent three hours sitting next to Francis at Nobu if he was so scared.

Aruffo explained he was just trying to stay on Francis's good side. "Leonard wanted friends. He wanted people to respect him. He wanted people to love him. He wanted people to tell him how generous he is.

But most important, he wanted people just around. And that's how you make friends, that's how you succeed with Leonard Francis."

By the time the waiter returned with their beverages, Aruffo had made up his mind to snitch in full. He described Glenn Defense as rotten to the core, a criminal enterprise built on deception and corruption.

"Fraudulent billings may be a nice way of saying it," he said. "It was so comical that he didn't even try and run a business. It was a cash grab."

McWhirter had interviewed many slippery criminals in his career. He knew Aruffo was trying to shift as much blame to Francis as possible.

"This is kind of a dumb question, but I've got to ask it," the agent said. "I mean, you knew that these things you were doing were illegal?"

"I knew they were wrong. I knew they were absolutely wrong," Aruffo admitted. "I can't tell you how many times I have woke up at four o'clock in the morning and thought that someone was going to be knocking on my door and put my kids on the floor."

He turned on his former mentor with a vengeance, describing him as a "master manipulator" with a monstrous ego. "I'll admit that I wanted to please him," he said, but added: "I'd be lying if I told you that I don't have at least a little bit of hostility for that son of a bitch you guys picked up and put in jail."

Once Aruffo started to snitch, he was hard to stop. He stayed with the agents at Marie Callender's long past closing time. The restaurant had run out of iced tea and the waiter had already clocked out when the manager told them to leave at 10:47 p.m.

Earlier that evening, the U.S. Attorney's Office in San Diego had issued its press release announcing that Francis, Misiewicz, and Beliveau had been arrested in a sex-for-secrets scandal. The news was overshadowed nationally by the Washington Navy Yard massacre, but the Associated Press posted a short item on its newswire and *The San Diego Union-Tribune* published a front-page story the next day. In the Navy, word spread quickly. People who had reason to feel nervous hurried to hide evidence of their involvement with Francis.

In the Philippines, Commander Troy Amundson, the recently retired former Navy Ball chairman, deleted emails from his Yahoo account. In Japan, Daniel Dusek, the former Seventh Fleet operations officer who had since been promoted to captain and become skipper of the USS *Bonhomme Richard*, likewise zapped emails that tied him to Glenn Defense. Within days, both would receive visits from federal agents.

In San Diego, Captain David Haas, the mole who had left the Seventh Fleet staff two months earlier, almost had a nervous breakdown. He had a new job as the deputy commander of a coastal protection unit and shipmates reported that the chiseled triathlete suddenly looked "panicky," "ragged," and "sleep deprived."

Haas barged into his boss's office to ask whether he had seen the news stories about Francis's arrest and declared, unprompted, "I'm no saint." Without specifying what he had done, he asked whether he could take a few days off, because he was worried NCIS would appear on his doorstep and take him to jail.

"I don't want to put my family through this," Haas said, according to his boss. "All I want to do is retire with benefits." He confided that he had reached out to a chaplain and a marriage counselor. His wife wanted him to get a blood test, for reasons left unsaid.

His shipmates worried that Haas, normally a "ball of energy," might try to kill himself. A senior enlisted sailor took him aside to ask whether he was okay.

Haas muttered about things that had gone on "under his nose" on the Seventh Fleet staff. "I am not without sin," he confessed.

Part Six
2013–2014

Spilling Some Beans

October 2013

SAN DIEGO, CALIFORNIA

After stewing in jail for two weeks, Leonard Francis was fed up and miserable. He complained that the guards at the Metropolitan Correctional Center in downtown San Diego treated him like an "animal," strip-searching him and tossing him in a cell with a junkie who couldn't stop vomiting. Unable to post bail because the government argued he was a flight risk, Francis saw his detention as a gross overreaction to the billing disputes between Glenn Defense and the Navy. He insisted to anyone who would listen that he was the owner of a highly successful company that protected American sailors and Marines, not a violent criminal. "This was just a financial matter. It was not hurting anybody," he said. "There was no blood spilled."

His attorneys took his plight more seriously, warning he could spend up to fifty years in prison. They badgered him "to spill the beans on the Navy," as he put it, and negotiate a plea deal. At first, he couldn't stomach the idea of pleading guilty. But he agreed to hold exploratory discussions with prosecutors and give them a taste of what he knew. The Justice Department didn't realize it yet, but he had enough beans to bury hundreds of Navy officers.

Francis had assembled a high-priced defense team: three attorneys from Holland & Knight, a multinational law firm that represented Glenn Defense in federal contracting cases, and Edward Patrick Swan Jr. a veteran San Diego trial lawyer who specialized in white-collar crime. They advised Francis to sign a proffer agreement, a contract to provide the Justice Department with information and evidence against other suspects. Informally known as a "Queen for a Day" letter, a proffer entitled a defendant to an hours-long respite from jail to meet with prosecutors and a promise not to use his statements against him. If his information proved reliable and worthy, it might lead to a favorable plea deal. Francis agreed.

On the morning of October 1, 2013, a Tuesday, U.S. Marshals fetched Francis from the jail, transporting him around the block to the federal building on Front Street for a meeting at the U.S. Attorney's Office. His four lawyers greeted him in a conference room as they all took seats at a long table.

On the other side was a team led by Mark Pletcher, an assistant U.S. attorney who had made his name prosecuting contract-fraud cases from the war in Iraq. The thirty-eight-year-old Pletcher could be imperious, prompting Francis to mock him as "Caesar" behind his back. He and two other prosecutors were joined by three investigators: James McWhirter, the DCIS agent who had half-jokingly predicted Francis would sell his kids to get out of jail; Trey DeLaPena, the youthful DCIS agent who had been pursuing leads in Thailand; and Mari Nash, an NCIS supervisory special agent from San Diego.

The prosecution team stared at the prisoner, unsure what to expect. The scope of the investigation had ballooned in recent months, but investigators still didn't know the extent of the Navy's entanglement in graft and depravity. In April, after Google released Francis's email cache, agents had drawn up a list of thirty persons of interest. In June, they'd added ten more names after analyzing messages from Francis's Facebook account. Since Francis's arrest in September, the list had gone through another growth spurt. It now exceeded one hundred names as agents pored over the emails, texts, and other data from the seized phones and laptops. The case resembled a constantly expanding puzzle, with millions of pieces. Investigators sorely needed someone to help them put it together.

Further complicating matters, the prosecutors were starting to realize their case could paralyze the Navy's chain of command. Witnesses reported that Francis had more admiral friends than anyone could count. In response to questioning, a defense attaché based in Asia predicted that Francis's allies in the Pentagon might try to squelch the investigation and that "it might get ugly" as agents discovered how many senior officers he knew.

The prosecution team opened the proffer session by broaching another raw subject: Francis's infiltration of NCIS. The agency was still reeling from John Beliveau's defection and struggling to understand how and why it happened—not to mention how he'd managed to keep his treachery undetected for so long. Francis smugly explained: He had diagnosed Beliveau as a lonely bachelor starved for sex, money, and attention. Then he appealed to Beliveau's vanity by seeking his advice on how Glenn Defense should respond to investigative queries from NCIS, an approach that made Beliveau feel like a "consultant" instead of a traitor. Soon, he was hooked.

Prosecutors wanted to know whether Francis had more moles in law enforcement and floated the names of three other federal agents based in Asia. Francis acknowledged meeting them for drinks or meals but said none had crossed the line like Beliveau.

Francis also told the backstories of his relationships with several officers atop the suspect list, including Mike Misiewicz, Ed Aruffo, Jose Sanchez, Jeff Breslau, and Dan Dusek. A born raconteur, Francis infused his narratives with juicy personal tidbits, including gossip about Dusek's extramarital affairs, Sanchez's "bar girls," and the spending habits of Misiewicz's wife. He characterized Misiewicz as a prized yet exasperating mole, a "loose cannon" whom he nicknamed "Mike Misfits" because of his undisciplined behavior.

As the proffer continued, Francis stunned the prosecution team with matter-of-fact accounts of how he had corrupted the Navy's contracting command in Singapore. He alleged that he had given $450,000 in bribes to Paul Simpkins, the contracting supervisor, to rig contracts for Glenn Defense. He regaled agents with his story of how he slipped a thick wad of cash to Sharon Kaur in the aisle of a Toys "R" Us. In an almost casual aside, he said he often spent tens of thousands of dollars on dinner parties to entertain officers—and had done so for a decade.

Francis felt flattered by the attention and the questions. But for now, he kept his most damning secrets in reserve. "I was just trying to give them some names for them to test out, to see where I was going to get with them," he recalled later. "I opened a Pandora's box."

For most defendants, proffer sessions last a few hours. Francis's initial debriefing took two full days. He could tell he had his adversaries right where he wanted them—eating out of his hand.

Francis's instincts were correct: The prosecution team wanted to hear more. Two weeks later, the U.S. Attorney's Office requested a follow-up session. On October 17, U.S. Marshals retrieved Francis from jail and escorted him to the federal building, where he delivered an encore performance lasting two days.

This time, he played to an audience of eleven, with five lawyers on his side and six attorneys and agents representing the government. For his opening monologue, he revealed how he had infiltrated the Seventh Fleet staff in 2006. He recounted how that fraternity of moles called themselves the "Band of Brothers," and he admitted to bribing them with fine wine, decadent dinners, swanky hotel stays, and "hostesses," as he euphemistically dubbed the prostitutes. He giggled when he said he organized so many sex parties that the USS *Blue Ridge* became known as "the Love Boat."

The prosecutors and agents had never heard a proffer like this. They had no idea the Seventh Fleet had been corrupted for so long.

They tried to conceal their horror as Francis bragged that Navy officers had leaked him classified information nonstop for seven years and that he—a convicted felon from Malaysia—had the power to reroute U.S. warships to ports of his choosing. They asked whether anyone ever rejected his "gifts." Rarely, he said.

To dispel any skepticism, Francis's attorneys brought documentation to back up a sampling of his claims, including $60,000 worth of invoices for Captain Jeff Breslau's ghostwriting services. The defense lawyers knew Glenn Defense's business records could be a huge bargaining chip in plea negotiations and indicated that Francis had a stockpile of other receipts that investigators would find invaluable.

Francis really captured the prosecutors' attention, however, when he started to sing about his friendships with admirals, describing how he spent years courting ambitious junior officers in hopes that they would rise to positions of power. He said an admiral's overt or implicit support for Glenn Defense was as "good as gold" and emphasized the value of Bravo Zulu letters as official endorsements.

Privately, Francis harbored hopes that some admirals might intercede on his behalf and persuade the Justice Department to drop charges against him, on national security grounds. So for the time being, he kept mum about most of his friends in high places. But to whet prosecutors' appetites, he spilled the names of eleven admirals, six of whom had not previously appeared on investigators' radar.

One name jumped out: Vice Admiral Ted Branch, the former commanding officer of the USS *Nimitz* aircraft carrier. Francis said he'd met Branch in 2005 and supplied him with cigars, wine, meals, a *Nimitz* ship model that cost about $1,000, and a "hostess."

The allegations unnerved the prosecution team. While Branch's purported sins were mild compared with those of some officers, he had been promoted three months earlier to Director of Naval Intelligence. If there was credible evidence that he had accepted bribes or prostitutes, he could easily be blackmailed—a nightmare scenario for U.S. counterintelligence officials.

Worse, Francis also claimed he'd supplied prostitutes to another intelligence officer: Bruce Loveless, the former captain on the Seventh Fleet staff. Like Branch, Loveless had been promoted three months earlier and was now a one-star admiral serving as a director of intelligence operations at the Pentagon.

Francis vividly described the nights he spent partying with Loveless, including the time the intelligence officer gave his business card to a prostitute. He mentioned Loveless's predilection for Mongolian women. The stories sounded crazy, but the agents had already seen Loveless's name in Francis's Facebook messages. They had no choice but to take the allegations seriously. Loveless, along with Branch, became an investigative priority.

By the time the second proffer session ended, agents had added seventy more names to their list of suspects. They were beginning to understand just how damaging the fallout from Francis's arrest could prove for the Navy. The case was growing so rapidly that NCIS and DCIS brought in reinforcements to work it full time.

Thinking that his information had earned him some goodwill from prosecutors, Francis pushed his lawyers to win his release on bond. He badly wanted to get out of jail to cope with crushing pressures at work and home. The Navy had terminated its contracts with Glenn Defense after his arrest, forcing the company to lay off hundreds of employees. With his revenue streams drying up, Francis had to liquidate personal assets, including his fleet of Rolls-Royces. Meanwhile, his mother and children had vacated the family's two rented mansions in Singapore for more-affordable quarters in Kuala Lumpur.

The defense team knew it would be difficult to persuade a judge to set bail. As a wealthy foreign citizen facing a potentially stiff prison sentence, Francis had the means—and incentive—to skip town. To alleviate concerns, his attorneys dreamed up a novel proposal to prevent him from escaping.

Under the plan, Francis would be released to home detention and forced to wear a GPS-equipped ankle bracelet to monitor his whereabouts—a common practice for defendants awaiting trial. But he also would be required to live in an upper-story apartment in downtown San Diego, with cameras and alarms installed on all exterior doors and windows. The court's Pretrial Services division would monitor the cameras and GPS tracker remotely, plus a guard would remain on the premises around the clock. Francis agreed to pay for all the security and housing expenses, plus $1.1 million in bail.

During a bond hearing in November, lead defense attorney Pat Swan argued that the combination of Francis's girth and notoriety—his case had generated waves of publicity in San Diego, Washington, and Singapore—made an escape unfeasible.

"His ability to flee and avoid detection and arrest is relatively minimal, if not nil," Swan said, pointing out that his client was "a large man" and that his "Fat Leonard" nickname had transformed him into an international celebrity. "He is almost bigger than life in certain respects," the lawyer added. "Since his arrest, his photo has been shown worldwide, making him a very recognizable public figure. . . . If he were to flee, frankly, there would be no place he could hide."

Prosecutors opposed bail, arguing that Francis posed too much of a flight risk, especially with the Mexican border just fifteen miles away. But they were overruled by Magistrate Judge Jan Adler. He approved the home detention plan and told Francis he could leave the apartment for pre-authorized appointments but had to remain in San Diego County.

"Mr. Francis, I want to make it very clear," the judge said. "You must not enter Mexico. You must not leave this county."

"Yes, your honor," Francis promised.

Francis's delight in his victory was short-lived. Before he could be freed, prosecutors asked for a stay so the trial judge assigned to Francis's case—U.S. District Judge Janis Sammartino—could review the unorthodox terms of his release.

Four days later in Sammartino's courtroom, Assistant U.S. Attorney Robert Huie argued vehemently that Francis needed to remain behind bars. He emphasized the pains the federal government had taken to trick Francis into visiting the United States and said authorities were "gravely concerned" that he would vanish if given the opportunity. "He will flee and he will not come back. He will not fall for a trick like that again, and all those efforts by law enforcement to investigate him and to get him here will have been in vain."

Ridiculing the home detention plan as "a do-it-yourself, self-designed jail," Huie predicted Francis would cut off his GPS transmitter in the middle of the night while no one at Pretrial Services was paying attention, bribe the guard to look the other way, hail a taxi, and run for the border. He estimated that it would take Francis fifteen minutes to reach Tijuana, Mexico, and that he'd be in the wind before U.S. Marshals could discover his absence.

"Even if all the technology works perfectly . . . there's still a very low probability that he would be physically caught," Huie said. "Once he makes it to Mexico, he has the means to pay for travel. He has the means to purchase travel documents and he can get to wherever in the world he wants to. . . . He can shop for a country that has no extradition treaty, like Russia."

This time, the judge sided with the prosecution. Sammartino had been assigned all the trials involving the Navy and Glenn Defense, and she didn't want to give the lead defendant a chance to disappear. Even with the extra layers of security, she said Francis's home confinement plan "provides no assurance against flight occurring" and no "real accountability."

With that, Sammartino gaveled the hearing to a close. The U.S. Marshals took Francis back to the Metropolitan Correctional Center in handcuffs and leg irons. He had remained silent during the proceedings, but inside he seethed. His lawyers had raised his hopes that he would be released. He had heeded their advice and cooperated with the U.S. Attorney's Office. Now he was stuck in jail indefinitely. He felt betrayed.

In that moment, he resolved to stop spilling the beans and call off his cooperation agreement. "I just got so mad," he recalled. "I basically said, 'Screw this.'" Without his help, he knew, investigators had no chance of finding all the Navy officers he had bribed. He wouldn't allow the U.S. government to treat him like this.

He would show all of them—the prosecutors, the agents, his lawyers, and the judge—that he was the Boss.

Chapter Twenty-eight

Twig

November 2013

JOINT BASE ANDREWS, MARYLAND

Few Navy officers could claim a more sterling, or colorful, career than that of Vice Admiral Ted Branch. The son of a fabled college football player from the Gulf Coast, Branch was raised outside New Orleans in small towns like Bogalusa, Louisiana, and Long Beach, Mississippi, before winning admission to the Naval Academy in 1975. Despite the school's punishing academic workload, he demonstrated a knack for maximizing its limited social opportunities. "Growing up 58 minutes away from Bourbon Street has got to have its effect on a person and Ted was no exception to the rule," observed *The Lucky Bag*, the Academy yearbook. "By the time he was 14, he knew what to order when he went to the bar—'J.D. on the rocks, please.'"

After graduation, Branch returned to the Gulf Coast to attend flight school in Pensacola, Florida. In a tongue-in-cheek military ritual, squadrons assigned junior pilots a call sign, or nickname, for radio identification purposes and to build esprit de corps among the swaggering brotherhood of aviators. Given Branch's slight, scrawny frame—he stood maybe five-foot-five with blow-dried hair—his squadron christened him "Twig."

Branch winced when he learned his call sign and pleaded with the squadron's commanding officer to reconsider. He explained that his father, Frank, already had been immortalized as "Twig" Branch decades earlier when he starred at quarterback for Mississippi State University despite weighing only 125 pounds.

The squadron commander looked down at the young officer. *You really don't like the name, huh?*

No sir, Branch said.

Good, the commander replied. *Then it's settled. Twig it is.*

Truth was, the call sign fit Branch to a T. With his squeaky twang, he sounded like another bantamweight Naval Academy alumnus— Texas billionaire H. Ross Perot—and told stories with the same homespun flair. "It's like Sunday in Mississippi," he told shipmates while training at sea. "You get up, go to church, eat some chicken, and shoot some guns. So enjoy it."

He thrived aboard a succession of aircraft carriers and flew A-7 Corsairs and F/A-18 Hornets in combat over Grenada, Lebanon, Bosnia-Herzegovina, and Iraq. Years later, as commanding officer of the USS *Nimitz*, he starred in *Carrier*, a ten-part PBS documentary about life aboard a nuclear-powered flattop that aired to acclaim in 2008. Subsequently, as commanding officer of the USS *Carl Vinson* carrier strike group, he led the Navy's humanitarian relief mission to Haiti in 2010 when an earthquake killed more than 200,000 people.

By the time he was promoted to Director of Naval Intelligence in July 2013, Pentagon insiders believed he stood a good chance of becoming a four-star admiral. Of the 324,000 active-duty sailors in the Navy at the time, only nine held that exalted rank.

But Branch's charmed career ran into turbulence. In November 2013, he received a request from the Justice Department to discuss the investigation of Commander Mike Misiewicz, the officer charged with leaking classified material to Leonard Francis. Prosecutors said that they wanted to gauge the seriousness of the leaks and hoped Branch, as chief guardian of the Navy's secrets, could help them understand the national security implications.

Branch had never met Misiewicz and wasn't eager to speak with prosecutors. But given his job he had little choice. On Tuesday, November 5, he arrived at the designated meeting place: a conference room at Joint Base Andrews, the suburban Maryland airfield that houses Air Force One and other aircraft for federal VIPs.

Admiral Branch was greeted by Mark Pletcher, the assistant U.S. attorney who had traveled cross-country from San Diego to direct the interview; Brian Young, a Justice Department trial lawyer; and NCIS Special Agent Eric Maddox. Pletcher thanked Branch for coming and innocuously explained that they were "talking to a number of people" about the Misiewicz leaks.

What he didn't say was that Francis, in his bid to strike a deal with prosecutors, had snitched on Branch, saying that he had accepted gifts and prostitutes. The real purpose of the meeting was to determine whether the head of Navy intelligence had committed a crime or was vulnerable to blackmail. Pletcher also didn't mention that Maddox worked on counterintelligence for NCIS and that the agent was covertly recording the interview.

At the outset, Pletcher asked the admiral to sign a boilerplate form waiving his rights to remain silent and have an attorney present, implying that the document was just a formality. Branch signed, but he saw through the facade and realized he was a suspect.

He volunteered that he'd met Francis in 2000 when he was executive officer of the USS *John C. Stennis* and saw him again five years later when he was the skipper of the *Nimitz*. That prompted more uncomfortable questions from the prosecutors.

Did he ever attend social events with Francis?

Yes, Branch said. The Glenn Defense owner would host dinners "from time to time" for the ship's senior staff, usually at a restaurant or hotel.

Did the officers chip in money for dinner? No, Branch said, not in his experience. He didn't know how much the meals cost.

Did Francis hand out gifts or party favors? Yes, Branch said. He once received a fancy pewter letter opener. "It's like a Malaysian sword. It's a curvy, saber-looking thing." And yes, Francis gave wine and cigars as presents. "He was very generous."

Prosecutors then zeroed in on Francis's after-parties. "Have you been present when hostesses or girls have either been brought in, or have sort of arrived on the scene?" Pletcher asked.

"I mean, there were hostesses, perhaps," Branch answered obliquely. "I don't have any idea if it was arranged."

Pletcher danced around the sensitive subject, trying to muster the nerve to ask the admiral directly whether he had ever had sex with a prostitute courtesy of Fat Leonard.

"The circumstance that I had in mind is that after dinner, my understanding is that you had sort of adjourned to the hotel," the prosecutor stammered. He asked whether Francis and another officer "brought girls back to the hotel, the two of them, and uh, and sort of met you—met you there."

"No," Branch said.

Pletcher tried a few more times, asking whether Branch had been provided with hostesses on other occasions. "I'm just asking the questions as they come up in the investigation," he said, half-apologetically.

"I told you that I didn't have a hostess provided to me," Branch snapped. "Does that answer the question?"

Pletcher said he had "an obligation" to pose the questions, based on information he had received "from other sources." He asked if Branch wanted to stop the interview or speak with an attorney.

"OK," Branch said. "I think we need to stop." He stood up and left.

The prosecutors didn't land the confession they were hoping for. But Branch had admitted enough to warrant getting fired. Investigators had confirmed that the Director of Naval Intelligence accepted dinners and gifts from Leonard Francis, a foreigner with a history of bribing U.S. personnel for military secrets. Plus, Branch had acknowledged that "hostesses" may have been present at those dinners.

The revelations about Branch's involvement with Francis weren't the most embarrassing moment for the Office of Naval Intelligence that day. Four hours earlier, in the same conference room, Pletcher and his team had interviewed Rear Admiral Bruce Loveless, the former Seventh Fleet intelligence officer working under Branch at the Pentagon. Maddox, the NCIS agent, recorded the conversation with a device hidden in the pocket of his suit jacket.

Loveless tied himself into knots with his evasive answers. Waiving his right to remain silent, he spoke smoothly at first about classification procedures and his assessment of the damage caused by Misiewicz's leaks and Francis's bribes. ("I guess I'd say I'm not too concerned.")

Halfway through the interview, Pletcher shifted gears and asked the admiral whether he had met Francis. Loveless acknowledged he had but downplayed the extent of their relationship. He claimed that he paid his share of the tab whenever he dined with Francis and denied seeing him provide "hostesses" or "girls" to anyone.

Pletcher accused Loveless of lying and said he had a receipt proving that Francis had spent $8,100 in March 2012 to treat him and nine others to dinner at a Nobu restaurant in Honolulu. (Loveless acknowledged being there with his wife and said the couple reimbursed Francis $200.) The prosecutors kept hammering, asking whether he had accepted "anything" else from Francis, including hostesses. Loveless insisted he had not.

But the admiral cracked when Pletcher confronted him about his reputed fondness for Mongolian prostitutes.

"The sources that we have talked to have described very specifically that after dinner in one of the locations, that two Mongolian girls were provided, and that one of the Mongolian girls actually became— my understanding is, in a real close relationship to you, and in fact you gave her a business card," Pletcher said. "This is the relationship that we're concerned about."

"I—I do remember a business card," Loveless sputtered. "I did not have a close relationship, significant or not significant, to remember."

"This is the hostess who was provided by Leonard Francis," Pletcher pressed.

"I—I'm not sure of that part of it," Loveless said. "I'm just aware of—of a woman."

He acknowledged socializing with the Mongolian woman over drinks at a hotel but denied having a romantic or sexual relationship. He said he'd shared his business card to show "this is who I am, this is what I do."

Asked whether he had patronized prostitutes supplied by Francis on other occasions, he again said no. "Yeah, let's be clear," he insisted. "I did not accept that—that—whatever that—that service is."

The prosecutors told Loveless they didn't believe him. "I'm just going to be honest with you," said Young, the Justice Department attorney. "I'm still going to leave this interview with concerns about the Mongolian girl and that aspect. So if there's anything else you can tell us . . . now would be the time to do it."

"No," Loveless said. "No additional comment."

For the Navy, the Glenn Defense investigation was becoming a counterintelligence horror show. The next morning, November 6, federal agents returned to Tampa to arrest Commander Jose Sanchez on charges that he had leaked classified information and other material to Francis for prostitutes, luxury travel, and $100,000 in cash.

Investigators were desperately trying to measure the volume of the classified material leaked to Francis and whether any of it had landed in the hands of U.S. adversaries. During his interviews with prosecutors and agents, Francis said he never knowingly divulged U.S. ship schedules to a foreign power. But he said he couldn't rule out that foreign spooks might have hacked Glenn Defense's computers or gleaned his stash of secrets by other means. For example, he acknowledged that his IT manager had access to the classified information and was friendly with Chinese diplomats in Singapore, including the defense attaché, with whom he golfed regularly.

Around the time of Sanchez's arrest, the Justice Department confidentially informed aides to Navy Secretary Ray Mabus that two senior intelligence officials—Branch and Loveless—were under criminal investigation and had failed to clear themselves of suspicion during interviews. Mabus was astonished. While admirals sometimes got in trouble for personal misconduct or professional incompetence, the Navy handled those cases administratively. It was almost inconceivable that the Justice Department might prosecute officers of such senior rank. No active-duty admiral had ever been convicted of a federal crime.

When Mabus heard the story about Loveless giving his business card to the Mongolian prostitute, he couldn't believe an intelligence officer could be so stupid. But he was stunned that Branch was under suspicion at all. As a former governor of Mississippi, Mabus had been acquainted with Branch's father, or "Big Twig," as he called him. As Navy secretary, he had been impressed by Little Twig's leadership during the Haiti earthquake relief operation.

The Justice Department divulged few other details to Mabus's aides but left him with the impression that indictments were imminent and that the case against Branch was one of the strongest that prosecutors from the U.S. Attorney's Office in San Diego had ever seen. Mabus's general counsel and chief of staff advised him to suspend both admirals' access to classified material immediately instead of waiting for the legal process to play out. Mabus agreed.

The Navy announced the suspensions at 7:21 p.m. on a Friday night, three days after the interviews at Joint Base Andrews. A sparsely worded press release stated that the Navy had placed Branch and Loveless on temporary leave on suspicion of "illegal and improper relations with Leonard Francis," citing "the sensitive nature of their current duties."

The announcement kicked news coverage of the Glenn Defense investigation into hyperdrive, with the *Washington Post* and *New York Times* publishing banner headlines about the admirals' suspensions. Sensing the scandal was worse than officials were letting on, reporters intensified their digging. Navy officials deflected queries, saying they couldn't release more information, because it might interfere with the investigation.

Several weeks passed, with no indictments. The investigation had hit a wall after Francis, furious over his bail denial, ceased cooperating. Meanwhile, the Justice Department kept Navy leaders in the dark, leaving Mabus exasperated. He agonized over what to do with Branch. He couldn't restore the admiral's access to military secrets with the investigation still under way, yet he felt it would be unfair to relieve Branch of command until he knew more details about what he had allegedly done.

Meanwhile, Mabus was under pressure from the uniformed brass to stand up for them and for the Navy as an institution. Many admirals had bitter memories of the Tailhook scandal from the early 1990s and felt prosecutors and the news media—especially *The Washington Post*—were after them again.

The Navy's reputation was at stake, but so was Mabus's. He launched his political career in Mississippi in 1983 as an anticorruption crusader, running for election as state auditor. When he won in an upset, he told staffers at his new agency that their days of pocketing gifts and accepting political favors were over. "If I find out that you so much as take a tomato from somebody's garden, I will fire you," he recalled warning them. Now, thirty years later, a major scandal involving Navy officers was brewing under his watch. Would he hold them accountable or try to whitewash the Navy's image?

On December 20, Mabus held a news conference in the Pentagon briefing room. It was the first time any Navy official had fielded questions on camera about the corruption investigation since Francis's arrest three months earlier. Mabus looked miserable, puffy-faced and raspy-voiced from a cold. He promised to crack down on contracting fraud and to appoint a four-star admiral with the authority to court-martial or impose discipline on anyone involved in the Glenn Defense case whom the Justice Department declined to prosecute.

He hinted that more arrests were likely and promised that the Navy would be transparent, especially about its handling of misconduct allegations against high-ranking officers. "It's the right thing to do," he said. "I would rather get bad headlines than let bad people get away."

Mabus's pledge to be transparent didn't last long. Neither he nor anyone in the Navy would hold another news conference about the epic sex-for-secrets scandal.

With Francis refusing to cooperate, the federal investigation of Branch slowed. But gradually, over many months, agents pieced together a clearer picture of their relationship.

Investigators confirmed that Branch attended dinners with Francis on four occasions, including a $14,700 meal that Glenn Defense hosted for *Nimitz* officers at the Petrus restaurant in Hong Kong in June 2005. In turn, Branch hosted Francis for lunch aboard the aircraft carrier and wrote a Bravo Zulu note, praising Glenn Defense for its "outstanding" and "over the top customer service" in Hong Kong.*

---

* In addition, Branch attended a lobster Thermidor dinner at the Chalet in Kuala Lumpur in February 2000 that Francis hosted for officers from the USS *John C. Stennis* carrier strike group and another dinner in Kuala Lumpur in July 2005 that was sponsored by the Royal Malaysian Navy but secretly financed by Francis. Branch also dined with Francis and other Navy officers at a Thai restaurant in Coronado, California, in April 2007, though the officers paid for their shares of that meal.

At the *Nimitz's* stop in Kuala Lumpur one month later, Branch approved Francis's recommendation to protect the ship with the Ring of Steel. The decision generated a windfall for Glenn Defense, which charged a hefty $400,000 for use of the contraption during the five-day port visit. One *Nimitz* officer told federal agents that he suspected Francis had concocted a security threat to justify its necessity.

Agents could not corroborate Francis's claim that he had provided Branch with prostitutes on three occasions. But they found plenty of smoke swirling around his allegations. Several Navy witnesses reported seeing the *Nimitz* skipper in the company of women who they suspected might have been sex workers. Three *Nimitz* officers who attended the Petrus dinner in Hong Kong said they joined Francis and Branch at an after-party where women appeared. One officer said he presumed the women were prostitutes hired by Francis, though no one observed Branch doing anything improper with them.

In a separate encounter that had nothing to do with Francis, an enlisted sailor on the *Nimitz* reported that he had witnessed Branch partying with "Russian girls" at a cabaret in the Persian Gulf port of Manama, Bahrain, in August 2005. The American sailor, who spoke Russian, told federal agents that the cabaret employed the women as dancers and surmised that they may have worked as prostitutes on the side. When the women learned that Branch was the commanding officer of an American warship, the sailor said, they treated the captain like a celebrity.

Coincidentally, around seven o'clock the next morning, that same enlisted sailor was on duty on the fantail of the *Nimitz* when he saw Branch coming aboard with several "very attractive" performers from the Russian cabaret in tow. According to the sailor, Branch was visibly struck by an "oh shit" moment when he realized his subordinate had seen him in the club with the women the night before. But the captain didn't say anything and proceeded to give the women a tour of the ship. (Branch's attorney later acknowledged that he visited a nightclub in Bahrain and invited a "band comprised of five or six men and women" to tour the *Nimitz* but said "there was no inappropriate activity involved.")

While Branch's interactions with women raised suspicions, the eyewitness accounts were hardly enough to find him guilty of a crime. But from a counterintelligence perspective, they were still alarming—credible allegations that the Director of Naval Intelligence had partied with Russian-speaking and Chinese-speaking foreigners who may have been prostitutes. The risk of blackmail was obvious.

The Branch investigation dragged on for more than three years. Inexplicably, he remained in charge of Navy intelligence even though he was barred from reading or hearing military secrets. (He was permitted to perform managerial duties while his civilian and military deputies handled the classified aspect of his job.)*

The Justice Department finally closed the Branch case in 2017 without taking action. The Navy then conducted a disciplinary review and concluded that Branch had violated ethics rules by accepting the Hong Kong dinner and assorted minor gifts from Francis. Branch received a letter from the Navy reminding him of the regulations and advising him not to do it again, but otherwise he went unpunished.

By then, none of it mattered—Branch had retired from the Navy in October 2016, with an honorable discharge and his pension and rank intact. Pledges of transparency notwithstanding, Navy officials announced only that they had taken "appropriate administrative action" in the admiral's case and kept the details under wraps.

---

* Key lawmakers expressed incredulity when *The Washington Post* reported in January 2016 that the Navy had quietly allowed Branch to remain as director of intelligence for years even though he was forbidden from knowing any military secrets. "Common sense tells me that the decision to leave a senior admiral, who was stripped of his clearances, in charge [of] Naval Intelligence operations in the midst of the global war on terror needs top-level scrutiny now," Senator Charles Grassley, a Republican from Iowa, wrote in a letter to the Pentagon. Still, the Navy allowed Branch to stay in his post until he retired.

Chapter Twenty-nine

Crazy Bob

November 2013

KABUL, AFGHANISTAN

By 2013, Rear Admiral Robert Gilbeau had moved on from his stints as a supply officer in the Pacific and was leading a joint military logistics unit in Kabul, overseeing defense contractors in the war zone. But in the weeks since Leonard Francis's arrest he had grown paranoid, hoarding junk in his office, staring blankly into space, and mumbling incoherently about women and dinners in Singapore. He looked like a wreck and stayed up all night at his military compound binge-watching episodes of *Californication*, a show about a brooding novelist addicted to sex and booze.

Aides to the fifty-two-year-old admiral didn't know what to do. They had never seen a senior officer go to pieces like this. One day Gilbeau whispered conspiratorially to his chief of staff, Navy Captain Jack Moreau, professing to be an undercover operative for the CIA. "And I'm like, okay, you're in crazytown," Moreau recalled. "We're just living in some kind of weird fantasy world at that point."

On November 7, Moreau intervened. He entered Gilbeau's cluttered office, expressed concern for his well-being, and begged him to hand over his military-issued sidearm before anyone got hurt. Gilbeau stared back blankly. After a long pause he surrendered his pistol, but not before scaring the bejesus out of Moreau, who feared he might do something rash.

With the gun secured, Moreau and a few colleagues crowded into Gilbeau's office and urged him to get help. The admiral broke down sobbing. He said he couldn't sleep or see straight and conceded he might be a danger to himself. Medics flew him by helicopter from Kabul to the hospital at Bagram Air Base, where he told doctors that long-repressed memories from a deployment to Iraq six years earlier had resurfaced to torment him. The doctors diagnosed him with post-traumatic stress disorder, hooked him to an intravenous drip, and put him on the next flight to a U.S. military hospital in Germany.

Several of Gilbeau's subordinates, however, suspected he was faking the whole thing. He had a long-standing reputation as a manipulator who spun fanciful stories to avoid getting in trouble. He had received a Purple Heart medal for combat wounds suffered in Iraq in 2007 but was dogged by rumors that he had exaggerated or made up his injuries. In his retellings, the story changed constantly. Sometimes he said he had sustained a traumatic brain injury. Other times, it was shrapnel in his leg or in his lungs.

Gilbeau's staffers noted his mental health had seemed perfectly fine until news of Francis's arrest reached Kabul. And he had admitted to some of them that he was worried investigators would come after him, too. Pretending to be crazy so he could avoid being tarred by the bribery scandal was just the kind of nutty stunt they thought he might try to pull.

A native of Fremont, California, Gilbeau said he grew up in a family with "a strong moral compass." He became an Eagle Scout and won a senatorial nomination to attend the Naval Academy. After graduation, he joined the Navy's Supply Corps and served as logistician aboard the USS *Guadalcanal*, USS *Harry W. Hill*, and USS *Boxer* in the 1980s and 1990s.

He impressed his shipmates with his keen intellect but also became known for his irreverent hijinks and willingness to flout regulations. He traveled on the government's dime to questionable destinations, racked up dubious expenses, and partied a lot. Other officers nicknamed him "Gilbeau the Clown."

"Bob is just, he's always kind of living on the edge," recalled David Pimpo, a fellow officer in the Supply Corps. "He's always kind of out there and having a good time and I know sometimes I just scratch my head." Jim Maus, the retired captain who became a thorn in Francis's side, had mentored Gilbeau early in their careers. He thought Gilbeau was "brilliant" but craved unnecessary risks. "He loved pressure. He loved anxiety," Maus said. "It was his adrenaline rush. He was like a fly near a flame. It's what turned him on."

He made a perfect companion for Fat Leonard. They met in Bali in 1997, and Francis found him "wild" and entertaining. Even better, he said that Gilbeau was the kind of supply officer who "would sign anything" during a port visit if he received a share of the spoils.

After an earthquake devastated Southeast Asia in December 2004, Gilbeau deployed to Singapore to lead a disaster-relief team for several months. With his wife and three daughters living far away in California, he heartily accepted Francis's dinner invitations. According to Francis, they partied together with prostitutes at the Brix nightclub and the Tiananmen KTV karaoke bar. During that time, Gilbeau became enamored of a European woman living in Singapore. To enhance his allure, the pudgy-faced, middle-aged supply officer invented a cover story that he was an F/A-18 Hornet fighter pilot and persuaded Francis to lend him his green Jaguar for a romantic night out. The gambit worked and the woman fell for him.

After a while, according to Francis, Gilbeau tired of the relationship but didn't have the spine to end it himself. Instead, he had a Navy friend email the woman with the tragic news that her pilot boyfriend had been shot down over Iraq and captured as a prisoner of war. Francis thought the saga was hilarious and began calling his buddy "Crazy Bob." (Gilbeau said the story was "not true." He explained that he was friends with the woman and stayed at her home to babysit her children, but added, "I wouldn't come close to classifying it as dating.")

Whenever Gilbeau passed through Singapore, Francis was happy to entertain him. But their final meeting, in September 2012, ended awkwardly. Over dinner at Singapore's Grand Hyatt hotel, Francis revealed that NCIS was investigating Glenn Defense but boasted that he had moles who "let me know what's going on." Gilbeau stayed quiet. The talk of NCIS spooked him. He needed to cover his tracks.

A few weeks later, he submitted a "Foreign Contact Questionnaire" to NCIS. Servicemembers were supposed to fill out the two-page counterintelligence form if they had an unofficial, prolonged encounter with a foreigner. Most sailors saw the requirement as a hassle and often ignored it.

But Gilbeau took the initiative to disclose his contact with a foreign citizen named Leonard Francis—under "physical description," he typed "very large Malaysian man"—over dinner in Singapore. He reported that they had been friends for years but that this time Francis said something NCIS might want to know: that he had a mole on the Navy's logistics staff who leaked him information about the Pacific Fleet's campaign to curtail husbanding expenses.

That much was true. But Gilbeau lied on another part of the form by declaring that he had never accepted gifts from Francis and that they split their dinner bill "50/50 as always."

The scheme was clever. By pre-emptively disclosing his relationship with Francis, Gilbeau made a show of obeying the rules while simultaneously protecting himself. And by tipping off NCIS that Francis had a mole, Gilbeau hoped investigators would view him as a conscientious officer instead of a suspect.

Six months after he saw Francis in Singapore, Gilbeau arrived in Afghanistan to take command of a logistics unit with a mouthful of a name: the Operational Contract Support Drawdown Cell. The assignment was supposed to last a year.

The admiral was hard to work for. Staffers described him as a "pathological liar" with a "God complex" who thought "laws don't apply to him." Heather Failla, a civilian who had known Gilbeau for three years, called him a "passive-aggressive" leader with "controlling behavior" whose primary missions were self-enjoyment and self-promotion. "It was all about making himself look good," she said. Instead of tending to his duties in Kabul, he traveled around Afghanistan to shop for gemstones and carpets.

As news coverage of the Glenn Defense case snowballed, Gilbeau's oddball behavior reached new heights. He destroyed documents, deleted computer files, and bought an Afghan burner phone. He talked about having visions of severed heads and "little blue men in little blue suits" doing construction projects in his bathroom. By the time he told Moreau that he was a secret agent for the CIA, his chief of staff couldn't tell whether he had truly lost touch with reality or was pretending to appear insane.

"Maybe he is in the freaking CIA, I don't know. I don't freaking care," Moreau recalled thinking. "If you're in the freaking CIA, all right, good on you man." He added: "I knew he was an idiot. I knew he was a freaking idiot. But I didn't know what he was doing, why he was doing it."

Other staffers warned Moreau not to fall for the bonkers act, suspecting Gilbeau was just creating a smokescreen to avoid culpability for his history with Fat Leonard. "This guy is playing us," they said. (Gilbeau denied that he was faking anything. "It was not an act," he insisted years later. Regarding his purported work for the CIA, he said: "I had a relationship with agencies that was highly classified. That's the only thing I was allowed to say.")

Two days after his evacuation from Afghanistan, Gilbeau was relaxing in a massage chair at the USO Warrior Center, adjacent to the U.S. military's sprawling medical center in Landstuhl, Germany. Two DCIS agents had been surveilling him since lunch. They walked up to him in the recliner, introduced themselves, and asked whether he was okay.

"I don't think I'm okay," Gilbeau replied, chuckling nervously. "Something is wrong with my brain."

DCIS and NCIS had been looking into Gilbeau since Francis had spilled the beans on the admiral at the U.S. Attorney's Office in San Diego three weeks earlier. When investigators learned Gilbeau had departed Afghanistan unexpectedly, they assigned two European-based DCIS agents, Victor Sanguanboon and Tim Robertson, to interrogate him at the hospital.

The agents escorted Gilbeau into a conference room and read him his legal rights. They didn't tell him they were covertly recording the interview.

"We'll cut to the chase," Sanguanboon said. "We know that you have a relationship with Leonard Francis."

Gilbeau said he'd cooperate but apologized for his foggy mental state.

"Forgive me because I took one of my anti-anxiety drugs here a little while ago. So it makes my brain go slow, but that's probably good," he said. "For lack of a better term, I said I went crazy, but they said it's PTSD, and I think it stems from when I got wounded and a bunch of stuff back in 2007 and 2008. And I've been trying to keep a lock on it for all this time. And many things transpired over the course of the last four or five months where my—sorry—maybe I'm really acting weird."

He admitted Francis was a friend but added, "I didn't really trust Leonard Francis, if that makes sense." He reassured the agents that he paid for his half of the tab whenever they had dinner and pointed out he had dutifully filed a Foreign Contact Questionnaire about Francis.

The agents let Gilbeau ramble before telling him they suspected he was putting on a show. "You have some issues with the PTSD going on right now," Sanguanboon said sarcastically. "I want to venture to guess that a lot of this pressure comes [from] an association with Francis."

Gilbeau acknowledged that news about the Glenn Defense case had been "causing me anxiety." He said he had expected to be called as a witness but didn't think he could be helpful.

"I have holes in my recollection right now," he said. "My brain is getting that knob feeling again. . . . I've had it all morning, and I'm going to take another lorazepam and lie down."

Sanguanboon told the admiral that instead of popping another pill, he'd feel better if he unburdened himself. The agents pressed him to name Navy officers whom Francis had bribed with prostitutes.

"Unfortunately, I can't even remember the name of my doctor right now," Gilbeau replied.

"Okay, well, what about you?" Sanguanboon asked. Had he slept with any prostitutes?

Gilbeau hesitated. He said he was uncomfortable talking about the subject, but for a different reason than the agents might expect.

"So here is my personal problem, and I would like this to stay as personal and private as possible," the admiral explained. "I have a pretty significant case of erectile dysfunction, so it would be a pretty big waste of money if I were to buy a prostitute. . . . I don't do sexual intercourse, and the only way that I can is if I don't have any alcohol and if I take a Cialis or Viagra or something like that. And that's been going on now for probably eight years."

It was exactly the kind of tale that inspired Francis to dub him "Crazy Bob." But it didn't stop there.

For investigators to buy his impotence story, Gilbeau knew he'd have to explain why Francis had provided him with women. He said that Francis had "arranged" for two "Thai ladies" to give him a massage a year earlier in Singapore, but he insisted that it was not sexual and that he paid for the rubdown himself. He also said he drank too much while singing karaoke with the Thai masseuses and caught a stomach bug, which put a further damper on the evening.

"This will be embarrassing if people read this, but I then remember something about bad diarrhea. I think I had bad diarrhea or something, and I just was like, 'Oh my God, I really need to lie down.' And then got into the room and I laid down and I got the massage," he said. "So I got a massage, half-hour, fell asleep, and again my erectile dysfunction wouldn't have even allowed me to do anything else."

The hospital interview dragged on for five surreal hours. Whenever the agents tried to nail Gilbeau with a hard question, he got the vapors. "Would you mind if I went and got one of my pills?" he asked. "It's just that I get these hallucinations."

"I'm having difficulty realizing what is reality and what is truth and what isn't," he added. "The docs evidently say it's PTSD, it's not craziness. I think it's craziness but that's been going on for a long time."

The agents ended the interrogation when Gilbeau said he was feeling "very paranoid" and a little suicidal. "There is no one out here to get you," Sanguanboon said. "I hope you feel safe here with us because we're not out to do anything bad."

"I feel—I feel very safe here and the medicine is helping me," Gilbeau replied.

As the interview wound down, he mentioned again that he had been wounded in a mortar attack in Iraq years before and his doctors believed that was the source of his PTSD.

"They think that's the root of all this bullshit," he said wearily. "Plus a bunch of other things. So anyways, that's my little wah-wah-wah."

As investigators scrutinized Gilbeau's ties to Francis, they heard from several witnesses who conveyed serious doubts about the admiral's PTSD diagnosis and his Purple Heart medal. Even Francis had heard the award was bogus. He said Gilbeau had told him that he staged the incident so he could win promotion.

Still, investigators found it hard to believe that a Navy officer—an Annapolis graduate, no less—would fake a war injury to receive the hallowed medal. Combat decorations are a sacred recognition of courageous sacrifice. In military culture, nothing is more disgraceful than to lay claim to an award to which a servicemember is not entitled.*

Federal agents interviewed veterans who had served with Gilbeau in Iraq when he was purportedly wounded on Thanksgiving Day 2007. At the time, Gilbeau was a captain serving in a joint contracting command in the heavily guarded Green Zone in Baghdad.

Shortly before dinnertime, sirens warned of an incoming mortar attack by insurgents. Gilbeau's colleagues took shelter in the building where they worked.

Once the all-clear was given, Gilbeau couldn't be found. His unit was about to launch a search when he showed up, limping. He said he had been caught outside during the shelling, saw a servicemember in distress, and dragged him to a bunker. While performing the rescue, however, Gilbeau said metal shrapnel struck him in the knee.

Three officers who were present when Gilbeau reemerged told investigators that his story didn't add up. For starters, nobody could find the person he had supposedly rescued. Gilbeau's right pants leg was badly torn, but there were no visible injuries—all they could see was a light scratch below his knee that wasn't bleeding. Navy Commander Kenneth Broomer said the consensus in the unit was that Gilbeau's story was dubious. Broomer, who admittedly disliked Gilbeau and thought he was the "worst" naval officer he had ever worked with, said he suspected Gilbeau had ripped his pants intentionally and inflicted the scratch himself.

Federal agents tracked down Gilbeau's medical records, which showed he had sought treatment after the mortar attack for ringing in

---

* The issue was especially sensitive in the Navy. In 1996, Admiral Jeremy Boorda—the service's top-ranking officer—fatally shot himself in the chest upon learning that *Newsweek* magazine was about to publish an article suggesting he was not entitled to wear two combat decorations from his service in Vietnam.

his ears. According to the records, he sustained a scratch on his right knee that "does not ooze, does not bleed and is not swollen." A medic applied a Band-Aid.

The paperwork for his Purple Heart was also fishy. After NCIS inquired about the award, Navy officials at the Pentagon conducted a review and concluded that "there are several administrative errors in the award entry that call into question its authenticity." The serial number and awarding authority appeared to have been falsified. And the clerk whose name was listed as having assembled the award package could not recall doing so.

If the findings had been made public, they would have given the Navy yet another black eye. As a result, the review of Gilbeau's Purple Heart remained confidential, and he was allowed to keep the award. (Gilbeau said he was never told about the review. He acknowledged that the leg wound he sustained in Iraq "was not that serious" and that his commanding officer presented him with the Purple Heart over his objections.)

The criminal inquiry into Gilbeau progressed slowly while he received medical treatment. In 2015, however, a Navy Physical Evaluation Board determined that Gilbeau was medically fit to continue service. The board concluded his symptoms were "situationally driven" and "temporally correlated to anxiety over his legal situation."

As part of a deal with prosecutors, Gilbeau pleaded guilty in 2016 to lying to agents about his relationship with Francis, making him the first active-duty admiral in American history to be convicted of a federal crime.

But he continued to insist he was unwell. He submitted medical reports to the court showing he was suffering from traumatic brain injury, shrapnel in his knee, crushed discs in his spine, "major depressive disorder . . . with psychotic features," chronic post-traumatic stress, "residual paranoia," loss of hearing, and "survivor guilt."

During court hearings, he appeared with a tiny therapy dog,

a fluffy white Cavachon crossbreed named Bella who sat on his lap to ease his anxiety. When U.S. District Judge Janis Sammartino sentenced Gilbeau to eighteen months in prison, Bella started yapping.

"That's quite all right," the judge said. "This has been a difficult morning for everyone."

Chapter Thirty

The Admirals Strike Back

July 2014

ANNAPOLIS, MARYLAND

Well-wishers packed the Naval Academy's Alumni Hall on a muggy July day for a change-of-command ceremony to honor a guardian of the Navy's core values. Vice Admiral Mike Miller, the academy's superintendent, was stepping down from the prestigious post after four years and preparing to retire from active duty. His mission had been to drill "the highest ideals of duty, honor and loyalty," into 4,500 midshipmen and to uphold the heart of the school's Honor Concept: "Midshipmen are persons of integrity. They stand for that which is right."

Miller's naval career had come full circle. He first set foot on "the Yard," as the academy campus is known, in 1970 as a gangly plebe from North Dakota who had never seen the ocean. Over the next four decades, he flew combat missions, commanded the USS *Ronald Reagan* carrier strike group, directed the White House Military Office, and represented the Navy as its chief liaison to Congress before returning to the Chesapeake Bay to oversee the Academy. Navy Secretary Ray Mabus, the keynote speaker at Miller's farewell ceremony, said the service could not have picked a better leader to mold the character of the next generation of officers: "His vision here in Annapolis went far beyond bricks and mortar and academics. The moral, mental and ethical development of our future leaders is also central to his legacy."

But Miller had a secret that he didn't want anyone at the ceremony to know.

Eight days earlier, two federal agents had visited his campus office to inform him that he was a subject of a criminal investigation, suspected of accepting illicit gifts from Leonard Francis. Instead of owning up to his history with Francis, Miller had been cagey and evasive. If a midshipman or an enlisted sailor had responded in the same manner, the punishment would have been swift and unforgiving. As a three-star admiral, however, Miller played by a different set of rules. He used his clout and connections to fight back and resist accountability, making a mockery of the academy's Honor Concept.

The agents had not told Miller exactly why they wanted to see him, but the admiral figured out what was afoot. That summer, word had spread that investigators were interviewing Miller's former *Reagan* shipmates about the carrier's 2006 deployment to Asia and the three indulgent dinners that Francis had hosted in Singapore, Kuala Lumpur, and Hong Kong. Miller was under scrutiny because he had reached out to Francis before the port visits seeking his hospitality.

Miller retained a high-powered defense team led by Louis Freeh, a pugnacious former director of the FBI who had overseen some of the biggest federal investigations of the 1990s, including the arrest of the Unabomber and the deadly terrorist attack on the Khobar Towers military complex in Saudi Arabia. Since leaving the FBI in 2001, Freeh had built a lucrative legal practice and developed close ties to the Naval Academy. His eldest son graduated from the school and Freeh got to know Miller while serving on the board of the Naval Academy Foundation, the school's fundraising arm. He agreed to represent the superintendent for free.

When DCIS Special Agent Jerry Crosby and NCIS Special Agent James Curry walked into Miller's office on July 15 to interrogate the admiral, Freeh was lying in wait and cut them off before they could ask a question. "We're assuming you're going to ask us about Glenn Marine," he said. "We don't think [Miller] has any liability there. We don't think he's done anything wrong or unethical."

The agents were braced for a tough interview. They knew Miller had lawyered up with the former FBI director and Washington power broker. But they bristled at Freeh's domineering tone. Crosby had helped convict a member of Congress and a senior CIA official for corruption during his twenty-four years in law enforcement. He let Freeh know that he and his partner wouldn't roll over.

"I want to emphasize that, number one, we're a little bit older than the normal average bear, OK?" Crosby growled. "Neither one of us is trying to earn our spurs here."

The agents pulled an old trick and asked Freeh for permission to record the interview.

"We prefer not to," Freeh replied.

"You prefer not to. OK," Crosby said, pretending to back off. He made a show of pressing the stop button on an audio recorder. "All right."

In fact, the agents had a second recording device that remained hidden. They kept that one running, hoping Miller and Freeh would lower their guard and say something dumb. It took audacity to deceive an admiral and a former FBI director and record their words against their will. But like other agents who were interviewing suspects in the Glenn Defense case, they had obtained approval from DCIS and the U.S. Attorney's Office in San Diego, so legally they were in the clear.

The agents held another advantage. Francis had blabbed about his relationship with Miller nine months earlier during his meetings with prosecutors and agents in San Diego. That led investigators to a bunch of incriminating emails between the two.

The agents began with an easy question: Had Miller met Francis while he served on the Seventh Fleet staff between 1997 and 1999? Without hesitation, the admiral said no, that he didn't meet Francis or socialize with him until several years later.

Crosby then pulled out a printout of an email that made Miller look like a liar. It was the fawning message that Miller had sent Francis as the *Reagan* prepared to visit Singapore in 2006, calling him "Mr. Make-It-Happen" and saying he was looking forward "to renewing our friendship" from the late 1990s when he was on the Seventh Fleet staff.

Miller faltered as he read the document. "Well, that's clearly from me," he said. "Uh, I—I must tell you I don't—I don't recall, uh, interacting with him at all when I was there at Seventh Fleet."

The rest of the interview unfolded with a similar lack of candor. Miller downplayed his contacts with Francis and said he remembered almost no details about the three pricey dinners they shared, except that he was sure everything was on the up-and-up. All told, he responded to questions by saying "I don't recall" or "I don't know" or "I don't remember" a total of forty-seven times.

Even so, at the end, Freeh sounded as if his client had been a model of cooperation: "I think he answered your questions completely and truthfully."

Almost a year had passed since Francis's arrest. Any faint hope among the Navy brass that the investigation would blow over had dissipated. Dozens of admirals who had frolicked with Francis over the previous two decades now feared it was only a matter of time before investigators summoned them for an interview. But with their reputations on the line, few would act with integrity and "stand for that which is right," in accordance with the Honor Concept taught at the Naval Academy. Instead, like Miller, most girded for battle.

Fortunately for the admirals, there was a high bar for federal criminal charges. To convict on a bribery count, prosecutors would have to prove a quid pro quo—that a Navy official not only had accepted cash, prostitutes, or other things of value from Glenn Defense, but also had done something tangible and improper to benefit the company in return.

Within the military justice system, however, the bar was much lower. The Navy could court-martial personnel for serious crimes, but it also had wide latitude to impose administrative discipline for minor offenses, such as conduct unbecoming an officer or violating travel regulations. Technically, an admiral could be rung up for palming a single Cuban cigar, though such outcomes were rare.

On the same day that Miller was interviewed, two other federal agents visited the Naval Postgraduate School in Monterey, California, to question David Pimpo, who had been promoted to rear admiral since he served as the *Reagan's* supply officer in 2006 and 2007. They found the hulking, baldheaded officer in a hostile mood. Pimpo had played defensive tackle for the Naval Academy football team, and he was ready to lock horns.

He bristled at having to answer questions and said he was meeting the agents only because the Pentagon had ordered him to. "I'm not in bed with Leonard Francis. He's not my friend. OK?" he declared. "I'm an ethical person."

Pimpo had dined with Francis four times in Asia but was reluctant to admit it. First, he acknowledged attending one meal, then two. Eventually, he conceded that "there were a bunch" of dinners, but put the onus on Francis, saying: "Leonard was very aggressive with trying to push a personal relationship."

Investigators later determined that Francis spent between $750 and $1,000 per guest on the four alcohol-drenched dinner parties that Pimpo attended. Yet the admiral claimed they were nothing special. "Nice dinner, you know, wine, you know, decent restaurant." He insisted he did the right thing by reimbursing Francis $50 each time. When the agents suggested he might have lowballed the true cost, he blew his stack and sounded offended that anyone would question the integrity of an alumnus of the Naval Academy.

"Really? You're going to make me flush away thirty, twenty-eight years of my career in embarrassment because when I was a younger guy I didn't know the difference between a $50 steak and a lot more expensive steak?" he said. "Certainly, I didn't do anything illegal on purpose. That was never my intent. It's not the way I was raised. That's not what I've ever known. I'm a Naval Academy grad. Trust me. 'Do not lie, cheat, or steal.' I get it. OK? Lived that way my whole life."

The next day, in Yokosuka, DCIS Special Agent Trey DeLaPena tried to question another Naval Academy grad: Terry Kraft, who had captained the *Reagan* in 2006 and 2007, and attended the same four dinners as Pimpo. Since then, Kraft had been promoted to rear admiral, and commanding officer of all U.S. Navy forces in Japan. When he learned he was a suspect, he invoked his right to remain silent and ended the interview.

Kraft then consulted with an attorney and submitted a four-page statement to agents saying he was "surprised that I am in any way involved" in the Glenn Defense investigation. "Upon taking command, I made it clear that we would adhere to all ethical standards without exception," he wrote. He acknowledged attending the four meals but, like Pimpo, couldn't remember basic details. He deflected blame to Miller, his former boss, claiming the strike group commander had "directed" him to attend.

In a follow-up interview two months later at the U.S. Attorney's Office in San Diego, Kraft shifted the blame again. He said two JAG officers on the *Reagan* had formally approved the dinners. Asked whether he had any records to back up his assertion, Kraft grew snippy. "Are you really asking me for something from eight years ago?"

Agents running the Glenn Defense investigation knew they had to handle cases involving admirals differently because of their power. Unlike lower-ranking personnel, admirals weren't afraid to get in a legal or political brawl. They usually had influential connections and enough money to hire high-powered attorneys who would try to pick apart the evidence.

•   •   •

After a review, the Justice Department decided not to bring criminal charges against the three admirals. But prosecutors shared the evidence they had gathered with Admiral John Richardson, the Navy's disciplinary authority for the Glenn Defense case. A career submariner, Richardson was selected for the role partly because he was one of the few four-star admirals who had never crossed paths with Francis.

Under the military justice system, Richardson had the power to convene a court-martial or impose other punishments for misconduct. He soon heard from Freeh, who aggressively lobbied him to let Miller off the hook.

In early November 2014, Freeh met with two attorneys on Richardson's staff to present what he described as "newly discovered" evidence—glowing statements from Miller's former JAG officer calling the admiral an "extremely ethical boss." Freeh also accused federal agents of conducting a "seriously unfair and embarrassing" investigation by omitting "exculpatory" information provided by the JAG officer.

Agents had already interviewed the JAG officer and did so again to mollify Freeh. Instead of clearing Miller, however, the JAG this time signed an eighteen-page sworn statement in which he accused his former boss of not being "completely forthcoming" about his relationship with Francis. He also blasted the admiral for attending the dinners, highlighting one meal in Hong Kong that cost about $800 per person. "You do not need any ethics training to know this is not right," the JAG officer wrote.

The unflattering statement helped sink Miller. In December, Richardson concluded that the Naval Academy superintendent had committed "egregious" misconduct during his command of the *Reagan* strike group.

"Miller's repeated acceptance of gifts from Mr. Francis and his failure to take action to stop the pattern of blatant influence peddling by

Mr. Francis leads a reasonable person to believe that [Vice Admiral] Miller used his official position for his own personal gain," Richardson wrote in a confidential memo. "His overly friendly relationship with Mr. Francis paved the way for greater ethical abuses and opportunity for manipulation."

Richardson reached almost identical conclusions in the cases involving Kraft and Pimpo. Luckily for the admirals, however, most criminal offenses under military law were subject to a five-year statute of limitations. Because more than seven years had passed, they couldn't be court-martialed for accepting freebies from Francis.

Instead, Richardson recommended to Mabus, the Navy secretary, that the three admirals be censured for their misbehavior. The formal reprimand was only a slap on the wrist, though the officers would be forced to retire from the military.

Mabus wrestled with the decision. During his six years as the Navy's top civilian, he had become close with Miller and considered him one of his best friends; their families ate steamed crabs together when Mabus visited Annapolis. Yet he knew he had to hold the admiral accountable and decided to approve the censures. "I didn't feel good about it, but I also didn't have a second thought about it," he said. "You've got to set an example."

Many of Miller's fellow admirals thought the censures were excessive and felt strongly that the Navy should not air its dirty laundry. In a tense meeting at the Pentagon, Admiral Michelle Howard, the vice chief of naval operations, and two other admirals debated with Mabus's chief of staff whether to make the censures public. The Navy had a long-standing policy to disclose censures and other disciplinary measures taken against commanding officers. But Howard forcefully argued against doing so this time, saying it would be unfair to humiliate three high-ranking officers after a lifetime of service.

Mabus held firm and the Navy announced the censures on February 10, 2015. But the late-night press release revealed only that Miller,

Kraft, and Pimpo had "demonstrated poor judgment and a failure of leadership" by engaging in an "inappropriately familiar relationship" with Francis. The embarrassing details about their dinners and gifts remained a secret. The senior brass had won a critical concession in their campaign to protect their reputations and hide their misconduct from the public.*

* The Navy released redacted copies of the admirals' censure letters six months later, but only after I and other journalists filed public records requests under the Freedom of Information Act.

Part Seven
2015–2022

Chapter Thirty-one

Flipped

January 2015

SAN DIEGO, CALIFORNIA

As he waited for his moment in the limelight, Leonard Francis combed his jet-black hair and tried to make himself presentable in his green, double-extra-large prison jumpsuit. He was making his first public appearance in more than a year. Gawkers, curiosity seekers, and legal busybodies crammed the benches in Courtroom 2B of the federal courthouse in downtown San Diego, while a pack of news reporters staked claim to the jury box. They all wanted to catch a glimpse of the celebrated con man. Had he lost weight in jail? Would he speak?

Shortly after 3 p.m., the clerk called the final case on the docket for Thursday, January 15: *United States of America versus Leonard Glenn Francis and Glenn Defense Marine Asia*. A marshal escorted the defendant to his lawyers' table.

"Good afternoon, Mr. Francis," Magistrate Judge Jan Adler said.

"Good afternoon," Francis replied.

The court listed the case as a change-of-plea hearing. Like 97 percent of federal criminal defendants, this one had decided to cut a deal with the Justice Department instead of taking his chances at trial. When the judge asked how he wanted to plead, Francis stood, held his hands behind his back, and wiggled his fingers.

"Guilty," he said.

Specifically, he pleaded guilty to three crimes: bribery, conspiracy to commit bribery, and conspiracy to defraud the United States. He confessed that he had corrupted "scores" of Navy officers with cash bribes, prostitutes, five-star hotel rooms, and ornate gifts. On the surface, it looked like the Justice Department had gotten the better end of the plea deal. Under federal guidelines, Francis would probably be sentenced to between fifteen and twenty-two years in prison. He also agreed to pay back $35 million in ill-gotten gains to the U.S. government.

After the hearing, prosecutors crowed, predicting that more Navy personnel would face charges in what was shaping up to be the most extensive corruption case in U.S. military history. "Today is the next step in this giant investigation," Assistant U.S. Attorney Mark Pletcher told reporters. "It's gathering momentum."

Francis had stubbornly resisted making a deal for fourteen months because he was mad about being denied bail. Eventually he set aside his emotions and made a cold business decision. "I don't have a choice," he said. He knew he was unlikely to win at trial. Investigators had accumulated a boatload of damning evidence. In addition, several other defendants—Captain Dan Dusek, Commander Jose Sanchez, NCIS agent John Beliveau Jr., Ed Aruffo, and Francis's cousin Alex Wisidagama—had already pleaded guilty to bribery or fraud charges and agreed to testify against him if necessary.

Yet Francis felt strangely upbeat and confident. The fifty-year-old chiseler was a genius at exploiting an adversary's weakness, and he knew the federal investigation of the Navy had slowed to a crawl after he stopped cooperating in 2013. He held the power to make or break a multitude of cases. He intended to exert his leverage. "I had the Navy by their balls," he recalled.

Francis and the Justice Department signed a secret addendum to his plea agreement that required him to provide unlimited assistance to investigators building cases against other suspects. If his cooperation proved beneficial, prosecutors promised to ask a judge to impose a lighter punishment than he would otherwise receive under federal guidelines. The deal carried risks for Francis. He would remain in jail while the investigation continued, and his fate would depend on how much goodwill he could build with the prosecution team. But he was willing to gamble because he had tons of dirt on the Navy.

Since the early 1990s, Francis had hoarded compromising material about hundreds of Navy officials: photographs, dinner invitations, brothel receipts, thank-you notes, Bravo Zulu messages, credit card statements, classified ship schedules, travel records, restaurant bills, hotel invoices, bank documents, even personally inscribed Christmas cards. He stored the stuff in warehouses, closets, file cabinets, and other hidey-holes in a maze of locations in Malaysia and Singapore. Five weeks before signing his plea deal, Francis sent one of his attorneys and a private investigator on a two-week trip to Southeast Asia to collect a sampling of the goods. They'd returned with three jam-packed suitcases just before Christmas.

Francis also agreed to hand over Glenn Defense's corporate computer server and multiple hard drives, which contained millions of emails, text messages, and financial records that investigators didn't already have.

Prosecutors couldn't wait to dive in. By the time Francis entered his guilty plea in court on the afternoon of January 15, they had already spent the whole morning debriefing him about the massive collection of evidence.

A dozen people crowded into a conference room at the U.S. Attorney's Office for the debriefing. Pletcher led the prosecution team and was joined by two Justice Department lawyers and two federal agents: Trey DeLaPena from DCIS and Mari Nash from NCIS. Having fired his first team of lawyers after he failed to make bail, Francis was represented by four new attorneys from Covington & Burling, a white-shoe international firm. His team also included Sarah Sloviter and Esteban Hernandez, the San Diego–based lawyer and private investigator who had lugged the suitcases of evidence back from Southeast Asia.

Sometimes, a proffer session—a confidential meeting to review evidence with prosecutors—might stretch into a second or third day for a major case, such as a drug cartel investigation. But the Glenn Defense corruption case, and Francis's trove of evidence, was unprecedented in scope. He had bribed so many Navy officials that investigators would conduct fifty meetings with him over the next twenty months, questioning him for more than three hundred hours.

Francis bragged that he had an elephant's memory and delighted in the retelling of his criminal capers. He liked to shock federal agents, especially female ones, with raw descriptions of his sex parties and the intimate secrets of his Navy moles. More important, he could usually back up even his most fantastical stories with hard evidence. His attorneys organized binders of material about dozens of Navy officers. If agents needed further corroboration, Francis directed his staff in Malaysia and Singapore to track down additional documentation—photographs, receipts, and so forth—and transmit copies by email.

Sometimes his cooperation produced immediate results. On January 29, two weeks after his plea, agents questioned Francis about Paul Simpkins, the civilian who headed the Navy's contracting office in Singapore between 2005 and 2007. Francis explained how he had bribed Simpkins with $450,000 to rig contracts for Glenn Defense. More importantly, he documented how he had evaded detection by wiring much of the money to a Japanese bank account in the name of Simpkins's since-deceased wife. On the vulgar side of the ledger, he also dished about Simpkins's germaphobia and his preference for "clean, disease-free" prostitutes.

Federal authorities swore out a warrant for Simpkins's arrest four days later. DCIS agents arrived at Simpkins's home in Haymarket, Virginia, at 7:30 a.m. and handcuffed him as he was leaving to go have breakfast at the International House of Pancakes.

"This is not the way to start my day," he told the agents. He later pleaded guilty to taking $350,000 in bribes from Francis.

•   •   •

Other cases were more sensitive for national security reasons. As soon as Francis signed his plea agreement on January 15, the first person the prosecution team wanted to question him about was Admiral Samuel Locklear III, the commander of all U.S. military forces in the Pacific.

Locklear was under consideration for chairman of the Joint Chiefs of Staff, the highest-ranking job in the military. The White House and Pentagon urgently needed to know whether the admiral had any embarrassing encounters with Fat Leonard during his thirty-eight-year career.

In an earlier interview, Locklear had assured federal investigators there was nothing to worry about. He acknowledged crossing paths with Francis at the 2012 Navy League birthday ball and at change-of-command ceremonies, as well as at two group dinners in Singapore in 2003 when he was commanding officer of the USS *Nimitz* carrier strike group. He told agents that the U.S. embassy coordinated his attendance at the dinners and that he was unaware Francis was hosting or paying for the meals. He denied accepting other gifts or favors from Francis, except for a wooden name plate and some cigars that he said his staff threw away.

Over the course of three proffer sessions, however, Francis portrayed the 2003 events in a completely different light. He said Locklear was the ranking guest of honor at both dinners—"very high-end" multi-course feasts at the Jaan restaurant with "top shelf" alcohol, Cuban cigars, and live entertainment. He said Locklear must have known that Glenn Defense paid for the meals because the company logo had adorned the menus and place cards on the table. Moreover, he sat next to Locklear both times and the admiral sent him effusive thank-you letters.

Francis had receipts to back up his story. He and his attorneys furnished restaurant contracts, spreadsheets, and other documentation showing he had spent tens of thousands of dollars on the two dinners. More vividly, he shared a stack of forty photographs from the second meal, depicting boozy *Nimitz* officers dancing in a conga line and Francis sharing glasses of cognac and wine with a beaming Locklear. In one picture, the admiral jokingly posed with his arms wrapped around Francis's waist, pretending he was strong enough to lift Fat Leonard off the floor.

That was bad enough, but Francis also claimed he'd hired several prostitutes for the second dinner to entertain the *Nimitz* officers, including a "totally wasted" Locklear. Once his guests finished eating, Francis recalled, he asked the admiral whether he wanted some "oriental dessert." When Locklear assented, Francis said he discreetly escorted him to a guest floor in the hotel where prostitutes were waiting. Francis said he picked out a Chinese woman for Locklear and handed him a card key to a room with a king-sized bed, a supply of condoms, and Viagra. When Locklear emerged thirty minutes later, according to Francis, the admiral had the "glowing eyes" of a man who had just had sex.

With the chairmanship of the Joint Chiefs on the line, agents re-interviewed Locklear on March 3. The admiral remained adamant that he had done nothing wrong and said he didn't observe any "red flags" at the two dinners that indicated they might be ethically problematic. He added that he "ate and left" the second dinner quickly and returned to the ship because he was ill with bronchitis. (Locklear also later denied that Francis had offered him a prostitute or that he saw any women who might have been one.)*

Investigators scrambled to locate other witnesses to the decade-old event to sort out who was telling the truth. Locklear's former flag aide supported his account, saying he did not see any women and left with the admiral. Two more officers concurred and described Locklear as a model of rectitude.

---

* In a letter to the author, Locklear was categorical in his denial. "Let me be clear: I was never offered a prostitute by Leonard Francis. I never requested a prostitute from him, and I never discussed prostitutes or escorts with him."

But four other officers from the *Nimitz* strike group corroborated important parts of Francis's story. When the meal ended, they said, numerous young women who were obviously prostitutes paraded into the private dining room. Soon afterward, they saw Locklear stand up and leave.

In fact, one of those officers kept a diary during the *Nimitz*'s deployment and shared the relevant pages with investigators. "Very expensive deal of 7 course dinner, wine, champagne," he wrote. "Admiral left when Leonard brought in the hookers—supposedly free. I made it back . . . somehow and passed out."

Some officers said they assumed Locklear skedaddled the party because it was apparent things were getting out of hand. But NCIS agents obtained copies of the *Nimitz*'s deck logs, which meticulously tracked senior officers' comings and goings from the ship. The logs reported that Locklear returned to the *Nimitz* at 12:45 a.m., undercutting his story that he left the dinner early because he was sick.

In the end, agents uncovered no proof that Locklear had sex with a prostitute. But there was enough concern about his association with Francis to doom his chances of becoming the nation's top military officer.

Investigators turned over their findings to Admiral John Richardson, the Navy's disciplinary authority. In a confidential ruling on April 24, Richardson concluded that Locklear had done nothing wrong because his staff had advised him it was permissible to attend the dinners. Instead, Richardson pinned the blame on Locklear's JAG officer for not protecting him from Francis, even though the staff lawyer wasn't present at the meals and said he didn't learn about their "extravagance" until after the fact.

On May 5, the White House announced that another four-star officer, Marine General Joseph Dunford Jr., had been nominated to become the chairman of the Joint Chiefs.

Locklear retired several weeks later. The Navy buried details of his investigation from public view.

For more than two years, Francis shuttled constantly between his jail cell and the U.S. Attorney's Office in downtown San Diego. For each debriefing, he woke before dawn and endured a succession of security checkpoints so U.S. Marshals could deliver him to the conference room by 8 a.m. The cast of characters that investigators wanted to quiz him about kept expanding.

By the end of 2016, he had provided evidence against 240 current and former Navy officers. Hundreds more would follow.

Officially, as federal prisoner #45415-298, Francis had no special standing. Unofficially, thanks to his wealth, chutzpah, and indispensability as a cooperating witness, he collected more perks and privileges than perhaps any inmate in America.

Despite his foreign background, Francis quickly figured out how to work the U.S. justice system. Still enriched by the money he had looted from the Navy, he hired a legion of lawyers, paralegals, and private investigators. On mornings when he wasn't at the U.S. Attorney's Office, a member of his defense team would visit him at the jail for a daily "legal prep" session that lasted two to four hours.

The prep sessions were mainly an excuse to give the prisoner time to relax. In the privacy of a huddle room reserved for lawyers and their clients, he'd manage his business and family affairs. Because he was unable to connect freely to the internet from jail, his defense team would bring him a laptop preloaded with emails, news stories, shopping websites, and other material. Upon returning to the office, they'd transmit draft emails he had written and download new files and websites for him to review the next day.

Francis hired a separate staff within the jail to attend to his personal needs. He put fellow inmates on his payroll by depositing funds in their commissary accounts, enabling them to make phone calls and buy snacks and cigarettes. His jail staff acted as domestic servants, making his bed, rubbing his swollen feet, and changing the television channel in the common rooms. They also ran interference for him with the guards and other prisoners.

But his creature comforts in the jail were nothing compared to the delights he enjoyed during his many visits to the U.S. Attorney's Office.

When Francis arrived for a proffer session, his defense team would ensure that a sumptuous breakfast awaited him in a conference room. He usually ordered from St Tropez, a French bistro, and devoured a double order of eggs Benedict, Chobani yogurts, fresh fruit cups, and two carafes of coffee. During lunch breaks, he often feasted on take-out from Hane Sushi, a popular Japanese restaurant, or pork belly and delicacies from eateries in Chinatown. He ate with unrestrained gusto and loudly smacked his lips.

No other inmate had access to such luxuries. Prosecutors and federal agents plugged their ears and looked the other way, partly because Francis covered his own expenses but mostly because he was an irreplaceable witness. The prisoner learned he could get away with almost anything and began acting like a diva.

Soon, he pushed to spend even more time at the U.S. Attorney's Office, saying he wanted a full day to prepare for each proffer session with agents and prosecutors. Francis and his lawyers also argued that they needed real-time internet access and more physical space than was available in the jail to sift through his storehouse of evidence. Such requests from prisoners were unheard of, but prosecutors granted his wishes and let him spend his prep days in a reserved conference room with minimal interference.

While Francis did some work on these occasions, he mostly exploited them to focus on self-care. His legal team dubbed the sessions "spa days" because he devoted more hours to primping than prepping. His female "paralegals" massaged his feet and tended to his toenails with a pedicure drill while he relaxed in a chair, resting his eyes. He took long breaks in the prosecutors' restroom, where he whitened his teeth, gave himself sponge baths, and colored his lustrous black hair in the sink. Afterward, he'd dab his face with French creams and cologne.

Francis also used his spa days to reconnect with his five children and his two Japanese-Brazilian girlfriends via FaceTime. His three youngest kids didn't know he had been arrested, only that Daddy was working in America; the video chats helped put their minds at ease. He compensated for his absence by spoiling the children rotten with gifts he purchased online, including Legos, video game consoles, and fancy clothes from boutiques in London.

By the time the U.S. Marshals returned Francis to jail for the evening, he smelled like a rose. Besides making him feel good, the spa treatments sent an unmistakable message to the guards and other inmates that he was important and well connected. To reinforce the point, he'd casually mention how he wasn't hungry for dinner because he had his fill of shrimp and other delicacies while he was out for the day.

Francis unapologetically viewed the VIP treatment as his justified reward for helping the Justice Department. "Uncle Sam loves me," he said. "My well-being is more important than anything else. I am their star witness."

Chapter Thirty-two

Bad Memories

March 2017

SILVERDALE, WASHINGTON

For scores of U.S. Navy officers who thought they had gotten away with breaking the law or violating ethics rules, Leonard Francis's decision to plead guilty and cooperate with the Justice Department was a nightmare come true. For years they had banked on the passage of time and their shipmates' code of silence to conceal their misdeeds. But Francis's willingness to share his immense repository of compromising material changed everything. When federal agents finally came knocking, most officers could only squirm.

Captain Jesus Cantu, a former assistant chief of staff for logistics with the Seventh Fleet, had initially balked when he was ordered to attend one of Francis's dinners in Singapore in 2006, but then he became hooked on the Boss's bribes. He greedily accepted meals and prostitutes until just prior to Francis's arrest. Agents had interviewed Cantu twice in 2013. At that point, they knew little about his sordid relationship with the Malaysian businessman, and he'd talked his way out of trouble. But his anxiety level spiked when he received a call three and a half years later from another agent who wanted to visit his Pacific Northwest home to ask some follow-up questions.

DCIS Special Agent Mari Nash seemed pleasant at first when she and a colleague arrived on the morning of March 9, a Thursday, at Cantu's residence near the Navy's submarine base on the Kitsap Peninsula. She offered to take off her shoes and complimented his beige, two-story house surrounded by towering hemlocks. "What a beautiful home, what a beautiful area," she said, hiding that she and her partner were secretly recording the conversation.

After some chitchat about Stanford University—Cantu's alma mater—Nash dropped her friendly mien. She revealed that Francis had handed over explosive evidence that incriminated the fifty-nine-year-old Cantu and a horde of other officers.

"We have a ton of information," she said. "We have pictures. You want to see?" She pulled out a color photograph of a playful Cantu enjoying a drink with Francis and warned the captain not to lie as he did the last time he had been interviewed.

"First off, I need the truth from you," Nash demanded.

"I—I think I've been truthful. I mean, I—I feel that I've been truthful," Cantu said.

"You weren't truthful about the prostitutes," Nash countered. "And we know that happened for sure."

Cantu tried to collect himself, unsure which prostitutes she was referring to. "OK," he mumbled, bracing himself for the next question.

To his chagrin, Nash proceeded to grill him about the 2007 sex party that Francis hosted for Seventh Fleet officers in the MacArthur Suite of the historic Manila Hotel. In his proffer sessions, Francis had mischievously recounted how he and Cantu shared a bed and engaged in a threesome with a prostitute. Calling Cantu his "bed buddy," Francis later joked: "We were embedded together. It's called embedded, really embedded." The Malaysian high school dropout chortled at the memory of being intimate with a Stanford man. "Of course, he was too embarrassed to admit anything," Francis recalled. "The straitlaced Jesus Cantu, brilliant Stanford graduate. Can you imagine? Stanford graduate. When they're too smart, this is what happens."

Special Agent Nash didn't hold back or spare Cantu's feelings. She told him investigators knew that the MacArthur Suite party was "a straight orgy," that officers had used the replica of General MacArthur's corncob pipe as a sex toy, and that Cantu was in the middle of the shenanigans.

"With the prostitutes, you slept in a bed with Francis," she said accusingly.

"Well—yeah," Cantu said.

"You guys shared the prostitute," she pressed.

"I did not. I did not," he insisted. "No, really. I did not."

Cantu was mortified. He worried his teenage daughter, who was home that day, could overhear the humiliating inquisition. Eventually he admitted that he was at the party in Manila, that prostitutes were present, and that he wound up in a bed with the 350-pound defense contractor. But he denied having sex with anyone.

"I was not attracted to them," he said of the women. "I was not drunk. I was not plastered. I was not partaking of that orgy." He said he "fell asleep and Leonard was next to me" but swore they did not have a ménage à trois.

Nash mocked him. "To date, I think you're the only man who has ever slept in a bed with Leonard Francis. What a distinction."

"There was no physical contact," Cantu said. "I think I put a pillow between us." He clung to his story that he chastely dozed off, unaware a sex party was unfolding around him. "That orgy that you're referring to," he said. "Either I have amnesia, but I did not participate. I did not see it. I did not know about it."

"I'm being honest," he added.

After two hours, Cantu ended the interview because he had to take his daughter to an appointment. As he walked the agents to the door, he recognized his performance hadn't gone over well.

"That's that Stanford education," he said. "Lot of good it did me, right?"

"No," the agents replied simultaneously.

The walls were also closing in on several of Cantu's former colleagues on the Seventh Fleet staff. In early March, federal agents tracked them down one by one to ask similarly uncomfortable questions about their escapades in Asia. Like Cantu, they tied themselves in knots with improbable stories of their virtuous resistance to Francis's temptations.

Captain David Newland, the former Seventh Fleet chief of staff with expensive tastes in champagne, was ambushed by two DCIS agents at his San Antonio financial services office, where he had worked since retiring from the Navy. Newland acknowledged attending the debaucherous party in the MacArthur Suite at the Manila Hotel but, like Cantu, insisted he did not succumb to the prostitutes' charms.

Newland said that his memory was fuzzy because "there was alcohol involved" and that he wasn't even sure whether he spent the night at the hotel. Nonetheless, he was certain he did not have sex with any of the female guests. "I didn't partake," he said. "I remember it was very uncomfortable."

"The girls are pushing themselves on you, sitting on your lap, that kind of stuff," he added. "But I did not have sex or go into a room with any of them."

Six days later, two federal agents showed up unannounced at the Gettysburg, Pennsylvania, home of Captain James Dolan, another former Seventh Fleet assistant chief of staff. Under questioning, Dolan conceded that he spent an evening with Francis at Pegasus, the members-only sex club in Bangkok, and socialized with flirty young female guests during other Glenn Defense parties. But he said it hadn't occurred to him that the women were sex workers or escorts.

"I thought they were just, for lack of a better term, party friends of Leonard's. I really did not recognize that they were prostitutes. So they appeared friendly, friendly with Leonard. They were lively people and all that," Dolan said. "But as far as me having an actual prostitute, no."

Meanwhile, Marine Colonel Enrico DeGuzman, another former Seventh Fleet staff officer, received a surprise visit from federal agents Mari Nash and Trey DeLaPena on a military base in Hawaii. Unaware that his interrogators had voice recorders hidden in their pockets, De-Guzman admitted that he'd cheated on his wife, had a "mistress," and joined in Francis's parties. Yet he maintained he drew the line at having sex with a prostitute.

"Yes, I was there. There was a girl sitting next to me. And yes, it was offered," he said. "But I will stand by this until I die," he added. "I didn't take any prostitutes from Leonard."

Prosecutors didn't buy the protestations of innocence and lowered the boom on March 10. In the biggest single criminal case to arise from the Glenn Defense investigation, a federal grand jury indicted Newland, Dolan, DeGuzman, and six other former Seventh Fleet staff officers on bribery and conspiracy charges.*

More than a dozen other officers who served on the USS *Blue Ridge*, the Seventh Fleet flagship, avoided federal prosecution but were cited by the Navy for misconduct or forced to retire. Confronted with evidence of their wrongdoing, many of those officers adhered to the same dubious script: Yes, they consorted with Francis's prostitutes, but no, they did not have sex with them.

In another awkward meeting with federal agents, Commander David Snee, a former admiral's aide on the Seventh Fleet staff, said other officers warned him to stay away from Francis. But he admitted he couldn't resist the defense contractor's magnetism.

Snee recalled one visit to Singapore in 2007 when he went out

---

* In a related case, Cantu pleaded guilty to a bribery charge six months later, admitting that he accepted prostitutes and other gifts from Francis.

drinking. Next thing he knew, he and another officer found themselves riding in the backseat of Francis's car with two "very touchy-feely" women. He said one tried to invite herself into his hotel room, but he fended her off.

"I can assure you that . . . I went up alone" and "did not, you know, partake in that, that offering from, from Leonard Francis," he said.

But Snee's story crumbled under pressure. One agent said a witness had seen him that evening "with a blond Russian female sitting on your lap" and spotted him again the next morning with the same woman, looking "chapped-lipped and hung over."

Snee confessed the blond woman did in fact spend the night with him. Still, he said he didn't realize she was a prostitute and didn't remember having sex. "I mean, I was really drunk and I woke up with her."

"In hindsight I'm sure it appears that she was a prostitute but I—I don't know that I knew that," he added. "I mean, she wasn't your typical prostitute. She was a white girl that I was talking to."

Instead of disciplining Snee, the Navy inexplicably later promoted him to captain. He was also awarded command of the USS *Vicksburg*, a guided-missile cruiser.

Past encounters with prostitutes came back to haunt other former Seventh Fleet staffers who had ascended to sensitive jobs. Investigators learned that a Glenn Defense executive had treated a vanload of officers to an unusual dinner party in May 2010 while the USS *Blue Ridge* was visiting the port of Vladivostok in Russia's Far East.

By Glenn Defense standards, the setting and food were downright déclassé: a dingy hotel near the terminus for the Trans-Siberian Railway. At a club in the hotel basement, the officers slurped bowls of borscht and drank vodka and beer while sitting at wooden tables. Oddly, the borscht restaurant featured a sauna, whirlpools, and a pair of adjoining bedrooms, the purpose of which became clear when a flock of young women walked in to befriend the Americans.

From a counterintelligence standpoint, the scene was an obvious debacle: at least six officers from the Seventh Fleet flagship, wearing dress-blue Navy uniforms, drinking with prostitutes on Russian soil. When Navy leaders were briefed several years later about the incident at the borscht café, however, they realized the episode also posed a public relations threat.

Based on witness reports, federal agents determined that two Navy officers had shed their uniforms and frolicked with prostitutes in the sauna before having sex with them in the adjacent rooms. One was Commander Dan Dusek, who had been promoted to captain since the night in Vladivostok and admitted to his misconduct at the café.

The other was Commander Lon Olson, who had since received a prestigious faculty appointment at the Naval Academy. That was embarrassing enough for the Navy, but not the worst part: Olson was responsible for teaching ethics and moral character to classes of midshipmen. (Olson's attorney later sought to excuse his behavior in Vladivostok by saying it was apparent only "in hindsight" that the women were prostitutes.)*

There was another twist. Also attending the borscht blowout was Captain Jeff Davis, a public affairs officer who had since taken a highly visible job as the Pentagon's director of press operations. Moreover, he had recently been selected for admiral and was in line to become the Navy's top spokesman. Davis admitted to federal agents that the night in Vladivostok had "turned ugly." He also acknowledged it was the second time in a month that he had attended a Glenn Defense party with prostitutes present, though he denied having sex with any of the women or violating ethics rules.

Mindful of the potential damage to its public image, the Navy cited both officers for misconduct but kept the whole affair a secret. Olson was quietly forced to retire. Davis withdrew from consideration to become an admiral after it became clear his nomination would face resistance in the Senate. He retired voluntarily.

---

* Receipts showed Glenn Defense paid the prostitutes at the borscht joint $600 each.

•　•　•

As federal agents pursued suspects up the chain of command, they interrogated an astonishing number of officers with stars on their uniforms. By 2018, ninety-one admirals had been placed under investigation or queried about their contacts with Francis. Some were retired, but most were still on active duty.

Instead of coming clean about the dinners or gifts they accepted from Glenn Defense, however, many admirals suffered memory blackouts and debilitating cases of amnesia under questioning.

Kenneth Norton, a retired one-star admiral, told DCIS agents that he could barely recall anything about his deployments to Southeast Asia in 2008 and 2009 as the skipper of the USS *Ronald Reagan*, let alone particulars about hobnobbing with Francis.

He said he did not remember staying at a $1,500-per-night villa in Phuket, with a private chef and prostitutes, that Francis had rented for him and other officers; attending a $5,000 boozefest with Francis and prostitutes at the Bintang Palace nightclub in Kuala Lumpur; or enjoying a $700-per-person dinner hosted by Francis at the Mezza9 restaurant in Singapore followed by a $9,000 after-party with sex workers at the Tiananmen KTV karaoke bar.

The agents tried to jog his memory by showing him a copy of a thank-you note he had sent Francis after partying with the prostitutes in Singapore.

"Greetings Leonard. Wow," it read. "I reflect back on last night and can't help but smile. The entire evening, from dinner to karaoke, will always be one of those experiences etched permanently in my mind."

Nevertheless, Norton insisted his mind had gone blank. When agents reminded him that lying to federal law enforcement officials was a felony, he terminated the interview.

The Navy's disciplinary authority later concluded that Norton had "brought ill-repute and disgrace upon our honored institution." The

Navy censured him for "truly reprehensible" conduct and blasted him for dishonesty. "It is clear that you did not care about the reputation of the Navy or the example you were setting for the officers in your command," his censure letter read. "You failed these officers, you failed your ship, and you failed the Department of the Navy."

Norton was no longer on active duty, however, so the censure amounted only to a scolding. In a rebuttal letter, he apologized but downplayed his behavior with Francis, saying he was just doing his job by engaging with the husbanding contractor.

"I only attended these events to show a professional courtesy," he wrote, "and certainly did not direct anyone else to attend."

The magnificent dinner in Hong Kong that Francis hosted for senior officers from the USS *Kitty Hawk* strike group on April 29, 2008, seemed unforgettable at the time. The grand banquet on the top floor of the Mandarin Oriental hotel commemorated the *Kitty Hawk*'s final visit to the former British colony after forty-seven years of patrolling the seas. The venerable aircraft carrier, based in Japan, was scheduled for decommissioning the following year.

Francis had invited a "small inner circle" of nine senior officers to savor an indelible meal at Pierre, a two-starred Michelin restaurant founded by celebrity chef Pierre Gagnaire. Billed as "a celebration among friends," the gathering took place in a private room overlooking Hong Kong's opalescent skyline.

To impress the Americans, Francis selected a world-class tasting menu with an exotic combination of ingredients:

A kombou seaweed jelly covered plate: seasonal vegetables.
Curried shellfish «à l'étuvée». Satay prawns with tomato heart.
Wild seabass carpaccio; baby artichoke and Oscietra.
Oyster pannequet, romaine salad and Culatello.

Warm blue lobster and crab salad, Toscana olive oil
"De Santa Tea," lemon paste and honey emulsion.
Crustacean jelly with carrot mousseline.

Traditional foie gras soup

Grilled Aubrac beef fillet, poached marrow and black
truffle mash potato.
Onion tempura and old port wine sauce.

La sélection de fromages Français.

Les Desserts de Pierre Gagnaire.

Francis covered the bill, which amounted to $3,252 per person. In return, the Navy officers paid homage to their Malaysian friend by signing their names and inscribing words of appreciation on a personalized menu.

When federal agents interviewed the nine *Kitty Hawk* strike group officers several years later, however, none could remember any details about the splendid affair.

Rear Admiral Barry Bruner said he had zero recollection of the dinner even after agents showed him the menu with his handwritten note of gratitude to Francis. ("Absolutely Fantastic! Thanks for everything"). Also professing total memory loss were Captain Alan Abramson ("Thank you again!") and Captain Todd Zecchin, the *Kitty Hawk*'s commanding officer. ("Yet another wonderful evening. Thank you so much for all that you do!").

Rear Admiral Dale Horan ("THANK YOU FOR SHARING HISTORY!") was the only officer who retained a vague idea of what happened. "I think Fat Leonard was there," he told investigators. "I just don't remember the restaurant. I just followed the group, we went in, had a dinner. I remember it being a nice dinner, but I don't remember it being more lavish."

The officer who helped Francis organize the dinner and the guest

list was Rear Admiral Mark Montgomery, who had been the commodore of a destroyer squadron in the *Kitty Hawk* strike group. Widely
recognized as a brilliant naval strategist, Montgomery boasted two
degrees from the University of Pennsylvania, a master's from Oxford,
and a diploma from the Navy's nuclear power school. He had also
served in highly selective assignments as a White House fellow and on
the National Security Council.

But when agents interrogated him in September 2017 about the
Hong Kong feast, his sharp brain entered a dense fog. He acknowledged his signature on the menu looked authentic ("It was an honor
and pleasure to eat with you!") but said he had a hard time believing
he actually attended a dinner that cost more than $3,000 a head.

Montgomery said he was just as surprised to learn from investigators that Glenn Defense had once paid $2,261 to subsidize his
three-day stay at the Grand Hyatt in Hong Kong and $1,608 to defray
a family vacation in Singapore. He likewise couldn't recall attending
a Francis-hosted dinner for several Navy officers at the Ritz-Carlton
hotel in Tokyo, even though he had praised the meal as "exquisite" in
an email to Francis.

The most hopeless amnesiac was Rear Admiral Richard Wren, the
commander of the *Kitty Hawk* strike group and the highest-ranking
officer present at the Pierre restaurant in Hong Kong.

Documents provided by Francis showed that Wren, a Naval Academy graduate, lapped up indulgent gifts on a regular basis. In addition
to the Hong Kong banquet and other meals, Francis spent almost
$9,000 on an intimate, three-person dinner in Wren's honor at the
InterContinental Hotel in Yokohama, Japan. To top off the party, the
admiral received two wrapped presents: a box of Cuban cigars and a
1959 vintage bottle of Bordeaux.

For three years running, Glenn Defense also gave Wren Christmas
gift baskets featuring $2,000 packages of Kobe beef, Dom Pérignon,
Scotch whisky, and boxes of cigars.

In a letter his lawyer sent to investigators, however, Wren claimed none of the gifts or meals had left the slightest impression. He had "no memory" of the $9,000 dinner in Yokohama, couldn't recall signing the menu at Michelin-starred Pierre ("Another perfect evening!"), and "never knowingly accepted" the Christmas baskets from Glenn Defense.

The Navy's disciplinary authority was unamused by the plague of forgetfulness. It concluded that the *Kitty Hawk* officers who toasted Francis in Hong Kong had committed misconduct and it singled out Wren and Montgomery for censure, blasting both admirals for lying to investigators and for setting "the worst type of example for subordinate officers within your chain of command."*

Even so, they received only a written tongue-lashing. For admirals in the Navy, the unofficial threshold for serious discipline and accountability was far higher than for ordinary sailors.

---

* The Navy also determined that Montgomery had "committed the offense of graft" by performing business favors for Glenn Defense. Montgomery acknowledged making "ethical errors" but said he believed "the evidence in no way supported" the allegations of graft or making a false official statement.

Chapter Thirty-three

A Secret Prognosis

December 2017

SAN DIEGO, CALIFORNIA

On the Monday morning before Christmas, Leonard Francis was sprung loose from the Otay Mesa Detention Center, a privately run jail two miles north of the Mexican border in San Diego County. The detention center held several hundred undocumented immigrants for U.S. Immigration and Customs Enforcement and a smaller number of inmates for the U.S. Marshals Service. Francis had spent twenty months at Otay Mesa, his third jail in four years, but a judge had secretly agreed to give him a reprieve.

The fifty-three-year-old Francis was in a world of pain. His health, never good, had deteriorated since his arrest in 2013. He sorely needed a hernia operation, but the prison doctors feared the surgery wouldn't work, because he was so obese. He struggled to lose weight; meniscus tears in his knees hindered him from walking. Most of the time, he sat in an extra-large wheelchair. He had become diabetic and depressed.

Francis and his defense team consulted a private physician who recommended gastric bypass revision surgery at Scripps Memorial Hospital in La Jolla, California, about fifteen miles north of downtown San Diego. Francis had undergone a similar weight-loss operation about fifteen years earlier to reduce the size of his stomach.

But over time his stomach pouch had stretched. His doctor hoped a follow-up gastric bypass procedure would enable him to shed enough mass to treat his other ailments.

But the Marshals Service, which had legal custody of Francis, was reluctant to release a prisoner for elective weight-loss surgery, let alone to pay for it. In response to the objections, Francis and his lawyers drew up an unorthodox proposal: If a judge granted him a temporary medical furlough, he would wear an ankle bracelet equipped with a GPS tracker, hire private security officers to ensure he didn't escape from the hospital, and cover all the expenses himself.

The plan was very similar to the bail scheme Francis had floated four years earlier. The U.S. Attorney's Office had vigorously opposed that idea, arguing that the notorious fraudster was likely to flee the country.

But the prosecutors' view of Francis had changed since then. Now, he was a government asset whose cooperation had turbocharged the largest public corruption investigation in U.S. military history. By the spring of 2018, thirty people had been indicted or arrested on criminal charges and more cases were in the pipeline.

Though most of the defendants later pleaded guilty, the Justice Department needed to keep Francis happy and healthy so he could testify if any of the cases went to trial. The scope of the investigation kept mushrooming. The Navy had placed 550 other people under scrutiny for possible violations of military law or ethics rules, a number that would continue to grow. Almost all of those cases relied on evidence provided by Francis, including the voluminous material from his blackmail files.

With backing from prosecutors, Magistrate Judge Jan Adler approved Francis's request for a brief medical furlough, ruling that he would have to return to jail at the end of his hospital stay. The decision was kept secret, ostensibly to protect Francis's privacy but also to prevent reporters and the public from finding out that federal authorities had freed Francis from detention so he could have an operation to lose weight.

At the hospital, however, doctors discovered that Francis's condition was worse than they suspected. Scans showed tumors in a kidney. Surgeons removed the kidney, along with his gall bladder. Tests confirmed the tumors were malignant and indicated the cancer had probably spread to a lung. Doctors diagnosed him with Stage Four renal cancer, the most advanced form. His odds of surviving the disease for five years, according to statistics, were between 10 and 15 percent. "I thought he was going to die," recalled Dr. Sunil Bhoyrul, the surgeon overseeing his care. "We saw a very sick guy."

The grim prognosis carried major implications beyond Francis's mortality. Trials were pending for nine Navy officers in federal court. Five more defendants faced military court-martial proceedings. Federal agents were banking on Francis's assistance to help resolve scores of other investigations. How many cases would prosecutors have to drop if their star witness died or became incapacitated?

Francis spent two months at Scripps Memorial Hospital. As his condition stabilized, authorities had to decide what to do with him. According to his surgeon, he would need intensive follow-up care. The Marshals Service said the only place it could treat a prisoner with such complex needs was a facility in South Carolina. But the distance from California would render him largely useless as a cooperating witness. Instead, defense lawyers and prosecutors both came to support a plan than on its surface may have seemed absurd: to secretly release him into the community in San Diego.

On February 26, 2018, U.S. District Judge Janis Sammartino held a closed hearing with the attorneys to decide what to do. The sixty-seven-year-old jurist had served as a federal, state, and municipal judge over a span of two dozen years but had never had to deal with a medical furlough like this.

Known for her respectful and low-drama demeanor on the bench, Sammartino was accustomed to umpiring courtroom disputes. But in this case, both sides were asking her to do the same thing: to approve special treatment for a wealthy prisoner who had gotten rich by fleecing the government. As the judge overseeing most of the defendants in the Glenn Defense scandal, she understood that Francis was the keystone to the investigation. The case had generated more publicity than any other on her docket. Nonetheless, she was torn.

Francis had hired yet another set of attorneys, this time from a small but respected San Diego criminal defense firm, Warren & Burstein. One of the partners, Devin Burstein, a thirty-nine-year-old former federal public defender, asked the judge to permit Francis to live in a "satellite clinic" close to the hospital so his doctor and nurses could check on him daily. Under the proposal, Francis would continue to wear a GPS tracker and pay for his own medical care. Mark Pletcher, the lead prosecutor, supported the arrangement.

Sammartino wanted to know why Francis couldn't just move to a rehabilitation center. The Marshals Service and the Federal Bureau of Prisons had contracts with such places to care for prisoners. "The way this is being set up, he's going to have, probably, the best medical care anybody could ever have," she noted.

Burstein shrugged. He said Francis's doctor, who specialized in gastric bypass and cancer surgery, didn't want to deal with the red tape of a rehab facility and preferred to oversee Francis's daily care himself. "It's beyond me, but that's what they suggested," he said. "It seems the proper course."

The judge was in an uncomfortable position. She had no independent medical assessments to guide her. Neither the Marshals Service nor the court's Pretrial Services division wanted to take responsibility. All she had were secondhand reports from a physician paid by Francis.

"I guess what I'm having a hard time understanding at this point is his actual medical condition," Sammartino said. "I mean, a lot of people monitor and they maintain [cancer] treatment for years."

Burstein said his client was still in "the danger zone," adding: "The doctors feel that he needs to be monitored."

With no other good options, Sammartino extended Francis's medical furlough for ninety days. She also reimposed the peculiar

requirement that Francis pay his own security guards to ensure he
didn't escape.

"I would feel better having a U.S. Marshal, but I don't think they'll
do it," she told Burstein. "In the event that something were to happen
and the facility were to be empty one morning and he's not there and
he's back in Malaysia for whatever reason, Mr. Pletcher's name isn't on
it. Your name isn't on it. My name's on it."

A few days later, Francis moved into the "satellite clinic"—which was
really a $1 million condominium that he rented from a friend of his
doctor in the Carmel Valley neighborhood, a few miles north of the
hospital in La Jolla.

At first, he stayed in a studio apartment over the garage while a security guard lived in the rest of the house. Almost immediately, however, he began testing boundaries to see what he could get away with.

Though prosecutors were told he was prohibited from having electronic devices, he acquired several smart phones, laptops and tablet
computers, and a WiFi booster system that cost about $1,000. He also
installed cameras and motion detectors around the property because
he feared Navy officers he had double-crossed might come looking for
revenge.

The live-in guard, Ricardo Buhain, earned $10,000 a month and
had to sign a nondisclosure agreement pledging to keep Francis's identity confidential. He was responsible for driving Francis to medical
appointments and chasing away unauthorized visitors. But he soon
found himself with plenty of company: Francis's mother and three
youngest children arrived from Malaysia and moved into the four-
bedroom, 2,700-square-foot condo, accompanied by a cast of nannies,
cooks, and other servants.

The cooks prepared so much food that the household tossed two
or three trash bags of leftovers a day. The garage overflowed with Am-
azon packages and furniture deliveries. "He is one of those 'Crazy

Rich Asian' kind of people," said Buhain, referring to the movie about a super-rich Singapore family. "The servants really served him. They bathed all of his kids. They fed them 24-7."

Officials from the court's Pretrial Services division were responsible for checking on Francis. But they were not very strict, and he exploited their lax oversight. After six months, he replaced Buhain with a new guard and cut his hours in half to a twelve-hour daytime shift—ignoring the judge's mandate for round-the-clock security. Francis also ordered the new guard to stay in the windowless garage, where he spent his time staring at security cameras. Amazingly, none of Francis's court-appointed minders seemed to notice or care. Neither did the NCIS or DCIS special agents who visited to milk Francis for information about Navy officers they were investigating.

Every few months, Judge Sammartino summoned the lawyers to her courtroom for an update on Francis's health. Each time, they asked for an extension of the medical furlough but provided fuzzy answers to the most obvious questions: How long did Francis have to live? And would he be available to testify?

"What we're doing is we're trying to prolong his life. We're beyond the probability of cure," Dr. Sunil Bhoyrul, Francis's surgeon, explained to the judge at one hearing.

Bhoyrul promised Francis wouldn't try to escape, because his life depended on the specialized treatment he was receiving. "Mr. Francis, like many of my patients, they really are imprisoned by their diagnosis. This man is not going to run away, because he's dead if he leaves."

Unaware that Francis was already ignoring many of the constraints on his freedom, Sammartino kept signing orders that granted him additional liberties. At the request of his doctors and lawyers, she permitted him to attend Mass and physical therapy appointments.

Each time Sammartino held a status conference on Francis's furlough, she cleared the courtroom and sealed records of the proceedings. But it became increasingly difficult to keep his medical condition and whereabouts a secret.

In May 2018, Francis's lawyers received a military subpoena summoning him to the Navy base in Norfolk, Virginia, to testify at the court-martial of Commander David Morales, a two-time organizer of the annual Navy birthday ball in Singapore. Navy officials thought Francis was still in jail and didn't know he had been diagnosed with an incurable illness.

Anxious and unsure what to do, Burstein notified the judge, who scheduled an emergency hearing. When Burstein offered to escort his client to Norfolk so he could testify, the normally low-key Sammartino exploded. If Francis was too sick to be incarcerated, how could he travel 2,500 miles to Norfolk for a court-martial? If he was healthy enough to fly, she mused, maybe he should go back to jail.

"He is not getting on a plane and going cross-country with you, sir," she lectured Burstein. "In the event that we lost him somewhere, those in this room would look pretty foolish and pretty lacking in judgment."

Sammartino also said the secrecy surrounding Francis's furlough had gotten out of hand.

"Pretty soon you better go public with this, because somebody's going to see Mr. Leonard Francis—some media person is going to see him," she warned the prosecutors and defense attorneys.

She was right. Six days later, I broke the news in *The Washington Post* that Francis had been released from jail because of an undisclosed malady and that federal authorities were refusing to divulge his location. "Where's Fat Leonard?" the story began.

Sammartino's refusal to let Francis travel to Norfolk infuriated the military judge overseeing the court-martial. He blamed the U.S. Attorney's Office in San Diego and other officials for making "misrepresentation after misrepresentation" about Francis's health and whether he was available to testify. The accusation was wholly justified. Federal prosecutors had been trying to keep a lid on the information because they didn't want any suspects to find out that the government's indispensable witness was critically ill.

In the end, the Navy accepted a compromise. Francis's defense team and the Justice Department agreed to make him available in San Diego for a deposition—an opportunity to obtain sworn testimony from a witness prior to a trial—in lieu of him traveling to Norfolk.

The three-day deposition was held in a military courtroom in July 2018 at the main Navy base in San Diego. For the first time, Francis had to answer questions under oath about his corruption of the Seventh Fleet. But Navy officials shrouded his statements in secrecy. They ordered the deposition sealed and prohibited the public—especially reporters—from attending the sessions.

Meanwhile, Francis steadily finagled more roaming privileges. During a closed court hearing in October 2018, Burstein asked Judge Sammartino to allow his client to attend church more often, go to the grocery store, take his kids to school, and meet their principal.

Prosecutors didn't object. They wanted to keep Francis in a good mood so he would continue to help NCIS and DCIS agents. But Sammartino questioned whether the extra freedoms were necessary. "I'm a little concerned about making it home detention kind of in name only," she said. "I need to think this through."

Still, she didn't say no—which Francis took to mean yes. The Pretrial Services staffers who were supposed to monitor his GPS tracker weren't very strict about his jaunts around town. They believed his doctor's assertions that he was too sick to flee. As long as he didn't board a plane or disappear to Las Vegas for the weekend, they let him do as he pleased. After hearing no objections, Sammartino let the matter drop.

For the next two years, Francis's doctor and lawyers gave the judge mixed messages about his health. Sometimes they portrayed his condition as dire. Other times they sounded hopeful. But they were never definitive. Worried that he could still die at any moment, Sammartino sounded genuinely concerned for his welfare. "Everyone wishes

Mr. Francis well as he treats on some very, very serious issues," she said during a closed hearing in 2019.

Critically ill or otherwise, Francis continued to play an essential role in the federal investigation, meeting regularly with agents and prosecutors. By 2019, criminal charges had been brought against thirty-three defendants in federal court and five in the military justice system—a remarkable number for a single corruption case.

While most eventually pleaded guilty—obviating the need for Francis to testify—the nine former Seventh Fleet officers indicted as a group in 2017 contested their charges while they remained free on bail. They were in no rush to defend themselves before a jury, and their attorneys filed a blizzard of legal motions that helped drag the cases out for years.

Though none would say it out loud, they hoped Francis's cancer would kill him before they had to go to trial.

The wheels of justice ground to a halt in March 2020 when the coronavirus pandemic paralyzed life in the United States. With his weakened immune system, Francis holed up with his family and servants. He communicated with investigators and prosecutors via Zoom. If his lawyers needed to visit, he met them in the backyard wearing a mask or plastic face shield.

On November 24, 2020, a few weeks before Covid-19 vaccines first became available to the public, Sammartino received an unexpected and perplexing one-page letter from Dr. Bhoyrul, Francis's physician.

"This letter is to notify you that Mr. Leonard Francis has been dismissed from our practice. We wish to congratulate him on his clean bill of health," it read. "Please contact me if you have any questions."

The judge was shocked and furious. She had plenty of questions. How does a terminally ill man suddenly get a "clean bill of health"?

She called an urgent closed hearing with the defense lawyers and prosecutors.

"It surprises me that I hear this from the doctor directly and not from all of you when there was a change of circumstances," Sammartino said. "I mean, it's bizarre, counsel, that he says, 'We wish him well on his clean bill of health.'" She wanted to know: Was Francis getting medical care from someone else? Had he parted ways with his security guards too? Was he still wearing his GPS tracker? "I went so far as to wonder if he is still in this country," she added.

Left unspoken was a damning question: Had Francis—the celebrated con man—paid people off to exaggerate his illness?

A shamefaced Burstein promised the judge that his client was "not going anywhere." He said that Francis and his surgeon had quarreled over medical bills, leading to "a breakdown in trust." Francis had refused to pay and hired two new doctors instead.

Burstein insisted Francis was very sick. "I do take real issue with a doctor saying he has a clean bill of health when clearly that cannot be true, and it is clearly not true, and he has no basis to say that." (Years later, Bhoyrul said Francis's condition had in fact improved. "Things had changed. He had gotten much better," he recalled. "I personally didn't feel that I, as a physician, needed to look after him anymore." He said it was true there was a dispute over Francis's unpaid medical bills but that it was "not a big deal.")

But Sammartino feared her compassion had backfired. She had given Francis a get-out-of-jail card for the past three years on the assumption that he was a dying man. Now she had a letter from his doctor proclaiming him cured.

She demanded that Francis's new doctors provide a detailed update on his condition. To justify the medical furlough, she needed a statement attesting that his health was still precarious. "Tell them they may be subpoenaed by the government to come and testify," she told Burstein. "That should motivate them to write these."

Two weeks later, however, the judge received more unsettling news. A staffer with the court's Pretrial Services division had inspected Francis's rental house for the first time in six months—and found no guards on the premises. Though Francis was present and claimed the security officer was taking a brief lunch break, the Pretrial Services staffer reported the guard went AWOL for three hours. (If Pretrial Services noticed Francis's other violations of his furlough—the internet access, the fact that he was living large in the main house—nobody mentioned them to the judge.)

Sammartino convened a teleconference with the lawyers. "Maybe I can make it simple for everybody. Security means security. It's a 24-hour, seven-day-a-week situation," she said sternly.

This time, Francis dialed into the meeting to grovel and perform damage control.

"I'm so sorry for what has happened. And I just want to let you know that this will never happen again," the con artist promised Sammartino. "I'm so sorry, ma'am."

The judge hadn't heard his voice in years. The apology mollified her.

"Mr. Francis, we all wish you good health and a long life, so it has nothing to do with that," Sammartino said. "But I've granted this medical furlough to help you achieve that, sir, and to not put you in custody, where you might not get the treatment that really you need to stay alive."

"Yes, your honor," he replied meekly.

But Francis recognized he had everybody—the judge, the prosecutors, his lawyers, the security guards—over a barrel. He knew the U.S. government needed him to testify. He could do almost anything he pleased.

Chapter Thirty-four

The Great Escape

December 2020

SAN DIEGO, CALIFORNIA

While Leonard Francis was making excuses in court about his missing security guard, he kept quiet about something else he knew would tick off the judge. He had decided to upgrade his lifestyle by moving to a $7,000-per-month mansion with a swimming pool and a three-car garage.

Two days earlier, he had secured a lease to relocate his home jail to a fabulous property shaded by palm trees in the gated community of Collins Ranch. His three youngest children were entering their teenage years, and the family needed more elbow room. In addition, Francis's love life had blossomed. He had a new girlfriend, a younger woman in her mid-thirties. With five bedrooms, seven bathrooms, and 5,500 square feet overall, the Spanish-Mediterranean-style house had space for everyone, including the servants and the kids' beloved English bulldog, Puteri.

Francis and his attorneys notified Pretrial Services and the U.S. Attorney's Office that he was changing addresses. Neither objected. All they cared about was that he was still breathing and still in San Diego. They didn't mind if he lived high on the hog as long as he answered the door when federal agents needed to discuss a case.

For a sickly felon who had been unemployed for the past seven years, Francis spent money like someone who had won the Powerball lottery several times over. He didn't blink at the thirty-month, $210,000 lease for his new residence. He paid private school tuition for his younger children, living expenses for his two adult sons and his parents, as well as salaries for several full-time staffers and servants in San Diego, Singapore, and Kuala Lumpur. And he still could afford his soaring medical and legal bills.

Yet he claimed to be a pauper. During his court-martial deposition, he testified that he'd "lost everything" after his 2013 arrest when creditors seized control of Glenn Defense and forced him to sell his real estate holdings. "I was fully indebted," he said. "Everything was controlled by my banks. I owed them a lot of money."

The subject of Francis's finances was a touchy one within the Justice Department. When he signed his plea agreement in 2015, he promised to forfeit $35 million to the U.S. government for defrauding the Navy. He paid $5 million up front to demonstrate his commitment to the deal. Since then, however, he hadn't paid another penny.

Whenever prosecutors nagged him about the rest of his $30 million debt, he wailed that they were trying to squeeze blood from a stone and throw his family onto the street. Given his profligate spending, it was obvious he still had a fortune stashed away. But prosecutors needed his help with their investigation so they let it slide.

They also looked the other way as evidence mounted that his cancer had gone into remission, eliminating the justification for his medical furlough. His new doctors reported to the court in early 2021 that his health had improved substantially.

"Really the messaging from both letters is that Mr. Francis is doing quite well," Mark Pletcher, the lead prosecutor, said during a closed March 2021 hearing. "While it requires a careful eye and diligent attention, it appears from the letters that his prognosis is good."

Judge Janis Sammartino asked Pletcher whether he was suggesting the medical furlough was no longer necessary. No, he replied.

Prosecutors knew Francis would go ballistic if they tried to send him back to jail, and they didn't want to alienate their prized collaborator.

Sammartino extended the furlough for three more months. But she gently warned Francis, who was listening to the proceedings by phone, that she might have to put him back behind bars if he continued to heal.

"A diagnosis of cancer that is acceptably treated and managed does not necessarily mean that somebody . . . warrants a medical furlough," she said. "But we wish you a long life, and I think that's definitely possible."

More than six years had passed since Francis had pleaded guilty, but he still didn't know when he would be sentenced for his crimes. He had agreed to defer his punishment until prosecutors wrapped up their other cases, with the understanding that the more help he provided, the more time would get knocked off his sentence. But because of the pandemic, the remaining cases were taking forever to resolve.

His mansion was far preferable to jail, but Francis grew bored. He missed the publicity that had once swirled around his case and swelled his ego. Before his cancer diagnosis and furlough, Francis proudly showed off front-page *Washington Post* stories to guards and other inmates so they could see what a big shot he was. He boasted it was a matter of time before a Hollywood studio bought the rights to his life story, predicting that the hulking action star Dwayne "The Rock" Johnson would be the natural choice to play him on screen.

Fed up with the endless delays in the Navy prosecutions, Francis decided to create a little excitement. In February 2021, he asked a mutual friend to reach out to Tom Wright, a British author living in Singapore, to see whether he'd be interested in telling his story. Francis had turned down interview requests from American journalists because they were unwilling to offer him money or bend to his editorial dictates. But he liked that Wright had cowritten a semi-flattering book about Jho Low, another chubby Malaysian businessman who had allegedly embezzled billions of dollars so he could party with celebrities and live the high life.

Wright had spent much of his career in Asia but didn't know Francis personally and had never written anything about the Glenn Defense scandal. He agreed to talk by phone and listened while Francis expressed interest in publishing his memoirs and filming a movie. Wright had another idea. He appealed to Francis's vanity by suggesting a podcast—that way he could tell his story how he wanted, in his own voice.

Francis agreed, and Wright shipped a high-quality microphone to his mansion in San Diego. Over the next six months, they conducted more than twenty hours of interviews over the internet, with Francis staying up past midnight to gab about his colorful life and how he had corrupted the Navy. "If the Navy would've charged every officer or admiral that were involved with me, the Navy would not have any more admirals," he said, exaggerating for effect. "Everybody would've been put away."

Wright was thrilled by his subject's flair for storytelling and eagerness to prattle away. "I'm pumped. You have an amazing memory!" he said. "I think you were born to do this."

"That's why Uncle Sam loves me," Francis replied. "The agents, when they speak to me, they go: 'This is amazing. This is an amazing story.' When I talk to them, it just comes out naturally."

While Francis loved the attention, his hubris would again trigger his comeuppance. His lawyers had cautioned him not to talk to reporters, because anything he said on the record could be used against him in court. Francis didn't take the warning seriously. All the federal prosecutions in the Glenn Defense case had resulted in plea bargains so far instead of going to trial. As the pandemic ebbed in 2021, however, Sammartino set a tentative trial date for several former Seventh Fleet officers who refused to plead guilty. Prosecutors said they expected to call Francis as their chief witness.

Wright was ecstatic. He figured Francis's testimony would generate tons of publicity, and he scrambled to finish the podcast before the trial. In August, he informed Francis that he planned to release nine episodes in a few weeks.

The timetable floored Francis, who had assumed the podcast would take much longer to produce. He realized he had made a bone-headed mistake by opening his mouth. If the podcast aired before he took the witness stand, everything he said in the interviews—all his wild stories—would become fair game for cross-examination. Attorneys for the accused Navy officers would play the most sensational audio clips to the jury and try to shred his credibility. The Justice Department would view his self-indulgent commentary as a double cross. Instead of urging the judge to give him a light sentence, prosecutors might argue for the maximum.

Panicked, he called Wright and begged him to hold off until the trial was over.

"I'm not saying there's anything wrong with your story. It's just the timing, Tom," he pleaded. "It's going to be a shipwreck in the middle of everything and I'm going to be the one that's going to get hurt the most."

Wright had never made any promises about the timing, and Francis's reaction flabbergasted him.

"But Leonard, you came to me. You came to me. Don't forget it," he said. "I can't change it now. It's just hard."

Wright stuck to his plan. He posted the first two episodes of the podcast on October 5, 2021, and followed up with a new installment each week through the end of November.

As Francis feared, lawyers for the Seventh Fleet defendants pounced on his inflammatory comments. Hoping to uncover more juicy material to use against him in court, the attorneys subpoenaed the podcast's production studio for all of Wright's recorded conversations with Francis. (Wright contested the subpoena but lost.) The defense lawyers said the interviews indicated Francis had lied about his need for a medical furlough and violated his plea agreement by withholding evidence.

The trial eventually got under way in March 2022. Former Seventh Fleet officers David Newland, James Dolan, David Lausman, Mario Herrera, and Bruce Loveless stood accused of bribery and conspiracy charges. The big question was whether prosecutors would dare to call Francis as a witness. While his testimony was expected to be damning for the Navy officers, defense attorneys were champing at the bit to discredit him.

For several weeks, prosecutors refused to tip their hand, relying on other witnesses and documentary evidence about Francis's sex parties, splashy dinners, and infiltration of the Seventh Fleet. In the end, they did not present Francis to the jury. Defense lawyers made a big show of his absence. "The government's entire case is built upon Leonard Francis. He's the elephant in the room," Joseph Mancano, Newland's attorney, told jurors. "Why wasn't he here to explain anything? Why not? I think you know the answer. Because the government deemed him too untrustworthy to testify."

For the most part, the prosecutors' gamble worked. The jury found Newland, Dolan, Lausman, and Herrera guilty but was unable to reach a verdict on Loveless. (Prosecutors later dropped charges against Loveless after deciding that their chances of obtaining a conviction in a retrial were low.)

The Justice Department was pleased with the outcome of the Glenn Defense investigation. Of the thirty-four people charged with federal crimes, thirty-three pleaded guilty or were convicted at trial. But Francis's usefulness had abruptly come to an end. Prosecutors no longer needed him.

Nine years after his arrest at the San Diego Marriott Marquis hotel, his sentencing was finally scheduled for September 22, 2022.

Ever since he pleaded guilty, Francis had banked on the proposition that the U.S. government would allow him to go free in exchange for his help. But after the tempest over the podcast, he was terrified he would have to go back to jail. Once the Seventh Fleet trial ended in June, he secretly hatched a plan to flee the country.

Unwittingly, nine years earlier, prosecutors had sketched out an escape route for him. In bail hearings after his arrest, they warned he might cut off his GPS transmitter in the middle of the night and catch a taxi from San Diego to the Mexican border, estimating that he could reach Tijuana in fifteen minutes. From there, they predicted, he would obtain forged travel documents and fly to a country that lacked an extradition treaty with the United States.

Federal authorities had stopped worrying that Francis might bolt for the border after he was diagnosed with cancer—his attorneys and doctors had said repeatedly he was too sick to flee. Once his health improved, however, they failed to reconsider the possibility he might make a run for it.

Outwardly, Francis focused on preparations for his sentencing hearing. He reviewed documents and drafted a letter seeking leniency from the judge. Acting on the pretext that he needed to downsize his living quarters—he told some people he was moving to an apartment but hinted to others that he had become resigned to a fate in prison— he ordered his staff to pack his family's belongings and clear out the house. His three youngest children returned to Malaysia to live with his mother in Kuala Lumpur.

He appeared beaten and deflated. "He became more and more morose as time went on," said Perla Nation, a paralegal whom Francis hired that summer to help put his affairs in order. "I remember the last time I saw him, and I could just see his face and it was so sad."

A closer look would've revealed that things weren't quite as they seemed. The security guard who was supposed to watch Francis at the mansion all but disappeared, with visitors only catching occasional glimpses of him in the garage. Francis broke his seclusion to go on short walks around the neighborhood, trying to build up his leg strength.

In another strange development, a television crew descended on the property at the end of August. The crew was led by Sarah

Macdonald, a documentary filmmaker and former BBC journalist who had fruitlessly tried for years to land an interview with Francis. Without revealing the real reason behind his sudden change of heart, Francis summoned the filmmaker from Europe on short notice and agreed to talk on camera.

The documentary team arrived on Monday, August 29, and spent four full days filming Francis inside the increasingly vacant house while moving vans carted away his remaining possessions. Toward the end of the week, staffers from the court's Pretrial Services division showed up to conduct a welfare and security check. Francis hid the television crew in one part of the house while he received his court-appointed minders in an adjoining room. The documentary producers listened from the other side of a locked door as the con man put on a stage-worthy act, pretending to be hopelessly feeble and promising that he was abiding by the restrictions of his home detention. The Pretrial Services staffers left a few minutes later, none the wiser.

The television crew left Friday morning. By Saturday night, the house had been emptied except for Francis's bedroom. According to Nation, who left around 8 p.m., Francis looked "distraught" and moped that he would probably spend the rest of his life in federal prison.

On Sunday, September 4, Francis woke up early. The neighborhood was quiet, with many people out of town for Labor Day weekend. Using a heavy pair of shears, he cut off his ankle bracelet with the GPS transmitter. He submerged the device in water in a portable ice chest, hoping that the Pretrial Services staff would assume the bracelet had malfunctioned as he was taking a shower or a dip in his pool. Then he summoned an Uber driver and headed south to the border crossing near Tijuana.

Luckily for Francis, his absence didn't trigger immediate alarms. At 7:35 a.m., Pretrial Services received an electronic alert that his ankle monitor had been tampered with. But nobody bothered to check on him for six hours. Finally, at the behest of Pretrial Services, one of Francis's attorneys arrived at his mansion at 1:28 p.m. Knocks on the door went unanswered.

San Diego police officers arrived at 2:42 p.m., forced their way inside, and found the sliced-up ankle bracelet in the water-filled cooler. Standing nearby was a life-sized posterboard cutout of Elvis that Francis had left behind as an in-your-face joke, a taunting reminder of his ability to repeatedly outsmart the U.S. government. By then, he was long gone, far across the border in Mexico.

On Monday afternoon—Labor Day—*The San Diego Union-Tribune* broke the news of Francis's escape. The U.S. Marshals Service and NCIS offered a $40,000 reward for information, but embarrassed federal officials refused to answer journalists' questions about how the legendary fraudster had outwitted them again.

After entering Mexico, Francis hopped a flight from Tijuana to Cancún and then another to Havana, Cuba, hoping that the communist government—a longtime foe of Washington—would grant him refuge. But Cuban authorities wouldn't allow him to stay. They advised him to try his luck in Venezuela, another country that was hostile toward the United States.

Traveling on a Malaysian passport, Francis departed Cuba and flew 1,400 miles southeast across the Caribbean Sea to Venezuela. Malaysians didn't need a visa to gain entry, and he slipped past immigration officials, who didn't notice or didn't care that he was the target of an international manhunt by U.S. authorities. He spent several days in Caracas, the capital, and on Margarita Island, a faded tourist destination off the South American mainland. To blend in, he acted like he was on vacation, staying at the beach and shopping at malls.

Still, the fugitive wanted to get further away from the United States. He decided Russia was his best option and applied for asylum at the Russian embassy in Caracas. Consular officials accepted his paperwork and said they'd get back to him.

On September 20, 2022, however, Francis's luck ran out after sixteen days on the lam. Acting on an Interpol alert for his arrest, Venezuelan authorities detained him at Simón Bolívar International Airport as he was attempting to board a flight back to Margarita Island. His booking photo showed him wearing a blue tropical-print shirt and looking downcast, haggard, and unshaven.

Francis's dash for freedom had fallen short. But bringing him back to San Diego wouldn't be easy.

While Venezuela had an extradition pact with the United States, the countries severed diplomatic relations in 2019, and Washington did not recognize the legitimacy of the rule of Venezuelan president Nicolás Maduro. As a result, the Justice Department lacked an official channel to request Francis's extradition.

The diplomatic impasse entrapped Francis. Though he hadn't committed any crimes in Venezuela, the country's secret police—the Bolivarian National Intelligence Service, known by its Spanish acronym, SEBIN—locked him up in El Helicoide, an infamous pyramid-shaped jail for political prisoners. SEBIN saw him as a bargaining chip to trade for Venezuelans held in U.S. custody. The spy agency had a history of taking foreign businessmen as hostages and was willing to hold Francis indefinitely because of his perceived value to the Americans.

Francis hired a local lawyer and filed another asylum claim, this time to remain in Venezuela on humanitarian grounds. But with SEBIN in control of his case, his appeals dragged on for more than a year. He remained imprisoned at El Helicoide, a pawn in a much bigger power struggle between Caracas and Washington.

For Francis, the disappointing outcome was nonetheless preferable to incarceration in the United States. He clung to the hope that the Venezuelans would eventually grant him asylum, and with it, his freedom. For the moment, the master trickster took solace in the knowledge that he had pulled off his greatest con yet: He had escaped the clutches of the Americans.

Epilogue

Leonard Francis's easy escape from home detention in San Diego left the U.S. government with egg on its face. Worse, his vanishing act coincided with the unraveling of the Justice Department's efforts to hold key Navy officers accountable for the most extensive corruption scandal in U.S. military history.

Prosecutors' biggest single accomplishment—the conviction of four former Seventh Fleet officers on bribery and conspiracy charges in 2022—crumbled months after Francis fled to Venezuela. Though a jury had pronounced Captain David Newland, Captain David "Too Tall" Lausman, Captain James Dolan, and Commander Mario Herrera guilty, defense attorneys petitioned Judge Janis Sammartino to throw out the verdict because of prosecutorial misconduct.

Testimony and court filings revealed that the prosecution team, led by Assistant U.S. Attorney Mark Pletcher, withheld evidence favorable to the defense. During opening statements to the jury, prosecutors declared that Lausman had sex with a prostitute at a raucous Glenn Defense party in Manila. The assertion was based on information from Francis, but federal agents hadn't spoken with the woman. When they finally tracked her down after the trial began, she admitted that Francis paid her to spend the night with an officer who matched the description of Lausman but said he had rebuffed her advances. "Nothing happened, I even slept on the couch lol," she texted the agents.

The discrepancy was a problem for prosecutors. It hurt their credibility and made their case preparation look shabby. Yet they dug a deeper hole for themselves by failing to promptly disclose their new findings to the defense, as required by law.

Defense lawyers found out anyway. Over time, they accused the U.S. Attorney's Office in San Diego of hiding other material facts, including the cushy privileges Francis received in exchange for his cooperation and details of how investigators obtained his blackmail files. While the omissions didn't change the core truth about Francis's corruption of the Seventh Fleet, they were fundamental legal errors that deprived the defendants of a fair trial. Judge Sammartino called the prosecutorial misconduct "outrageous." Though she stopped short of overturning the guilty verdicts against the four officers, she delayed their sentencings while defense attorneys dug up further evidence of the government's shady legal tactics.

The U.S. Attorney's Office assigned a fresh set of prosecutors to review the case and eventually admitted wrongdoing. In September 2023, one year after Francis's escape, it vacated the felony convictions—which ordinarily would have resulted in long prison sentences—and instead let Newland, Lausman, Dolan, and Herrera each plead guilty to a single misdemeanor. Their only punishment: a $100 fine.

The bottom line was that the four retired Navy officers won get-out-of-jail-free cards because prosecutors got caught cheating. "There were pretty obviously serious issues that affect our ability to go forward," Assistant U.S. Attorney Peter Ko acknowledged during a court hearing.

The legal reversal enabled the four defendants to deflect blame for accepting Francis's lavish gifts and helping him to infiltrate the Seventh Fleet. In public, they portrayed themselves as victims of a witch hunt by the Justice Department. "China couldn't have done as much damage to the Navy as the prosecutors did by some of these false allegations," Lausman told The Wall Street Journal.

Joseph Mancano, the defense attorney for Newland, the former Seventh Fleet chief of staff, described the bungled trial as another example of U.S. officials succumbing to Fat Leonard's temptations. "Leonard Francis was like a puppet master," he told *The Washington Post*. "He played the Navy and all the Navy officers he dealt with. Then he played the Department of Justice. He played everybody."

Fallout from the prosecutorial malpractice caused several related cases to come unglued. In early December 2023, the U.S. Attorney's Office handed get-out-of-jail-free cards to four more officers—Captain Don Hornbeck, Commander Steve Shedd, Marine Colonel Enrico DeGuzman, and Chief Warrant Officer Robert Gorsuch—who had been charged in the same indictment as Newland and the other Seventh Fleet defendants. A fifth officer, Commander Jose Luis Sanchez, a longtime Francis mole, received the same lenient treatment.

The collapse of those five cases was particularly humiliating for the Justice Department because the defendants had already pleaded guilty to felony bribery charges and were waiting to be sentenced. Nevertheless, prosecutors said they felt compelled to let Hornbeck, DeGuzman, Gorsuch, and Sanchez plead guilty to misdemeanors instead, with no time behind bars. Shedd got an even sweeter deal: Prosecutors filed a motion to dismiss the entire case against him, even though he had admitted under oath to betraying his country and leaking military secrets to Francis for $105,000 worth of bribes.

But the disintegration of these cases was too much for Judge Sammartino to stomach. On December 20, 2023, she temporarily blocked the new plea deals and the dismissal of Shedd's charges, saying that the public deserved a clearer explanation for why the cases had fallen apart. The judge knew that if she let some offenders slide without meaningful punishment, she would hear loud objections from the twenty-three others who were forced to serve time in prison.

During her ten years of presiding over the Glenn Defense cases, Sammartino had bent over backward to avoid sentencing disparities. But the prosecution's screwups, and Francis's escape to South America, were making it nearly impossible to uphold the principles of fairness and justice in her courtroom.

In 2016, she sentenced Commander Michael Misiewicz, the former golden boy of the Seventh Fleet, to six and a half years in prison. His offenses were almost identical to Shedd's—they both leaked reams of classified material to Francis in exchange for prostitutes, dinners, and free travel. The only difference was that Shedd cooperated with investigators after he got caught, while Misiewicz did not.

More recently, in February 2023, Sammartino had sentenced retired Captain Jesus Cantu—the supply officer who once shared a bed with Francis—to thirty months in prison for conspiracy to commit bribery. Like Shedd, Cantu expressed remorse for his crimes and cooperated by testifying against his former Seventh Fleet shipmates. Unlike Shedd, however, he did not leak any classified information and only pleaded guilty to one felony, whereas Shedd had copped to two.

The prospect of no jail time for Shedd, Sanchez, Gorsuch, Hornbeck, and DeGuzman, despite their admissions of taking bribes, was also hard to square with the punishment meted out to John Beliveau Jr., the dirty NCIS agent. In 2016, Sammartino had sentenced him to twelve years in prison, more than any other defendant.

As a federal law enforcement agent who betrayed his badge, Beliveau occupied a heinous category of his own. Prosecutors had urged the judge to show him no mercy. "What he did was absolutely unconscionable," said Assistant U.S. Attorney Brian Young. But was it defensible to lock up Beliveau for a dozen years while turning a blind eye to others—including Sanchez and Gorsuch—who had in effect sold classified information to Francis, a threshold that Beliveau never crossed?

In the star-crossed quest for accountability, another disparity had become glaringly obvious. Of the ninety-one admirals investigated for taking gifts, or questioned about their connections to Fat Leonard, only one went to prison: Robert "Crazy Bob" Gilbeau, who received a sentence of eighteen months. (The Navy also busted him down in rank to captain and forced him to retire with a less-than-honorable discharge.)

Like many officers, Gilbeau tried to minimize his misbehavior even after he pleaded guilty. In a letter to the judge, he apologized only for "my misrepresentation of my relationship with Leonard Francis." At his 2017 sentencing, he continued to blame post-traumatic stress and "survivor's guilt" for his actions, adding: "I know in my heart of hearts that I'm not corrupt."

Americans are supposed to be treated equally under the law. But veterans have a saying—"different spanks for different ranks"—to describe their widespread belief that enlisted personnel are punished far more harshly than officers. Indeed, while admirals largely avoided culpability in the Glenn Defense scandal, enlisted sailors and junior officers got hammered.

Brooks Parks III, a chief petty officer who worked on the Seventh Fleet staff, received a sentence of twenty-seven months after he pleaded guilty to providing Glenn Defense staffers with proprietary, but unclassified, information in exchange for hotel rooms and other gifts. (Sammartino freed him from prison after five months on compassionate release grounds.) While Parks violated the law, he had no direct dealings with Francis himself and received fewer illicit perks than many admirals and commanding officers. "I was a little man on the totem pole," Parks told me.

One mid-ranking officer, Commander Bobby Pitts, was sentenced to eighteen months in prison after he pleaded guilty to conspiracy to commit fraud. Pitts, who was stationed in Singapore between 2009 and 2011, leaked Francis an unclassified email about overbilling investigations into Glenn Defense and lied about it afterward. Strangely, however, prosecutors could not prove that he received anything of value from Francis other than a few cups of tea.

"They didn't find any money, no pictures of me with any hookers or anything like that, no hotel stays or anything," Pitts told me. He said he pleaded guilty because he "just flat ran out of money" to defend himself. Asked why he thought he was arrested while so many senior officers skated, he replied: "Rank has its privileges."

Federal agents admitted there was a higher bar for investigating admirals. "They're a lot more financially able to take apart your investigation and say that you did a bad job and accuse you of malfeasance," said Trey DeLaPena, the DCIS special agent.

A few convicted Navy officers faced the consequences without making excuses. "I have only myself to blame," said Commander David Kapaun, who worked as an unofficial consultant for Francis in the early 2000s and received an eighteen-month prison term. Captain Michael Brooks, the former naval attaché who let Francis infiltrate the U.S. embassy in Manila, did not whitewash the damage he caused. "As a senior naval officer, my actions in the Philippines are inexcusable," he told the judge during his sentencing hearing in 2017. He received a prison term of thirty-five months.

But most ducked taking full responsibility for their crimes. Captain Jeff Breslau, Francis's ghostwriter, pleaded guilty to a criminal conflict of interest charge and received a six-month prison term. At his sentencing in 2019, he suggested he had committed only a technical violation of the law by failing to disclose his work for Francis while on active duty, not that he had betrayed his officer's oath by taking money from a con man to help manipulate admirals. "It was out of character for me to assume my activities fell outside the scope of conflict-of-interest rules," he said.

Many officers blamed booze and other vices. "My relationship with alcohol is unhealthy," said Captain David Haas, the Seventh Fleet triathlete, when he was given a two-and-a-half-year sentence in 2023. Captain Dan Dusek, another former Seventh Fleet officer, said "excessive amounts of alcohol" and the "tortuous ending of my second marriage" spurred him to barter military secrets for prostitutes. He received nearly four years in prison. The attorney for Lieutenant Commander Gentry Debord, a supply officer, said he accepted cash bribes and prostitutes in part because of his "sex addiction." He was sentenced to thirty months.

A lawyer for Paul Simpkins, the contracting supervisor in Singapore who took hundreds of thousands of dollars in bribes from Francis, also alluded to "an alcohol problem." In a rambling letter to the judge, however, Simpkins called himself "a scapegoat" and a casualty of "the cover up." He received a six-year prison term.

In contrast, few proved more adept at dodging legal bullets than Ed Aruffo, the Seventh Fleet wedding planner and Francis protégé who confessed to orchestrating kickbacks when he worked as Glenn Defense's country manager for Japan. Aruffo pleaded guilty to conspiracy to defraud the United States but had to spend only eighty-three days in jail because he cooperated with federal agents and testified as a government witness.

Despite his felony record, Aruffo persuaded the Thomas Jefferson School of Law in San Diego to admit him as a student. He earned his juris doctor degree and passed the California bar exam in 2020. As of December 2023, the state had not licensed him to practice law, partly because he was still on probation. But Thomas Jefferson hired the admitted fraudster as an adjunct professor to teach a new generation of law students. He also wrote a popular book, *Bar Exam Essay Rules: Your Guide to Passing the Bar Exam.*

Meanwhile, as an institution, the U.S. Navy did everything it could after Francis pleaded guilty in 2015 to hide the extent of the rot in its ranks and avoid a full public accounting.

Apart from the thirty-four defendants prosecuted in federal court, the Justice Department referred cases involving 685 U.S. servicemembers—almost all of them Navy personnel—to military disciplinary authorities for review.

The Navy adjudicated almost all its cases in the dark. It publicly identified only nineteen individuals who were found to have violated military law, regulations, or ethical standards. Of those, five were court-martialed. Eleven received letters of censure—a professionally embarrassing reprimand, but otherwise a punishment of little consequence.

I filed dozens of Freedom of Information Act (FOIA) requests seeking thousands of pages of military disciplinary records from the Fat Leonard scandal. For the most part, the Navy released only fragments, blacking out the names of those who were investigated, among other details. Fortunately, in many instances, I was able to obtain uncensored copies from other sources.

Those documents show that the Navy exonerated a small number of personnel because of a lack of evidence. Likewise, it was unable to court-martial some suspects because the statute of limitations under military law had lapsed. But in most instances, the Navy excused misconduct on the dubious grounds that its personnel didn't know any better. In case after case, the Navy let people off the hook for enjoying Francis's extravagant feasts or sleeping in five-star hotels at Glenn Defense's expense because they were following the lead of an admiral or senior officer who did the same thing.

Notably, there was no sign that the Navy stripped anyone of their military pensions or other retirement benefits, even those offenders who admitted to selling out their country by taking bribes or giving Francis military secrets. (Veteran benefits can be substantial, with retired admirals and captains receiving six-figure annual pensions for life, courtesy of U.S. taxpayers.)

Meanwhile, another big mystery remained: Exactly how much money did Francis steal from the U.S. government during his twenty-five years of doing business with the Navy? It was a question that neither the Justice Department nor the Navy answered definitively, in part because the figure would be such an embarrassment.

When Francis pleaded guilty in 2015, he admitted to defrauding the Navy of $35 million over a nine-year period. But investigators suspected him of fleecing U.S. taxpayers of far more. In a 2017 court hearing, Assistant U.S. Attorney Pletcher stated that Francis "serially defrauded the United States of upwards of $50 million," a number echoed in several confidential NCIS documents. Others guessed the total was higher. In one internal report, an NCIS official estimated that the figure was "more towards possibly $100 million."

One person knew for sure, and he wasn't telling. A year before both men were arrested, John Beliveau Jr., the crooked NCIS agent, tipped off Francis in a text that some officials suspected the Navy had "lost $$ Billions due to fraud."

Francis didn't bite. Instead, he texted a teasing reply.

"Ha Ha"

Throughout 2023, nobody paid closer attention to the faltering Navy prosecutions than Francis. Though he was stuck in a jail cell in Caracas, he obsessively read news coverage about the prosecutorial misconduct in San Diego and prodded family members, ex-girlfriends, and other contacts to text him updates.

Despite his guilty plea eight years earlier, Francis still saw himself as an unfairly maligned victim. In his mind, he had faithfully served the U.S. Navy for decades and then provided an unprecedented amount of assistance to the Justice Department. If the U.S. Attorney's Office **was** going to throw in the towel with so many cases, he hoped that maybe—just maybe—it would drop charges against him, too.

El Helicoide was a notorious, cockroach-filled prison in the center of Caracas where detainees complained of being subjected to electric shocks and other forms of torture. Yet Francis was held in comparative comfort in a VIP wing for special prisoners. He was permitted to keep a phone and receive food deliveries, though he was denied medical care. He worried constantly that his cancer might come back.

As the months passed, Francis became more hopeful that the Venezuelan government would grant his asylum claim and free him from custody. He was jolted, however, in June 2023, when the Venezuelan secret police told him he had some visitors. They turned out to be a group of diplomats, led by an American: Roger Carstens, the State Department's special envoy for hostage affairs.

Francis panicked. The last person he was hoping to see was someone from the U.S. government. He told Carstens that he opposed any effort to return him to the United States. He wanted to stay in Venezuela or go back to his native Malaysia.

Though neither side told Francis, U.S. and Venezuelan officials were secretly negotiating a prisoner swap. The Venezuelan government was offering to exchange Francis and several detained Americans for Alex Saab, a businessman and close ally of President Nicolás Maduro who was being prosecuted in Miami on federal money laundering charges. But the U.S. government was reluctant to part with Saab, whom it considered a bigger fish than Francis in terms of national security and foreign policy.

The negotiations stalled. By November 2023, Francis felt optimistic again. Rumors spread through El Helicoide that a political decision had been made to let him go because the Americans were unwilling to trade for him. Prison informants told Francis that he would be freed through informal channels if there was no pending litigation to gum up the works. As a result, he ordered his Venezuelan attorney, Marco Rodríguez-Acosta, to drop a habeas corpus petition seeking to compel his release.

Rodríguez-Acosta was shocked and told Francis he was making a huge mistake. But Francis was convinced his freedom was near. He stiffed Rodríguez-Acosta for $49,000 in unpaid legal bills, just as he had stopped paying his doctor, landlord, and lawyers in San Diego when he felt he didn't need their services anymore.

A week before Christmas, Francis texted his mother in Kuala Lumpur to say that Venezuelan officials had promised to let him out of El Helicoide to receive medical treatment, and that he expected to win his complete freedom by the end of the year. He sent similar messages to Sarah Macdonald, the British journalist and filmmaker who had interviewed him in his San Diego mansion shortly before his escape from U.S. custody.

In fact, it was all a ruse. The Venezuelan secret police had planted false rumors about Francis's pending release. They wanted him to abandon any legal obstacles that could block his transfer back to the United States.

On December 20, Venezuelan authorities removed him from prison, bundled him onto a small jet, and flew him to Canouan, a tiny Caribbean island. There, along with ten Americans who had been held prisoner in Venezuela, he was handed over to U.S. officials in exchange for Saab.

The prisoner swap made international headlines. President Joe Biden welcomed the release of the "wrongfully detained" Americans and bragged that the long arm of the law had nabbed Francis again. "He will face justice for crimes he committed against the U.S. government and the American people," Biden promised.

While most of the freed American prisoners were flown to San Antonio, where they received medical checkups at a U.S. Air Force base, Francis was taken in shackles on a separate flight to Miami, where he was presented to a federal magistrate.

Wearing a tan jumpsuit, Francis appeared haggard and about forty pounds lighter than he did fifteen months earlier when he fled from California. Prosecutors said he would be charged with absconding from justice and moved to transfer him to San Diego to face the music. When the judge asked Francis if he could afford a lawyer, he replied: "Not right now."

Instead of ringing in the New Year by celebrating his freedom, Francis found himself in the custody of U.S. Marshals and the Federal Bureau of Prisons. In San Diego, he landed back on Judge Sammartino's court docket. She would spend 2024 deciding his punishment, once and for all.

Acknowledgments

For ten years, I have been captivated by the hard-to-believe and outrageous saga of Leonard Francis and the U.S. Navy. My curiosity was ignited in October 2013, when I was wandering the halls of the Pentagon as a military beat reporter for *The Washington Post* and bumped into a Navy officer I was acquainted with. Offhandedly, I asked if he knew anything about the defense contractor who had recently been arrested in San Diego on bribery charges, a story that had received a smattering of press coverage on the West Coast. "Oh, you mean Fat Leonard," he replied, smiling. "Everybody in the Navy knows about Fat Leonard." The revelation that Francis was a semi-legendary figure in Navy circles and had a tabloidesque nickname smelled like an irresistible story. I started digging and was instantly hooked. When I had to turn my attention to other assignments, the Fat Leonard scandal continued to exert a magnetic hold on me. This book is the final product of my decade-long fixation.

I had an enormous amount of help along the way. *The Washington Post*, my professional home for the past twenty-five years, is an inspirational place to work and places the highest premium on investigative reporting that holds people in power to account. The *Post* gave me endless encouragement to cover the story, as well as that most precious commodity for journalists—time.

When I first started working on the story, my editors on the *Post*'s National Security Desk, Peter Finn and Jason Ukman, gave me the freedom to dive in and edited dozens of articles that I wrote between 2013 and 2016. When I moved to the Investigative Desk, my editors

Jeff Leen and David Fallis encouraged me to dig deeper and write bigger. They lead the best team of investigative journalists in the world. A special thanks to David, who edited the early drafts of this manuscript and guided me in the right direction at pivotal moments. He is a spectacular journalist who also served as the primary editor on my first book, *The Afghanistan Papers*. Mary Pat Flaherty, another outstanding editor on the Investigative Desk, also provided invaluable feedback.

The *Post*'s senior editors unflinchingly back their reporters to the hilt and I am privileged to work for Executive Editor Sally Buzbee and her team of managing editors: Justin Bank, Matea Gold, Scott Vance, and Krissah Williams. Former managing editors Cameron Barr and Tracy Grant encouraged me to turn my newspaper reporting into a book. I'd also like to thank a host of treasured colleagues in the newsroom who humored me along the way and never seemed to tire of my Fat Leonard updates: Michael Robinson-Chavez, Mark Gail, Dan Lamothe, Greg Jaffe, Mary Jordan, Kevin Sullivan, Ian Shapira, John Woodrow Cox, Lynda Robinson, Nate Jones, Paul Schwartzman, Sarah Childress, Jenn Abelson, Nicole Dungca, Amy Brittain, and Dalton Bennett. Special shout-outs go to Jonathan O'Connell, Robert Miller, and Maria Luísa Paúl, who helped keep the story alive.

Several other talented *Post* colleagues played critical roles in producing this book. J. J. Evans is an editor and fact-checker of unparalleled skill who took a rough draft and magically transformed it into something I'm very proud of. Laris Karklis, a top-notch cartographer, drew the beautiful map of Southeast Asia. Kevin Uhrmacher is a first-rate graphics editor who first teamed up with me on this story in 2016 and designed the terrific charts illustrating Navy officer ranks and a selection of ships from the Seventh Fleet. Andrew Ba Tran, one of the country's best data journalists, helped me organize several terabytes of records.

I am exceptionally grateful to the team at Simon & Schuster for recognizing the narrative potential of this story and for devoting so much enthusiasm to the project. Vice President and Editor-in-Chief Priscilla

Painton is a gem of an editor who has always been a lifeline: patient, accessible, and unfailingly supportive. This is our second book together and she has a special touch. It has also been my good fortune to work with Ian Straus, a true wordsmith and natural storyteller whose energy and hard work helped this book reach its maximum potential. Fred Chase, a marvelous copy editor, polished the entire manuscript. Thanks also to John Pelosi and Felice Javit for their thorough legal review, and to Anna Hauser for helping to deliver the final product.

I would never have become an author without the backing and motivation of my all-star literary agent, Christy Fletcher, the co-head of publishing for United Talent Agency. Christy is the person who first saw the potential for writing a book about Leonard Francis and the U.S. Navy. She is the best in the business, and I treasure her steadfast support and wise counsel. Thanks also Zoë Balestri for always being there in a pinch.

This book would not have been possible without help from a host of sources who trusted me to tell the story with accuracy, depth, and nuance. Many of them risked retaliation for talking to a journalist. Even after ten years, I can't name them all here because of fears that they would be subject to reprisal for spilling the Navy's secrets.

A heartfelt thanks to the following individuals who granted on-the-record interviews and were generous with their time: David Schaus, Chris Statler, Jonathan Greenert, Thomas Oppel, Ray Mabus, Jeff O'Neal, David Adelman, David Meyers, Marty Fields, Sunil Bhoyrul, Spencer Driscoll, James Paris, John Durkin, Joel Rolley, Lance Don, Mark Ridley, John Smallman, Greg Ford, Andrew Hogan, Marcy Misiewicz, Lora Amundson, Morena De Jesus, Claudia Risner, Mike Lang, Mike Seaman, David Warunek, Ron Carr, Ron Horton, Steve Barney, Adrian Jansen, Mike Ryan, Keith Maly, Tim Giardina, Doug Crowder, Jeff Davis, Scott Thompson, Sarah Macdonald, Christopher Kirchhoff, and David Fravor. A special note of gratitude to Jim Maus, who knows Leonard Francis better than most and who spent countless hours teaching me about logreqs, Z-peller tugboats, demurrage, and other intricacies of the husbanding business. Ed Hanel made sure I understood the difference between a husbanding contractor and a husbanding agent, as well as other intricacies of contracting law. Jim Piburn and Robert Gonzales were unfailingly tolerant of my pesky questions and understood the importance of telling the full story. Stephen Wrage was a valuable sounding board, and the U.S. Naval Academy is fortunate to count him among its faculty.

While the Navy may have wished the story would go away, the following public affairs officers were always professional and responded to my queries in good faith: Rear Admiral John Kirby, Rear Admiral Dawn Cutler, Rear Admiral Ryan Perry, Captain Amy Derrick, Captain Greg Hicks, and Captain Mike Kafka. Karen Richman, NCIS's assistant counsel and the head of its Freedom of Information Act office, and her colleague Erin Roberge, went beyond the call of duty in responding to my dozens of FOIA requests. Kelly Thornton, the media relations director for the U.S. Attorney's Office in San Diego, was equally responsive and helpful in providing public records.

I extend a special measure of respect to several defendants in the Glenn Defense Marine Asia case who granted me on-the-record interviews, including Troy Amundson, Jeff Breslau, Robert Gilbeau, Dave Kapaun, David Morales, Brooks Parks III, and Bobby Pitts. It would have been understandable for them to stay silent, but they forthrightly answered difficult questions. John Beliveau Jr. sent me numerous letters from prison and didn't duck any of my queries. A heartfelt thanks to his mother, Mary Beliveau, for acting as a go-between so we could dodge the censors at the Bureau of Prisons. Attorneys for numerous defendants helped me better understand their clients' cases, including Joseph Mancano, Vincent Ward, Frank Spinner, Gary Myers, Eric Montalvo, Suresh Damodara, Mark Adams, and Jeremiah J. Sullivan III. Thanks also to Devin Burstein, Marco Rodriguez-Acosta, and Ethan Posner, who represented Leonard Francis.

Matt Topic and Josh Loevy, two of the nation's leading FOIA attorneys from the firm Loevy and Loevy, took on my FOIA lawsuit against the Department of Defense and the Navy. It takes mettle to sue the federal government, and they never flinched. I also benefited from the reporting of several other journalists who broke important ground on the Fat Leonard case, including Geoff Ziezulewicz of *Navy Times*, Kristina Davis, Alex Riggins, and Greg Moran of *The San Diego Union-Tribune*, Andrew Dyer of KPBS, and Tony Perry of the *Los Angeles Times*.

Finally, for someone who writes for a living, it is difficult for me to put into words how thankful I am for the unconditional support of my family. My wife, Jennifer Toth, is the love of my life and I am forever grateful for her wisdom, insights, patience, and advice. More than anyone, she understood why I felt I had to write this book and the dedication that it required. Her indispensable feedback and editing suggestions improved every chapter. Our son, Kyle Whitlock, spent his high school and college years cheerfully listening to my stories about Leonard Francis and the Navy. I'm proud of him beyond belief and lucky to be his father.

Note on Sources

There's an old saying in journalism: If your mother says she loves you, check it out.

That means reporters and authors should never assume anyone—not even Mom—is telling the truth. Sometimes well-meaning sources get their facts mixed up. Other times people inadvertently omit important parts of the story. Not infrequently, those with agendas or something to hide try to deceive. As a result, it is critically important for journalists to verify whatever they are told with independent sources.

Investigative journalists consider documents to be the gold standard of source material. There is nothing better than having government, corporate, or personal records to corroborate information gleaned from first-person interviews. Fortunately, I managed to collect a bonanza of documents during my decade of digging into the Fat Leonard scandal—more, by far, than for any other project I have tackled during my thirty-four-year career as a journalist, including my previous book, *The Afghanistan Papers: A Secret History of the War.*

This trove includes notes from law enforcement interviews of hundreds of witnesses and suspects in the case, as well as court records, affidavits, transcripts of surreptitious audio recordings, Navy disciplinary records, documents from court-martial proceedings, military personnel files, warship deck logs, husbanding invoices, Bravo Zulu letters, diary entries, and declassified intelligence reports. The material also includes emails, text messages, spreadsheets, and other data which federal investigators obtained from Leonard Francis's smartphones, laptops, and Glenn Defense computer servers.

Last but certainly not least, this book draws on material from Francis's voluminous "blackmail" files: photographs, prostitute testimonials, hotel receipts, bar tabs, restaurant menus, thank-you notes—even Christmas cards that he received from Navy officers.

These documents enabled me to check, and cross-check, what I learned while conducting more than 150 on-the-record interviews. I made repeated attempts to contact everyone profiled in the book, or their legal representatives, to ask for comment. Responses from those who agreed to answer questions or provide statements are reflected throughout the chapters and in the Endnotes. Military personnel are identified by the rank they held at the time of the events described.

While reporting and writing *Fat Leonard*, I had to constantly gauge people's credibility. It will come as no surprise to readers that many of those tarred by the scandal had incentive to lie or minimize their involvement.

In trying to ascertain the truth, I gave the greatest weight to official findings from federal court cases and the military justice system, especially sworn witness testimony, jury verdicts, and stipulations of fact. Similarly, I lent extra credence to notes and transcripts of what people said during interviews with federal agents because those individuals knew they could be prosecuted if they made false statements to law enforcement officials. Even then, however, it was not uncommon for Navy personnel to fib or obfuscate or profess amnesia when questioned about their dealings with Francis. I took nothing at face value.

The character who merits the most skepticism is Francis himself, an admitted con artist. Leonard has an outsized ego and loves to brag about how easy it was for him to seduce, corrupt, and manipulate so many Navy officers. In his podcast interviews, he made several dubious or exaggerated statements. (Full disclosure: Francis declined repeated interview requests from me.) It is important to note that federal prosecutors declined to call him as a witness during the 2022 criminal trial of several former Seventh Fleet officers. They knew defense attorneys would have questioned his veracity and his motives for cooperating with the Justice Department.

In reviewing notes of Francis's interviews with prosecutors and federal agents, however, I generally found what he said during those sessions to be credible. Unlike other suspects in the scandal, most of whom tried to cover up their wrongdoing, Francis volunteered details of his many crimes. What made his interviews even more compelling was that he usually had hard evidence to confirm his stories, such as contemporaneous emails, text messages, photographs, and hotel bills. Even so, I applied the same hard-and-fast rule to Francis as I did to everyone else: I never took his word for it. I used information attributable to him only if it checked out with other sources or documents.

Endnotes

PROLOGUE

1 *he cut off the GPS tracking device:* María Luisa Paúl, "'Fat Leonard' Escapes Weeks Before Sentencing in Navy Bribery Scandal," *Washington Post,* September 6, 2022.

3 *"Every sailor has a weakness somewhere":* Leonard Francis email to Commander Jose Sanchez, September 2, 2009.

4 *"The Soviets couldn't have penetrated us better than Leonard Francis":* Author interview with retired Captain Jim Maus, February 15, 2015.

4 *"The KGB could not have done what he did":* Author interview with retired Captain Jim Maus, February 1, 2016.

4 *nearly one thousand people were swept up:* Transcript, Status Hearing, *USA v. David Newland, et al.,* U.S. District Court, Southern District of California, September 13, 2019. At the hearing, Assistant U.S. Attorney Mark Pletcher said the investigation had "between 700 and 1,000 subjects."

4 *including 685 U.S. servicemembers:* Declaration of Lieutenant Commander Ann Oakes, Judge Advocate General's Corps, *Craig Whitlock v. U.S. Department of Defense and U.S. Department of the Navy,* U.S. District Court, District of Columbia, November 1, 2021. Responding to the author's Freedom of Information Act (FOIA) lawsuit against the Navy, Oakes stated that the Justice Department "has referred approximately 685 subjects to the military adjudication authorities for all of the services."

4 *"A Global Force for Good":* The Navy stopped using the recruiting slogan in 2015.

5 *my first article about the case:* Craig Whitlock, "Senior Officer, NCIS Agent Are Among Those Arrested in Navy Bribery Scandal," *Washington Post,* October 19, 2013.

6 *the Navy grew tired of my questions:* G. E. Lattin, Director, General Litigation Director, Office of the Judge Advocate General, Department of the Navy, in letter to author, June 3, 2020.

CHAPTER ONE: A GOOD WHIPPING

11 *two unlicensed .38-caliber Smith & Wesson revolvers:* Criminal Appeal, *Public Prosecutor v. Leonard Glenn Francis,* High Court (Penang), March 1, 1989, as published in *The Malayan Law Journal,* June 16, 1989.

11 *Detectives had nabbed Francis:* Ibid.

12 *"Young dumb-dumb":* Tom Wright interview #4 with Leonard Glenn Francis. (Hereinafter Francis interview #[ ], Wright.) Wright conducted twenty hours of interviews with Francis and used them for a 2021 podcast titled *Fat Leonard.* In response to a judicial subpoena, Wright made eighteen audio recordings of his interviews with Francis publicly available, posting them at www.dropbox.com on December 22, 2021. The interview dates were not disclosed.

12 *"the burly businessman":* "Trader Charged with Robbery After Acquittal," *New Straits Times,* Kuala Lumpur, Malaysia, April 2, 1986.

12 *"undesirable characters":* Criminal Appeal, *Public Prosecutor v. Leonard Glenn Francis,* High Court (Penang), March 1, 1989.

12 *separated from her philandering husband:* Ibid.

12 *A psychiatrist from Penang General Hospital:* Ibid. The consulting psychiatrist, Dr. Varughese Thomas, wrote a medical report stating that Francis was "in need of prolonged psychiatric help" and that his obesity "was also to be regarded as a serious physical disorder."

13 *"I am giving him another chance":* "Trader Charged with Robbery After Acquittal, *New Straits Times,* April 2, 1986.

13 *"cannot be justified either in law or on principle":* Criminal Appeal, *Public Prosecutor v. Leonard Glenn Francis,* High Court (Penang), March 1, 1989.

13 *"whipping with six strokes":* Ibid.

13 *about a year behind bars:* Francis interview #5, Wright.

13 *Even the whipping went better than expected:* Ibid.

14 *fathered two sons and a daughter:* Adrian David, "Penang's Prominent Shipping Agent Dies," *New Straits Times,* April 29, 2021.

14 *left his wife and children behind:* Leonard Francis email to author, November 23, 2017.

14 *Portuguese explorers and Tamil merchants:* Francis interview #5, Wright.

14 *baptized him in the church:* Francis interview #2, Wright.

15 *enrolled at St. Christopher School:* Author interview with Jeff O'Neal, October 26, 2021.

15 *"My father was very violent":* Francis interview #5, Wright.

15 *"always messing around":* Francis interview #1, Wright.

15 *"I'm a survivor":* Francis interview #13, Wright.

15 *"a pretty difficult child to manage"*: Francis interview #1, Wright.

16 *"He was a natural-born leader"*: O'Neal interview with author.

16 *expelled fifteen-year-old Leonard*: Ibid.

16 *"He was too busy womanizing"*: Francis interview #2, Wright.

16 *called the old man "Gaddafi"*: O'Neal interview with author.

17 *Leonard drew up the paperwork*: Francis interviews #1 and #3, Wright. Francis has given varying accounts of when he started Glenn Marine Enterprise, but he was likely between eighteen and twenty years old.

17 *"a taste for going big"*: O'Neal interview with author.

17 *regaled him with tales of their international adventures*: Ibid.

18 *renamed it Tropicana*: Francis interview #4, Wright.

CHAPTER TWO: THE STRIVER

20 *Francis cut a vivid figure that evening*: Francis kept about thirty photographs that show him partying with the USS *Acadia* officers in May 1992.

20 *made-up stories about his college days at the University of North Carolina*: Notes from DCIS interview of retired Captain Harry Guess, August 10, 2017. Francis often told people he went to UNC. The university registrar's office said it has no record of Francis attending the school.

20 *he knew he wasn't supposed to accept freebies*: Ibid. Guess told DCIS agents that he and the other *Acadia* officers wanted to pay for their share of the meal, but Francis refused, so they decided "to chalk it up to a life lesson and never do something like that again."

20 *"Thanks so much for everything. With Love, Ruth"*: Lieutenant Ruth Christopherson letter to Leonard Francis, May 28, 1992. In an interview with DCIS agents on August 11, 2017, Christopherson—who had since retired from the Navy as a captain—said she could only vaguely recall going to dinner with Francis.

21 *a storefront office near a new Malaysian navy base*: Francis interview #4, Wright.

21 *so small that it shared a squat toilet*: Ibid.

22 *"It all just kind of fell in my lap"*: Ibid.

22 *After his stint in prison, he met and married*: Ibid. Deposition of Leonard Francis, *General Court-Martial of Commander David Morales*, Naval Base San Diego, July 18, 2018. Francis told Wright that he was twenty-seven when he married, but he was evasive when asked at the deposition how old he had been.

22 *"I kind of got a liking to her"*: Francis interview #4, Wright.

23 *Francis almost drowned*: Notes from joint DCIS-NCIS interview of Rear Admiral Cynthia Thebaud, February 15, 2016. Francis email to Thebaud, September 20, 2003.

23 *squashed on purpose so Leonard could fit in the car:* Notes from NCIS interview of retired Commander Tracy Brown, September 7, 2017.

23 *"a bend-over backwards type guy":* Ibid.

23 *Some called him "Fat Bastard":* Notes from NCIS interview of retired Lieutenant Commander John Van Gorp, March 10, 2016.

23 *"Mr. Francis's untiring devotion to United States Navy ship visits":* Vice Admiral Robert Natter letter to Glenn Marine Enterprise, February 5, 1997.

23 *He bragged that he once handed a $20,000 bribe to a supply officer:* Notes from joint NCIS-DCIS interview of Leonard Francis, January 30, 2015. Notes from joint DCIS-NCIS interview of Neil Peterson, former vice president for operations, Glenn Defense, May 11, 2017. Peterson corroborated Francis's story that he provided cash bribes to Navy officials who would hide the money in a ballcap to get it back onto the ship.

24 *"He was huger than huge then":* Author interview with retired Captain Robert Gilbeau, October 17, 2023. In a 2013 interview with DCIS, Gilbeau estimated that Francis weighed "like 450, 500 pounds" at the time.

24 *"Oh, sit, sit—spend some time!":* Transcript, DCIS interview of Rear Admiral Robert Gilbeau, November 10, 2013. Notes from joint DCIS-NCIS interview of Leonard Francis, May 4, 2015. Francis confirmed Gilbeau's account that they first met in Bali in 1997.

25 *jamming roads leading to the harbor:* "More than 100,000 Visit Two US Warships," *New Straits Times,* May 1, 1997.

25 *"He looked like Jabba the Hutt sitting out there":* Author interview with retired Captain Jim Maus, February 17, 2019.

26 *"The guy was unbelievably charming":* Ibid.

26 *"I was thinking, 'Wow, this guy is really prepared for us'":* Ibid.

26 *Francis arranged for the sailors to travel by rail:* Ibid. Notes from DCIS interview of Leonard Francis, November 23, 2015.

27 *a Royal Selangor pewter tankard:* Maus interview with author, February 17, 2019.

27 *"I was just absolutely livid":* Ibid.

27 *"I was so pissed":* Ibid.

CHAPTER THREE: RING OF STEEL

29 *"No little boat is going through that":* Author interview with retired Captain Jim Maus, June 14, 2019.

30 *"The Navy went crazy and paranoid over the Cole":* Author interview with retired Commander David Kapaun, February 5, 2021.

30 *stopped by Glenn Marine's "floating barrier of barges":* USS *Blue Ridge* Command

History for Calendar Year 2001, Naval History and Heritage Command, Washington, D.C. Notes from joint DCIS-NCIS interview of retired Captain Alan Abramson, April 7, 2016. Abramson, who attended the Chalet dinner, said several barges surrounded the *Blue Ridge* to provide extra security during the port visit but he did not recall an attempted terrorist attack.

31 *"Everybody had to use the Ring of Steel"*: Francis interview #10, Wright.

31 *"a well-trained, well-led and highly capable ship"*: Navy JAGMAN Investigation into the attack on USS *Cole* in Aden, Yemen, October 12, 2000.

32 *they knew if "you had a second* Cole, *that the shit would hit the fan"*: Transcript, NCIS interview of Captain James Dolan, March 15, 2017.

32 *Some mocked it as "the Ring of Gold"*: Notes from NCIS interview of retired Lieutenant Commander Ryan Kight, March 1, 2017. Kight, a supply officer, told federal agents that he "hated" Glenn Defense because the firm was "ripping us off."

32 *or the "Ring of Death"*: Transcript, NCIS interview of retired Lieutenant Commander Fred Higgs, March 2, 2017.

33 *"It's nothing sophisticated or fancy"*: Notes from joint NCIS-DCIS interview of retired Captain Al Collins, September 26, 2017.

33 *never subjected the Ring of Steel to rigorous field testing*: Notes from joint DCIS-NCIS interview of retired Commander Jonathan Mosier, September 16, 2014.

33 *Wackenhut reported the Ring of Steel had "a robust appearance"*: Wackenhut, "Report: Assessment of Contracted Force Protection Services, US Navy, Western Pacific AOR," December 26, 2006.

33 *complained that the Ring of Steel was "ridiculously expensive"*: Notes from DCIS interview of retired Commander David Warunek, February 17, 2015.

34 *"silent, quiet weirdo"*: Notes from joint DCIS-NCIS interview of Leonard Francis, November 6, 2015.

34 *"a whole lot of expensive prostitutes"*: Ibid.

34 *in from Jakarta*: Ibid. Government Sentencing Memorandum, *USA v. David Kapaun*, U.S. District Court, District of Hawaii, September 8, 2017.

34 *He rated prostitutes by their looks*: Francis interview, DCIS-NCIS, November 6, 2015. Francis provided federal agents with copies of ten email exchanges that he had with Kapaun between 2003 and 2006. Francis also alleged that Kapaun provided him with classified ship schedules. In an interview with the author, Kapaun acknowledged giving ship schedules to Francis on one occasion but was unsure if they were classified or not. The Justice Department did not charge Kapaun with leaking military secrets.

35 *"[Leonard's] written English was terrible"*: Kapaun interview with author.

35 *He suggested how Francis could tweak his plans for the Ring of Steel*: Ibid.

35 *$50,000 worth of prostitutes, meals, hotel rooms, tickets, and other gifts*: Government Sentencing Memorandum, *USA v. Kapaun*. In June 2017, Kapaun

pleaded guilty to making false statements about his relationship with Francis and received an eighteen-month prison sentence. He agreed to pay $50,000 in restitution and a $25,000 fine.

35 *"I knew the banshees might come to roost for me"*: Kapaun interview with author.

35 *he now weighed about five hundred pounds*: Author interview with Jeff O'Neal, October 26, 2021.

35 *Leonard thought the operation sounded promising*: Ibid.

36 *He was carrying $40,000 in cash*: Ibid.

36 *"off to Graceland"*: Ibid.

CHAPTER FOUR: LEONARD THE LEGEND

37 *the $30,000 feast*: Notes from joint DCIS-NCIS interview of Leonard Francis, October 21, 2013.

37 *massaged their necks*: Notes from joint DCIS-NCIS interview of retired Marine Corps Sergeant Major Jeffrey Morin, October 21, 2015.

37 *the scene resembled a "Roman orgy"*: Notes from joint DCIS-NCIS interview of retired Commander Thomas Reynolds, October 26, 2015. Reynolds said it was obvious that Francis was trying to bribe his Navy guests with the prostitutes and that anyone who fell for it was an "idiot."

37 *One prostitute flashed her breasts at Rear Admiral Robert Conway Jr.*: Notes from joint DCIS-NCIS interview of Rear Admiral Cynthia Thebaud, February 15, 2016. Thebaud said Conway, her boss, had been "friendly" with the prostitutes and that one of them flashed him. In a separate interview with federal agents, Conway denied that anyone had flashed their breasts at him, saying: "I did not see that." When asked if any of the prostitutes had sat on his lap, he said he could not recall. Notes from NCIS interview of retired Vice Admiral Robert Conway Jr., April 6, 2016. In an email to the author, Conway said the accounts of what happened at the dinner party were "based on hearsay and not ground truth," but he declined to comment further.

37 *mouthed the words to "Y.M.C.A."*: Reynolds interview, DCIS-NCIS. Reynolds said Regner's singing shocked him because he had previously thought of the Marine colonel as "strict" and a "robot." In a 2015 interview with federal agents, Regner—by then a major general—acknowledged attending the dinner but said he could not recall who sponsored it. He said there were "many pretty girls" serving alcohol but that he would have remembered if there were prostitutes. Navy disciplinary authorities concluded there was no evidence that Regner patronized a prostitute or behaved inappropriately.

38 *a "self-impressed" blowhard*: Notes from joint DCIS-NCIS interview of retired Captain Dennis Schulz, January 28, 2016. Schulz was the operations officer for

Expeditionary Strike Group One aboard the USS *Peleliu*. He said he skipped the dinner because he was too exhausted from work.

38 *Conway showed the invitation to a uniformed Navy lawyer:* Notes from joint DCIS-NCIS interview of Captain William Boland, September 9, 2015. Boland said he advised Conway that it was okay to attend the dinner based on a "foreign area gift exception" to federal ethics rules but didn't know it would be a catered affair at the top of a skyscraper. When federal agents told him the cost of the event exceeded $30,000, he replied, "holy shit."

*38 *he told the admiral stories, in graphic detail:* Notes from joint DCIS-NCIS interview of retired Vice Admiral Robert Conway Jr., February 26, 2016. Conway said it never occurred to him that accepting the meal might be a violation of federal ethics rules. When federal agents asked him if, in hindsight, he might do anything differently, Conway said no.

39 *"dressed to the nines":* Notes from joint DCIS-NCIS interview of retired Commander David Cole, August 27, 2015. Cole was the Navy SEAL liaison officer for Expeditionary Strike Group One. When the women entered the room, he recalled, all eyes swung toward Conway to gauge his reaction. He said the admiral did not object or protest.

39 *"This is your entertainment for the evening!":* Notes from NCIS interview of retired Captain Lowell Crow, September 4, 2015. Crow, the commanding officer of the USS *Ogden* in 2003, described the women as wearing "hooker shoes" and said it was obvious they were prostitutes. He said he and Thebaud became uneasy and left.

39 *She bit her tongue:* Thebaud interview, DCIS-NCIS.

39 *a meal that cost $880 per person:* Admiral Philip Davidson memo to Chief of Naval Personnel, March 9, 2018. An estimated twenty-five to thirty-five guests attended the dinner. Navy disciplinary authorities determined that the value, per person, "exceeded $880." In March 2018, the Navy concluded that Conway—by then retired—had committed misconduct by improperly accepting dinner and entertainment "in excess of ethical limits." But the Navy kept the matter a secret and took no further action against Conway.

39 *Conway dismissively told his staff:* Conway interview, DCIS-NCIS, February 26, 2016.

39 *"you made our stay a memorable one":* Rear Admiral R. T. Conway Jr. letter to Leonard G. Francis, September 22, 2003.

40 *"Their egos allowed them to feel like they should be treated in a certain way":* Transcript, NCIS interview of retired Captain Ted Algire, September 25, 2013.

40 *Francis engrossed the admiral:* Notes from joint DCIS-NCIS interview of Admiral Samuel Locklear, October 30, 2014. Locklear told federal agents that he

did not want to attend the dinner but went anyway because Navy officials stationed in Singapore had arranged it. He said he was unaware that Francis had
paid for the meal.

41 *Francis said he paid some prostitutes:* Notes from joint DCIS-NCIS interview of
Leonard Francis, May 4, 2015.

41 *"Catch my drift?":* Commander Robert Gilbeau email to Leonard Francis, October 1, 2003.

41 *"The Kahuna above has heard our prayers":* Leonard Francis email to Commander Robert Gilbeau, October 1, 2003.

41 *Francis spent $35,000 on the feast:* Notes from joint DCIS-NCIS interview of
Leonard Francis, April 1, 2015.

41 *After dessert, things turned rowdy:* Ibid.

41 *"Fat Leonard brought in the girls":* Craig Whitlock, "'Fat Leonard' Affected Pentagon's Pick to Lead Joint Chiefs," *Washington Post*, April 1, 2018.

42 *"The food was absolutely magnificent!":* Rear Admiral S. J. Locklear III letter to
Leonard Francis, October 13, 2003.

42 *asked him to buy $200,000 worth of flat-screen televisions:* Francis interview,
DCIS-NCIS, May 4, 2015.

42 *"Help out an old buddy":* Ibid.

42 *Gilbeau obliged:* In a October 17, 2023, interview with the author, Gilbeau
confirmed that he approved the purchase of the flat-screen televisions. He said
the captain of the Nimitz told him to buy the televisions and that Glenn Defense offered the best deal in terms of cost, quality, and delivery time. "It was
all above board," he said.

42 *Glenn Defense further overcharged the* Nimitz: Government Sentencing Memorandum, *USA v. Robert Gilbeau*, U.S. District Court, Southern District of California, April 11, 2017. A federal audit showed that Glenn Defense charged
the *Nimitz* for nearly triple the usual amount of wastewater removal during its
2003 visits to Singapore and that Gilbeau approved the invoices.

42 *in exchange for a $40,000 cash bribe and two prostitutes:* Government Sentenc-
ing Memorandum, *USA v. Gilbeau*. Francis interview, DCIS-NCIS, May 4,
2015. According to prosecutors, Glenn Defense bank records partially corroborated Francis's allegation.

42 *"He doubled it up just so that he could get a kickback from me and get laid":* Francis interview #10, Wright.

42 *Gilbeau confirmed that he approved:* Gilbeau interview with author.

42 *"I never accepted a bribe from Leonard Francis":* Ibid. Gilbeau pleaded guilty in
2016 to lying to federal officials about his contacts with Francis.

43 *He asked his JAG officer:* Notes from NCIS interview of retired Captain Scott
Thompson, October 6, 2015.

43 *he double-checked with a senior JAG officer:* Ibid. Thompson said he sought the guidance from then-Commander Nanette DeRenzi, the Seventh Fleet JAG. DeRenzi later became a vice admiral and the Navy's top JAG.

43 *"I ran the traps":* Author interview with retired Captain Scott Thompson, October 26, 2023. In an October 19, 2023, interview with the author, Admiral Crowder took responsibility for authorizing attendance at the dinner. "The only reason why anyone went to that event is because I said it was OK."

44 *"I said, 'All his profits are coming from overcharging us for services'":* Craig Whitlock, "Admiral Tapped for Promotions Despite Dinners with 'Fat Leonard,'" *Washington Post,* September 24, 2018.

44 *only two guests were unaffiliated with the Navy or Francis's firm:* NCIS report, "Identification of Christmas 2004 Hong Kong Reception Attendees," August 28, 2015. Federal agents identified seventy-eight people who attended, about sixty of whom were uniformed Navy personnel.

44 *Glenn Defense spent more than $60,000 on the dinner:* Ibid.

45 *"fanciest dinner I'd ever been to":* Notes from NCIS interview of retired Commander George Stanley, August 17, 2015.

45 *"full of himself, pretty large and in charge":* Transcript, NCIS interview of Rear Admiral Craig Faller, November 10, 2015. When federal agents questioned Faller in 2015 about the Christmas Cheer party, he asked: "Is there a picture of me with one of those elves?" They showed him two. Faller said he had no reason to think the elves were prostitutes, adding: "I have never engaged in the services of prostitutes in my life."

45 *his Santa Niñas, or Santa Girls:* Francis interview, DCIS-NCIS, October 21, 2013.

45 *"Is this illegal?":* Notes from joint NCIS-DCIS interview of retired Captain Donald Hornbeck, April 5, 2017. Hornbeck said the party was "unlike anything [I've] ever been to." When federal agents showed him a photo of the female elf sitting on his lap and asked if she was a prostitute, he replied that he "absolutely did not take their services."

46 *crashed the stage to play drums:* Notes from DCIS interview of retired Commander David Dunn, June 5, 2017. Dunn served as the executive officer of the USS *Benfold.* He said Hornbeck was very shy but became the "life of the party" when he drank.

46 *Thompson realized he'd made a colossal error:* Thompson interview, NCIS. After an investigation of the Christmas Cheer party, Navy disciplinary authorities determined in January 2018 that Thompson had committed misconduct by failing to take proper action after it became apparent that the dinner violated federal ethics rules. He received a confidential rebuke. No one else from the *Abraham Lincoln* strike group got in trouble. After his retirement from the

Navy, Thompson was named as the top ethics official in the Office of the General Counsel at the Pentagon.

46 *"I definitely felt snookered"*: Thompson interview with author. "I'm not making excuses," he added. "But the ethics rules don't tell you what to do if you show up to a widely attended gathering that turns out to be something else."

46 *Francis kept digital copies*: Francis saved 252 photographs from the Christmas Cheer party and distributed them on CDs to partygoers as souvenirs. One Navy officer shared his CD with federal agents twelve years later.

47 *Francis handed him a $600,000 invoice*: Notes from joint DCIS-NCIS interview of Commander Chris Statler, December 16, 2014.

47 *"He laughed in my face"*: Author interview with retired Commander Chris Statler, March 24, 2022.

47 *"And what an event it was!!"*: Rear Admiral Doug Crowder letter to Leonard Francis, December 28, 2004. In his 2023 interview with the author, Crowder said he was just minding his manners by writing the thank-you letter to Francis. "This was according to my upbringing by Mrs. Crowder, my mother," he said.

CHAPTER FIVE: MR. MAKE-IT-HAPPEN

51 *"Win one for the Gipper!"*: "Navy Carrier USS Reagan Sails from San Diego on First Deployment," Associated Press, January 4, 2006.

51 *"Undoubtedly Mike will go far"*: The Lucky Bag, U.S. Naval Academy yearbook, Annapolis, Maryland, 1974.

52 *"We always called you 'Mr. Make-It-Happen'"*: Rear Admiral Michael Miller email to Leonard Francis, February 5, 2006.

52 *"I'm wondering if you would have any suggestions"*: Ibid.

52 *"Looking forward to our visit"*: Ibid.

52 *Francis barely remembered him*: Notes from joint DCIS-NCIS interview of Leonard Francis, January 16, 2015.

52 *"Of course I remember you"*: Leonard Francis email to Rear Admiral Michael Miller, February 5, 2006.

53 *"has expensive tastes and likes to buy nice things"*: Written statement to DCIS by Captain Joel Doolin, Navy JAG Corps, November 21, 2014. Doolin served as the JAG and ethics counselor on Miller's staff in 2006.

53 *"very entitled" with "two hands and two legs" out*: Notes from joint DCIS-NCIS interview of Leonard Francis, January 30, 2015.

53 *a "British racing green" Jaguar*: Francis interview, DCIS-NCIS, January 16, 2015.

54 *He held parties on the ship*: Notes from joint DCIS-NCIS interview of Leonard Francis, October 21, 2013.

54 *gave him a wooden-and-brass plaque:* Affidavit of DCIS Special Agent James McWhirter, March 22, 2016.

54 *Miller admired a collection of burgundy Chesterfield-style chairs:* Francis interview, DCIS-NCIS, January 16, 2015.

54 *Francis had recently bought the chairs for about $1,700 each:* Ibid.

54 *he swore he could see the curvature of the earth:* Notes from joint NCIS-DCIS interview of retired Captain William Hart, July 3, 2014. Hart was the executive officer of the USS *Ronald Reagan* at the time of the dinner.

54 *a raven-haired "catwalk model":* Francis interview #6, Wright.

54 *one officer called her "drop-dead gorgeous":* Notes from joint DCIS-NCIS interview of retired Captain Howard Trost, June 25, 2014. Trost served as the *Reagan* strike group chief of staff.

54 *Francis noticed the admiral gazing at her with a "lusty" look:* Francis interview, DCIS-NCIS, January 16, 2015.

55 *"She was very striking":* Transcript, joint NCIS-DCIS interview of Vice Admiral Mike Miller, July 15, 2014.

56 *Francis honored Miller by presenting him with an elaborate model:* McWhirter affidavit, March 22, 2016.

56 *"one of the best evenings of my life":* Rear Admiral Mike Miller email to Leonard Francis, February 10, 2006.

56 *Some worried Francis had become an "ethics time bomb":* Notes from DCIS interview of retired Commander Joseph Boveri, October 20, 2017. Boveri served as the JAG officer for a Navy task force based in Singapore.

56 *called the Hong Kong soiree the "last straw":* Notes from joint DCIS-NCIS interview of retired Commander David Warunek, January 13, 2017.

57 *The only one who kept a record was Miller:* Miller provided copies of the checks to federal agents when they interviewed him in 2014. In an October 20, 2023, email to the author, Miller's attorney, Louis Freeh, wrote: "We proved to the Navy that our client actually paid for anything of possible value which he received, and have the checks to prove it." After completing their investigation, however, Navy authorities disagreed. On January 23, 2015, Navy Secretary Ray Mabus censured Miller for "repeatedly paying Mr. Francis for personal expenses at a rate far below the market value." Mabus concluded that Miller "knew or should have known that $50.00 per person was not the market value for these extravagant dinner parties."

57 *"like a well-oiled machine":* Navy message from Rear Admiral M. H. Miller, February 12, 2006.

58 *"trust me, Leonard can make it happen":* Rear Admiral Mike Miller email to Rear Admiral John Goodwin, commanding officer, Carrier Strike Group Nine, March 31, 2006.

58 *"I'm still full from that wonderful spread"*: Commander David Pimpo email to Leonard Francis, March 30, 2006.

58 *Miller's chief of staff emailed with discouraging news:* Captain Howard Trost email to Leonard Francis, May 8, 2006.

59 *Risner said she always made it "crystal clear"*: Author interview with retired Captain Claudia Risner, June 28, 2021.

59 *"It's not like they bolted from the room"*: Ibid.

59 *"Thanks again for the magnificent support"*: Rear Admiral Mike Miller letter to Leonard Francis, June 5, 2006.

59 *"Mr. Francis can truly do it all"*: Navy message from Rear Admiral Mike Miller, June 8, 2006.

59 *Miller again reimbursed Francis for the meal at a rate of $50 per person:* Miller letter, June 5, 2006.

59 *The company paid $28,000:* McWhirter affidavit, March 22, 2016.

60 *"The service you provide is head and shoulders above all others"*: Rear Admiral M. H. Miller letter to Leonard Francis, June 15, 2006.

60 *Glenn Defense submitted a fraudulent invoice:* NCIS Report of Investigation, Special Inquiry, USS *Ronald Reagan*, June 19, 2006.

60 *Glenn Defense had overbilled the carrier by $68,000:* Ibid.

60 *"He became furious, accusing me of calling him a liar"*: Craig Whitlock, "The Man Who Seduced the 7th Fleet," *Washington Post*, May 27, 2016.

60 *the agent inexplicably closed the case:* NCIS Report of Investigation, Special Inquiry, USS *Ronald Reagan*.

60 *Nothing happened after that:* Craig Whitlock, "Navy Repeatedly Dismissed Evidence That 'Fat Leonard' Was Cheating the 7th Fleet," *Washington Post*, December 27, 2016.

61 *"everyone knew they were rotten"*: Whitlock, "The Man Who Seduced the 7th Fleet."

61 *"Leonard, you are already a legend"*: Commander David Pimpo email to Leonard Francis, March 7, 2007.

62 *"Thank you for an amazing night!"*: NCIS and DCIS agents questioned then-Rear Admiral Gilday on April 2, 2015, at the NCIS Washington Field Office about his attendance at the Hong Kong dinner. Gilday told the agents that he paid either $30 or $50 in cash for his share of the dinner but acknowledged that the real cost was probably far higher. He said the dinner made him feel uncomfortable but thought it had been "cleared through legal channels." On June 1, 2015, Navy disciplinary authorities determined that the dinner had not been cleared and that the cost exceeded federal gift limits. But the Navy cleared Gilday of wrongdoing, finding that he "honestly and reasonably believed [his] attendance was ethically permissible."

CHAPTER SIX: NAKED BRIBERY

64 *he had been married five times:* NCIS Investigative Action, Reference Check for Paul Simpkins, October 17, 2013.

64 *he was cheating on her:* Notes from joint DCIS-NCIS interview of Leonard Francis, February 3, 2015. Transcript, Motion Hearing, *USA v. Paul Simpkins,* U.S. District Court, Southern District of California, January 8, 2016. Assistant U.S. Attorney Mark Pletcher highlighted Simpkins's complicated romantic life during the hearing: "While his wife was receiving money in Japan, he was consorting with a number of other people, including his now wife, who was then his mistress."

64 *Francis wanted to build a rapport without spooking his target:* Francis interview, DCIS-NCIS, February 3, 2015.

64 *What was in it for him?:* Ibid.

64 *a stack of $100 bills—$50,000 worth:* Ibid. A March 2015 federal indictment also alleged that Simpkins pocketed the $50,000 cash bribe. Simpkins later pleaded guilty to bribery and conspiracy charges but did not admit to accepting money on this occasion.

65 *he bribed Simpkins with an additional $350,000 by wiring the money:* Plea Agreement, *USA v. Paul Simpkins,* June 23, 2016. In court papers, Simpkins admitted that Francis wired $350,000 to his wife's account in five different payments.

65 *he provided Simpkins with prostitutes on more than ten occasions:* Francis interview, DCIS-NCIS, February 3, 2015.

65 *rigged government business in the company's favor:* Simpkins Plea Agreement.

65 *"Yes we have conquered Thailand":* Leonard Francis email to Captain David Newland, March 2, 2006.

65 *Francis fed Simpkins spurious allegations:* Notes from joint NCIS-DCIS interview of Leonard Francis, May 4, 2015.

66 *"I did the research myself":* Paul Simpkins email to Leonard Francis, May 18, 2006.

66 *"the $$ will flow":* Leonard Francis email to Paul Simpkins, May 15, 2006.

66 *he made good on his word:* Simpkins Plea Agreement.

66 *when the Philippines contract came up for renewal, Francis wired:* Ibid.

66 *Two months later, on Simpkins's recommendation:* Ibid.

66 *"Now the Bitch Rose is suing":* Leonard Francis email to Lieutenant Commander Edmond Aruffo, February 20, 2007.

66 *sent him police records:* NBI Record of Ms. Rose [Baldeo] Siy, National Bureau of Investigation, Republic of the Philippines, undated.

67 *The two-bit cases were later dismissed:* In an email to the author, Baldeo said Francis's "smear campaigns against me were not true" and that the bounced-check charges were the result of "some misunderstanding."

67 *he leaked details:* Leonard Francis email to Paul Simpkins, with attachments, March 29, 2007.

67 *viewing him as "standoffish":* Notes from DCIS interview of retired Lieutenant Michael Lang, February 13, 2015.

67 *and incompetent:* Notes from joint DCIS-NCIS interview of retired Commander David Warunek, January 13, 2017.

67 *Warunek regarded the Ring of Steel as his "pet peeve":* Notes from DCIS interview of retired Commander David Warunek, February 17, 2015.

67 *he recommended against awarding an extension:* Service Contractor-Performance Rating, Glenn Defense Marine (Asia), December 6, 2006.

68 *Simpkins overruled him:* Sharon Kaur and Paul Simpkins, Memo for the Record, FISC Detachment Singapore, December 13, 2006.

68 *Lang thought it strange:* Lang interview, DCIS.

68 *"I was just getting sick of the Navy getting bilked":* Author interview with retired Lieutenant Mike Lang, March 27, 2021.

68 *"Do not request any invoices from the ship":* Paul Simpkins email to Dickson Luk, June 16, 2006.

68 *Simpkins liked to take "dirty weekend" trips to Bangkok:* Francis interview, DCIS-NCIS, February 3, 2015.

69 *he attacked Schaus as a "prick":* Leonard Francis email to Paul Simpkins, July 8, 2006.

69 *"Meters solved ha ha":* Leonard Francis email to Howard Patty, Alex Wisidagama, and Neil Peterson, January 29, 2007.

69 *"What else could I have done to expose this racket?":* Craig Whitlock, "Navy Repeatedly Dismissed Evidence That 'Fat Leonard' Was Cheating the 7th Fleet," *Washington Post*, December 27, 2016.

70 *The most valuable was Sharon Kaur:* Statement of Facts, *Public Prosecutor v. Gursharan Kaur Sharon Rachael*, State Courts of the Republic of Singapore, June 30, 2017. Kaur, also known as Gursharan Kaur Sharon Rachael, pleaded guilty to four corruption-related charges for taking bribes from Francis. An appellate court sentenced her to forty months in prison in 2019. Selina Lum, "High Court: Those Convicted of Bribing Foreign Public Officials Should Expect Jail Time," *The Straits Times*, Singapore, September 6, 2019.

70 *a deluge of confidential information:* Ibid.

70 *With Francis's guidance:* Francis interview, DCIS-NCIS, May 4, 2015.

70 *the company paid for her to take luxury vacations:* Kaur, Statement of Facts.

70 *her "heart, soul and mind":* Francis interview, DCIS-NCIS, May 4, 2015.

70 *Behind his back, she called him "Mottu," or "Fatty":* Notes from NCIS interview of Evelyn Progasom, October 7, 2013. Progasom was a contract specialist who worked with Kaur and Francis at the Navy Fleet Logistics Center in Singapore.

70 *a holiday gift basket was delivered to her apartment:* Kaur, Statement of Facts.

71 *slipped her 50,000 Singapore dollars:* Francis interview, DCIS-NCIS, May 4, 2015. According to the Statement of Facts in her criminal case, Kaur admitted to accepting a bribe of this amount from Francis, but described the circumstances differently, saying that Francis's driver passed her an envelope with the cash.

71 *they arranged to meet at a Toys "R" Us store:* Ibid. Kaur did not admit to accepting this bribe as part of her plea agreement in the Singapore courts.

71 *They twice honored her with the Singapore office's "On-the-Spot" Award:* NCIS Report of Investigation, "Seizure and Review of Personnel Records for Sharon Kaur," October 9, 2013.

71 *"Ms. Kaur's superb performance":* Ibid.

CHAPTER SEVEN: SEDUCING THE SEVENTH FLEET

73 *Giardina complimented Francis:* Author interview with retired Rear Admiral Timothy Giardina, April 29, 2020.

73 *"Leonard would throw prostitutes at me":* Transcript, joint DCIS-NCIS interview of Vice Admiral Timothy Giardina, September 19, 2013. The following year, in an unrelated case, the Navy disciplined Giardina for conduct unbecoming an officer after finding him guilty of using fake gambling chips at an Iowa casino while he was the deputy leader of U.S. Strategic Command. He reverted in rank to a two-star admiral and retired.

73 *"impeccable character and integrity":* Testimony of Glenn Cooper, *USA v. David Newland et al.,* U.S. District Court, Southern District of California, May 23, 2022.

73 *Another called him a "total pro":* Testimony of John Spear, *USA v. Newland et al.,* May 23, 2022.

74 *"I knew I wasn't going to be an admiral":* Transcript, DCIS interview of retired Captain David Newland, March 2, 2017.

74 *"a tremendous level of hatred":* Testimony of Edmond Aruffo, *USA v. Newland et al.,* March 10, 2022.

75 *"I don't know what he has planned for your folks":* Captain George "Terry" Foster email to Captain David Newland and Commander Steven Barney, February 16, 2006.

75 *wrote his own email to officers:* Commander Steven Barney email to Seventh Fleet officers, February 16, 2006.

75 *Newland assured Barney that he'd take care of it:* Testimony of Steven Barney, *USA v. Newland et al.,* March 22, 2022.

75 *"It was one of the most extravagant things I've ever seen":* Testimony of Edmond Aruffo, *USA v. Newland et al.,* March 9, 2022.

76 *"We are getting too many complaints"*: Paul Simpkins email to Leonard Francis, March 2, 2006.

76 *he claimed a Hong Kong travel agency, Richmond Travel*: Leonard Francis email to Paul Simpkins, March 3, 2006.

76 *In reality, Richmond Travel was a front*: Notes from DCIS interview of Leonard Francis, March 11, 2015.

76 *large duty-free shopping bags filled with alcohol*: Aruffo testimony, March 10, 2022.

76 *"He was in my cabin in every port"*: Newland transcript, DCIS.

77 *Francis secretly paid for the event*: Barney testimony. Barney said Greenert mentioned that he saw Francis at the dinner and suspected the Glenn Defense owner had been the actual host.

77 *Navy officers piled into his Hummer*: Notes from joint DCIS-NCIS interview of retired Commander Jon "Gerry" Benavente, December 12, 2016. After federal agents showed Benavente an email in which he thanked Francis for the dinner and "great entertainment," he admitted that Francis took him and several others in his Hummer to a party.

77 *Francis explained that it would "assist with blowing away" criticism*: Aruffo testimony, March 9, 2022.

77 *had instructed his aides to refuse gifts*: Notes from DCIS interview with Commander Christopher "Adam" Kijek, January 20, 2015. Kijek, who served as Greenert's flag aide from 2004 to 2005, said part of his job was to keep the admiral away from Francis.

77 *Greenert said his encounters with Francis*: Author interview with retired Admiral Jonathan Greenert, October 25, 2023.

77 *"Can do easy!"*: Captain David Newland email to Leonard Francis, March 8, 2006.

77 *Francis received a letter*: Vice Admiral J. W. Greenert letter to Leonard Francis, March 9, 2006.

78 *"am comparing if it's better looking than my wife, ha ha"*: Aruffo testimony, March 9, 2022. Prosecutors introduced the letter as an exhibit and Aruffo read it aloud during his testimony.

78 *a stream of "six-star perks"*: Francis interview, DCIS, March 11, 2015.

79 *Newland made a show of dumping his glass of Dom Pérignon*: Aruffo testimony, March 9, 2022.

79 *laughed about their insolent disregard for the ethics warning*: Ibid.

79 *Even the Seventh Fleet chaplain*: Craig Whitlock, "Leaks, Feasts and Sex Parties: How 'Fat Leonard' Infiltrated the Navy's Floating Headquarters in Asia," *Washington Post*, January 31, 2018. The chaplain, Captain William Devine,

said in an interview that he "vaguely" remembered the dinner. "I guess in my naivete I never saw that as going against any rules," he said. "Shame on me."

80 *had been uncomfortable with the idea:* Testimony of Jesus Cantu, *USA v. Newland et al.,* March 24, 2022.

80 *"'You need to get your ass down here'":* Ibid.

80 *"My initial thought was, 'This is the height of decadence'":* Ibid.

80 *"I'm trying to get on Leonard's good side there":* Newland transcript, DCIS.

CHAPTER EIGHT: GRAND AMBITIONS

81 *It was the first time a large-deck U.S. warship:* Sopaporn Kurz, "City at Sea," *The Nation,* Bangkok, Thailand, April 25, 2006.

82 *by underbidding his rival, Papa Chin:* Notes from DCIS interview of Chief Petty Officer Michael Higley, December 5, 2016. Higley, who worked with Navy contracting officials in Singapore from 2005 to 2008, said if the contract had been based on "best value" versus the lowest cost, Chin would have won.

82 *"everybody is approved into Laem Chabang":* Grand Jury Indictment, *USA v. Newland et al.,* U.S. District Court, Southern District of California, March 10, 2017.

82 *a glowing thank-you note:* Ambassador Ralph L. Boyce letter to Leonard Francis, May 11, 2006.

82 *Glenn Defense earned $1.9 million in revenue:* Grand Jury Indictment, *Newland et al.*

82 *including a $500,000 security charge for the Ring of Steel:* Notes from NCIS interview of retired Captain Kevin Campbell, August 18, 2015. Campbell served as the operations officer aboard the USS *Abraham Lincoln* from 2004 to 2006.

83 *"No one cared about costs":* Notes from DCIS interview of Leonard Francis, March 11, 2015.

83 *Francis had close ties to every four-star admiral:* Notes from NCIS interview of retired Captain Jeffrey James, August 14, 2017. James commanded the USS *Hopper* from 2007 to 2008.

84 *"You can't put a value on happiness":* Natasha Ann Zachariah, "Nassim's Cheer: A Home Owner's Festive Light-up Is Drawing Camera-Happy Visitors," *The Straits Times,* Singapore, December 22, 2012.

84 *a paranoid micromanager:* Notes from joint DCIS-NCIS interview of Alexander Wisidagama, November 18, 2013.

84 *signed all company checks himself:* Ibid.

85 *He installed security cameras:* Notes from NCIS interview of Andre Francis, January 27, 2014.

85 *He carried as many as fifteen cell phones:* Notes from joint NCIS-DCIS interview of retired Captain James Maus, July 7, 2016.

85 *a handbag that his American friends mocked as a "man purse":* Testimony of Stephen Shedd, *USA v. Newland et al.,* May 5, 2022.

85 *Leonard once punched him in the face:* Andre Francis interview, NCIS, January 27, 2014.

85 *"I am the general and you are the soldier":* Ibid.

85 *The White House was trying to seal a nuclear cooperation agreement:* Notes from joint DCIS-NCIS interview of Rear Admiral Michael Manazir, October 23, 2015. Manazir commanded the USS *Nimitz* from 2007 to 2009.

85 *the Pacific Fleet ordered the USS* Nimitz: Transcript, DCIS interview of Captain James Dolan, December 10, 2014. Dolan served as a logistics officer on the Pacific Fleet staff from 2005 to 2007.

85 *Rising to the challenge, Leonard agreed:* Francis interview, DCIS, March 11, 2015.

86 *Some crewmembers clamored to turn back:* Ibid. Francis said the crew almost mutinied.

86 *One of the company's trash barges rammed into the* Nimitz: Manazir interview, DCIS-NCIS, October 23, 2015.

86 *"Please accept my sincere appreciation":* Rear Admiral J. T. Blake letter to Leonard Francis, July 8, 2007.

86 *He billed the Navy $4.5 million:* Andre Francis interview, NCIS, January 27, 2014.

86 *"They know there's nobody else":* Francis interview #10, Wright.

86 *"He loved getting the glory":* Andre Francis interview, NCIS, January 27, 2014.

86 *Glenn Defense subsidized hotel rooms:* Notes from DCIS interview of Alex Wisidagama, April 7, 2015. Glenn Defense kept a spreadsheet with details of the hotel reservations and costs.

87 *a sublime dinner at the Jaan restaurant:* Admiral Philip Davidson memo to Chief of Naval Personnel, October 6, 2017. Navy disciplinary authorities determined that Blake committed misconduct by attending the dinner and improperly endorsing Glenn Defense with two Bravo Zulu letters. The Navy estimated the Jaan dinner cost between $730 and $1,095 per person but took no further action against Blake and kept the findings a secret. In an August 9, 2017, letter to the Navy, Blake said "at no time did I engage in any immoral or criminal activity and did not perform any act that I thought was improper or unethical in any way." Regarding the opulent meal, Blake wrote: "I am not a wine or food connoisseur. My recollection is that the dinner was very good but the event does not otherwise stand out in my memory."

87 *Francis signed a $55 million deal:* Annual Report 2009, Genting Hong Kong Limited.

87 *its ships jostled for space with cargo ships:* Grand Jury Testimony of retired Admiral Mohammed Anwar, *USA v. Newland et al.,* September 15, 2015. Grand jury proceedings are ordinarily kept secret but defense attorneys posted a transcript of Anwar's testimony on the public docket.

87 *dredged the channel:* Ibid.

88 *he recommended that the USS* Pinckney *order bigger fenders:* Leonard Francis email to Commander Errin Armstrong, January 30, 2010. Armstrong was the commanding officer of the USS *Pinckney.*

88 *Glenn Defense "cannot be held liable":* Ibid.

89 *the price to rent them was $60,000 extra:* Notes from DCIS interview of Captain Errin Armstrong, April 20, 2016.

89 *just as Francis predicted, a fuel barge slammed into the* Pinckney: Ibid.

CHAPTER NINE: THE WEDDING PLANNER

90 *He called himself "the wedding planner":* Notes from joint NCIS-DCIS interview of retired Lieutenant Commander Edmond Aruffo, September 23, 2014.

91 *"I wanted to impress him":* Transcript, joint DCIS-NCIS interview of retired Lieutenant Commander Edmond Aruffo, September 17, 2013.

91 *"Leonard Conquers Tokyo":* Lieutenant Commander Edmond Aruffo email, with attachment, to Leonard Francis, August 31, 2006.

91 *to set aside eight bottles of Cristal:* Testimony of Edmond Aruffo, *USA v. Newland et al.,* March 10, 2022.

91 *paid for the dinner and hotel bills:* Ibid. The total cost was about $23,000, according to Francis's American Express card statement.

91 *"uneasy feeling":* Craig Whitlock, "Leaks, Feasts and Sex Parties: How 'Fat Leonard' Infiltrated the Navy's Floating Headquarters in Asia," *Washington Post,* January 31, 2018.

92 *"I didn't like the way he kind of hoodwinked us":* Author interview with retired Vice Admiral Doug Crowder, October 19, 2023.

92 *"What is Fat Leonard doing in my backyard?":* Ibid.

92 *Crowder blew his stack:* Ibid.

92 *"I called the chief of staff and said, 'He's gone'":* Ibid.

92 *"complete and total nonsense":* Author interview with Edmond Aruffo, January 6, 2024.

93 *"what are you going to do? Cause a scene?":* Whitlock, "Leaks, Feasts and Sex Parties: How 'Fat Leonard' Infiltrated the Navy's Floating Headquarters in Asia."

93 *Aruffo grew up poor with three sisters:* Defendant Sentencing Memorandum, *USA v. Edmond Aruffo,* U.S. District Court, Southern District of California, October 18, 2022.

93 *made the cut for a highly selective program:* Ibid.

93 *the skipper of the* Blue Ridge *invited him to a dinner:* Testimony of Edmond Aruffo, *USA v. Newland et al.*, March 15, 2022. Aruffo identified the skipper as Captain Steve Maynard.

93 *"For some reason, he considered me a friend":* Aruffo transcript, DCIS-NCIS, September 17, 2013.

93 *he mailed Francis a compact disc:* Aruffo testimony, March 10, 2022.

94 *"don't need people running their mouths":* Edmond Aruffo email to Leonard Francis, February 1, 2007.

94 *"a sly guy, cocky, Italian":* Notes from joint NCIS-DCIS interview of Lieutenant Commander Todd Malaki, December 28, 2014. Malaki served as supply officer aboard the USS *Blue Ridge* from 2005 to 2007. Malaki pleaded guilty in 2015 to conspiracy to commit bribery and was sentenced to forty months in federal prison.

94 *"a little shady":* Transcript, joint NCIS-DCIS interview of Commander Stephen Shedd, September 17, 2013.

94 *"very flashy":* Transcript, DCIS interview of Commander Ron Thornton, November 5, 2014. Thornton served on the Seventh Fleet staff from 2010 to 2012 and attended several of Francis's parties.

94 *"a glad-hander":* Transcript, joint NCIS-DCIS interview of retired Captain Jeffrey Bartkoski, March 8, 2017. Bartkoski commanded the USS *Blue Ridge* from 2005 to 2007 and attended several of Francis's parties.

94 *"sneaky":* Notes from joint DCIS-NCIS interview of retired Commander Jon "Gerry" Benavente, December 12, 2016.

94 *"kind of slick":* Transcript, joint NCIS-DCIS interview of retired Captain Jonathan Will, March 9, 2017. Will served on the Seventh Fleet staff from 2005 to 2007 and attended several of Francis's parties.

94 *a "used-car salesman":* Notes from DCIS interview of retired Navy Commander Michael Thibodeau, December 1, 2016. Thibodeau served on the Seventh Fleet staff from 2007 to 2008. He said Aruffo tried to recruit him to attend Francis's parties, but he always declined.

94 *a "wheeler-dealer":* Notes from DCIS interview of retired Captain Phil Kessler, December 1, 2016. Kessler served on the Seventh Fleet staff from 2006 to 2008.

94 *"a greasy dude":* Notes from NCIS interview of retired Chief Petty Officer Michael Seaman, October 6, 2014. Seaman served on the Seventh Fleet staff from 2010 to 2013.

94 *a "partying type of officer" who was only "70 to 75 percent reliable":* Notes from DCIS interview of Master Chief Hilton Todd Owens, January 21, 2015. Owens served on the Seventh Fleet staff from 2003 to 2006.

94 *his protégé could be "overbearing":* Francis interview #10, Wright.

95 *"You must exercise extreme caution"*: Commander Steven Barney email to Seventh Fleet officers, February 2, 2007.

95 *Aruffo dismissed the JAG as a Grinch*: Aruffo interview, NCIS-DCIS, September 23, 2014.

95 *"All it would take is some double crosser"*: Howard Patty Sr., email to Leonard Francis, February 6, 2007.

95 *"Rather than one type, I'd like to compare"*: Aruffo testimony, March 10, 2022. Aruffo read Newland's email aloud in court.

96 *Francis invited Newland, Aruffo, Captain Jesus Cantu, and a few other officers*: Newland, Aruffo, and Cantu admitted to federal agents that they attended.

96 *Francis directed Aruffo to find prostitutes*: Aruffo testimony, March 10, 2022.

96 *things turned "wild and crazy"*: Francis interview #7, Wright.

96 *a replica of his iconic corncob pipe and used it as a sex toy*: Ibid. Notes from joint DCIS-NCIS interview of Leonard Francis, February 19, 2015.

96 *Francis posed for a photo with the pipe in his mouth*: Aruffo testimony, March 10, 2022.

96 *including the presidential suite for Newland*: Testimony of Edmond Aruffo, *USA v. Newland et al.*, March 14, 2022.

96 *hosted another party with prostitutes*: Notes from joint DCIS-NCIS interview of Leonard Francis, February 26, 2015.

96 *he began referring to the* Blue Ridge *as "the Love Boat"*: Notes from joint DCIS-NCIS interview of Leonard Francis, October 21, 2013.

96 *Francis threw a party aboard the* Glenn Braveheart: Notes from DCIS interview of Lieutenant Commander Todd Malaki, February 19, 2015.

97 *marred by an incident involving Aruffo*: Malaki interview, NCIS-DCIS, December 28, 2014.

97 *the furious soldiers had threatened to shoot*: Transcript, DCIS interview of Marine Colonel Enrico DeGuzman, March 1, 2017. "The soldiers were ready to shoot Aruffo on sight," DeGuzman recalled. "I had to go negotiate. 'Don't shoot Aruffo.'"

97 *"Gonzales is someone I need to build a strong relationship with"*: Leonard Francis email to Edmond Aruffo, February 20, 2007.

97 *he realized the event broke every ethics rule*: Author interview with retired Captain Robert Gonzales, May 13, 2021.

97 *"It was unbelievably 100 percent obvious"*: Ibid.

98 *Aruffo proclaimed it "tremendously tasty"*: Aruffo testimony, March 14, 2022.

99 *"Well, this looks like the end of the road"*: Edmond Aruffo email to Leonard Francis, June 1, 2007.

99 *"I was almost sure that night would be used in a court of law someday"*: Aruffo testimony, March 14, 2022.

99 *two computer disks containing military secrets:* Notes from DCIS interview of Leonard Francis, April 10, 2015. Francis reviewed two spreadsheets from the disks with federal agents and said he was certain Gorsuch—and not anyone else at the dinner—had handed him the military secrets in Sydney. Both spreadsheets were marked SECRET. In 2021, Gorsuch pleaded guilty to a bribery charge. He admitted giving Francis classified ship schedules, though not specifically at the time of the Sydney dinner. Plea Agreement, *USA v. Robert Gorsuch*, U.S. District Court, Southern District of California, August 31, 2021.

CHAPTER TEN: LEAKY EMBASSIES

103 *They lunched at the Hyatt Hotel:* Notes from joint DCIS-NCIS interview of Leonard Francis, March 12, 2015.

103 *Brooks emailed Francis a note thanking him:* Plea Agreement, *USA v. Michael George Brooks*, U.S. District Court, Southern District of California, November 15, 2016.

104 *He also attached his first leak:* Ibid.

104 *he supplied the naval attaché with prostitutes:* Transcript, Sentencing Proceedings, *USA v. Michael George Brooks*, June 16, 2017. Assistant U.S. Attorney Mark Pletcher told the court that Brooks "received prostitutes on scores of nights, on a frequency without peer in this case." Brooks pleaded guilty to conspiracy to commit bribery in 2016 and admitted accepting prostitutes from Francis.

104 *an acute threat to U.S. national security:* Ibid. Pletcher called Francis's corruption of Brooks "a foreign intelligence threat. . . . It was pervasive. It was enduring. It was deliberate."

104 *"I lost my moral compass":* Ibid.

104 *he discovered that Brooks led two separate personal lives:* Francis interview, DCIS-NCIS, March 12, 2015.

105 *he paid running tabs for two prostitutes:* Ibid.

105 *in the mood for "high tea" or "chocolate shakes":* Brooks Plea Agreement.

105 *"Anytime Leonard came into town, it was girls at the hotel":* Transcript, joint DCIS-NCIS interview of retired Captain Michael Brooks, May 25, 2016.

105 *he'd show up for a quickie wearing gym clothes:* Francis interview, DCIS-NCIS, March 12, 2015.

105 *invited the defense contractor over to his house:* Brooks interview, DCIS-NCIS, May 25, 2016.

105 *He even chartered a limousine:* Francis interview, DCIS-NCIS, March 12, 2015.

105 *When the family vacationed in Thailand:* Ibid.

105 *"It was just fucking stupidity"*: Brooks interview, DCIS-NCIS, May 25, 2016.

105 *"Did I fall into the trap of Leonard Francis?"*: Ibid.

106 *Brooks leaked internal correspondence to Francis*: Government Sentencing Memorandum, *USA v. Michael George Brooks*, June 19, 2017.

106 *he secretly allowed the company to ghostwrite its own job evaluation*: Ibid.

106 *Brooks gave his own "strongest recommendation"*: Ibid.

106 *"We are looking great!"*: Leonard Francis email to Howard Patty Sr., and Neil Peterson, November 29, 2007.

106 *In another scheme*: Francis interview, DCIS-NCIS, March 12, 2015.

106 *Brooks declared that the ships were allied with the U.S. Navy*: Brooks Plea Agreement.

106 *it was "unheard of" for a contractor to be granted unfettered access*: Francis interview, DCIS-NCIS, March 12, 2015.

107 *"I'm not even a U.S. citizen and I had diplomatic immunity!"*: Francis interview #6, Wright.

107 *a "slippery character" and a "master manipulator"*: Transcript, NCIS interview of Captain Clayton Grindle, September 19, 2013.

107 *He also asked Francis to broker meetings*: Ibid.

107 *"Leonard Francis would have made a wonderful intelligence officer"*: Transcript, joint NCIS-DCIS interview of Captain Clayton Grindle, October 25, 2016.

108 *"He tries to feel you out"*: Grindle interview, NCIS, September 19, 2013.

108 *Moss said he tried to avoid Francis at first*: Transcript, joint DCIS-NCIS interview of A. W. Moss, August 7, 2014.

108 *"He puts his arm around my shoulder"*: Ibid.

108 *"Just meeting with this guy was a stupid thing"*: Ibid.

108 *Jansen thought Francis was a "scumbag"*: Author interview with retired Captain Adrian Jansen, November 12, 2021.

108 *He said he wanted to build a relationship*: Ibid. Transcript, NCIS interview of Rear Admiral Adrian Jansen, June 18, 2015. "Did I get used by Leonard? Okay, maybe I did. And I'm surely the sucker," Jansen told federal agents. "But I used him, too. And I used him in the sense that I got to Stanny, and I could use Stanny for my own purposes."

109 *"Did Leonard play me? Yeah, he played me"*: Jansen interview, NCIS, June 18, 2015. Navy disciplinary authorities determined in 2017 that Jansen, who had been promoted to rear admiral after he served as the naval attaché to Indonesia, had violated federal ethics rules for accepting more than $5,000 worth of dinners and gifts and was derelict in the performance of his duties for failing to report his contacts with Francis. He was reprimanded and fined $7,500. The following year, the Navy reduced him in rank and he retired as a captain. In an interview with the author, Jansen acknowledged that he was wrong to

accept the dinners but accused the Navy of making him a scapegoat. "I'm still trying to understand why the Navy found it so important to crucify me," he said.

CHAPTER ELEVEN: DIRTY SECRETS

110 *Patiently waiting at the gate:* Robert Gorsuch email to Leonard Francis, October 24, 2007.

111 *Gorsuch handed him an envelope:* Notes from joint NCIS-DCIS interview of Leonard Francis, April 10, 2015.

111 *"No worries about helping you out":* Gorsuch email to Francis, October 24, 2007. Gorsuch admitted giving Francis the classified information at Yokosuka. Plea Agreement, *USA v. Robert Gorsuch*, U.S. District Court, Southern District of California, August 31, 2021.

112 *Gorsuch couldn't leak the information as quickly as Francis wanted:* Francis interview, NCIS-DCIS, April 10, 2015.

112 *Gorsuch transferred his leaking duties:* Grand Jury Indictment, *USA v. Newland et al.*, U.S. District Court, Southern District of California, March 10, 2017. Plea Agreement, *USA v. Stephen Shedd*, U.S. District Court, Southern District of California, January 26, 2022.

113 *his chances of being selected for a command job were "very precarious":* Testimony of Stephen Shedd, *USA v. Newland et al.*, May 4, 2022.

113 *having an opportunity to "rub elbows":* Notes from DCIS interview of Commander Stephen Shedd, January 6, 2022.

113 *"I honestly thought I hit the lottery":* Shedd testimony, May 4, 2022.

113 *"in deep-crap territory":* Ibid.

113 *Though he realized he would be "crossing the bribery line":* Shedd interview, DCIS, January 6, 2022.

113 *"It only took me a few seconds":* Shedd testimony, May 4, 2022.

113 *"We had an understanding of mutually assured destruction":* Testimony of Stephen Shedd, *USA v. Newland et al.*, May 5, 2022.

113 *began leaking classified ship schedules to Francis:* Shedd Plea Agreement. Shedd pleaded guilty to bribery and conspiracy to commit bribery.

114 *He thought Shedd had the potential:* Notes from joint DCIS-NCIS interview of Leonard Francis, October 21, 2013.

114 *his-and-her Swiss watches:* Shedd testimony, May 4, 2022.

114 *worth $25,000:* Shedd Plea Agreement.

114 *a weeklong vacation at a Malaysian resort:* Ibid.

114 *an expensive promotion party in Hornbeck's honor:* Grand Jury Indictment, *USA v. Newland et al.*

114 *a culinary internship for Hornbeck's oldest son:* Ibid. Notes from joint NCIS-DCIS interview of retired Captain Donald Hornbeck, April 5, 2017.

114 *Francis nicknamed him "Bubbles":* Francis interview, DCIS-NCIS, October 21, 2013.

114 *Shedd had to coordinate the trip:* Shedd testimony, May 4, 2022.

115 *where the Boss had prepaid for their rooms:* Ibid.

115 *"a lot of craziness goes on":* Notes from joint NCIS-DCIS interview of Leonard Francis, March 9, 2015.

115 *about twenty prostitutes wearing cocktail dresses:* Shedd testimony, May 4, 2022.

115 *"a lot of boobs flying":* Transcript, NCIS interview of Captain James Dolan, March 15, 2017.

115 *Hornbeck showed his wild side:* Notes from joint DCIS-NCIS interview of Leonard Francis, March 8, 2015.

115 *the officers took women back to the hotel:* Shedd testimony, May 4, 2022. Hornbeck interview, NCIS-DCIS, April 5, 2017. Dolan admitted to federal agents that he went to Pegasus but denied having sex with anyone. "I never received a prostitute. I don't—honestly, I don't—that's not my thing." Transcript, DCIS interview of Captain James Dolan, March 8, 2017.

115 *"kids in a candy store":* Shedd interview, DCIS, January 6, 2022.

115 *the officers "were all smiles on the drive home":* Lieutenant Commander Stephen Shedd email to Leonard Francis, May 4, 2008.

115 *it dawned on him that Francis could blackmail the officers:* Shedd interview, DCIS, January 6, 2022.

115 *Loveless's "egregious" conduct of consorting with prostitutes:* Ibid.

115 *impressed Francis as a poker-faced "spook":* Francis interview, NCIS-DCIS, March 9, 2015.

115 *assessing him as an "up and comer":* Ibid.

116 *Loveless became infatuated with a Mongolian prostitute:* Ibid.

116 *lectured him about the need for discretion:* Hornbeck interview, NCIS-DCIS, April 5, 2017. Hornbeck confirmed to federal agents that Loveless had told him about giving his business card to the Mongolian prostitute and that Francis had chewed out the intelligence officer for being stupid.

116 *"What I gave them was beyond their wildest dreams":* Francis interview, NCIS-DCIS, March 9, 2015.

116 *"really enjoyed my new Mongolian friend":* Captain Donald Hornbeck email to Leonard Francis, May 7, 2008.

116 *the officers "were all grins this morning":* Lieutenant Commander Stephen Shedd email to Leonard Francis, May 10, 2008.

116 *"get hookers":* Shedd interview, DCIS, January 6, 2022.

117 *Shedd said he and the three captains:* Shedd testimony, May 5, 2022.

117   *"They were going to listen to my agenda before the pants came down"*: Francis interview, NCIS-DCIS, March 9, 2015.

117   *draining the hotel's entire supply of Dom Pérignon:* Grand Jury Indictment, *USA v. Newland et al.* Shedd testimony, May 5, 2022.

117   *"I went by that room and holy—debauchery like nothing you've ever seen before"*: Transcript, joint DCIS-NCIS interview of retired Captain Michael Brooks, May 25, 2016.

117   *the suite looked like a "disaster"*: Notes from DCIS interview of retired Captain Michael Brooks, October 26, 2016.

118   *Francis got "out of control" drunk and ate a wineglass:* Hornbeck interview, NCIS-DCIS, April 5, 2017.

118   *"What's this whore doing here?"*: Shedd interview, DCIS, January 6, 2022.

118   *threatening to douse her face with acid and toss her out a window:* Ibid.

118   *threatening to get an Uzi to "shoot these bitches"*: Ibid.

118   *"I finally detoxed myself from Manila"*: Lieutenant Commander Steven Shedd email to Leonard Francis, May 30, 2008.

118   *a "quite intoxicated" Dolan:* Shedd testimony, May 5, 2022.

119   *"I want to fuck! Let me in!"*: Ibid.

119   *"Get your fucking hands off me"*: Ibid.

119   *the lieutenant commander was drowning in debt:* Ibid.

119   *"I'll think about it"*: Ibid.

119   *a "washed-up asset"*: Shedd interview, DCIS, January 6, 2022.

120   *"probably the most extravagant, salubrious surrounds I've been in"*: Transcript, Australian Federal Police interview of Alexander Gillett, November 1, 2016. Gillett pleaded guilty in 2018 to abuse of public office. He admitted to leaking ship schedules to Francis on six occasions from 2008 to 2009. He received a suspended prison sentence of twenty-three months. *Crown v. Alexander Gillett,* Supreme Court of the Australian Capital Territory, July 5, 2018.

120   *a muleheaded sailor with "crazy-ass bug eyes"*: Transcript, DCIS interview of retired Commander Alan Munoz, October 23, 2014. Munoz served as an officer on the Seventh Fleet staff. Herrera pleaded guilty to a misdemeanor charge of illegally leaking the USS *Blue Ridge*'s port visit schedule to Francis on one occasion in 2009. *USA v. Mario Herrera,* U.S. District Court, Southern District of California, September 6, 2023. He did not admit to leaking classified information. His attorney acknowledged that he attended three parties with Francis.

120   *"wasn't the brightest of bulbs"*: Dolan interview, DCIS, December 10, 2014. Sanchez admitted to leaking classified ship schedules to Francis. Plea Agreement, *USA v. Jose Luis Sanchez,* U.S. District Court, Southern District of California, January 6, 2015.

120 *"just a big mouth, braggart, showoff"*: Transcript, DCIS interview of Lieutenant Commander Joseph Klapiszewski, December 14, 2014.

121 *"Please be in touch with your needs"*: Lieutenant Commander Alexander Gillett email to Leonard Francis, November 3, 2008.

121 *"Lets work a plan"*: Leonard Francis email to Lieutenant Commander Alexander Gillett, November 5, 2008.

121 *spending a total of $55,000 on meals, alcohol, and lodging*: Grand Jury Indictment, *USA v. Newland et al.*

CHAPTER TWELVE: THE NEMESIS

123 *"I felt I wasn't earning my money"*: Author interview with retired Captain Jim Maus, June 14, 2019.

123 *"Sometimes I'd just walk around the harbor"*: Author interview with retired Captain Jim Maus, February 24, 2019.

123 *Hinting that Glenn Defense was a financial house of cards*: Ibid. The executive with the coffee mug was Dr. Wong Wee Chwee.

123 *"I wasn't doing much anyway"*: Ibid.

124 *"It was clear Leonard was playing us"*: Author interview with retired Captain Jim Maus, March 2, 2019.

125 *Maus slowly won most of them over*: Ibid.

125 *"There was never an intention to put him out of business"*: Author interview with retired Captain Jim Maus, February 17, 2019.

126 *"Maus is stirring shit now"*: Leonard Francis email to Commander Jose Sanchez, September 2, 2009.

126 *Piburn had never met Leonard Francis*: Author interview with retired Captain James Piburn, February 9, 2021.

126 *he had no interest in getting chummy*: Ibid.

127 *"Let's study Capt Piburn"*: Francis email to Sanchez, September 2, 2009.

127 *"Will pull out the magnifying glass"*: Commander Jose Sanchez email to Leonard Francis, September 2, 2009.

127 *described him as a "Boy Scout"*: Notes from joint NCIS-DCIS interview of Captain Christopher French, December 19, 2017. French served as a JAG officer on the Seventh Fleet staff from 2009 to 2011.

127 *mocking Piburn privately as Captain "Pubic Hair"*: Grand Jury Indictment, *USA v. Newland et al.*, U.S. District Court, Southern District of California, March 10, 2017. Leonard Francis email to Edmond Aruffo, February 10, 2010.

127 *"Piburn is a moron"*: Edmond Aruffo email to Leonard Francis, February 14, 2010.

127 *"Piburn is a Cancer"*: Leonard Francis email to Edmond Aruffo, February 14, 2010.

127 *"Leonard hates your guts"*: Piburn interview with author, February 9, 2021.

127 *"This is a personal agenda driven by my Ex staff"*: Leonard Francis text message to Commander Michael Misiewicz, November 23, 2011.

128 *"Jesus, I'd better do something"*: Author interview with retired Captain Jim Maus, March 10, 2019.

128 *"you do whatever it takes to win"*: Ibid.

129 *"When it came to taking on Leonard"*: Ibid.

129 *yet accepted his invitations to two dinners*: Admiral John Richardson letter to Rear Admiral Timothy Giardina, December 10, 2014. Richardson, who served as the Navy's first disciplinary authority for the Glenn Defense case, issued a Nonpunitive Letter of Caution to Giardina for accepting two dinners from Leonard Francis.

129 *he knew Francis would try to butter him up*: Transcript, joint DCIS-NCIS interview of Vice Admiral Timothy Giardina, September 19, 2013. The Navy subsequently stripped Giardina of a star and he retired as a rear admiral because of an unrelated disciplinary matter.

129 *"He's got a big-ass shopping bag that looks like Santa Claus"*: Author interview with retired Rear Admiral Timothy Giardina, April 29, 2020.

129 *He demanded that the Navy open an ethics review*: Rear Admiral Timothy Giardina letter to Chief of Naval Personnel, March 19, 2015.

129 *Personally, Giardina had no problems with Maus*: Giardina interview with author.

130 *"There was clearly bad blood between them"*: Giardina interview, DCIS-NCIS, September 19, 2013.

130 *accused Maus of "retaliatory activities"*: Charles Black letter to U.S. Pacific Fleet, May 2, 2011.

130 *"'Well, do we need to suspend Jim at this point?'"*: Author interview with Edward Hanel Jr., March 16, 2019.

130 *Hanel told the admiral no*: Ibid.

131 *Hanel drafted a tough reply*: Ibid.

CHAPTER THIRTEEN: MIKEY

133 *"I could not imagine taking him from his mother and father"*: Maryna Misiewicz letter to U.S. District Judge Janis Sammartino, March 1, 2016.

133 *the only nonwhite kid in school*: John Gruhn letter to U.S. District Judge Janis Sammartino, March 1, 2016. Gruhn was a childhood friend of Misiewicz's.

133 *elected him president four years running*: Edward Nelson letter to U.S. District

Judge Janis Sammartino, March 1, 2016. Nelson was a teacher and athletic director at Lanark High School.

133 *his father and two other sisters, along with sixteen other relatives, had died:* Eddie Khem letter to U.S. District Judge Janis Sammartino, February 26, 2016. Eddie Khem is Misiewicz's older brother.

133 *sobbed for hours when they met:* Ibid.

134 *"Greetings, Auntie":* Mike Eckel, "U.S. Navy Commander Returns to Cambodian Roots," Associated Press, December 4, 2010.

134 *"Anything is possible":* Press release, U.S. Pacific Fleet Forces Command, December 3, 2010.

135 *"He had me convinced he was my true friend":* Commander Michael Misiewicz letter to U.S. District Judge Janis Sammartino, April 22, 2016.

135 *He also gave Misiewicz tickets:* Notes from joint NCIS-DCIS interview of Edmond Aruffo, December 31, 2014.

135 *She thought Aruffo was "a cheesy, smarmy used-car salesman":* Marcy Misiewicz letter to U.S. District Judge Janis Sammartino, March 1, 2016.

135 *"I'm sure it just came across as another ping from the nagging wife":* Ibid.

135 *another mole who had leaked classified ship schedules:* Plea Agreement, *USA v. Daniel Dusek,* U.S. District Court, Southern District of California, January 15, 2015.

136 *"Do you have a place/person to use for girl delivery?":* Edmond Aruffo email to Leonard Francis, February 13, 2011.

136 *"you're in MANILA DUDE they are everywhere":* Leonard Francis email to Edmond Aruffo, February 13, 2011.

136 *Aruffo ordered half that number and hosted a dinner:* Notes from joint DCIS-NCIS interview of Edmond Aruffo, September 6, 2014.

136 *Dusek passed out:* Notes from DCIS interview of Captain Daniel Dusek, November 17, 2015.

136 *ended up flat on his back on the mat:* Government Sentencing Memorandum, *USA v. Michael Vannak Khem Misiewicz,* U.S. District Court, Southern District of California, April 27, 2016.

136 *"Just wanted to say thanks":* Commander Michael Misiewicz email to Ed Aruffo, February 17, 2011.

136 *"I am grooming Mike to be a good mole":* Edmond Aruffo email to Leonard Francis, March 4, 2011.

137 *Francis had lined up prostitutes and hotel rooms:* Affidavit of DCIS Special Agent James McWhirter, *USA v. Misiewicz,* September 12, 2013.

137 *"It was pretty much the hardest job I ever had":* Transcript, joint NCIS-DCIS interview of Commander Michael Misiewicz, September 16, 2013.

137 *"We gotta get him hooked on something":* Leonard Francis email to Edmond Aruffo, May 23, 2011.

137 *He bought Misiewicz plane tickets:* Plea Agreement, *USA v. Misiewicz,* January 28, 2016.

137 *provided him with several prostitutes of "different flavors":* Notes from joint NCIS-DCIS interview of Leonard Francis, March 26, 2015.

138 *"Take care gents":* McWhirter affidavit, *USA v. Misiewicz,* September 12, 2013.

138 *"We got him!!:)":* Ibid.

138 *The tipster suspected Misiewicz of committing espionage:* NCIS Report of Investigation, Misiewicz Special Inquiry, Far East-Yokosuka Field Office, November 23, 2011. The report was declassified by NCIS on June 4, 2015.

139 *"This dude was the golden boy of the Seventh Fleet":* Transcript, DCIS interview of Commander Ron Thornton, November 5, 2014.

139 *Francis considered Misiewicz to be on his "payroll":* Francis interview, NCIS-DCIS, March 26, 2015.

139 *"I am disappointed with Mike":* Leonard Francis email to Edmond Aruffo, August 19, 2011.

139 *"We are not a nonprofit organization":* Leonard Francis email to Edmond Aruffo, October 15, 2011.

139 *"As yet, he hasn't been worth the effort":* Edmond Aruffo email to Leonard Francis, August 19, 2011.

139 *"See, you ask—I deliver!":* Misiewicz Plea Agreement.

139 *Francis offered to pay for a divorce lawyer:* Francis interview, NCIS-DCIS, March 26, 2015.

140 *Mike allegedly became violent:* "Episode Five—Marcy," Fat Leonard podcast, October 26, 2021. "He grabbed me and pushed me and then pushed me up the stairs," Marcy Misiewicz said. "It wasn't until a couple days later that I had a friend notice that I had some bruising."

140 *Marcy reported it to the Seventh Fleet staff:* Author interview with Marcy Misiewicz, October 28, 2023.

140 *"He has been feuding with his wife":* Edmond Aruffo email to Leonard Francis, September 12, 2011.

140 *she assumed it was about her quarrels with her husband:* Misiewicz Special Inquiry, NCIS.

140 *The spying allegation stunned Marcy:* Ibid.

140 *Moss wrote in a report that he "expressed some sympathy":* Ibid.

141 *whether Mike had any "suspicious foreign contacts":* Ibid.

141 *he had called a woman in Malaysia ninety times:* Ibid.

141 *the NCIS agent interviewed Mike about the espionage allegations:* Ibid.

141 *He denied having affairs or sex with anyone other than Marcy:* Ibid. Years later, when federal agents questioned Misiewicz about the Malaysian woman again and asked if they were "still dating," he replied: "We still correspond." Francis

independently described the woman as Misiewicz's "mistress" and said he had met her on multiple occasions.

141 *"This investigation revealed marital stress"*: Ibid.

142 *where Francis allegedly paid $20,000 for them:* Grand Jury Indictment, *USA v. David Williams Haas*, U.S. District Court, Southern District of California, August 16, 2018.

142 *Francis bought plane tickets for Misiewicz:* Misiewicz Plea Agreement.

CHAPTER FOURTEEN: THE SPECIAL AGENT

143 *asking for a meeting to discuss "some billing discrepancies":* NCIS Special Agent Tony Sanz email to Glenn Defense Marine, June 15, 2011.

143 *the firm billed the Navy for $110,000:* Affidavit of DCIS Special Agent James McWhirter, *USA v. John Bertrand Beliveau Jr.*, U.S. District Court, Southern District of California, September 12, 2013.

143 *In fact, Navy contracting officers had noticed:* Notes from NCIS interview of Teresa Kelly, April 15, 2014. Kelly was the director of contracting for the Fleet Logistics Center in Singapore.

144 *blew off his request:* Leonard Francis email to John Beliveau Jr., July 2, 2011.

144 *The agency had sharply de-emphasized such cases after 9/11:* Craig Whitlock, "Navy Repeatedly Dismissed Evidence That 'Fat Leonard' Was Cheating the 7th Fleet," *Washington Post*, December 27, 2016.

144 *pinning the blame on a handful of suspects:* John Lancaster, "Tailhook Probe Implicates 140 Officers," *Washington Post*, April 24, 1993.

145 *"he just had a ton of information":* Author interview with John Smallman, March 18, 2022.

145 *"Everyone knew Leonard was dirty":* Ibid.

146 *"I never busted his balls about being fat":* Ibid.

146 *Michell liked to "sit and talk" at bars with prostitutes:* Notes from joint DCIS-NCIS interview of Leonard Francis, March 25, 2015.

146 *divulged details about planned ship movements:* Ibid.

146 *he knew it was a "big no-no":* Notes from joint DCIS-NCIS interview of NCIS Deputy Assistant Director Darrick Kennedy, March 19, 2015. Kennedy was stationed on the USS *Blue Ridge* from 2002 to 2004.

146 *he was relieved of duty:* Notes from NCIS interview of NCIS Executive Assistant Director Alexander MacIsaac, March 18, 2015. MacIsaac was the NCIS assistant special agent in charge and Michell's direct supervisor when he was relieved of duty from the USS *Blue Ridge*.

146 *wouldn't find out for years:* Admiral Philip Davidson memo to Director, NCIS, January 20, 2017. Davidson, serving as the Navy's Consolidated Disposition

Authority for Glenn Defense matters, forwarded findings of his misconduct investigation of Michell to NCIS "for disposition as you deem appropriate." An NCIS spokesman declined to say whether the agency took further personnel action against Michell.

147 *"People just weren't paying attention to fraud stuff"*: Smallman interview with author.

147 *NCIS opened twenty-seven criminal investigations:* Whitlock, "Navy Repeatedly Dismissed Evidence That 'Fat Leonard' Was Cheating the 7th Fleet."

147 *NCIS received an anonymous letter, accompanied by incriminating paperwork:* NCIS Report of Investigation, Cost Mischarging, Resident Agency Manila, August 16, 2007.

147 *Two years later, NCIS opened another investigation:* NCIS Report of Investigation, Possible Fraudulent Fuel Order, Resident Agency Singapore, May 24, 2010.

147 *In 2009, the agency opened a counterintelligence investigation:* NCIS Report of Investigation, Counterintelligence Support to U.S. Navy Port Visits in Japan, Resident Agency Atsugi (Japan), December 4, 2009. The report was originally classified SECRET/NOFORN. It was declassified by NCIS on June 9, 2016.

148 *"I don't think there was an invoice"*: Transcript, joint DCIS-NCIS interview of Edmond Aruffo, September 17, 2013.

148 *had picked up hints that he was vulnerable:* Letter from John Beliveau Jr. to author, June 27, 2021. "He knew I was exhausted and a drinker and used that to cope," Beliveau wrote.

148 *he was diagnosed with obsessive-compulsive disorder:* Defendant Sentencing Memorandum, *USA v. Beliveau,* October 5, 2016.

149 *compounding his insecurities about sex and women:* Ibid.

149 *He first saw Leonard Francis in Kuala Lumpur:* Letter from John Beliveau Jr. to author, July 31, 2020.

149 *"He was affable, eccentric, with a jolly laugh"*: Ibid.

149 *his anxieties and compulsions returned in force:* Letter from John Beliveau Jr. to author, September 6, 2020.

149 *the traumatic episode left him "shocked, numb and scared out of my fucking mind"*: Beliveau Defendant Sentencing Memorandum.

149 *To cope, Beliveau drank and sought solace from prostitutes:* Ibid.

149 *"He was a good groomer"*: Beliveau letter to author, June 27, 2021.

149 *But he was agonizingly shy:* Beliveau Defendant Sentencing Memorandum.

150 *a twenty-eight-year-old Filipina who looked like a fashion model:* Beliveau letter to author, June 27, 2021. "He said he knew a girl he could set me up with, a real girl, not a working girl," Beliveau wrote.

150 *"Joyce your kind of babe?"*: McWhirter affidavit, *USA v. Beliveau.*

150 *He paid her about $665 per day:* Notes from NCIS interview of Joyce, March 5,

2014. I am withholding Joyce's surname to protect her privacy. In her interview with NCIS, Joyce said she was anxious about cooperating because she did not want anyone to know about her work for Francis.

150 *He got sick, blacked out, and woke up hungover:* Notes from joint DCIS-NCIS interview of John Beliveau Jr., September 23, 2013.

150 *"Gosh john is unbelievable":* Email from Joyce to Leonard Francis, March 8, 2011.

150 *"Papi honestly I had a hardtime with him":* Ibid.

151 *"I was kind of like his fake friend":* Francis interview #7, Wright.

151 *insisted he hadn't done anything wrong:* Beliveau letter to author, June 27, 2021. "He always claimed and was emphatic to the end that he was doing nothing wrong, he got the job done and people (like his competitors) were out to get him," Beliveau wrote.

151 *he rationalized that he was assisting both Glenn Defense and the Navy:* Ibid.

151 *"I would be distraught and almost crazed":* Transcript, Sentencing Proceedings, *USA v. Beliveau*, October 14, 2016.

151 *Then he stepped further over the line:* Plea Agreement, *USA v. Beliveau*, December 17, 2013.

152 *"Im so drunk hehe":* John Beliveau Jr. text message to Leonard Francis, January 3, 2012.

152 *"Yeah Bro take it easy":* Leonard Francis text message to John Beliveau Jr., January 3, 2012.

152 *"She a hotty, what u think":* John Beliveau Jr. text message to Leonard Francis, February 3, 2012.

152 *"a nut case" with "this really split personality":* Francis interview #7, Wright.

CHAPTER FIFTEEN: SPOUSAL PRIVILEGES

155 *had studied the two women closely:* Notes from joint DCIS-NCIS interview with Leonard Francis, May 5, 2015.

156 *To put the women at ease:* Ibid.

156 *the dinner, which cost $320 per person:* A copy of the customized menu from Spoon lists the cost, including the service charge, as $2,516 Hong Kong dollars per person—the equivalent of $323 USD based on the currency exchange rate from November 12, 2011.

156 *Charlene Haley was "overjoyed" with the Gucci purse:* Francis interview, DCIS-NCIS, May 5, 2015.

156 *after consulting with a JAG officer on his staff:* Notes from joint DCIS-NCIS interview of Commander Brian Halliden, September 29, 2014. Halliden was the staff judge advocate for the USS *George Washington* carrier strike group from 2010 to 2012.

156 *to get around the Navy's "seemingly illogical ethics rules"*: Letter from Rear Admiral J. R. Haley to Leonard Francis, December 11, 2011.

156 *"The enclosed money is not your 'Santa's Present'"*: Ibid.

157 *Carol Lausman frowned at her present*: Notes from NCIS interview of Leonard Francis, April 23, 2015. Francis estimated to agents that the purse cost about $3,000. He later produced a receipt from the Versace store showing that he purchased two purses there on November 11, 2011, one for $2,700 and the other for $2,500. Carol Lausman acknowledged to federal agents that she accepted a Versace purse from Francis. David Lausman's attorney suggested it was probably a knockoff.

157 *"I am very disappointed that they sold me a damaged product"*: Leonard Francis email to Angie Kong, November 14, 2011.

157 *the wives "tended to keep track of Leonard"*: Transcript, joint DCIS-NCIS interview of Rear Admiral J. R. Haley, September 17, 2013.

158 *"He always has these women who, you look at them and say"*: Ibid.

158 *considered him almost like family*: Notes from joint NCIS-DCIS interview of Carol Lausman, September 25, 2013.

158 *She first met Francis around 2006*: Ibid.

158 *making reservations at five-star hotels*: Notes from joint DCIS-NCIS interview of Leonard Francis, March 19, 2015.

158 *who knew her favorite shopping haunts*: Notes from joint DCIS-NCIS interview of Edmond Aruffo, April 9, 2015.

158 *"Loving it here and having a glass of champagne as I type"*: Carol Lausman email to David Lausman, May 5, 2008.

159 *The next night, Francis hosted an $11,000 dinner*: According to federal prosecutors, Francis's credit card records showed the meal cost $11,748 for ten guests.

159 *"Of course we would pay . . . yea right, but at least we could try"*: Ibid.

159 *Carol told the other women beforehand that it was common*: Notes from joint DCIS-NCIS interview of Susan Cloyd, August 3, 2015. Susan Cloyd was the wife of Rear Admiral Dan Cloyd, the commanding officer of the USS *George Washington* carrier strike group from 2010 to 2011, and the commander of U.S. Naval Forces-Japan from 2011 to 2013.

159 *The arrangement sounded good to the other spouses*: Ibid. Navy disciplinary authorities determined that Susan Cloyd attended two dinners and one brunch with Francis at his expense. Admiral Philip Davidson memo to Chief of Naval Personnel, January 12, 2018.

159 *They let Francis cover the $3,300 bill*: Notes from joint DCIS-NCIS interview of Leonard Francis, April 16, 2015. The dinner was held at the Mezza9 restaurant at the Grand Hyatt. Francis's credit card records show he spent $3,300 on the meal. In an October 27, 2023, email to the author, Laura Schaefer, an

attorney for David and Carol Lausman, said "the authenticity and completeness" of Francis's business records was "highly questionable" but declined to comment about the Lausmans' attendance at specific events.

159 *an $8,600 dinner at a rooftop restaurant:* Ibid. Francis told federal agents that he hosted a "ladies' night" dinner at the Sirocco restaurant in Bangkok on October 4, 2010. His credit card records showed that the meal cost $8,600.

159 *"thank you for all your kindness wherever we go":* Carol and David Lausman letter to Leonard Francis, December 2010.

159 *he spent more than $100,000 on the couple:* Francis interview, NCIS, April 23, 2015.

159 *"completely untrustworthy":* Laura Schaefer email to author, October 27, 2023.

160 *Rose agreed to run a "shaping" operation:* Plea Agreement, *USA v. Enrico DeGuzman,* September 3, 2021.

160 *Rose reported back that he had "bedazzled":* Rose DeGuzman email to Leonard Francis, March 29, 2007.

160 *"It's so cute, but she even told me how she touched your hand":* Ibid.

160 *He arranged a romantic weekend for the couple:* Letter of Censure from Navy Secretary Richard Spencer to Captain Heedong Choi, April 26, 2019.

161 *Francis told the Navy officer to let him take care of everything:* Notes from joint DCIS-NCIS interview of Leonard Francis, October 19, 2015.

161 *"I never in a million years could have imagined or planned":* Commander Heedong Choi letter to Leonard Francis, June 18, 2009.

CHAPTER SIXTEEN: CHANGE OF COMMAND

162 *among the one thousand VIPs:* Tina Reed, "Naval Academy Grad Takes Top Post; Roughead, Former Commandant, Retires as Chief of Naval Operations," *The Capital,* Annapolis, Maryland, September 24, 2011.

163 *"one of the most revered and fabled titles":* Remarks by Ray Mabus, Secretary of the Navy, U.S. Naval Academy, September 23, 2011.

163 *"I see the storm warnings out there":* Remarks by Admiral Jonathan Greenert, U.S. Naval Academy, September 23, 2011.

164 *his "Personal A-list" of guests:* Geoff Ziezulewicz, "How Did Fat Leonard Attend This Former CNO's Change of Command? He Was on the VIP List," *Navy Times,* July 23, 2021. *Navy Times* obtained Roughead's guest list with a Freedom of Information Act request. In an email to the author, Roughead said he couldn't "recall particulars" about those invited to the event.

164 *his "steadfastness in holding naval leaders to exceptionally high standards":* Mabus remarks, U.S. Naval Academy.

165 *the service had fired twenty-nine commanding officers:* Craig Whitlock, "Navy

Has Spike in Commanding-Officer Firings, Most for Personal Misconduct," *Washington Post*, June 17, 2011.

165 *"It is your responsibility to meet the highest standards"*: Admiral Gary Roughead, "The Charge of Command," Memorandum for all Prospective Commanding Officers, June 9, 2011.

165 *a jilted lover reported he had been carrying on two extramarital affairs*: Report to Commander, Carrier Strike Group One, "Preliminary Inquiry into Allegations of an Inappropriate Personal Relationship [Involving] Capt Donald Hornbeck," April 26, 2011. According to the Navy's investigative report, Hornbeck, who was married, had a long-running affair with the wife of a junior officer. After Hornbeck's girlfriend discovered that he was cheating on her with a third woman, however, she reported his adulterous conduct to the Navy. "Over several years, Don led me to believe that he desired to get a divorce and spend his life with me," the girlfriend wrote in a letter to Navy officials. "I foolishly believed him and protected him."

166 *"The ceremony was a near-religious experience"*: Leonard Francis email to Rear Admiral J. R. Haley, September 27, 2011.

166 *Francis's anticipated presence had triggered concern*: Author interview with retired Captain Jim Piburn, February 9, 2021. Notes from NCIS interview of retired Commander Joseph Carilli, May 17, 2016. Carilli, the JAG officer, confirmed Piburn's account.

167 *He nodded and thanked the officers*: Piburn interview with author, February 9, 2021.

167 *"I look over and there's Leonard"*: Ibid.

167 *The aide confessed that the admiral had ignored Piburn's warning*: Ibid. In an interview with federal agents on September 23, 2016, Van Buskirk denied inviting Francis to the ceremony, but acknowledged he was there.

167 *"We never made the mistake of thinking that we were smarter"*: Ibid.

167 *"a very intimate, small party"*: Author interview with Edward Hanel Jr., March 23, 2019.

167 *"and about two feet behind me, lo and behold, is Leonard Francis"*: Ibid.

168 *"I kind of swore to myself"*: Ibid.

168 *"We kind of looked at each other and laughed"*: Ibid.

168 *Both admirals later insisted they had no idea*: Craig Whitlock, "'Fat Leonard' Probe Expands to Ensnare More than 60 Admirals," *Washington Post*, November 5, 2017.

168 *"Leonard Francis had a way of showing up"*: Ibid.

168 *he had sent a polite email to Walsh's chief of staff*: Leonard Francis email to Captain Bill Kearns, December 16, 2011.

168 *"Admiral Walsh looks forward to seeing you"*: Captain Bill Kearns email to

Leonard Francis, December 16, 2011. Kearns declined to speak with federal agents when they requested an interview in 2018.

168 *Francis returned to Hawaii to pay homage to yet another pair of four-star admirals:* In a 2018 letter to the author, Admiral Locklear confirmed that Francis was present at the ceremony but said that neither he nor Admiral Willard had invited him.

169 *He hosted a dinner for several Navy officers and their wives at Nobu:* Deposition of Leonard Francis, General Court-Martial of Commander David Morales, Naval Base San Diego, July 18, 2018.

CHAPTER SEVENTEEN: THE GHOSTWRITER

170 *The job interview took place over lunch:* Notes from joint DCIS-NCIS interview of Leonard Francis, October 30, 2015.

171 *But he was tempted by the money:* Author interview with retired Captain Jeffrey Breslau, April 27, 2020.

171 *he would be in legal peril if anyone found out:* Transcript, Sentencing Proceedings, *USA v. Jeffrey Breslau,* February 9, 2019. Breslau pleaded guilty to federal criminal conflict-of-interest charges and was sentenced to six months in prison. "I knew Mr. Francis was a foreign contractor and decided, foolishly, that as long as I did not accept payments directly from Mr. Francis or his company while I was on active duty, the part-time employment did not need further ethics review," Breslau told the court.

171 *Francis would pay Breslau by depositing funds into a bank account:* Francis interview, DCIS-NCIS, October 30, 2015.

171 *"I just said I'll not take any money":* Author interview with retired Captain Jeffrey Breslau, April 27, 2020.

171 *viewed him as "a smooth operator" with a "huge ego":* Author interview with Edward Hanel Jr., March 23, 2019.

172 *he presented Francis with an "action plan":* Government Sentencing Memo, *USA v. Breslau,* February 4, 2019.

172 *"I like your ghost writing it truly helps me":* Ibid.

173 *Livid, he asked Breslau to help him devise a "whisper" campaign:* Ibid.

173 *"It was almost always tied to Maus":* Breslau interview with author, April 27, 2020.

173 *"Important not to compromise me even to your closest Navy brothers":* Captain Jeffrey Breslau email to Leonard Francis, April 9, 2012.

173 *"Rest assured your identity is protected":* Leonard Francis email to Captain Jeffrey Breslau, April 10, 2012.

174 *he wanted "the freedom, to put it bluntly, to make some money":* Retired Admiral Gary Roughead email to Leonard Francis, April 21, 2012.

174 *asking for the admiral's "informal guidance"*: Leonard Francis email to retired Admiral Gary Roughead, April 18, 2012.

174 *a six-page, three-thousand-word set of talking points:* Proposed Talking Points, meeting between Leonard Francis and ADM (ret) Roughead, April 30, 2012.

174 *his "unethical" former employee was trying to "vilify"*: Ibid.

175 *"The goal is to get Roughead to offer solutions"*: Ibid.

175 *"That's exactly what he was trying to do"*: Breslau interview with author, April 27, 2020.

175 *"I really enjoyed our wide ranging conversation"*: Retired Admiral Gary Roughead email to Leonard Francis, May 2, 2012. After a review, Navy disciplinary authorities determined in November 2018 that Roughead did not violate any post-government employment restrictions and did not improperly accept any gifts from Francis. Admiral C. W. Grady memo to Chief of Naval Personnel, November 20, 2018.

176 *might "care to share a meal" and "catch up"*: Leonard Francis email to Rear Admiral J. R. Haley, May 5, 2012.

176 *Breslau went into overdrive:* Notes from joint DCIS-NCIS interview of Leonard Francis, April 16, 2015.

176 *"She can help distract the other spouses"*: Captain Jeffrey Breslau email to Leonard Francis, May 11, 2012.

177 *Francis quickly stashed the gifts in the kitchen:* Notes from DCIS interview of Lieutenant Commander Frank Sanchez, March 23, 2015. Sanchez served as the flag aide to Rear Admiral Dan Cloyd from 2011 to 2013.

177 *Based on ethics advice from his JAG officer:* Ibid. Lieutenant Commander B. J. Halliden memorandum for the record, June 8, 2013. Halliden was the judge advocate on Haley's staff.

177 *He accused his former employee of "unethical practices"*: Captain Jeffrey Breslau memo to Leonard Francis, Proposed Talking Points for dinner with RDML Haley and RADM Cloyd, version 2, undated.

177 *"The food was fantastic, the conversation enjoyable as always"*: Leonard Francis email to Rear Admiral John Haley, May 17, 2012.

177 *gloated that the admiral's wife "kissed my cheeks"*: Leonard Francis email to Captain Jeffrey Breslau, May 26, 2012.

178 *"Dance around the Maus issue but tread very lightly"*: Captain Jeffrey Breslau email to Leonard Francis, May 28, 2012.

178 *a "brilliant strategist"*: Leonard Francis email to Captain Jeffrey Breslau, May 24, 2012.

178 *an "awesome mentor and advisor"*: Leonard Francis email to Captain Heedong Choi, May 31, 2012.

178 *"We have made new inroads and will work in the shadows"*: Leonard Francis email to Howard Patty Sr., May 21, 2012.

178 *Breslau put Francis in touch with Mark Zaid, a Washington power lawyer*: Transcript, NCIS interview of Captain Jeffrey Breslau, September 17, 2013. Zaid declined to comment.

178 *He thought Zaid was a "pit bull"*: Leonard Francis text message to Commander Jose Sanchez, February 2, 2013.

178 *"I will finish Maus off this time"*: Ibid.

178 *The two-page instruction*: Message from Commander, Pacific Fleet, "Judiciousness in Dealing with Husbanding Contractors," July 19, 2012.

179 *"Maus is behind this"*: Leonard Francis email to Captain David Haas and Commander Michael Misiewicz, August 5, 2012.

179 *"I know you are familiar with the principles of Judo"*: Captain Jeffrey Breslau email to Leonard Francis, August 3, 2012.

180 *He wired a total of $65,000 to the officer's bank account*: Plea Agreement, *USA v. Jeffrey Breslau*, November 13, 2018. As part of his guilty plea, Breslau admitted that Francis paid him approximately $65,000.

CHAPTER EIGHTEEN: SPY VS. SPY

182 *"He was my husband. I loved him"*: Author interview with Marcy Misiewicz, October 28, 2023.

182 *She shared her suspicions with a senior officer*: Ibid.

182 *"He doesn't miss too many meals"*: Notes from NCIS interview of Merrick Misiewicz, September 5, 2012.

182 *"Don't be bragging that you ate dinner with Mr. Francis"*: Ibid.

182 *Merrick's ten-year-old sister*: Marcy Misiewicz interview with author.

182 *Miss Hani and Mike had been carrying on a long-distance affair*: Notes from joint NCIS-DCIS interview of Leonard Francis, March 26, 2015.

183 *Marcy thought she was reporting her husband to NCIS for infidelity*: Marcy Misiewicz interview with author.

183 *Mariner, the special agent, stunned her*: Ibid.

184 *More than half the amount was fraudulent*: Plea Agreement, *USA v. Pornpun "Yin" Settaphakorn*, U.S. District Court, Southern District of California, August 4, 2021. Settaphakorn pleaded guilty to defrauding the United States and served a total of three years in prison in Thailand and the United States.

184 *Yin fumed that the coworker was "evil"*: Transcript, NCIS Oral/Wire Intercept, Yin Settaphakorn, June 13, 2012.

184 *"She's going to cause problems for everybody"*: Ibid.

185 *He drank too much and was depressed and burdened by debt:* Notes from joint DCIS-NCIS interview of John Beliveau Jr., September 23, 2013.

185 *"I have 30 reports for u":* Text message exchange between John Beliveau Jr. and Leonard Francis, August 17, 2012.

185 *"No way!":* Ibid.

185 *"I warned you about this":* Ibid.

186 *his wife had "fucked things up" by ratting them out:* Francis interview, NCIS-DCIS, March 26, 2015.

186 *"You give whores more money than me":* John Beliveau Jr. email to Leonard Francis, April 26, 2012.

187 *"You are a sore Bitch":* Leonard Francis email to John Beliveau Jr., April 27, 2012.

187 *Francis had been bribing Jose Sanchez:* Plea Agreement, *USA v. Jose Luis Sanchez,* U.S. District Court, Southern District of California, January 6, 2015.

187 *"Hey boss, how are things?":* Commander Jose Sanchez email to Leonard Francis, July 20, 2010.

187 *he alerted Francis to yet another set of fraud allegations:* Sanchez Plea Agreement.

187 *"I just wanted to make sure you are protected":* Captain Heedong Choi email to Leonard Francis, December 4, 2012.

188 *He ignored Beliveau's warning:* Francis interview, NCIS-DCIS, March 26, 2015. Grand Jury Indictment, *USA v. David Williams Haas,* U.S. District Court, Southern District of California, August 16, 2018.

188 *he met Misiewicz again in Singapore:* Francis interview, NCIS-DCIS, March 26, 2015. Another officer, Commander Jason Starmer, confirmed Misiewicz's presence at Francis's party at the Tiananmen KTV club in September 2012. Stipulation of Fact, *General Court-Martial of Commander Jason Starmer,* Norfolk Naval Station, Navy-Marine Corps Trial Judiciary, February 28, 2018.

188 *"Mike wanted to go out and meet girls wherever he went":* Transcript, joint DCIS-NCIS interview of Edmond Aruffo, September 17, 2013.

188 *he told his Big Bro not to worry:* Francis interview, NCIS-DCIS, March 26, 2015.

188 *When Marcy heard about the award, in November 2012, she felt sick:* Notes from joint DCIS-NCIS interview with Marcy Misiewicz, September 19, 2013.

188 *accused her of "trying to bite the hand that feeds you":* Ibid.

CHAPTER NINETEEN: THE BIRTHDAY BALL

191 *"Are locations such as Australia, New Zealand, Beijing":* Petty Officer First Class Christopher Egan email to Rosemary Chng, September 21, 2010. Egan was an enlisted sailor stationed in Singapore. Chng was a Glenn Defense executive.

191 *"The Navy wanted bigger and brighter":* Author interview with retired

Commander Troy Amundson, August 25, 2021. Amundson pleaded guilty in 2018 to conspiracy to commit bribery. He was sentenced to thirty months in federal prison.

192 *"what I got was the Predators' Ball"*: Author interview with John Durkin, January 30, 2019.

192 *"That's basically giving everyone a green light for graft"*: Ibid.

192 *The evening also troubled someone sitting with Locklear at the head table:* Author interview with former Ambassador David Adelman, February 8, 2019.

193 *"The whole night felt over the top"*: Ibid.

194 *some officers reported as much as $30,000 in revenue had gone unaccounted for:* Notes from joint DCIS-NCIS interview of Commander Troy Amundson, October 2, 2013. Amundson denied the money had been stolen. In an interview with the author, he said he was not responsible for handling ticket sales or accounting for the ball's finances. He blamed a junior officer who served as treasurer for the Navy ball for poor recordkeeping. Navy officials tried to conduct an audit but were unable to reconstruct accounting records from the ball.

194 *he "gave the Navy Ball the middle finger"*: Testimony of Daniel Bryan, General Court-Martial of Commander David R. Morales, Navy Region Mid-Atlantic, August 30, 2018. Bryan was stationed in Singapore as a lieutenant commander on active duty from 2006 to 2010. He served there again as a Navy contractor from 2012 to 2016.

194 *Amundson was what Francis called a "turncoat"*: Notes from joint DCIS-NCIS interview of Leonard Francis, August 3, 2015.

195 *"In my mind, I was done, done with the Navy"*: Transcript, Sentencing Proceedings, *USA v. Troy Amundson*, U.S. District Court, Southern District for California, October 19, 2018.

195 *he hired several Vietnamese and Mongolian prostitutes:* Notes from joint DCIS-NCIS interview of Commander Troy Amundson, June 2, 2017. Amundson acknowledged to federal agents that Francis provided the prostitutes.

195 *He became an ardent mole for Glenn Defense:* Plea Agreement, *USA v. Troy Amundson*, January 30, 2018.

195 *He was thrilled when Locklear gave him a shoutout:* Notes from joint NCIS-DCIS interview of Leonard Francis, March 25, 2015. In a 2018 letter to the author, Admiral Locklear said that as the banquet's guest speaker, he gave an "impromptu brief acknowledgment" of Francis because the master of ceremonies had described the Glenn Defense owner as a major supporter of the event.

195 *Francis bad-mouthed him to others as "a cock"*: Deposition of Leonard Francis, *General Court-Martial of Commander David Morales*, Naval Base San Diego, July 17, 2018.

195 *King noticed that people carrying cameras often followed him around:* Notes from NCIS interview of Commander Jerry King, January 27, 2014.

196 *Francis had rigged the raffle:* Amundson interview, DCIS-NCIS, June 2, 2017, and Amundson interview, DCIS-NCIS, October 2, 2013. Amundson has given differing accounts of how the Lucky Draw was conducted and who drew the winning ticket. He told federal agents that there was nothing improper about drawing the winner of the Rolex watches giveaway ahead of time in secret, calling it a "showmanship" tactic to increase suspense. He first told federal agents that Ray Corrigan, the head of the Navy League chapter in Singapore, selected the winning ticket, but later changed his story and said Francis had done so. In an interview with the author on August 25, 2021, Amundson changed his account again, saying: "I think that Ray picked it. And then Leonard had it in his pocket or something."

196 *His handpicked winner:* Ibid.

196 *King told Amundson there was no way he could accept:* Ibid.

CHAPTER TWENTY: LOOSE LIPS SINK SHIPS

197 *a thick brown envelope stuffed with forty pages of military secrets:* Notes from joint NCIS-DCIS interview of Leonard Francis, March 26, 2015. Plea Agreement, *USA v. Michael Vannak Khem Misiewicz,* U.S. District Court, Southern District of California, January 28, 2016. Misiewicz pleaded guilty in 2016 to bribery and conspiracy and was sentenced to six and a half years in prison.

197 *He was allegedly accompanied by his boss, Captain David Haas:* Grand Jury Indictment, *USA v. David Williams Haas,* U.S. District Court, Southern District of California, August 16, 2018. Haas pleaded guilty in 2018 to conspiracy to commit bribery.

197 *The papers were stamped SECRET:* Ibid.

198 *highly sensitive details of the Navy's ballistic missile defense operations:* Government Sentencing Memorandum, *USA v. Misiewicz,* April 27, 2016.

198 *Misiewicz and Haas suggested a few candidates:* Francis interview, NCIS-DCIS, March 26, 2015. Misiewicz Plea Agreement.

198 *escorted the Seventh Fleet officers to Seventh Heaven:* Notes from joint DCIS-NCIS interview of Leonard Francis, October 19, 2015.

198 *the Boss had blown nearly $7,000:* Grand Jury Indictment, *USA v. Haas.*

198 *John Beliveau Jr. had tipped Francis off to a new threat:* Government Sentencing Memorandum, *USA v. John Bertrand Beliveau Jr.,* U.S. District Court, Southern District of California, October 7, 2016.

199 *bordered on treason:* Government Sentencing Memorandum, *USA v. Misiewicz.* Prosecutors accused Misiewicz of providing Glenn Defense with classified

ship schedules "dozens of times and whenever specifically asked to do so." In his plea agreement, Misiewicz admitted leaking classified material on eight occasions.

199 *Haas acknowledged accepting prostitutes, meals, and hotel rooms:* Plea Agreement, *USA v. Haas,* June 9, 2020.

199 *he didn't know that Misiewicz was passing classified ship schedules:* In a November 1, 2023, letter to the author, Haas added: "Had I known this, I would have put a stop to it and removed Mike Misiewicz from my Deputy position immediately."

199 *"Brother you must have copied me by mistake":* Leonard Francis email to Commander Michael Misiewicz, May 20, 2012.

199 *"Oh crap":* Commander Michael Misiewicz email to Leonard Francis, May 20, 2012.

200 *he slipped printouts under the door:* Transcript, joint DCIS-NCIS interview of Edmond Aruffo, September 17, 2013.

200 *calling him "very pro-U.S. and patriotic":* Transcript, joint NCIS-DCIS interview of Commander Michael Misiewicz, September 16, 2013.

200 *Haas called him "Uncle Arleigh":* Defendant Sentencing Memorandum, *USA v. Haas,* January 26, 2023.

200 *gloated that they were "in bed" together:* Francis interview, NCIS-DCIS, March 26, 2015.

200 *Francis had pegged Haas as a "bright star":* Ibid.

200 *treating the married officer to dinners and entertainment:* Ibid.

201 *Haas never gave Francis classified information himself:* Defendant Sentencing Memorandum, *USA v. Haas.*

201 *Haas and Misiewicz denied that they had the authority:* In his letter to the author, Haas added: "Francis' boast that he controlled carrier movement was simply ego and ignorance."

201 *The port had never hosted a carrier:* Notes from DCIS interview of Commander Jerry King, December 20, 2015.

201 *But Haas and Misiewicz squashed their protests:* Grand Jury Indictment, *USA v. Misiewicz,* January 6, 2015. Misiewicz denied steering ships to Glenn Defense's Pearl Ports, though he "occasionally weighed in on port visit decisions where he believed it was appropriate," according to the 2016 sentencing memorandum filed by his attorney.

201 *with one officer saying he was ordered to "shut the fuck up":* Notes from joint NCIS-DCIS interview of Captain Michael Lockwood, March 30, 2016. Lockwood was an operations officer for a combined Navy task force in Asia in 2012. He said Misiewicz's rationale for sending the *Stennis* to Kota Kinabalu was "bullshit."

201 *Francis crowed about his triumph over the "pork chops":* Leonard Francis email to

Captain John Segura, September 12, 2012. Segura was the U.S. defense attaché to Malaysia.

201 *"We ambushed them ha ha"*: Leonard Francis email to Neil Peterson, September 15, 2012.

201 *Haas "consistently, routinely and often" protected Glenn Defense*: Notes from DCIS interview of Captain Ronald Carr, October 20, 2014. Carr was the Seventh Fleet's assistant chief of staff for logistics from 2012 to 2014.

201 *"completely dirty or living on a different planet"*: King interview, DCIS, December 20, 2015.

202 *a JAG officer heard Haas brag about having social plans with Francis*: Notes from NCIS interview of retired Commander Joseph Carilli, May 17, 2016.

202 *Francis spent $90,000 on prostitutes, meals, hotel rooms, and other favors for Haas*: Haas Plea Agreement. As part of his plea deal, Haas agreed to repay the Navy more than $90,000 in restitution.

202 *and about $95,000 on Misiewicz*: Transcript of Sentencing Proceedings, *USA v. Misiewicz*, April 29, 2016. Misiewicz agreed to repay $95,000 in restitution to the Navy.

202 *He was already on Francis's payroll*: Information, *USA v. Dan Layug*, U.S. District Court, Southern District of California, May 15, 2014. Layug pleaded guilty to conspiracy to commit bribery and was sentenced to twenty-seven months in prison.

202 *to pick up an envelope with $1,000 in cash*: Ibid.

202 *video game consoles, a digital camera, or other electronics*: Notes from joint DCIS-NCIS interview of Dan Layug, April 22, 2014.

202 *The twenty-five-year-old sailor embraced the assignment*: Government Sentencing Memo, *USA v. Layug*, January 19, 2016. According to prosecutors, Layug delivered classified ship schedules to Neil Peterson on four occasions.

203 *Layug scanned the documents and transmitted them*: Ibid.

203 *rolled down the window of his dark sedan*: Ibid.

203 *Over cocktails, the officers blabbed*: Notes from joint NCIS-DCIS interview of Captain Evan Piritz, April 7, 2016. Piritz was the chief of staff to the commanding officer of the USS *Carl Vinson* carrier strike group. He said the information about bin Laden's burial at sea was no longer classified. In an interview with federal agents on September 21, 2015, Francis confirmed that the *Vinson* officers told him how they had "bagged Osama."

204 *Francis knew the Chinese government had developed a keen interest*: Notes from joint DCIS-NCIS interview of Leonard Francis, October 21, 2013.

204 *golfing buddies with Glenn Defense's IT manager*: Ibid.

CHAPTER TWENTY-ONE: FAMILY MAN

207 *"Leonard, pls don't hide my children to me"*: Morena De Jesus text messages to Leonard Francis, January 20, 2013.

207 *"i just wanna see my children"*: Ibid.

207 *He refused to let their mother anywhere near them:* Plaintiff's Submissions, Morena Galvizio De Jesus v. Leonard Glenn Francis, State Courts of the Republic of Singapore, March 19, 2014.

208 *"I don't think I could live a boring life"*: Francis interview #8, Wright.

208 *"just a little bar girl"*: Francis interview #18, Wright.

208 *"They came to me with their eyes open"*: Francis interview #13, Wright.

209 *"When I first met him, he is good"*: Episode 6, *Fat Leonard* podcast, November 2, 2021.

209 *Francis wanted more children:* Francis interview #6, Wright.

209 *Francis visited sporadically and promised they'd get married:* De Jesus plaintiff's submissions.

209 *a Glenn Defense staffer shocked Morena:* Episode 6, *Fat Leonard* podcast.

209 *he had another part-time girlfriend in Manila*: Morena De Jesus email to author, April 24, 2017.

210 *calling her a "bitch prostitute" and worse:* Episode 6, *Fat Leonard* podcast.

210 *she discovered that he had evicted her:* De Jesus plaintiff's submissions.

210 *"He left me with nothing"*: De Jesus email to author.

211 *"Hugs n kisses for Leandro n Luisa"*: Morena De Jesus text messages to Leonard Francis, March 16–18, 2013.

211 *"Morena claims to be in Spore and wants to see the children!"*: Leonard Francis text message to Bernice Loo, May 7, 2013.

211 *a "deep, deep practicing Catholic"*: Francis interview #5, Wright.

211 *he formed unconventional "temporary wife" relationships:* Leticia Murakami Acosta text messages to Leonard Francis, August 22, 2013.

212 *"He was just here and spent all his time drinking"*: Ed Aruffo email to Howard Patty Sr., January 29, 2012.

212 *"Leonard never has clean, cordial breakaways"*: Ed Aruffo email to Howard Patty Sr., February 20, 2012.

212 *A few desperadoes pirated fuel from the company:* Joint DCIS-NCIS interview of Neil Peterson, March 24, 2017.

212 *shelling out $500,000 for a new Rolls-Royce Phantom:* Notes from joint DCIS-NCIS interview of Linda Raja, August 3, 2017. Raja worked as Glenn Defense's general manager for Singapore, Australia, and the Pacific Islands.

212 *Francis said the Rolls was critical for maintaining appearances:* Peterson interview, DCIS-NCIS, March 24, 2017.

212 *"Glad he continues to have fun":* Howard Patty Sr. email to Ed Aruffo, February 21, 2012.

213 *warning that a "perfect storm is developing over the horizon":* Howard Patty Sr. email to Ed Aruffo, February 22, 2012.

213 *"His wish was granted":* Ibid.

CHAPTER TWENTY-TWO: BAITING A TRAP

214 *A two-page letter explained:* Jennifer Stone, Google Legal Investigations Support, letter to NCIS Special Agent Amanda Blair, March 28, 2013.

215 *she made Fields sign a nondisclosure agreement:* Author interview with retired Captain Marty Fields, October 26, 2023.

216 *"I'm feeling pressure from everybody":* Ibid.

216 *NCIS had briefed only two Navy officers:* Ibid.

216 *a strategy session in March:* Author interview with James Paris, January 27, 2013. Paris, a government attorney, served as counsel to the commander, Naval Supply Systems Global Logistics Support, in San Diego, from 2011 to 2018. He attended the meeting in Bremerton.

217 *Fields suggested stringing a trail of bait:* Fields interview with author.

217 *He had warned Francis that Fields was in contact with NCIS:* Commander Jose Sanchez text message to Leonard Francis, February 28, 2013.

218 *he noticed that NCIS had a search warrant pending:* Government Sentencing Memorandum, *USA v. John Bertrand Beliveau Jr.,* U.S. District Court, Southern District of California, October 7, 2016.

218 *"They got a warrant for ur gmail account":* John Beliveau Jr. text message to Leonard Francis, April 9, 2013.

218 *"My boy Mike Miez just hung himself—dick":* Leonard Francis text message to John Beliveau Jr., April 10, 2013.

218 *"Dumbo didnt delete anything for several years":* John Beliveau Jr. text message to Leonard Francis, April 11, 2013.

219 *urged Francis to protect himself with "Sopranos" tactics:* John Beliveau Jr. text messages to Leonard Francis, April 13, 2013.

219 *"Don't trust him and never email or text him":* Ibid.

219 *he mocked Mariner as "the Japan bitch":* Leonard Francis text message to John Beliveau Jr., March 12, 2012.

219 *"the genius agent":* Leonard Francis email to John Beliveau, April 10, 2012.

220 *He told Beliveau he was "embarrassed":* Leonard Francis text messages to John Beliveau Jr., April 16, 2013.

220 *"Yeah, I know . . . emails kill":* John Beliveau Jr. text messages to Leonard Francis, April 15–17, 2013.

220 *"Don't even trust your admiral buddies"*: Ibid.

220 *"If they find that you sent me [anything], im screwed"*: Ibid.

220 *"I cleaned it out 6 months back"*: Leonard Francis text message to John Beliveau Jr., April 16, 2013.

220 *It contained a letter and CD from Google:* Mika Yukimura, Google Legal Investigations Support, letter to NCIS Special Agent Amanda Blair, April 16, 2013.

220 *If he had acted a few days sooner, he would have been in the clear:* Transcript, Sentencing Proceedings, *USA v. Beliveau*, October 14, 2016. Assistant U.S. Attorney Brian Young said if Francis had deleted his emails a little earlier "This case isn't here today. . . . Leonard is still under contract with the Navy and tens of millions of dollars are continuing to evaporate into thin air."

221 *"At that point, everything changed"*: Transcript, joint DCIS-NCIS interview of A. W. Moss, August 7, 2014. (DeLaPena made the remarks while interviewing Moss.)

222 *so a federal prosecutor and other agents could interview them:* Notes from joint NCIS-DCIS debriefing of confidential informant, Bangkok, Thailand, June 11, 2013.

222 *Francis had paid for Beliveau to go on sex trips to Southeast Asia:* Notes from joint DCIS-NCIS interview of John Beliveau Jr., September 23, 2013.

222 *"The thing that really kept me awake at night"*: Author interview with former NCIS Acting Director Mark Ridley, April 16, 2019.

223 *"Holy shit. Are you kidding me?"*: Author interview with former Navy Secretary Ray Mabus, May 10, 2019.

CHAPTER TWENTY-THREE: PARTY ON

225 *"Really arrogant bitch!"*: Leonard Francis text messages to Sompiak, his driver, June 24, 2013.

225 *or "Bang-cock" as he liked to call it:* Deposition of Leonard Francis, *General Court-Martial of Commander David Morales*, Naval Base San Diego, July 17, 2018.

226 *a "desperate" bid to recruit new moles:* Ibid.

226 *"He was just fun to hang out with"*: Author interview with retired Commander David Morales, October 26, 2013.

226 *immersed themselves in Singapore's luxury nightlife:* Notes from NCIS interview of Leonard Francis, April 25, 2018.

226 *a $10,000, six-liter bottle of champagne:* Francis deposition.

226 *a Gucci fashion show:* Ibid.

226 *a Julio Iglesias concert:* Special Findings, *General Court-Martial of Commander David Morales*, November 15, 2018. Morales was found guilty in September

2018 of conduct unbecoming an officer. He was sentenced to 165 days confinement.

227 *"Thanks for oink oinks x 4":* Record of Trial, Morales court-martial.

227 *escorted them to Pegasus, the ritzy sex club:* Francis deposition.

227 *Morales reacted with "shock and awe" and felt "like a rock star":* Ibid.

227 *"working girls" were present:* Morales interview with author. Morales said a female friend of his from Bangkok met him at Pegasus and later dropped him at the hotel.

227 *Francis slipped out to pick up Captain Haas:* Stipulation of Expected Testimony of retired Captain David Haas, Morales court-martial, August 27, 2018. In his interview with the author, Morales said he was "shocked to see" Haas at the club.

227 *After making a loud scene:* Francis text messages to Sompiak. The texts that Francis exchanged with his driver back up his version of what happened that night. "I came back from Club with 7 girls to pass to my 2 frens on different room floors," he wrote.

228 *Morales gave a slightly different account:* Morales interview with author. Morales said he observed Francis arguing with the front-desk clerk, the hotel manager, and a patron who tried to intervene. He said he got "the hell out of there" and went up to his room.

228 *Haas, in his version:* Haas Stipulation of Expected Testimony.

228 *creeped out his target, who said she "just wanted to get out of there":* Testimony of Lieutenant Commander Taeko McFadden, Morales court-martial, August 28, 2018.

228 *plying him with meals, prostitutes, and spa treatments:* Grand Jury Indictment, *USA v. David Williams Haas,* U.S. District Court, Southern District of California, August 16, 2018.

228 *Francis failed to seal the deal and "baptize" any of them:* Notes from joint NCIS-DCIS interview of Leonard Francis, March 26, 2015.

228 *"Most of the other officers were scared":* Francis deposition.

228 *an outlandish idea to capture him:* Author interview with Thomas Oppel, April 17, 2019. Oppel served as chief of staff to Navy Secretary Ray Mabus.

229 *"We didn't think Singapore would extradite":* Author interview with former Navy Secretary Ray Mabus, May 10, 2019.

229 *They would plant false updates into K-NET:* Government Sentencing Memorandum, *USA v. John Bertrand Beliveau Jr.,* U.S. District Court, Southern District of California, October 7, 2016.

230 *"Fyi Thai case was closed":* John Beliveau Jr. text message exchange with Leonard Francis, via phone and Skype, July 4, 2013.

230 *"Awesome!":* Ibid.

230 *"The Thai case was the best possible case"*: Ibid.

230 *Francis thanked Beliveau for his "stellar advice"*: Ibid.

231 *Given his rank and the sensitivity of his job*: Testimony of DCIS Special Agent James McWhirter, Evidentiary Hearing, *USA v. David Newland et al.*, U.S. District Court, Southern District of California, November 5, 2019.

231 *Ten other Navy officers surfaced in Francis's Facebook messages*: Ibid.

231 *Blair repeated the lie that the cases had stalled*: Notes from NCIS interview of Not Somnuek and Tu Kiatthisak, August 13, 2013.

231 *complained about the "amateurs" and "ignorant unintelligent fucks"*: John Beliveau Jr. text messages to Leonard Francis, June 6, 2013.

231 *"Cocks everywhere u go"*: Leonard Francis text message to John Beliveau Jr., June 6, 2013.

231 *"As I see it I saved your business"*: John Beliveau Jr. text message to Leonard Francis, July 23, 2013.

231 *"Stop being dramatic nd chill"*: Leonard Francis text message to John Beliveau Jr., July 25, 2013.

232 *"Work n play!"*: Leonard Francis text message to Ed Aruffo, August 21, 2013.

232 *where to shop in Beverly Hills for "high-end" XXL body-building gear*: Leonard Francis text message to Ed Aruffo, September 7, 2013.

232 *Aruffo told him that getting "ripped quick doesn't work"*: Ed Aruffo text message to Leonard Francis, September 7, 2013.

232 *He said he hoped the steroids would help him grow "a dick extension"*: Leonard Francis text message to Ed Aruffo, September 7, 2013.

233 *Adelman thought the fraud case against Francis sounded "airtight"*: Author interview with former Ambassador David Adelman, February 8, 2019.

233 *in a private room at Tatsuya*: Plea Agreement, *USA v. Jesus Vasquez Cantu*, U.S. District Court, Southern District of California, August 18, 2017. Notes from joint DCIS-NCIS interview with retired Captain Jesus Cantu, July 7, 2017. Cantu said that Francis also provided him with a prostitute that evening.

233 *"Unclassified good but can't do the classified"*: Commander David Morales text message to Leonard Francis, September 11, 2013.

233 *"I will join you"*: Leonard Francis text message to Commander David Morales, September 11, 2013.

234 *the check-in staff had a golf cart waiting*: Francis interview #8, Wright.

CHAPTER TWENTY-FOUR: BUSTED

235 *A plainclothes surveillance team of fourteen federal agents*: DCIS surveillance log, September 19, 2013.

235 *Around 2:30 p.m., an agent spotted Leonard Francis:* Ibid.

235 *From a distance, agents observed Francis and his cousin:* Ibid.

235 *the vanguard of an extraordinary force:* NCIS Interim Report of Investigation, Glenn Defense Marine Asia, February 6, 2014.

236 *execute search warrants in seven states:* Ibid.

236 *Secrecy was so tight:* Government Sentencing Memorandum, *USA v. John Bertram Beliveau Jr.*, U.S. District Court, Southern District of California, October 7, 2016.

236 *He had spent his law enforcement career toiling in unglamorous parts:* McWhirter affidavit, *USA v. Beliveau*, September 12, 2013.

237 *Francis had asked Ed Aruffo to make a reservation:* Leonard Francis text message to Ed Aruffo, September 5, 2013.

237 *Also present was Steve Shedd:* Transcript, joint NCIS-DCIS interview of Commander Stephen Shedd, September 17, 2013.

237 *refilled his belly with a late breakfast:* Transcript, joint NCIS-DCIS interview of Howard Patty Sr., September 16, 2013.

238 *They were escorted to a conference room:* James Paris email to author, January 26, 2023. Paris, the Navy attorney, attended the meeting.

238 *Heck was oblivious to the sting operation:* Ibid. Author interview with retired Captain Marty Fields, October 26, 2023.

238 *agents had installed a spy camera and microphone:* Results of Technical Investigative Support, NCIS, September 19, 2013.

238 *Investigators had briefed his boss:* Paris email to author. Fields interview with author.

238 *subcontractors for the Chinese government:* Transcript of NAVSUP conference, NCIS, September 16, 2013.

238 *"Our mission at Glenn Marine, of course":* Ibid.

238 *"Hi, is Mr. Francis here?":* Transcript, joint DCIS-NCIS interview of Leonard Francis, September 16, 2013. The transcript includes the entire exchange between McWhirter and Francis leading up to his arrest at 6:12 p.m.

242 *cornered the shellshocked retired Navy captain:* Transcript, joint DCIS-NCIS interview of C. Rivers Cleveland, September 16, 2013.

242 *"I mean, I have no idea what's going on":* Ibid. The transcript includes the entire exchange between the agents and Cleveland.

243 *told the fifty-seven-year-old Patty up front they weren't going to arrest him:* Patty interview, NCIS-DCIS, September 16, 2013.

243 *"Well, yeah":* Ibid. The transcript includes the entire exchange between the agents and Patty.

244 *"Hey dad, we had a situation at the house today":* Leonardo Francis text message to Leonard Francis, September 17, 2013.

CHAPTER TWENTY-FIVE: SHOCK WAVES

245 *He could tell something had gone horribly wrong:* John Beliveau Jr. letter to author, October 15, 2021.

246 *Beliveau talked his way past the closed gates:* Ibid.

246 *"I'm glad you're here":* Ibid.

246 *Beliveau thought the timing was odd:* Ibid.

247 *Beliveau looked around the squad room and recognized a couple of faces:* Ibid.

247 *"You know, Leonard is not your friend":* Ibid.

247 *They ordered Beliveau to strip off his NCIS polo shirt:* Ibid.

248 *he was "curious" to hear what this was all about:* Transcript, joint NCIS-DCIS interview of Commander Michael Misiewicz, September 16, 2013.

248 *"I'm good":* Ibid. The transcript includes the entire exchange between Misiewicz and Special Agent Erika Mariner.

250 *A manager had given them the passcode to the gate:* Results of Federal Search Warrant Executed at Sanchez's Residence, NCIS Investigative Action, October 16, 2013.

251 *He had just finished gulping down takeout from Steak 'n Shake:* Ibid.

251 *"I want to talk to an attorney":* Notes from NCIS interview of Commander Jose Sanchez, October 24, 2013.

251 *now the Samsung was ringing almost nonstop:* Results of Sanchez search warrant.

251 *Agents were banging on her door too:* Notes from NCIS interview of Priscilla Sanchez, September 20, 2013.

251 *"Emergency, apartment raided by 15 federal agents":* Commander Jose Sanchez text messages to Leonard Francis, September 16, 2013.

252 *"Dave!":* Transcript, joint NCIS-DCIS interview of retired Captain David Lausman, September 16, 2013.

253 *"He's as tall as I am and probably another 150 pounds heavier":* Ibid. The transcript includes the entire exchange between David Lausman and Special Agent Patricia Dempski.

253 *In the kitchen, Carol Lausman spun her own web:* Notes from joint NCIS-DCIS interview of Carol Lausman, September 16, 2013. The agents did not record Carol Lausman's interview.

253 *she did recall a purse, but she dismissed it as a cheap little thing:* Ibid.

253 *Lausman rummaged through a closet:* Notes from joint NCIS-DCIS interview of retired Captain David Lausman, February 19, 2014.

254 *he placed the devices on a flat surface and pulverized them with a hammer:* Plea Agreement, *USA v. David Lausman*, U.S. District Court, Southern District of California, September 6, 2023. Lausman pleaded guilty to a misdemeanor charge of destruction of government property causing damage of $1,000 or less.

CHAPTER TWENTY-SIX: PANIC ATTACKS

256 *a wave of nausea and fear engulfed him:* Author interview with retired Captain Jeffrey Breslau, May 7, 2020.

256 *he'd even supplied talking points for Francis's presentation:* Pre-sentence Investigation Report, *USA v. Jeffrey Breslau,* U.S. District Court, Southern District of California, January 4, 2019.

256 *just providing "advice":* Transcript, joint NCIS-DCIS interview of Captain Jeffrey Breslau, September 17, 2013.

256 *"I told him that he's got to be honest":* Ibid. The transcript includes the entire exchange between Breslau, NCIS Special Agent Jonathan Greenert, and DCIS Special Agent Joseph Johnson. Special Agent Greenert was the son of Admiral Jonathan Greenert, the chief of naval operations at the time.

256 *Each had a Sony digital voice memory stick in his pocket:* NCIS Investigative Action, Results of Interview of Breslau, September 18, 2013.

256 *Breslau raced to find an attorney:* Breslau interview with author, May 7, 2020.

257 *but found only his wife at home:* Notes from joint DCIS-NCIS interview of Charlene Haley, September 18, 2013.

257 *"If Leonard's guilty, you need to get all his money back":* Transcript, joint DCIS-NCIS interview of Rear Admiral J. R. Haley, September 17, 2013.

257 *"I guess the bottom line is I want to help you":* Ibid. The transcript includes nearly the entire exchange between Haley, DCIS Special Agent Alison Sutton, and NCIS Special Agent Terry Moreau, except for a small portion that is classified.

258 *Charlene Haley surrendered the Gucci purse:* Charlene Haley interview, DCIS-NCIS.

258 *appraised its value between $1,200 and $1,400:* Notes from NCIS interview of Jessica Haugen, December 18, 2013. Haugen was the legal coordinator for Gucci America, Inc.

259 *She welcomed them inside while she rounded up her "rugrats" for a bath:* Transcript, joint NCIS-DCIS interview of Commander Stephen Shedd, September 17, 2013.

259 *"So, who are we investigating?":* Ibid. The transcript includes the entire exchange between Stephen Shedd, NCIS Special Agent James Curry, and DCIS Special Agent Michelle Hendricks.

259 *the officer was gripped by "total shock" and "absolute panic":* Testimony of Stephen Shedd, *USA v. Newland et al.,* U.S. District Court, Southern District of California, May 5, 2022.

259 *Shedd lied and then lied some more:* Ibid. When asked by a federal prosecutor to describe how he had responded to the agents' questions when they visited his home, Shedd replied: "Yeah, generally it was obfuscation, denial and in some cases straight lying."

259 *In fact, he had accepted $105,000 worth of bribes:* Plea Agreement, *USA v. Stephen Shedd*, U.S. District Court, Southern District of California, January 26, 2022. Shedd agreed to pay $105,000 in restitution to the Navy.

260 *"Hello, is your daddy home?":* Transcript, joint DCIS-NCIS interview of Edmond Aruffo, September 17, 2013.

261 *"I'll be straight up with you":* Ibid. The transcript includes the entire exchange between Aruffo, DCIS Special Agent James McWhirter, and NCIS Special Agent Shannon Rachal.

263 *Amundson, the recently retired former Navy Ball chairman, deleted emails:* Plea Agreement, *USA v. Troy Amundson*, U.S. District Court, Southern District of California, January 30, 2018.

263 *likewise zapped emails that tied him to Glenn Defense:* Plea Agreement, *USA v. Daniel Dusek*, U.S. District Court, Southern District of California, January 15, 2015. Dusek pleaded guilty to conspiracy to commit bribery. He was sentenced to forty-six months in prison.

263 *the chiseled triathlete suddenly looked "panicky":* Notes from joint NCIS-DCIS interviews of Captain Chris Peterschmidt, November 15, 2013, and December 23, 2013. Peterschmidt was the commodore for Coastal Riverine Group One and Haas's direct supervisor.

263 *declared, unprompted, "I'm no saint":* Peterschmidt interview, NCIS-DCIS, November 15, 2013.

263 *"I don't want to put my family through this":* Ibid.

263 *normally a "ball of energy":* Notes from joint NCIS-DCIS interview of Command Master Chief Michael Wentzel, January 16, 2014. Wentzel was the command master chief for Coastal Riverine Group One, where Haas was assigned in 2013.

263 *"I am not without sin":* Ibid.

CHAPTER TWENTY-SEVEN: SPILLING SOME BEANS

267 *treated him like an "animal":* Francis interview #8, Wright.

267 *"This was just a financial matter":* Ibid.

267 *They badgered him "to spill the beans on the Navy":* Ibid.

268 *agents had drawn up a list of thirty persons of interest:* Testimony of DCIS Special Agent James McWhirter, Evidentiary Hearing, *USA v. David Newland et al.*, U.S. District Court, Southern District of California, November 5, 2019.

268 *In June, they'd added ten more names:* Ibid.

268 *in September, the list had gone through another growth spurt:* Ibid.

269 *"it might get ugly":* Transcript, NCIS interview of retired Captain Theodore Algire, September 25, 2013. Algire formerly served as the equivalent of the U.S. defense attaché to Hong Kong.

269 *The prosecution team opened the proffer session:* Notes from joint NCIS-DCIS interview of Leonard Francis, October 1–2, 2013.

269 *Francis infused his narratives with juicy personal tidbits:* Ibid.

269 *a "loose cannon" whom he nicknamed "Mike Misfits":* Ibid.

270 *"I was just trying to give them some names":* Francis interview #8, Wright.

270 *he revealed how he had infiltrated the Seventh Fleet staff:* Notes from joint DCIS-NCIS interview of Leonard Francis, October 17–18, 2013.

271 *They asked whether anyone ever rejected his "gifts":* Ibid.

271 *Francis's attorneys brought documentation:* Ibid.

271 *as "good as gold":* Ibid.

271 *he spilled the names of eleven admirals:* Ibid.

272 *Francis vividly described the nights he spent partying with Loveless:* Ibid.

272 *agents had added seventy more names:* McWhirter testimony.

272 *Francis had to liquidate personal assets:* NCIS Investigative Action, Leonard Francis Assets in Singapore, January 26, 2015.

273 *"His ability to flee and avoid detection":* Transcript, Bond Hearing, *USA v. Leonard Glenn Francis*, U.S. District Court, Southern District of California, November 21, 2013.

273 *"Mr. Francis, I want to make it very clear":* Ibid.

273 *"Yes, your honor":* Ibid.

274 *"He will flee and he will not come back":* Transcript, Bond Hearing, *USA v. Leonard Glenn Francis*, U.S. District Court, Southern District of California, November 25, 2013.

274 *"a do-it-yourself, self-designed jail":* Ibid.

274 *"Even if all the technology":* Ibid.

274 *"provides no assurance against flight occurring":* Ibid.

275 *"I just got so mad":* Francis interview #8, Wright.

CHAPTER TWENTY-EIGHT: TWIG

276 *"Growing up 58 minutes away from Bourbon Street":* The Lucky Bag, 1979.

276 *Branch winced when he learned his call sign:* Author interview with former Navy Secretary Ray Mabus, May 10, 2019.

277 *The squadron commander looked down at the young officer:* Ibid.

277 *"It's like Sunday in Mississippi":* Episode 3, *Carrier*, PBS documentary, April 28, 2008.

277 *Pentagon insiders believed he stood a good chance:* Mabus interview with author.

278 *Branch had never met Misiewicz:* Transcript, NCIS interview of Vice Admiral Ted Branch, November 5, 2013. Some portions of the transcript are described as inaudible.

280 *a device hidden in the pocket:* NCIS Assistant Director Eric Maddox testimony, *USA v. Newland et al.,* U.S. District Court, Southern District of California, May 12, 2022.

280 *"I guess I'd say I'm not too concerned":* Transcript, NCIS interview of Rear Admiral Bruce Loveless, November 5, 2013. Some portions of the transcript are described as inaudible.

281 *he couldn't rule out that foreign spooks:* Notes from joint DCIS-NCIS interview of Leonard Francis, October 17–18, 2013.

282 *Mabus was astonished:* Mabus interview with author.

282 *he couldn't believe an intelligence officer could be so stupid:* Ibid.

282 *left him with the impression that indictments were imminent:* Ibid.

282 *A sparsely worded press release:* Statement by Rear Admiral John F. Kirby, Navy Chief of Information, Navy News Service, November 8, 2013.

283 *leaving Mabus exasperated:* Mabus interview with author.

283 *"If I find out that you so much as take a tomato":* Ibid.

284 *"It's the right thing to do":* Transcript, Press Briefing by Navy Secretary Ray Mabus, Pentagon Briefing Room, December 20, 2013.

284 *Branch attended dinners with Francis on four occasions:* Admiral Philip Davidson memo to Chief of Naval Personnel, September 8, 2017.

284 *wrote a Bravo Zulu note:* Navy message from Captain Ted Branch, USS *Nimitz,* to Ship Support Office, Hong Kong, June 11, 2005.

285 *Branch approved Francis's recommendation to protect the ship:* Notes from joint NCIS-DCIS interview of Leonard Francis, March 4, 2016.

285 *The decision generated a windfall for Glenn Defense:* Ibid.

285 *Francis's claim that he had provided Branch with prostitutes:* Ibid. Francis told federal agents and prosecutors that he had provided Branch with prostitutes in Kuala Lumpur in 2000, in Hong Kong in 2005, and again in Kuala Lumpur in 2005. "I knew Branch's weakness," he said. In a May 11, 2017, letter to the Navy, Branch's attorney denied that he ever received a prostitute from Francis or Glenn Defense.

285 *Three Nimitz officers who attended the Petrus dinner:* Notes from DCIS interview of retired Captain Joseph Clarkson, July 10, 2015. Notes from joint NCIS-DCIS interview of Captain Evan Piritz, April 7, 2016. Notes from joint NCIS-DCIS interview of retired Captain Lance Massey, February 5, 2016. All three officers served on the USS *Nimitz* in 2005.

285 *One officer said he presumed the women were prostitutes:* Massey interview, NCIS-DCIS, February 5, 2016.

285 *he had witnessed Branch partying with "Russian girls":* Notes from joint DCIS-NCIS interview of Ensign Vladimir Sukharev, January 21, 2015. Sukharev was an enlisted sailor on the USS *Nimitz* in 2005. He left the Navy in 2006 but rejoined the Navy Reserve in 2014 as an intelligence officer.

285 *Branch was visibly struck by an "oh shit" moment:* Ibid.

286 *"there was no inappropriate activity":* In the letter to the Navy, Branch's attorney wrote: "Along with several others, my client did go to a nightclub a couple times while in port in Bahrain and he invited the band to tour the ship one day. All the band members, male and female, came for the tour."

286 *Inexplicably, he remained in charge of Navy intelligence:* Craig Whitlock, "The Admiral in Charge of Navy Intelligence Has Not Been Allowed to See Military Secrets for Years," *Washington Post,* January 28, 2016.

286 *"Common sense tells me":* Senator Charles Grassley letter to Defense Secretary Ashton Carter, February 22, 2016.

286 *concluded that Branch had violated ethics rules:* Davidson memo, September 8, 2017. Branch's attorney acknowledged that he attended "a few dinners and having drinks with Mr. Francis" but "perceived them to be part of his official duties."

286 *"appropriate administrative action":* Carl Prine, "Navy Won't Punish Vice Admiral Stripped of Security Clearance During 'Fat Leonard' Probe," *San Diego Union-Tribune,* September 22, 2017.

CHAPTER TWENTY-NINE: CRAZY BOB

287 *mumbling incoherently about women and dinners:* Notes from DCIS interview of Lieutenant Commander Michael Bono, November 10, 2014. Bono served as Gilbeau's flag aide in Afghanistan from July to November 2013.

287 *binge-watching episodes of Californication:* Transcript, joint DCIS-NCIS interview of Captain Thomas Jack Moreau, April 2, 2015.

287 *"And I'm like, okay, you're in crazytown":* Ibid.

287 *begged him to hand over his military-issued sidearm:* Ibid.

288 *but not before scaring the bejesus out of Moreau:* Statement to DCIS by Heather Failla, March 18, 2014. Failla, a civilian, served under Gilbeau in Afghanistan. She said Moreau told her that there was a split second when he thought he might die.

288 *Moreau and a few colleagues crowded into Gilbeau's office:* Ibid.

288 *The admiral broke down sobbing:* Notes from DCIS interview of Army Lieutenant Colonel Rodney LeMay, April 6, 2015. LeMay served as the deputy staff judge advocate to U.S. Forces-Afghanistan in 2013.

288 *He said he couldn't sleep:* Failla statement, DCIS.

288 *The doctors diagnosed him with post-traumatic stress disorder:* Notes from DCIS interview of Lieutenant Michael McClellan, November 13, 2013. McClellan accompanied Gilbeau on his medical flight from Kabul to Germany.

288 *He had a long-standing reputation as a manipulator:* Bono interview, DCIS.

288 *dogged by rumors that he had exaggerated or made up his injuries:* Ibid. Notes from joint DCIS-NCIS interview of Commander James Christopher Statler, December 16, 2014. Statler served under Gilbeau from 2008 to 2010.

288 *he was worried investigators would come after him, too:* Bono interview, DCIS.

288 *a family with "a strong moral compass":* Retired Captain Robert Gilbeau letter to U.S. District Judge Janis Sammartino, March 8, 2017.

289 *racked up dubious expenses:* Statler interview, DCIS-NCIS.

289 *Other officers nicknamed him "Gilbeau the Clown":* Ibid.

289 *"Bob is just, he's always kind of living on the edge":* Transcript, joint NCIS-DCIS interview of Rear Admiral David Pimpo, July 14, 2014.

289 *"He loved pressure. He loved anxiety":* Author interview with retired Captain James Maus, April 2017.

289 *Francis found him "wild" and entertaining:* Notes from joint NCIS-DCIS interview of Leonard Francis, May 4, 2015.

289 *the kind of supply officer who "would sign anything":* Ibid.

289 *they partied together with prostitutes at the Brix nightclub:* Ibid.

289 *Gilbeau became enamored of a European woman:* Ibid.

289 *Francis thought the saga was hilarious:* Ibid.

289 *Gilbeau said the story was "not true":* Author interview with retired Captain Robert Gilbeau, October 17, 2023. Gilbeau said the woman was divorced and explained that he babysat her children "as a kind of reciprocation" for being allowed to swim at her private club. He acknowledged that Francis nicknamed him "Crazy Bob" and "Casanova Bob."

290 *boasted that he had moles who "let me know what's going on":* Notes from NCIS interview of Rear Admiral Robert Gilbeau, February 20, 2013.

290 *he typed "very large Malaysian man":* Foreign Contact Questionnaire, Robert John Albert Gilbeau, November 27, 2012.

290 *But Gilbeau lied on another part of the form:* Ibid.

290 *Staffers described him as a "pathological liar" with a "God complex":* Bono interview, DCIS. Failla statement, DCIS.

291 *who thought "laws don't apply to him":* Moreau transcript, DCIS-NCIS.

291 *a "passive-aggressive" leader:* Failla statement, DCIS.

291 *"It was all about making himself look good":* Ibid.

291 *to shop for gemstones and carpets:* Bono interview, DCIS.

291 *He talked about having visions of severed heads:* Ibid.

291 *"little blue men in little blue suits":* Gilbeau interview with author.

291 *"Maybe he is in the freaking CIA":* Moreau transcript, DCIS-NCIS.

291 *Other staffers warned Moreau not to fall for the bonkers act:* Notes from NCIS interview with Heather Failla, January 22, 2015.

291 *"This guy is playing us":* Moreau transcript, DCIS-NCIS.

291 *"It was not an act"*: Gilbeau interview with author. Responding to subordinates who described him as a pathological liar, Gilbeau said: "I obviously can't refute what somebody thinks." He said he genuinely had suicidal thoughts while in Afghanistan. "I had a desire to be killed in action."

291 *relaxing in a massage chair*: Notes from DCIS interview of Rear Admiral Robert Gilbeau, November 12, 2013.

292 *"I don't think I'm okay"*: Transcript, DCIS interview of Rear Admiral Robert Gilbeau, November 10, 2013.

292 *"We'll cut to the chase"*: Ibid. The entire exchange between Gilbeau, Sanguanboon, and Robertson is reflected in the transcript.

293 *"So here is my personal problem"*: Ibid. In his 2023 interview with the author, Gilbeau said he still suffered from erectile dysfunction. "I wish I didn't. But I do."

294 *Even Francis had heard the award was bogus*: Francis interview, DCIS-NCIS, May 4, 2015.

295 *Gilbeau's story was dubious*: Notes from DCIS interview of retired Commander Kenneth Broomer, January 3, 2017.

296 *"does not ooze, does not bleed"*: Chronological Record of Medical Care, Robert John Gilbeau, November 22, 2007.

296 *the Pentagon conducted a review*: Notes from joint NCIS-DCIS interview of Mark Newman, April 3, 2015. Newland served as the deputy director of the Chief of Naval Operations Awards Branch.

296 *"there are several administrative errors"*: NCIS Executive Pacific Director memo to Chief of Naval Operations, January 21, 2015.

296 *And the clerk whose name was listed*: Statement by Jamie Blanco to NCIS, May 4, 2015. Blanco served as the administrative assistant to the Director of Air Warfare from 2006 to 2009.

296 *Gilbeau said he was never told about the review*: Gilbeau interview with author. During the interview, Gilbeau rolled up his pant leg to show me a tiny, faded scar near his knee. When he sustained the injury, he said, he told his commanding officer, "It's not that bad. I don't deserve a Purple Heart. It's just a small wound." He added that his commander, an Air Force general, insisted on submitting paperwork for the award anyway.

296 *a Navy Physical Evaluation Board determined that Gilbeau was medically fit*: Government Sentencing Memorandum, *USA v. Robert Gilbeau*, U.S. District Court, Southern District of California, April 11, 2017.

296 *his symptoms were "situationally driven"*: Ibid.

296 *He submitted medical reports to the court*: Defendant Sentencing Memo, *USA v. Gilbeau*, April 11, 2017.

297 *Bella started yapping:* Craig Whitlock and Tony Perry, "Former Admiral Sentenced to 18 Months in 'Fat Leonard' Case," *Washington Post,* May 17, 2017.

297 *"This has been a difficult morning for everyone":* Transcript, Sentencing Proceedings, *USA v. Gilbeau,* May 17, 2017.

CHAPTER THIRTY: THE ADMIRALS STRIKE BACK

298 *a gangly plebe from North Dakota: The Lucky Bag,* 1974.

298 *who had never seen the ocean:* Eloise Ogden, "North Dakota Native to Lead US Naval Academy," *Minot Daily News,* July 17, 2010.

298 *"His vision here in Annapolis went far beyond bricks and mortar":* Remarks of Navy Secretary Ray Mabus, U.S. Naval Academy, July 23, 2014.

299 *to inform him that he was a subject of a criminal investigation:* Notes from joint DCIS-NCIS interview of Vice Admiral Michael Miller, July 22, 2014.

299 *Miller had been cagey and evasive:* Transcript, joint DCIS-NCIS interview of Vice Admiral Michael Miller, July 15, 2014.

299 *He agreed to represent the superintendent for free:* Louis Freeh letter to DCIS Special Agent Jerry Crosby and NCIS Special Agent James Curry, July 18, 2014.

300 *"We're assuming you're going to ask us about Glenn Marine":* Miller transcript, DCIS-NCIS, July 15, 2014. The entire exchange among Miller, Freeh, Crosby, and Curry is reflected in the transcript.

300 *they had obtained approval:* Miller interview, DCIS-NCIS, July 22, 2014. Informed by the author that federal agents had secretly recorded the interview, Freeh responded by calling it a violation of his and Miller's privacy rights. "They deliberately lied to us in connection with their interview of our client, and deceitfully recorded our meeting," he wrote in an October 20, 2023, email. "You rely on their 'investigative files' and 'notes' at your journalistic peril." He said any suggestion that Miller had been evasive during the interview was "laughable."

302 *"I'm not in bed with Leonard Francis":* Transcript, joint NCIS-DCIS interview of Rear Admiral David Pimpo, July 14, 2014.

302 *he conceded that "there were a bunch" of dinners:* Ibid. The entire exchange between Pimpo, NCIS Special Agent Oscar Cunha, and DCIS Special Agent Mark Mayeda is reflected in the transcript.

303 *When he learned he was a suspect:* Voluntary Statement of Rear Admiral Terry Kraft, July 25, 2014. In his statement, Kraft recounts the DCIS attempt to interview him on July 16, 2014.

303 *"surprised that I am in any way involved":* Ibid.

303 *Kraft shifted the blame again:* Notes from joint NCIS-DCIS interview of Rear Admiral Terry Kraft, September 5, 2014.

303 *"Are you really asking me for something from eight years ago?":* Ibid.

304 *what he described as "newly discovered" evidence:* Louis Freeh letter to Captain Kirk Foster and Frank Futzu, November 7, 2014.

304 *a "seriously unfair and embarrassing" investigation:* Ibid.

304 *the JAG this time signed an eighteen-page sworn statement:* Statement to DCIS by Captain Joel Doolin, November 21, 2014.

304 *"You do not need any ethics training to know this is not right":* Ibid.

304 *committed "egregious" misconduct:* Admiral John Richardson memo to Secretary of the Navy, December 11, 2014.

305 *Richardson reached almost identical conclusions:* Admiral John Richardson memo to Naval Inspector General, Adverse Information ICO RADM Terry B. Kraft, February 13, 2015. Richardson criticized Kraft for "a weak ethical tone which permeated his command." In a June 4, 2021, email to the author, Kraft denied accepting gifts and said he had done nothing wrong. "I attended three dinners at the direction of my superior. I and my wardroom paid for each one. Two JAG officers approved my attendance."

305 *The formal reprimand was only a slap on the wrist:* The Navy stripped Pimpo of his admiral's star and made him retire as a captain. Miller and Kraft were permitted to retain their ranks and retire as a vice admiral and rear admiral, upper half, respectively. In his email to the author, Louis Freeh, Miller's attorney, wrote: "You can be sure that if there had been any credible and provable evidence of any unethical or improper conduct by our client, he never would have been allowed to retire honorably and with his highest, earned rank."

305 *he had become close with Miller:* Mabus interview.

305 *"I didn't feel good about it":* Ibid.

305 *But Howard forcefully argued against doing so:* Author interviews with Thomas Oppel, April 17, 2019, and May 2, 2019.

306 *"demonstrated poor judgment and a failure of leadership":* "SECNAV Censures Three Senior Officers," Navy News Service, February 10, 2015.

CHAPTER THIRTY-ONE: FLIPPED

309 *"Good afternoon, Mr. Francis":* Transcript, Change of Plea Hearing, *USA v. Leonard Glenn Francis,* U.S. District Court, Southern District of California, January 15, 2015.

309 *Francis stood, held his hands behind his back, and wiggled his fingers:* Julie Watson, "Contractor at Center of Navy Bribery Scheme Pleads Guilty," Associated Press, January 15, 2015.

310 *He confessed that he had corrupted "scores" of Navy officers:* Plea Agreement, *USA v. Francis,* January 15, 2015.

310 *He also agreed to pay back $35 million:* Addendum to Plea Agreement, *USA v. Francis,* January 15, 2015.

310 *"Today is the next step in this giant investigation":* Kristina Davis, "Contractor Pleads Guilty in Bribe Case Tied to Navy," *San Diego Union-Tribune,* January 16, 2015.

310 *"I don't have a choice":* Francis interview #13, Wright.

310 *"I had the Navy by their balls":* Ibid.

310 *Francis and the Justice Department signed a secret addendum:* Francis Plea Agreement Addendum.

311 *Francis had hoarded compromising material:* Lanny Breuer letter to Laura Duffy, U.S. Attorney for the Southern District of California, December 9, 2016. Breuer was a senior attorney with Covington & Burling, one of the law firms representing Francis. The seventeen-page letter details the cooperation that Francis provided to the Justice Department in 2015 and 2016.

311 *a two-week trip to Southeast Asia to collect a sampling of the goods:* Notes from DCIS interview of Esteban Hernandez, August 3, 2023.

311 *Francis also agreed to hand over Glenn Defense's corporate computer server:* Breuer letter.

312 *fifty meetings with him over the next twenty months:* Ibid.

312 *His attorneys organized binders of material:* Ibid.

312 *"clean, disease-free" prostitutes:* Craig Whitlock, "Former Navy Official Gets Six Years in Prison for Taking $350,000 in Bribes from 'Fat Leonard,'" *Washington Post,* December 2, 2016.

312 *"This is not the way to start my day":* Transcript, DCIS interview of Paul Simpkins, February 3, 2015.

312 *He later pleaded guilty to taking $350,000 in bribes:* Plea Agreement, *USA v. Paul Simpkins,* U.S. District Court, Southern District of California, June 23, 2016.

313 *the first person the prosecution team wanted to question him about:* Notes from joint NCIS-DCIS interview of Leonard Francis, January 15, 2015.

313 *Locklear had assured federal investigators:* Notes from joint DCIS-NCIS interview of Admiral Samuel Locklear, October 30, 2014.

313 *"very high-end" multi-course feasts at the Jaan restaurant:* Francis interview, NCIS-DCIS, January 15, 2015.

313 *the admiral sent him effusive thank-you letters:* Notes from joint NCIS-DCIS interview of Leonard Francis, March 25, 2015.

313 *he shared a stack of forty photographs:* Notes from joint DCIS-NCIS interview of Leonard Francis, April 1, 2015.

314 *Francis also claimed he'd hired several prostitutes:* Ibid. Francis waited until his third proffer session in 2015 to make his allegations about Locklear and the prostitutes. When investigators asked why he hadn't told them before, he said he had been afraid of retaliation because of Locklear's high-ranking position.

314 *Francis said he picked out a Chinese woman:* Ibid.

314 *The admiral remained adamant that he had done nothing wrong:* Notes from joint NCIS-DCIS interview of Admiral Samuel Locklear, March 3, 2015.

314 *he "ate and left" the second dinner quickly:* Ibid.

314 *Locklear also later denied that Francis had offered him a prostitute:* Retired Admiral Samuel Locklear letter to author, March 3, 2018. Locklear said investigators never gave him "a full or detailed explanation" of Francis's allegations about a prostitute. "I can tell you, however, that any assertions he may have made along these lines are false. Given my personal and professional reputation during nearly 43 years in uniform, it is inconceivable to me, as it is to others who know me, that I would engage in such activity."

315 *But four other officers from the* Nimitz *strike group corroborated:* Notes from DCIS interview of retired Rear Admiral Thomas Cropper, April 11, 2016. Cropper served as the deputy commander of the USS *Nimitz*'s air wing in 2003. He told federal agents that a large group of Chinese women walked into the private dining room toward the end of the dinner and that he was confident they were prostitutes. He also described Locklear as a "straight shooter" and said he would be surprised if he did anything unethical.

Another officer present at the party, David Fravor, told the author that he witnessed Francis bring in about fifteen prostitutes and that Locklear left "as soon as the hookers came in the room." Craig Whitlock, "'Fat Leonard' Affected Pentagon's Pick to Lead Joint Chiefs," *Washington Post*, April 1, 2018. "I didn't see Admiral Locklear do anything wrong at all," he added.

A third officer, retired Captain William Cone, told federal agents that numerous women whom he assumed were prostitutes arrived at the dinner and that one of them propositioned him in the elevator (he said he declined). Notes from DCIS interview of retired Captain William Cone, April 20, 2015.

315 *one of those officers kept a diary:* Notes from joint NCIS-DCIS interview of Captain Paul "Smack" Mackley, March 19, 2015. Mackley was the executive officer of an aviation unit on the *Nimitz.*

315 *Locklear returned to the* Nimitz *at 12:45 a.m.:* NCIS Investigative Action, Receipt of Ship's Deck Logs for USS *Nimitz*, April 13, 2015.

315 *Richardson concluded that Locklear had done nothing wrong:* Admiral John Richardson memo to Naval Inspector General, April 27, 2015.

316 *For each debriefing, he woke before dawn:* Breuer letter.

316 *evidence against 240 current and former Navy officers:* Ibid.

316 *his defense team would bring him a laptop:* Government Disclosures, *General Court-Martial of Commander David Morales,* Naval Base San Diego, July 16, 2018.

317 *a sumptuous breakfast awaited him:* Ibid.

317 *tended to his toenails:* Ibid.

318 *"Uncle Sam loves me":* Francis interview #5, Wright.

318 *"My well-being is more important than anything else":* Francis interview #13, Wright.

CHAPTER THIRTY-TWO: BAD MEMORIES

320 *"What a beautiful home":* Transcript, DCIS interview of Captain Jesus Cantu, March 9, 2017.

320 *"We have a ton of information":* Ibid. The transcript reflects the entire exchange between Cantu and Special Agents Mari Nash and Chris Somboon.

320 *Calling Cantu his "bed buddy":* Leonard Francis email to Howard Patty Sr., October 4, 2011.

320 *"We were embedded together":* Francis interview #8, Wright.

320 *"Of course, he was too embarrassed to admit anything":* Ibid.

321 *"With the prostitutes, you slept in a bed with Francis":* Cantu transcript, DCIS.

322 *his memory was fuzzy because "there was alcohol involved":* Transcript, DCIS interview of retired Captain David Newland, March 2, 2017.

322 *"The girls are pushing themselves on you":* Ibid.

323 *"I thought they were just, for lack of a better term, party friends":* Transcript, DCIS interview of Captain James Dolan, March 8, 2017.

323 *admitted that he'd cheated on his wife:* Transcript, DCIS interview of retired Colonel Enrico DeGuzman, March 3, 2017.

323 *"Yes, I was there. There was a girl sitting next to me":* Ibid.

324 *two "very touchy-feely" women:* Transcript, joint NCIS-DCIS interview of Commander David Snee, February 14, 2017.

324 *"I mean, I was really drunk":* Ibid.

324 *"In hindsight I'm sure it appears that she was a prostitute":* Ibid.

324 *a Glenn Defense executive had treated a vanload of officers:* Notes from NCIS interview of Captain Jeff Davis, August 18, 2016.

324 *a dingy hotel:* Ibid. Captain Jeff Davis letter to Navy Consolidated Disposition Authority, June 30, 2017.

324 *a sauna, whirlpools, and a pair of adjoining bedrooms:* Notes from DCIS interview of Captain Dan Dusek, November 17, 2015.

324 *wearing dress-blue Navy uniforms:* Davis letter.

325 *One was Commander Dan Dusek:* Dusek interview, DCIS.

325   *The other was Commander Lon Olson:* Admiral Philip Davidson memo to Chief of Naval Personnel, Adverse Information ICO CDR Lon Olson, January 17, 2018.

325   *it was apparent only "in hindsight":* Memo from Olson's attorney to Commander, Navy Personnel Command, August 24, 2018.

325   *the night in Vladivostok had "turned ugly":* Davis, NCIS interview. In his letter to the Consolidated Disposition Authority, Davis said he and two other senior officers retreated to a corner when the women arrived at the borscht restaurant. "We agreed that this was an awkward situation, but that as much as we wanted to leave, we were in uniform in a potentially unsafe area and at the mercy of our host for return transportation to the ship. The three of us agreed we should sit it out, and so we waited in a corner area where we watched TV and talked, politely but uncomfortably waiting for the event to end."

325   *he denied having sex with any of the women:* Davis letter.

325   *the Navy cited both officers for misconduct:* Davidson memo, Adverse Information ICO CDR Olson. Admiral Philip Davidson memo to Chief of Naval Personnel, Adverse Information ICO Capt Jeff Davis, August 18, 2017.

325   *Olson was quietly forced to retire:* Chief of Naval Personnel memo to Assistant Secretary of the Navy (Manpower and Reserve Affairs), December 12, 2018.

325   *Davis withdrew from consideration:* Author interview with retired Captain Jeff Davis, October 13, 2023.

326   *let alone particulars about hobnobbing with Francis:* Notes from DCIS interview of retired Rear Admiral Kenneth Norton, April 25, 2016.

326   *he did not remember:* Ibid.

326   *"one of those experiences etched permanently in my mind":* Captain Kenneth Norton email to Leonard Francis, June 28, 2009.

326   *"brought ill-repute and disgrace":* Secretarial Letter of Censure to retired Rear Admiral Kenneth Norton, November 28, 2017.

327   *"It is clear that you did not care":* Ibid.

327   *"I only attended these events to show a professional courtesy":* Retired Rear Admiral Kenneth Norton letter to Secretary of the Navy, December 18, 2017.

327   *Francis had invited a "small inner circle":* Leonard Francis email to Captain Mark Montgomery, April 20, 2008.

328   *Francis covered the bill, which amounted to $3,252 per person:* Admiral Philip Davidson memo to Secretary of the Navy, October 15, 2018.

328   *Bruner said he had zero recollection of the dinner:* Notes from DCIS interview of Rear Admiral Barry Bruner, November 14, 2016.

328   *Also professing total memory loss were Captain Alan Abramson:* Notes from joint DCIS-NCIS interview of retired Captain Alan Abramson, April 7, 2016.

328 *and Captain Todd Zecchin:* Notes from joint NCIS-DCIS interview of retired Captain Todd Zecchin, July 6, 2016.

328 *"I think Fat Leonard was there":* Transcript, joint DCIS-NCIS interview of Rear Admiral Dale Horan, November 9, 2015.

329 *He acknowledged his signature on the menu looked authentic:* Notes from joint DCIS-NCIS interview of Rear Admiral Mark Montgomery, September 25, 2017. In a November 20, 2023, email to the author, Montgomery noted that federal agents interviewed him nearly a decade after the events occurred. "I was unaware of the cost of the dinner, and obviously, in hindsight, I should have asked," he wrote. "As a non-drinker and not physically comfortable around cigar smoke, I leave dinners after dessert and consequently would not have known how expensive this outing became."

329 *Montgomery said he was just as surprised to learn:* Ibid.

329 *even though he had praised the meal as "exquisite":* Davidson memo, October 15, 2018. In his email to the author, Montgomery said he did not intend to deceive federal agents. "I specifically told the investigators that I did not recall attending a reception 10 years earlier," he wrote. "I still don't believe I attended this reception."

329 *Documents provided by Francis:* Francis interview, DCIS-NCIS, May 5, 2015.

329 *Glenn Defense also gave Wren Christmas gift baskets:* Secretarial Letter of Censure to retired Rear Admiral Richard Wren, June 14, 2018.

330 *He had "no memory":* Memo from Wren's attorney to Commander, Fleet Forces Command, October 26, 2017.

330 *blasting both admirals for lying to investigators:* Wren censure. Secretarial Letter of Censure to retired Rear Admiral Mark Montgomery, November 19, 2018.

CHAPTER THIRTY-THREE: A SECRET PROGNOSIS

331 *Francis had spent twenty months at Otay Mesa:* Government Disclosures, General Court-Martial of Commander David Morales, Naval Base San Diego, July 16, 2018.

331 *He sorely needed a hernia operation:* Ibid.

331 *doctors feared the surgery wouldn't work, because he was so obese:* Transcript, Status Hearing, *USA v. Leonard Glenn Francis*, U.S. District Court, Southern District of California, June 8, 2017.

331 *he sat in an extra-large wheelchair:* Government Disclosures, Morales court-martial.

332 *Francis and his lawyers drew up an unorthodox proposal:* Unopposed Motion for Temporary Release from Detention, *USA v. Francis*, November 14, 2017.

332 *Magistrate Judge Jan Adler approved Francis's request:* Order Granting Defendant's Unopposed Motion, *USA v. Francis,* November 14, 2017.

333 *Surgeons removed the kidney, along with his gall bladder:* Government Disclosures, Morales court-martial.

333 *Tests confirmed the tumors were malignant:* Ibid.

333 *"I thought he was going to die":* Author interview with Dr. Sunil Bhoyrul, October 22, 2023. Bhoyrul said multiple physicians reviewed scans of Francis's tumors and confirmed the diagnosis. "The scans don't lie," he added.

334 *to permit Francis to live in a "satellite clinic":* Transcript, Status Hearing, *USA v. Francis,* February 26, 2018.

334 *"The way this is being set up":* Ibid.

334 *"It's beyond me, but that's what they suggested":* Ibid.

334 *"I guess what I'm having a hard time understanding":* Ibid.

334 *"The doctors feel that he needs to be monitored":* Ibid.

335 *"I would feel better having a U.S. Marshal":* Ibid.

335 *The live-in guard, Richardo Buhain, earned $10,000 a month:* Jonathan O'Connell, "'Fat Leonard' Had Life of Leisure, Relaxed Security Before Escape, Capture," *Washington Post,* September 24, 2022.

335 *"He is one of those 'Crazy Rich Asian' kind of people":* Ibid.

336 *After six months, he replaced Buhain with a new guard:* Ibid.

336 *"What we're doing is we're trying to prolong his life":* Transcript, Status Hearing, *USA v. Francis,* June 14, 2018.

336 *"This man is not going to run away, because he's dead if he leaves":* Ibid.

336 *she cleared the courtroom and sealed records of the proceedings:* Sammartino signed an order to unseal transcripts of most of the closed hearings on January 20, 2022.

337 *"He is not getting on a plane":* Transcript, Status Hearing, *USA v. Francis,* May 16, 2018.

337 *"Pretty soon you better go public with this":* Ibid.

337 *Six days later, I broke the news:* Craig Whitlock, "'Fat Leonard' Is Ailing and the Feds Are Keeping His Whereabouts a Secret," *Washington Post,* May 22, 2018.

337 *for making "misrepresentation after misrepresentation":* Transcript, Status Hearing, Morales court-martial, May 24, 2018. The military judge was Captain Charles Purnell.

338 *"I'm a little concerned about making it home detention kind of in name only":* Transcript, Status Hearing, *USA v. Francis,* October 4, 2018.

338 *"Everyone wishes Mr. Francis well":* Transcript, Status Hearing, *USA v. Francis,* January 31, 2019.

339 *"This letter is to notify you that Mr. Leonard Francis has been dismissed from our*

practice": Dr. Sunil Bhoyrul letter to U.S. District Judge Janis Sammartino, November 24, 2020.

340 *"It surprises me that I hear this"*: Transcript, Status Hearing, *USA v. Francis*, December 2, 2020.

340 *Left unspoken was a damning question:* In his interview with the author, Dr. Bhoyrul said: "There was no fooling anyone. He was very ill. He got better."

340 *his client was "not going anywhere"*: Transcript, Status Hearing, *USA v. Francis*, December 2, 2020.

340 *"I do take real issue with a doctor saying he has a clean bill of health"*: Ibid.

340 *"Things had changed. He had gotten much better"*: Bhoyrul interview. Bhoyrul said he felt an obligation to write Judge Sammartino and provide an update to his statements in court about his patient's condition. "I had to absolve myself."

340 *"Tell them they may be subpoenaed"*: Transcript, Status Hearing, *USA v. Francis*, December 2, 2020.

341 *the guard went AWOL for three hours:* Transcript, Status Hearing, *USA v. Francis*, December 17, 2020.

341 *"Maybe I can make it simple for everybody"*: Ibid.

341 *"I'm so sorry for what has happened"*: Ibid.

341 *"Mr. Francis, we all wish you good health"*: Ibid.

CHAPTER THIRTY-FOUR: THE GREAT ESCAPE

342 *a $7,000-per-month mansion:* Complaint for Damages, *Mitesh Kathia v. Sandra Jenney and Leonardo Francis*, Superior Court of California, San Diego County, September 13, 2022.

342 *Two days earlier, he had secured a lease:* Ibid.

342 *He had a new girlfriend:* Declaration of Private Investigator Efren Lapuz, *USA v. Newland et al*, U.S. District Court, Southern District of California, March 29, 2023.

342 *the kids' beloved English bulldog, Puteri:* Jonathan O'Connell, "'Fat Leonard Had Life of Leisure, Relaxed Security Before Escape, Capture," *Wahington Post*, September 24, 2022.

343 *he testified that he'd "lost everything"*: Deposition of Leonard Francis, *General Court-Martial of Commander David Morales*, Naval Base San Diego, July 17, 2018.

343 *he promised to forfeit $35 million:* Plea Agreement Addendum, *USA v. Leonard Glenn Francis*, U.S. District Court, Southern District of California, January 15, 2015.

343 *He paid $5 million up front:* Ibid.

343 *"Really the messaging from both letters":* Transcript, Status Hearing, *USA v. Francis,* March 12, 2021.

344 *"A diagnosis of cancer that is acceptably treated":* Ibid.

344 *he asked a mutual friend to reach out:* Francis interview #18, Wright.

345 *Francis expressed interest in publishing his memoirs:* Ibid.

345 *"If the Navy would've charged every officer":* Francis interview #8, Wright.

345 *"I'm pumped":* Francis interview #5, Wright.

345 *"That's why Uncle Sam loves me":* Ibid.

346 *The timetable floored Francis:* Francis interview #18, Wright.

346 *"I'm not saying there's anything wrong with your story":* Ibid.

346 *"But Leonard, you came to me":* Ibid.

347 *"The government's entire case is built upon Leonard Francis":* Transcript, Closing Arguments, *USA v. Newland et al.,* June 6, 2022.

348 *drafted a letter seeking leniency from the judge:* Lapuz declaration.

348 *Acting on the pretext that he needed to downsize:* Ibid.

348 *"He became more and more morose as time went on":* Jonathan O'Connell, "'Fat Leonard' Had Life of Leisure, Relaxed Security Before Escape, Capture," *Washington Post,* September 24, 2022.

348 *Francis broke his seclusion to go on short walks:* Lapuz declaration.

348 *a television crew descended on the property:* Author interview with Sarah Macdonald, September 19, 2023.

349 *Francis summoned the filmmaker from Europe on short notice:* Ibid.

349 *Francis hid the television crew:* Macdonald interview with author.

349 *The television crew left Friday morning:* Ibid.

349 *he cut off his ankle bracelet:* O'Connell, "'Fat Leonard Had Life of Leisure, Relaxed Security Before Escape, Capture."

349 *He submerged the device in water:* Ibid.

349 *At 7:35 a.m., Pretrial Services received an electronic alert:* Petition for Warrant for Defendant on Pretrial Release, *USA v. Francis,* September 4, 2022.

350 *a life-sized posterboard cutout of Elvis:* Macdonald interview with author.

350 The San Diego Union-Tribune *broke the news of Francis's escape:* Kristina Davis and Greg Moran, "'Fat Leonard,' Set to Finally Be Sentenced in Long-Running Navy Bribery Scheme, Is on the Lam," *San Diego Union-Tribune,* September 5, 2022.

350 *several days in Caracas, the capital, and on Margarita Island:* Author interview with Marco Rodriguez-Acosta, June 26, 2023.

350 *To blend in, he acted like he was on vacation:* Ibid.

351 *locked him up in El Helicoide:* Francisco Olivares, "El oscuro caso de Fat

Leonard, el preso que Maduro protege para negociar con Biden," *El Estímulo*, Caracas, Venezuela, November 7, 2023.

351 *SEBIN saw him as a bargaining chip:* Ibid.

EPILOGUE

353 *"Nothing happened, I even slept on the couch lol":* Ynah text message to DCIS Special Agent Oscar Cunha, March 8, 2022. Francis referred to the woman by her nickname, Ynah. I am withholding her real name for privacy reasons because she said she no longer works as a prostitute. She said she falsely told Francis she had sex with the officer so she would get paid.

354 *Sammartino called the prosecutorial misconduct "outrageous":* Alex Riggins, "Federal Prosecutors Admit Errors, 'Serious Issues' in 'Fat Leonard' Trial of Former Naval Officers," *San Diego Union-Tribune*, September 6, 2023.

354 *"There were pretty obviously serious issues":* Ibid. In a December 11, 2023, statement to the author, Tara McGrath, the U.S. attorney in San Diego, added: "There are fair questions to be asked, and lessons to be learned from the trial in this case. But to focus only on the trial would obscure that the full investigation into [Glenn Defense] resulted in more than two dozen federal convictions of individuals who admitted to facilitating Leonard Francis's years-long corruption and defrauding of the United States Navy."

354 *"China couldn't have done as much damage to the Navy":* Aruna Viswanatha and Nancy A. Youssef, "Mastermind 'Fat Leonard' Gets the Last Laugh in Disastrous Navy Corruption Trial," *Wall Street Journal*, December 18, 2023.

355 *"Leonard Francis was like a puppet master":* María Luisa Paúl, "4 Convictions Thrown Out in Fat Leonard Case After Prosecutor Misconduct," *Washington Post*, September 7, 2023.

355 *she temporarily blocked the new plea deals:* Alex Riggins, "San Diego Judge Skeptical About Reducing or Dismissing More Charges in 'Fat Leonard' Prosecution," *San Diego Union-Tribune*, December 20, 2023.

356 *"What he did was absolutely unconscionable":* Transcript, Sentencing Proceedings, *USA v. John Bertrand Beliveau Jr.*, U.S. District Court, Southern District of California, October 14, 2016.

357 *"my misrepresentation of my relationship with Leonard Francis":* Retired Captain Robert Gilbeau letter to U.S. District Judge Janis Sammartino, March 8, 2017.

357 *"I know in my heart of hearts that I'm not corrupt":* Transcript, Sentencing Proceedings, *USA v. Robert Gilbeau*, U.S. District Court, Southern District of California, May 17, 2017.

357 *"I was a little man on the totem pole"*: Author interview with retired Chief Petty Officer Brooks Parks III, March 14, 2022.

357 *"They didn't find any money, no pictures of me with any hookers"*: Author interview with retired Commander Bobby Pitts, September 18, 2021.

358 *"They're a lot more financially able to take apart your investigation"*: Transcript, joint DCIS-NCIS interview of Captain Thomas Jack Moreau, April 2, 2015. (DeLaPena made his comments while questioning Moreau.)

358 *"I have only myself to blame"*: Transcript, Sentencing Proceedings, *USA v. David Kapaun*, U.S. District Court for Hawaii, September 11, 2017.

358 *"As a senior naval officer"*: Transcript, Sentencing Proceedings, *USA v. Michael George Brooks*, U.S. District Court, Southern District of California, June 16, 2017. Brooks originally received a sentence of forty-one months, but it was reduced by six months after he cooperated with investigators.

358 *"It was out of character for me"*: Transcript, Sentencing Proceedings, *USA v. Jeffrey Breslau*, U.S. District Court, Southern District of California, February 8, 2019. In an interview with the author on April 27, 2020, Breslau was more contrite about his dealings with Francis. "It was just stupid. I should have never even engaged in conversations with him. I should've just walked away."

358 *"My relationship with alcohol is unhealthy"*: Retired Captain David Haas letter to U.S. District Judge Janis Sammartino, January 26, 2023. Haas's sentence was later reduced to two years in prison.

358 *"excessive amounts of alcohol"* and the *"tortuous ending of my second marriage"*: Defendant Sentencing Memorandum, *USA v. Daniel Dusek*, U.S. District Court, Southern District of California, March 21, 2016.

358 because of his *"sex addiction"*: Craig Whitlock, "Another Navy Officer Gets Prison Time for Taking Bribes and Prostitutes from 'Fat Leonard,' " *Washington Post*, January 13, 2017. Debord's sentence was later reduced to twenty-seven months.

359 also alluded to *"an alcohol problem"*: Transcript, Sentencing Proceedings, *USA v. Paul Simpkins*, U.S. District Court, Southern District of California, December 2, 2016.

359 *Simpkins called himself "a scapegoat"*: Paul Simpkins letter to U.S. District Judge Janis Sammartino, April 23, 2017.

360 *"serially defrauded the United States"*: Transcript, Kapaun Sentencing Proceedings.

361 *"more towards possibly $100 million"*: Transcript, NCIS interview of Commander Matt Tritle, September 17, 2013. The rough estimate was made by NCIS Special Agent Thomas Ryan.

361 *"lost $$ Billions due to fraud"*: John Beliveau Jr. text message to Leonard Francis, February 9, 2012.

361 *"Ha Ha"*: Leonard Francis text message to John Beliveau Jr., February 9, 2012.

361 *El Helicoide was a notorious, cockroach-filled prison*: María Luisa Paúl, "VR Transports Users to Notorious Venezuelan Prison: 'The World Needs to Know,' " *Washington Post*, September 22, 2023.

362 *a group of diplomats, led by an American*: Marco Rodríguez-Acosta letter to author, June 26, 2023.

362 *to drop a habeas corpus petition*: Marco Rodríguez-Acosta letter to Leonardo Francis, December 21, 2023.

362 *He stiffed Rodríguez-Acosta for $49,000 in unpaid legal bills*: Ibid.

362 *Francis texted his mother*: Craig Whitlock, "Fat Leonard Thought He Was Going Free. Now He's Locked Up in Miami," *Washington Post*, December 21, 2023.

363 *bundled him onto a small jet, and flew him to Canouan*: Ibid.

363 *"He will face justice"*: Statement from President Joe Biden on Securing the Release of Americans Detained in Venezuela, White House Briefing Room, December 20, 2023.

363 *"Not right now"*: Joshua Goodman and Eric Tucker, "From Fugitive to Shackled Prisoner, 'Fat Leonard' Lands Back in US Court and Could Face More Charges," Associated Press, December 21, 2013.

Index

In this index "LGF" refers to Leonard Glenn Francis.

Photo Credits

1. Courtesy Jeff O'Neal
2. Courtesy Jeff O'Neal
3. NCIS-DCIS case files
4. U.S. Navy
5. NCIS-DCIS case files
6. NCIS-DCIS case files
7. NCIS-DCIS case files
8. NCIS-DCIS case files
9. NCIS-DCIS case files
10. NCIS-DCIS case files
11. NCIS-DCIS case files
12. NCIS-DCIS case files
13. NCIS-DCIS case files
14. NCIS-DCIS case files
15. NCIS-DCIS case files
16. Aaron Burden/U.S. Navy
17. Aaron Burden/U.S. Navy
18. NCIS-DCIS case files
19. NCIS-DCIS case files
20. Heng Sinith/AP
21. NCIS-DCIS case files
22. Courtesy Glenn Defense Marine Asia
23. NCIS-DCIS case files
24. U.S. Navy
25. NCIS-DCIS case files
26. NCIS-DCIS case files
27. NCIS-DCIS case files
28. Jay C. Pugh/U.S. Navy
29. U.S. Navy
30. Courtesy Morena De Jesus
31. NCIS-DCIS case files
32. NCIS-DCIS case files
33. U.S. Navy
34. NCIS-DCIS case files
35. Andrew Schneider/U.S. Navy
36. U.S. Navy
37. Lenny Ignelzi/AP
38. Obtained by the author
39. Obtained by the author
40. Lenny Ignelzi/AP
41. U.S. Marshals Service
42. Interpol

About the Author

Craig Whitlock is an investigative reporter for *The Washington Post* and the #1 *New York Times* bestselling author of *The Afghanistan Papers*. He has worked for *The Post* since 1998 as a foreign correspondent, Pentagon reporter, and national security specialist and has reported from more than sixty countries. His coverage of the war in Afghanistan won the George Polk Award for Military Reporting, the Scripps Howard Award for Investigative Reporting, the Investigative Reporters and Editors Freedom of Information Award, and the Robert F. Kennedy Journalism Award for international reporting. He is also a three-time finalist for the Pulitzer Prize. He lives in Silver Spring, Maryland.

Fat Leonard's world

CHINA

Hong Kong

Hanoi

VIETNAM

Hainan

South

China

Sea

LAOS

THAILAND

Spra
Islar

MYANMAR

Laem Chabang

CAMBODIA

Bangkok

Sihanoukville

Gulf of
Thailand

Andaman
Sea

SINGAPORE
Glenn Defense
headquarters

Phuket

Penang
Leonard Francis's birthplace

MALAYSIA

Kuala
Lumpur

Strait of
Malacca

Port Klang

INDONESIA

Indian
Ocean

Sumatra

Equator

Map by Laris Karklis